1982

Modeling and Analysis

An Introduction to System Performance Evaluation Methodology

Modeling and Analysis

An Introduction to System Performance Evaluation Methodology

HISASHI KOBAYASHI
IBM Corporation

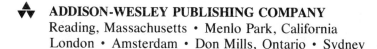

ADDISON-WESLEY PUBLISHING COMPANY
Reading, Massachusetts • Menlo Park, California
London • Amsterdam • Don Mills, Ontario • Sydney

To Masaye

THE SYSTEMS PROGRAMMING SERIES

*The Program Development Process Part I—The Individual Programmer	Joel D. Aron
The Program Development Process Part II—The Programming Team	Joel D. Aron
*The Structure and Design of Programming Languages	John E. Nicholls
Mathematical Background of Programming	Frank Beckman
Structured Programming: Theory and Practice	Richard C. Linger Harlan D. Mills Bernard I. Witt
*The Environment for Systems Programs	Frederic G. Withington
Coded Character Sets; History and Development	Charles E. Mackenzie

*An Introduction To Database Systems, Second Edition	C. J. Date
Interactive Computer Graphics	James Foley Andries Van Dam
*Sorting and Sort Systems	Harold Lorin
*Compiler Design Theory	Philip M. Lewis II Daniel J. Rosenkrantz Richard E. Stearns
*Communications Architecture for Distributed Systems	R. J. Cypser

*Recursive Programming Techniques	William Burge
Conceptual Structures: Information Processing in Mind and Machines	John F. Sowa
*Modeling and Analysis: An Introduction to System Performance Evaluation Methodology	Hisashi Kobayashi

*Published

IBM EDITORIAL BOARD

Foreword

The field of systems programming primarily grew out of the efforts of many programmers and managers whose creative energy went into producing practical, utilitarian systems programs needed by the rapidly growing computer industry. Programming was practiced as an art where each programmer invented his own solutions to problems with little guidance beyond that provided by his immediate associates. In 1968, the late Ascher Opler, then at IBM, recognized that it was necessary to bring programming knowledge together in a form that would be accessible to all systems programmers. Surveying the state of the art, he decided that enough useful material existed to justify a significant publication effort. On his recommendation, IBM decided to sponsor The Systems Programming Series as a long term project to collect, organize, and publish principles and techniques that would have lasting value throughout the industry.

The Series consists of an open-ended collection of text-reference books. The contents of each book represent the individual author's view of the subject area and do not necessarily reflect the views of the IBM Corporation. Each is organized for course use but is detailed enough for reference. Further, the Series is organized in three levels: broad introductory material in the foundation volumes, more specialized material in the software volumes, and very specialized theory in the computer science volumes. As such, the Series meets the needs of the novice, the experienced programmer, and the computer scientist.

The Editorial Board

Preface

During recent years a vast body of knowledge central to the problem of computer performance evaluation has accumulated. Unfortunately, however, the work on the subject demonstrates enormous disparity. On the one hand, we find numerous reports and documents that present masses of empirical data from measurement or simulation, and on the other hand, there are theoretical papers that are, more often than not, couched in advanced mathematics, not easily accessible to engineers. This book is an attempt to fill this undesirable gap between practitioners and theoreticians and to make the modeling and analysis of system performance more methodical and more realistic.

Among a number of mathematical disciplines related to system modeling, "queueing model," "simulation method," and "statistical analysis" are the most important quantitative techniques. I believe that anyone engaged in modeling and analysis should have a command of these subjects. This book provides a cohesive introduction to the modeling and analysis techniques, which will certainly be applicable to modeling activities of complex systems in general, and not merely computer systems. The development of the subject matter is sufficiently self-contained and augmented by an extensive list of important references. The book does not require a prior knowledge of advanced mathematics: Familiarity with college-level calculus and matrix algebra is sufficient. It is assumed that the reader has a basic knowledge of computer system hardware and software. Although lack of system knowledge may not handicap the reader in digesting most of the material, successful applications of these techniques to *actual* modeling activities certainly require a great deal of system knowledge. After all, any model we use is an *abstraction* of a system in the real world. The problem of *mapping* a given or hypothetical system into some kind of model is as important as (and sometimes more challenging than) that of solving the model itself. However, in order to successfully formulate the real system into an abstract form, one must be knowledgeable about which models are mathematically tractable, and how sensitive model solutions will be to specific assumptions and approximations introduced.

Chapter 1, "Computer Performance Evaluation: An Introduction," is an overview of the performance evaluation of computers. We briefly review some key developments and important concepts of general-purpose computing systems. Then we discuss the need and importance of the performance evaluation/prediction. Section 1.3 discusses the performance measures, which we will be dealing with in the rest of the book. The rest of this chapter reviews the current practice in performance evaluation and modeling, and discusses limitations of these techniques.

Chapter 2, "Probability Theory," is prerequisite material for the main subjects of this volume: analytic, simulation, and statistical techniques. We review important notions of probability theory such as statistical independence, random variables, and random processes. Then we follow selected topics relevant to the discussions in later chapters. In particular, the generating functions and the Laplace transform methods are extensively used in Chapter 3. The basic properties of Markov chain are discussed in the last section.

Chapter 3, "Basic Queueing Analysis," presents an introductory queueing analysis. We first discuss such fundamental notions as the Poisson process and formula $L = \lambda W$. Then a collection of queueing models is introduced in the order of their increasing complexity. In Section 3.9, we introduce several computational formulas and approximate and graphical solutions, which will be of practical importance in applications. Section 3.10 illustrates the use of the queueing network models through a case study of an interactive system with multiprogramming in virtual storage.

In Chapter 4, "The Simulation Method," we introduce basic techniques of computer system simulation: trace-driven simulation versus self-driven simulation, the generation of random variables, event-scheduling and data structures for simulation, etc. Two simulation languages, GPSS and SIMPL/1, are presented using simple case studies. The rest of the chapter discusses statistical considerations in simulation: the choice of sample size and the confidence intervals of simulation estimates. We also cover advanced materials such as the regenerative method and variance-reducing methods, which are within the realm of current research efforts.

Chapter 5, "Data Analysis," discusses how to apply statistical analysis methods to measurement data of real systems or simulation outputs. The chapter starts with an overview of the current practice in measurement and monitoring techniques, followed by a section on various graphical presentation methods: Plotting data in the right format is often the most crucial step in the exploratory stage of data analysis. Fundamental notions of experimental design and statistical inferences are also discussed. Then we proceed to selected topics that are relevant to the performance evaluation: factorial experiments, the analysis of variance and covariance, and regression models, followed by a section on a case study in which we illustrate how the effects of system changes can be assessed using these statistical techniques.

This book is appropriate for such courses as "performance evaluation," "modeling and simulation," and "operations research," which are listed among 34 subject areas of *Model Curriculums for Computer Science/Engineering Education*, recently prepared by the IEEE Computer Society. This volume contains material enough for two quarters. Many exercise problems are included within the chapters for the convenience of homework assignment and for self-study. Portions of the material in Chapters 2 through 4 of this book were used by the author in graduate courses of Computer Science and Electrical Engineering at the University of Hawaii and Stanford University in 1975 and 1976, respectively. It is my hope that this book will encourage more universities to offer a course on modeling and analysis in their regular computer science/engineering curricula.

It has turned out to be a rather challenging undertaking to select subjects from various disciplines and put them all into a single volume. In order to keep the volume within a reasonable size, I had to exclude some important topics, but the discussion and reference sections given at the end of each chapter will hopefully complement the main body of the text.

Yorktown Heights, New York   H.K.
June 1978

Acknowledgments

I am grateful to the Computer Science Department of the IBM Research Center for their support of my efforts in writing this book and for providing facilities. Without the generous management supports of Joel S. Birnbaum and W. Donald Frazer, I would not have completed this book. I would like also to express my gratitude to the past editor-in-chief, Joel D. Aron, and the present editor-in-chief, Richard P. Case, of the Systems Programming Series for their continuing encouragement.

I also thank the University of Hawaii and Stanford University for arranging my opportunities to visit there and teach parts of this material in their graduate courses during 1975–1976. I benefitted a great deal from comments and suggestions given by my students at Hawaii and Stanford.

Andrew S. Noetzel of Brookhaven National Laboratory read the entire manuscript and made many valuable corrections and suggestions for improvement. For this I wish to express my special gratitude to him. Others whom I should like to acknowledge for their constructive criticisms of portions of the manuscript are Arnold O. Allen, Harold Anderson, Herman Friedman, Philip L. Rosenfeld, Charles H. Sauer, Gerald S. Shedler, K. Y. Sih, Lin S. Woo, and Philip S. Yu. I am also deeply indebted to many past and present colleagues for their collaborative research efforts with me, which are reflected in various parts of this book. I wish also to acknowledge the kind permission of other authors and several journals and publishers to incorporate materials published elsewhere.

To Joanne Bennett and Betty Smalley, I give my deepest thanks for their thorough and rapid task of preparing the final manuscript. I also thank Martha Morong for her extremely careful editing of the manuscript, which led to numerous improvements in style. Finally, I owe a great debt of thanks to my wife, Masaye, not only for her encouragement during the writing of the book but also for her typing the original draft of the manuscript.

The author

Contents

1
Computer Performance Evaluation: An Introduction

1.1 THE EVOLUTION OF COMPUTERS

The evolution of computers from their infancy three decades ago to their sophistication and pervasiveness in our society has been startling; it is certainly one of the fastest technological developments in human history. In this introductory section, we glance at major developments in the history of digital computers. It is customary to divide the era of computers into "generations" (Denning, 1971; Rosen, 1969). The first-generation machines (from approximately 1940 to 1950), represented by the ENIAC, used vacuum tubes for arithmetic operations; the time per operation ranged from 0.1 to 1.0 msec. Main-memory components consisted of electrostatic tubes and delay lines. These were augmented by auxiliary memory such as paper tapes, punched cards, and delay lines.

The second-generation (1950–1964) computer systems, such as the IBM 7040 and 7094, adopted transistor technology for logical operations: Their time per operation ranged from 1 to 10 microseconds. Magnetic drums and magnetic core appeared as main memory with access time also ranging from 1 to 10 μsec. Magnetic tapes, disks, and drums became available as auxiliary memory. The development of the first software systems—assemblers, relocatable loaders, and FORTRAN—made significant impacts on the use of computers. Floating-point arithmetic, interrupt facilities, and special-purpose I/O equipments were developed, and software services, such as subroutine libraries, batch monitors, and I/O control routines, enhanced the efficiency of digital computers.

With the introduction of the IBM System/360 and CDC 6600, the era of third-generation computer systems began. Integrated circuits were used in the CPU: These achieved speeds on the order of 0.1 to 1.0 μsec per operation. Storage capacity also expanded, in both main memory and auxiliary memory. But at least an equally important advance in the third-generation computing systems was made in software, that is, in the introduction of powerful and sophisticated *operating systems*. An operating system is a collection of computer system software that is responsible for allocating and controlling the use of the hardware, program, and data resources. The operating systems were designed to affect the capability of allowing several programs (or tasks) to run simultaneously by sharing resources. The sharing is, of course, motivated by the effective use of expensive computer resources, thereby increasing the system's productivity and users' satisfaction. The operating systems were also developed to relieve users and programmers of the detailed and tedious tasks involved with the system operation, such as converting data to the formats required by the hardware of the various devices. An operating system called OS/360 was designed to serve all the IBM System/360 models for a variety of applications.

In the late 1960s and 1970s, the third-generation computer systems moved into what we may call the "late third" generation or what some people designate as the "fourth" generation. These systems are characterized by faster machines utilizing more advanced LSI (large-scale integration) technology and semiconductor memory. The advances in storage technology are most noteworthy in this phase of computer system evolution. Additional memory devices, including flexible media and magnetic recording, have been developed over a broad range of accessing speeds and costs-per-unit capacity. An optimum combination of these technologies from the viewpoint of performance-cost tradeoffs has resulted in storage structures of many levels, collectively referred to as *storage hierarchies* (or *memory hierarchies*). A typical storage hierarchy consists of *cache* (buffer storage interposed between the processing unit and main storage), main storage (also called the backing store), drum, disk, and tape storage, and possibly including on-line archival mass storage. The memory requirements of programs have often outpaced the growth of storage capacity, placing on users the great burden of allocating storage space within the storage hierarchy. Thus, highly automated procedures have been devised for the allocation of storage spaces to the individual tasks and for the transfer of pieces of the programs and data from one level to another in the hierarchy. Progress in conventional storage devices, both semiconductor and magnetic types, continues to make them even faster and cheaper. In the future, such devices as charge-coupled devices, magnetic bubbles, beam-addressed optical storage, and holographic storage will further enlarge the list of available technologies.

Dynamic address translation, based on paging or segmentation (or combinations thereof), came into vogue in the mid-1960s as a major advancement in memory management. A storage hierarchy supported by such a memory management policy has come to be known as a *virtual storage* or *virtual memory.* The MULTICS (Multiplexed Information and Computing Service) system jointly developed by MIT and GE, and the IBM System/370 virtual-storage operating systems represent systems that employ the virtual storage concept. The architectural concept of virtual storage has been extended further into the notion of *virtual machines,* which can accommodate simultaneously several operating systems by dynamically sharing the resources of a single *real* machine. CP-67 (which was developed for the System/360 Model 67) and its successor, VM-370, are examples of operating systems that support multiple virtual machines.

Also in the late 1960s and early 1970s a number of *multiprocessing* systems came into existence. The wider use of multiprocessing was spurred on by economies of scale in the production of processors, by the flexibility to obtain the desired processing power through the addition of processing units, and by the prospect of uninterrupted (although degraded) performance in the event of failure. Parallel computers, such as the IBM 2938 array processor, the ILLIAC IV, the CDC STAR-100, and the Texas Instruments ASC (Advanced Scientific Computer), have evolved as alternative architecture for faster computation in specific environments.

Recent advances in computer architecture and hardware/software technologies have not only introduced a number of new computer applications, but have also impacted the ways in which information processing takes place. On-line teleprocessing and interactive use of a system with a large *data base* is now widespread. As the emphasis in the information processing industry shifts from the conventional mathematical computations to information management, the data base has become increasingly central to an overall system design.

The growth of computer applications and the effort for improved human/machine interface are stimulating the development of new peripheral devices and data entry technologies. The fast growth of information processing and management has also led to the development of computer-communication networks, as represented by the ARPANET (Advanced Research Projects Agency Network) and its descendants. We can regard *networking* as an extension of the resource-sharing concept exploited in the multiprogrammed and time-shared systems: Resources of host computers (their computing powers, data bases, and functions) at geographically distributed locations are accessible to a program or user through terrestrial, radio, and satellite links. The bursty nature of message traffic from computers or user terminals has required new ways of sharing or *multiplexing* transmission links. The combination of time-division multiplexing with packet-switching techniques is a notable example. In parallel with the continuing growth of large-scale general-purpose computing systems, *minicomputers* and, more recently, *microcomputers* (or *microprocessors*) have emerged, creating new applications of information management and processing.

1.2 THE ROLE OF PERFORMANCE EVALUATION AND PREDICTION

The issue of performance evaluation and prediction has concerned users throughout the history of computer evolution. In fact, as in any other technological development, the issue is most acute when the technology is young; the persistent pursuit of products with improved cost-performance characteristics then constantly leads to designs with untried and uncertain features.

The need for computer performance evaluation and prediction exists from the initial conception of a system's architectural design to its daily operation after installation. In the early planning phase of a new computer system product, the manufacturer usually must make two types of *prediction*. The first type is to forecast the nature of applications and the levels of "system workloads" of these applications. Here the term *workload* means, informally, the amount of service requirements placed on the system. We shall elaborate more on workload characterization in Section 1.4. The second type of prediction is concerned with the choice between architectural design alternatives, based on hardware and software technologies that will be available in the development period of the planned system. Here the criterion of selection is what we call "cost-performance tradeoff." The accuracy of such prediction rests to a considerable extent on our capability of mapping the performance characteristics of the system components into the overall system-level performance characteristics. Such translation procedures are by no means straightforward or well established.

Once the architectural decisions have been made and the system design and implementation started, the scope of performance prediction and evaluation becomes more specific. What is the best choice of machine organization? What is the operating system to support and what are the functions it should provide? The interactions among the operating system components—algorithms for *job scheduling, processor scheduling,* and

storage management—must be understood, and their effects on the performance must be predicted. The techniques used for performance evaluation and prediction during the design and implementation phases range
from simple hand calculation to quite elaborate simulation. Comparing
the predicted performance with the actual achieved performance often
reveals major defects in the design or errors in the system programming.
It is now a widely accepted belief that the performance prediction and
evaluation process should be an integral part of the development efforts
throughout the design and implementation activities.

After a new product is developed, the computer manufacturer
must be ready to predict the performance for specific applications and
requirements of potential buyers. The manufacturer must propose an
optimal combination and organization of its hardware and software
products to offer the best solution to a customer's requirements. This activity
is often referred to as the *configuration process*. Although the performance
prediction and evaluation tools and methodologies that are utilized during
the system development phase can be used for the purpose of configuration, there is an additional factor required in this effort. The projected
user environment must be translated into a set of quantitative parameters
that can be used as inputs to a performance prediction model. This is
the workload characterization problem again, but more precision is called
for in this instance.

When a product system is installed at a customer's site, the computer
vendor or service company must see that the system realizes its full
potential and meets the promised performance level. Such *system tuning*
activities were (and quite frequently still are) traditionally based on
intuition and experience. The complexity and sophistication of contemporary large-scale computers are such that the globally optimum and stable
operating point can no longer be easily found by mere intuition or
trial-and-error procedures. The system tuning requires a clear understanding of the complex interactions among the individual system components. A systematic procedure of performing this task is yet to be
developed, and awaits our continuing research and development efforts.

1.3 PERFORMANCE MEASURES

In the previous section, we frequently used the term performance without
precisely defining it. In this section, we clarify the term so that we have a
well-understood common ground on which to develop the discussions of
the following chapters.

When we say that "the performance of this computer is great," it
means perhaps that the quality of service delivered by the system exceeds

our expectation. But "the measure of service quality" and "the extent of expectation" vary depending on the individuals involved, be they system designers, installation managers, or terminal users. If we attempt to measure the quality of computer performance in the broadest context, we must consider such issues as user response (as well as the system response), ease of use, reliability, user's productivity, and the like as integral parts of the system's performance. Such discussions, however, fall within the realm of *nonquantitative* sciences that involve social and behavioral sciences. Despite our full awareness that performance analysts cannot avoid what are ultimately behavioral questions, the scope of this text is quite limited: We discuss the computer performance only in terms of *clearly measurable* quantities. This is done with the same spirit with which we conventionally define, for instance, the signal-to-noise ratio and the probability of decoding errors as measures of performance of communication systems.

There is certainly more than one choice for the measure of performance. We can classify performance measures into two categories: user-oriented measures and system-oriented measures. The user-oriented measures include such quantities as the *turnaround time* in a batch-system environment and the *response time* in a real-time and/or interactive-system environment. The turnaround time of a job is the length of time that elapses from the submission of the job until the availability of its processed result. Similarly, in an interactive environment, the response time of a request represents the interval that elapses from the arrival of the request until its completion at the system. There are several variants of the response time measure in common use, due to differing definitions of the moment of the request arrival and the moment of completion. For instance, we may define the arrival time as the moment when the user pushes the RETURN key at his or her terminal; the completion time may be the moment when the first line from the system output is typed out at the terminal. When terms such as response time are used in making performance comparisons, they should be accompanied by unambiguous definitions.

In interactive systems, we sometimes use the term *system reaction time*, which is the interval of time that elapses from the moment an input arrives in the system until it receives its first *time slice* of service. It measures how effective a scheduler is in dispatching service to a newly arrived input. Turnaround time, response time, and reaction time are all considered *random variables;* hence, we can talk about their *distributions, expected values, variances,* and the like.*

---

* See Section 2.4.1 for the formal definitions of random variables and these related terms.

　　Usually we categorize jobs or requests in several different priority classes and assign to the individual job the *priority* value of its class. Many factors may determine the assignment of a priority to a job: the job's urgency, its importance, and its resource-demand characteristics. We often define and compute the turnaround time or response time separately for different job classes.

　　The system-oriented (or installation-oriented) measures are typically *throughput* and *utilization*. Throughput is defined as the average number of jobs processed per unit time. It measures the degree of productivity that the system can provide. If jobs arrive at a system according to some arrival mechanism that is *independent* of the state of the system, throughput is equivalent to the average arrival rate, provided that the system can complete the jobs without creating an ever-increasing backlog. But in this case throughput is not an adequate measure of performance; rather, it is a measure of system *workload*.

　　The notion of throughput makes sense when either (1) there is always some work awaiting the system's service, or (2) the job arrival mechanism depends on the system state. Case (1), in the context of queueing theory, means that the system is unstable in the sense that the queue, or backlog, will grow without bound. In practice, however, we may define and measure throughput over a finite interval in which the input queue is never empty. Throughput thus defined is a proper indicator of a system's *capacity*. Case (2) applies when we assume a finite number of job generation sources. Suppose that, in an interactive system, there is a finite number N of terminal users actually logged on. Assume further that a terminal is *blocked* while its request is in the system, either waiting for or receiving service. If there are n jobs in the system, only the remaining $N - n$ terminals are eligible for generating requests. Thus, the effective arrival rate is a (linearly) decreasing function of the system state, n.[*] We can envision a similar situation in a batch-system environment: There may be a sufficiently large number of users to keep the system continually busy. In reality, however, as the system congestion level increases, a user may be discouraged from submitting a new job. Again, the job arrival rate will be some decreasing function of the number of outstanding jobs. This *negative feedback* loop inherent in the job generation mechanism makes the system always stable.

　　The *utilization* of a resource is the fraction of time that the particular resource is busy. The CPU utilization is the most popular measure of system usage, although it is not necessarily the most important in complex systems. When the CPU is not idle, it may be in either of two busy states:

---

[*] See Sections 3.9 and 3.10 for a full description of such models.

the *problem program state* (or simply the *problem state*) and the *supervisory program state* (or the *supervisor state*). The former represents the portion of time when the CPU is actually executing the programs written or called by the users; the latter is the time consumed in executing such operating system components as the scheduler and various interrupt-handling routines. The distinction is commonly assumed to be synonymous with that of "useful work" versus "overhead." Yet it must be noted that much of the supervisor-state operation provides necessary and useful service for the user programs; hence the "overhead" categorization may be misleading.

If we assume a system with a single CPU, and if the CPU utilization figure excludes the supervisor state, then we find the following simple relationship between throughput λ (jobs per second) and the CPU utilization ρ_{CPU}:

$$\rho_{CPU} = \lambda \bar{S}_{CPU}, \qquad (1.1)$$

where $\bar{S}_{CPU}$ (seconds per job) represents the average CPU time required to process a job.

The mean response time, which we denote by $\bar{T}$, is found to have the simple relation with throughput

$$\lambda \bar{T} = \bar{n}, \qquad (1.2)$$

in which $\bar{n}$ represents the average number of jobs (waiting or being served) in the system. Both Formulas (1.1) and (1.2) are special cases of the formula $L = \lambda W$ that appear frequently in a more general context. (See Section 3.6 for details of this formula.)

1.4 WORKLOAD CHARACTERIZATION AND PERFORMANCE EVALUATION TECHNIQUES

As we stated earlier, by the term workload we mean the amount of *service demands* imposed on the system by a set of jobs in a given application. The job arrival rate, or more generally the job arrival mechanism, is certainly one factor that determines the system's workload. For example, the Poisson arrival assumption, which we shall discuss in Section 3.3, can be regarded as a part of the *workload model*. We remarked in the previous section that the job arrival process should depend on the degree of the system's congestion. Thus, the system's workload and the system's performance are not independent of each other.

The job arrival model is only a part of the workload characterization: We must also represent the work demands brought in by the individual jobs. Since a computer is an entity consisting of multiple resource components, the work demands of a job must be represented by at least (1) the CPU work demand, (2) memory space demand, (3) I/O (input/output) work demand, and (4) demands on software components. Thus, we must translate a given application environment into a set of work demands seen by system resource components. This translation procedure was a relatively simple matter in the early days when the CPU was the major critical resource in the system and each job was sequentially executed in isolation. In the following discussion we first review the conventional methods of workload characterization and performance evaluation: specifically, instruction mixes, kernel programs, and benchmarks.

Instruction mixes

One popular method of representing the workloads on the CPU is the *instruction mix*. By an instruction mix we mean the *distribution of relative frequencies* $\{f_i\}$ of instruction types (for the given instruction set) observed in a typical application environment of the system in question. An instruction mix is obtained by running a set of representative programs and counting the number of occurrences of individual instruction types— Add/Subtract, Multiply, Divide, Load, Store, Shift, branch operations, and the like. Since the instruction execution times t_i of each instruction type i are known for a given CPU, we can calculate τ, the average execution time per operation,

$$\tau = \sum_i f_i t_i, \tag{1.3}$$

where the sum is taken over all distinct instruction types i. If we choose the microsecond (μsec) as the unit of time $\{t_i\}$, then the quantity $1/\tau$ represents the speed of the CPU measured in MIPS (Million Instructions Per Second).

The instruction mix provides valuable information for the design and implementation of a processor: When the design of the CPU adopts microprogramming, the instruction mix gives a good indication whether to emphasize the performance efficiency or minimize the space occupancy of a particular instruction. There are, however, a number of shortcomings and limitations of the instruction mix. First of all, there is a question of the "representativeness" of the chosen instruction mix. Since it is expensive in machine time to produce a new instruction mix figure, we often rely on the relative frequencies $\{f_i\}$ measured by others. Even if we have program tracing facilities and can afford the machine time, the matter of selecting a set of representative programs is not trivial.

Second, the instruction mix $\{f_i\}$ is the first-order statistic; it completely lacks information on serial dependency and instruction overlap. In a system with buffer store (cache) or pipelined CPU, the effective execution speed depends on the sequence pattern of the instruction and data references, not just the relative frequency. Furthermore, because the instruction mix does not include demand for other system resources, such as I/O devices, it cannot be used for overall system performance evaluation.

Kernel programs

The second method used to represent loads on a CPU is the *kernel program method.* A kernel program is a small program segment that represents the inner loop of a frequently used program. For instance, in scientific applications, a matrix inversion routine and a differential equation solution program may be selected as kernel programs. A payroll program is an example of a business application. A kernel program is useful in the early stages of a CPU design for the evaluation of different instruction sets and different architectural ideas. This is because the kernel preserves such important information as the sequence of instructions and the relative positions of branch instructions. Kernels also allow evaluation of some software components. For instance, the quality of a compiler can be evaluated by programming and compiling the kernel and examining the object code.

Although kernel programs contain significantly richer information than instruction mixes, there are still a number of limitations on their use. First, a performance analysis based on kernels requires coding the kernel program for the machine in question, using the specific instruction set. Thus, any such study is usually done using only a small number of kernel programs. Then the question of "representativeness" will be a more critical issue here than with the instruction mix method, in which measurement over a wide range of programs is relatively easy, although expensive in terms of computer time. Second, although a kernel program allows the performance evaluation of CPU/main-memory usage, it does not normally include adequate information on I/O operations. Thus, kernel programs are not adequate for the evaluation of multiprogramming systems.

Benchmarks

A *benchmark* is a complete program that is written in a high-level language and is considered to be representative of a given class of application programs. Sort programs and file updating programs are popular examples of benchmarks. By running mixed benchmarks on the system under evaluation, the performance of the entire system in realistic circumstances can be estimated. The quality of compilers can also be assessed by measuring both the compilation time and the execution time of each benchmark. The so-called *benchmark test* is a common practice that takes place during the vendor selection process. A benchmark program is simply run on each proposed system; the comparison of the total run times provides a good indication of relative performance capabilities. But the questions of how to prepare good benchmark programs and of how to interpret the benchmark test results are certainly of central importance in this decision-making process.

A major advantage of benchmarks over instruction mixes and kernel programs is that they are closer to realistic workloads. But this advantage is at the same time a major limiting factor. First, the use of benchmarks is limited to existing systems; a proposed system for test must be available in its entirety, with all the required hardware and software, and in a specific configuration. Second, a specific benchmark program ought not to be used to compare systems of radically different structure, since an efficient version of any program must depend on the system and facilities available. For example, programs written for OS/360 are certainly not appropriate benchmarks for VS/370 systems. Both the collection and use of benchmarks will become increasingly complex and costly as the size and sophistication of computing systems grow. For example, benchmarks cannot be used meaningfully for an interactive system unless there are additional facilities that simulate terminal systems. This is usually done either with a separate computer or with an in-core program that places commands into the terminal handling software, following some scripts that simulate the user terminal's behavior.

Synthetic jobs or programs

Rather than selecting a set of benchmarks from existing programs, *synthetic jobs* are often used in the measurement and performance evaluation. A synthetic job, as the name indicates, is an artificial program, but it is supposed to contain all the important ingredients of programs to exercise various components of computer systems. It includes adjustable *parameters* to mimic a broad range of program characteristics. These parameters are, for instance, the amount of CPU processing demands, storage space requirements, and the number of disk accesses. The structure of a synthetic job can be quite simple: For instance, the computation phase in a synthetic program may be a loop that merely sums integers.

The development and usage of synthetic jobs is a rather recent phenomenon, but is drawing increasing attention from performance analysts. A major problem here is again the issue of representativeness. For a given synthetic program, how can we know whether a specific choice of adjustable parameters will reasonably approximate the workload of the actual installation? The goodness-of-fit may depend on the performance measure to be used. For instance, if the system throughput is the chosen performance criterion, a set of fairly simple synthetic jobs may be quite adequate. The same set of synthetic jobs may be a poor representation of the real workload if the performance measure is instead a set of response times for different priority classes. Workload characterization depends on its intended use, which cannot be divorced from the criteria chosen for performance comparison. Thus, the study of workload characterization is not separable from the progress in modeling and performance analysis.

1.5 TOTAL SYSTEM PERFORMANCE AND MODELING METHODOLOGIES

Performance analysis of a computer system by means of benchmarks or synthetic jobs is thus limited in many ways. Aside from the representativeness of chosen benchmark programs or synthetic programs, the intrinsic limitation of these techniques lies, as pointed out earlier, in that a system under test must be available *in its entirety*. Thus the techniques are limited only to the performance evaluation of an existing system.

When the performance predictions for each of a set of various design (or configuration) specifications are called for, it is essential to construct a *model* that can reflect the difference between the proposed alternatives. The first step is to list and examine the important system device parameters: the capacity and cycle time of cache and main memory, the speed of the CPU, the access time and data transfer rate (bandwidth) of rotating storage devices, and the types and characteristics of terminals and communication equipments. We also need to know software components: the job scheduling algorithm, the memory management algorithm, the CPU dispatching algorithm, the disk and drum scheduling algorithm, the sizes of page and block, and the file organization. In addition, we may want to find the amount of traffic (or loads) anticipated for each of these components: the job arrival rate, the amount of CPU time (or instructions) per job, the memory space requirements, the page fault rate, the number of disk arm movements per second, the request rate on the drums, and the required data transfer rate between main memory and auxiliary storage.

It is relatively easy to make such lists, which include all the system components and parameters that may have a bearing on the system performance: It is less easy to identify a set of critical parameters, much less to find the relationships or equations that relate the overall system performance to these parameters. The difficulty is that the total system is more than the sum of its components. The catalogued values of system devices and the performance analyses of the individual components of an operating system give little more than a clue as to how the overall system will perform. The device parameters, the operating system components, and the load or traffic parameters are strongly interrelated.

1.5.1 System Bottlenecks and Instability

Prediction of the overall system performance is difficult since the nature of the interactions is highly *nonlinear* and *nondeterministic.* Yet we tend to extrapolate things linearly and deterministically. In this section we give a brief account of some important notions that are useful in understanding the computer performance. The first is the notion of *system bottlenecks.* We use the term bottleneck to refer to a resource or service facility whose capability seriously limits the performance of the entire system. A bottleneck is created at some resource when the job traffic to that resource approaches the resource capacity, whereby a saturation of the resource is incurred. A saturation is, informally, the level of congestion at which the jobs begin to feel strong interference from one another. (A more formal definition of saturation will be introduced in Section 3.9.) We should be aware that a saturation generally occurs at a congestion level substantially lower than the value predicted by a simple *deterministic* model—a model in which we use constant parameters, ignoring the statistical fluctuations inherent in the arrival and service demands mechanisms.

Once a bottleneck is created in the system, a disproportionately large load will be placed on the critical resource: All other resources will be lightly loaded, their potential productivity wasted. What will happen if we add N more jobs to the system? We merely increase the queue size of the critical resource approximately by N, with practically no increase in other queues, however large N may be! (See Section 3.9.1 and Exercise 3.8.18.) When we identify the system's bottleneck, we expect to improve the overall performance, either by expanding the capacity of the limiting resource or by improving its management. But if another resource of approximately equal saturation level happens to exist in the system, this resource will immediately turn to a new bottleneck, and its queue size will jump to the level previously found at the original bottleneck resource.

Another important type of interaction is a *feedback loop* in the system. There are two types of feedback loops: positive and negative. There are many situations in which a negative feedback loop governs the overall behavior of the system or subsystem. A simple example is a situation in which the job arrival rate decreases as the backlog increases. Such a situation was described earlier in Section 1.3 in connection with the definition of throughput. In the presence of a negative feedback loop, a *restoring tendency* plays a dominant role in governing the system behavior; stability is maintained since the queue length tends to remain centralized around the mean value. The negative feedback loop decreases the variation or fluctuation in congestions and makes the analysis substantially simpler. In fact, a deterministic model becomes quite acceptable in such a circumstance. The *fluid approximation* model and the corresponding *graphical analysis* to be discussed in Section 3.9.3 are examples of deterministic models.

On the other hand, a positive feedback loop will have the opposite effect. Positive feedback may occur, for instance, in a virtual storage system with paging, when the job scheduler makes a poor judgment of paging activities. Suppose that the operating system observes that the CPU is underutilized with moderate paging-device utilization. It may then direct that the multiprogramming level be increased, with the intent of better utilizing the CPU. The inclusion of additional programs into the multiprogramming mix decreases the amount of memory space allocatable to each program; hence the page fault rate may begin to rise. But the CPU utilization may remain low or even decrease, due to the increased congestion at the paging device. If the low CPU utilization causes the operating system to introduce even more programs into the multiprogramming mix, an excessive amount of paging activity—a phenomenon called "thrashing"—will result (Denning, 1968). Then the system throughput will virtually decline to zero: The positive feedback created by the poor control mechanism may drive the system into an unstable region, and finally into a very undesirable operating point.

Cases of instability due to positive feedback can also be found in packet-switching communication networks. An example is the ALOHA system, a random-access multiplexing communication system developed by the University of Hawaii (Abramson, 1973). Its basic operation is roughly as follows. A user transmits data messages into the random-access channel (a radio or satellite channel, although in principle it can be any shareable communication medium) in the form of packets. If a packet occupies the channel by itself for the entire packet duration, it will be successfully received by a message-switching processor at the other end of the channel. If several users transmit packets simultaneously and these transmission times overlap each other even partially (an event called a *collision*), then all of the transmissions are considered unsuccessful. The senders become aware of the failures by not receiving positive acknowledgments from the message-switching processor. These packets must then be retransmitted, after randomly chosen delays. When the number of backlogged messages increases beyond some critical level (that depends on the retransmission strategy), the channel throughput decreases as the congestion level rises, because more frequent collisions are incurred. Then the message arrival rate from the user terminals exceeds the channel throughput, whereby the message backlog further increases and the throughput gets even worse. Once the system operating point is driven into such a region of positive feedback, the system's performance suddenly collapses: Throughput decreases virtually to zero level, and the channel delay becomes immensely large. See Kleinrock and Lam (1975) for quantitative analyses of the instability problem.

The user behavior in a conventional batch-processing environment may provide another example of positive feedback (even though it was previously used as an example of negative feedback!). As the turnaround time gets exceedingly longer, many users begin to be impatient, and rather than completely debugging their programs they may start submitting multiple production runs with various sets of data parameters. Clearly, many of these will be unproductive runs that could be avoided if the system were more responsive. Such user behavior contributes to a potentially unstable feedback loop: The increased turnaround time causes the users to create more jobs, which in turn causes a further increase in the turnaround time.

1.5.2 Structured Modeling and Modularity

The notions of bottleneck, saturation, and feedback discussed in the previous section are examples of interactions observed among system components which lie *horizontally* to each other or at the same level in our conceptualization of the system. Many of the difficulties we may face in the construction of an overall model are frequently due to our failure to structure the model *vertically* or *hierarchically*. Figure 1.1 is an example of what we call a hierarchical model structure. In this representation, module A is at the lowest layer and the performance analysis results

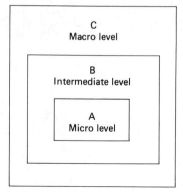

Fig. 1.1 A hierarchical model structure.

of the module A should be summarized in a form easily usable in the next layer above, that is, module B. Usually, a scaling factor (such as the effective processing rate) or a random variable with some distribution is used as a summarized statistic for an interface. Similarly, the results of the module B are incorporated into the higher level, module C, and so forth.

The decomposition of a total system into submodels in a manner as clear as that shown in Fig. 1.1 may be rarely feasible. But, in practice, these submodels are often "near-completely" decomposable. In the sense that Courtois (1975) defines the term, the basic requirement for near-complete decomposition is that the time constant of a given layer is sufficiently smaller than the interevent times of the layer above it. To be more concrete, let us consider the example of Fig. 1.1. When the time between events in the module A is expressed in nanoseconds or microseconds, we shall say that the module A is at the *micro level* (Baskett and Muntz, 1973). An example of a model at this level is that of multiple CPU's, each of which has a cache and occasionally makes read/write requests to main memory. Such performance issues as memory interference, the effect of interleaving, and cache mapping algorithms should be analyzed at this level of model. When the time between events in the module B is expressed in milliseconds, we shall say that the module B is at the *intermediate level*. An example of a model at this level is a multiprogramming model. The programs (sometimes called processes or tasks) are either engaging in data transfer on I/O devices, executing instructions with a CPU, or waiting for one of these servers. Operating system components such as processor scheduling, I/O scheduling, and memory management should be studied using a model at this level. When the time between events is expressed in seconds, we shall say that we have a *macro-level* model. An example at this level is a time-sharing system model. Studies of job scheduling and the analysis of terminal response time are typical issues addressed by using a model at this level. In Section 3.10.5 we present an example of a two-level model for a time-shared interactive system with multiprogramming in virtual storage.

The specific hierarchical structure we should choose in constructing an overall model of a given system depends not only on the machine configuration, but also on the structure of the operating system. Clearly, the model structure should closely reflect the modular structure of the operating system. In this respect, the increasing interest in *structured programming* constitutes a desirable trend toward greater "modelability" of the total system. Using the structured approach, the designer of an operating system modularizes the system software vertically: The function of each layer is composed of the functions of the underlying layers. In the system design specifications, the *top-to-bottom* procedure is desirable: We start with the overall function and performance requirements, and determine what supporting functions and performance levels are required in order to meet the objectives. This procedure is repeated, giving rise to a series of layers, until the system is finally implemented in terms of the available primitives, usually the hardware of the machine itself.

For successful system design and performance prediction, the specification of performance should be incorporated as an integral part of the design of each layer. To ensure that the performance objectives set for each layer are met, performance modeling, prediction analysis, measurement, and evaluation are all required at every layer. In the remainder of this text, we will discuss a collection of quantitative techniques that are available to serve such purposes. We cannot overemphasize, however, that the most important and critical step of any performance study lies in the way in which we decompose the total system model into a set of submodels of manageable complexities and clear interfaces.

There are various approaches to solving both total models and submodels. We often classify them into the following three types: (1) analytic models, (2) simulation models, and (3) empirical models. This classification, however, is not always appropriate for reasons that will become clear as we discuss them.

1.5.3 Analytic Models

When we speak of an analytic model, we usually mean a solution technique that allows us to write a functional relation between system parameters and a chosen performance criterion in terms of equations that are analytically solvable. A simple "paper-and-pencil" calculation certainly belongs to this category, and such a calculation ought to be tried wherever possible so that we may acquire a gross understanding of the overall performance before more elaborate mathematical analysis is attempted.

Among a number of mathematical disciplines pertinent to analytic modeling, *queueing theory* plays the most important role. We view a computer system as a *multiple-resource system*, where the resources are the CPU, memory, auxiliary storage, and I/O channels and devices. Jobs or programs demand services from these resources or servers. A major function of the operating system is, as we discussed earlier, to manage the use of resources among many programs. Most performance problems are therefore related to queueing delays caused by contention for resources. The theory of queues provides a mathematical framework for formulating such problems. The solution techniques that we present in Chapter 3 are useful in analyzing the effects of various resource contentions on such performance measures as throughput, utilization, and the mean response time. Many of the assumptions made in simple queueing models may seem unrealistic or oversimplified, yet the prediction results obtained are often found to agree surprisingly well with either the actual observations or the estimates obtained through more realistic simulations (see Section 3.10.5). These agreements are not coincidental; some measures of performance are rather *insensitive* or *robust* with respect to the distributional forms of service time and to the scheduling rules adopted, as we shall discuss in Sections 3.6, 3.7, 3.9.1, and 3.9.3. It is important for the system analysts to acquire some feeling as to when bold assumptions can be introduced without seriously affecting the prediction results.

There is an important constraint in queueing theory that intrinsically limits its applications to multiple-resource systems—that is, a job (or customer) cannot occupy more than one resource (or server) simultaneously. Certainly this rule is violated in modeling a computer system: A job in execution holds at least main-memory space and the CPU simultaneously. The hierarchical modeling approach discussed above may sometimes overcome difficulties of this kind.

1.5.4 Simulation Models

An analytic model should be sought wherever possible, since it can evaluate the performance with minimal efforts and costs over a wide range of choices in the system parameters and configurations. Even with simplifying assumptions and decompositions, however, the resultant analytic model is often not mathematically tractable. Then the only alternative for predicting the performance of a nonexisting system is a *simulation*. The term simulation has a number of connotations. In our discussion a simulation means a numerical technique for conducting an experiment (by a digital computer) of a system evolving in time. Therefore, in a simulation the concept of time is explicit. A simulation model describes the *dynamic* behavior of a system, even when the system analyst may ultimately be interested in only the mean value of some measure (e.g., CPU utilization, the response time) in the steady state.

The structure and complexity of a simulator depends on the scope of the simulation experiment. The hierarchical structure should be adopted as much as possible in the construction of a simulation model also, though the motivation here is somewhat different. There are at least two features that make such a structure attractive. First, a hierarchical (or, more generally, decomposable) structure allows *modularization* of a simulation program into a set of subprograms. Modularization leads to a flexible structure of the program, so that further extensions and changes are easily handled. Second, an ingenious use of the hierarchical structure may shorten a simulation run time substantially. In general, the length of a simulation run is determined by the required accuracy of simulation estimates and the amount of *correlation span* (or, equivalently, the magnitude of *transient time*) of the stochastic process observed in the simulation outputs. In the model structure of Fig. 1.1, we said that the interevent time in the micro-level model is in microseconds. Then the number of events observed over the simulated time of, say, one second will be in the order of 10^6; this subsystem easily reaches its steady state within that period. During the same period, the number of events that take place at the intermediate model is in the order of 10^3. The stochastic process that characterizes the intermediate-level model may possibly reach its steady state, but the sample size of 10^3 is perhaps not large enough to allow a reasonably accurate estimate of a chosen performance measure. But at the macro-level model, it is quite evident that one second of simulated time is too short to understand the system behavior, since the interevent time itself is in the order of seconds. Perhaps a simulated time of 10^3 seconds or more will be required at this level to obtain an accurate estimate of the overall performance measure. If we were to run this simulator *in its entirety* over the period of, say, 10^3 seconds in simulated time, the total number of events observed at the micro level would amount to the order of 10^9 events! Note that the actual length of computer running time for the simulation experiment is governed not by the length of simulated time, but by the *total number of events* handled. What the simulator performs is essentially to record all the system changes caused by the individual events. Therefore, a "brute-force" simulation often leads to an extremely costly experiment, but this is unfortunately the way in which most simulators have been structured in the past.

A more efficient approach to the simulation effort is to run different submodels *separately*, thereby avoiding the waste of running the micro-level model for such a long period. Interfacing a lower-level model to a higher-level model should be achieved through summarized statistics, such as scaling constants and service time distributions. Since the equilibrium state solution of a model of a given level depends on its surroundings, we must have separate runs of the model for different sets of parameters that determine its surroundings. For example, if the intermediate-level model of Fig. 1.1 represents a multiprogramming model, we need to run the simulator of that level for different values of the degree of multiprogramming. These simulations will determine the whole range of *effective processing rates* that the individual jobs receive under different congestion environments. The values of the effective processing rates are then used as parameters of the macro-level model.

The above decomposition formulation naturally leads to the notion of what is sometimes called *hybrid modeling:* a combination of analytical procedure and simulation.* So long as the interfaces between different levels or submodels are clearly established, the mixing of analytic and simulation techniques should present no technical problems. In fact, this approach deserves special attention, since it allows us to take the best of both worlds: the efficiency of analytic modeling and the realism of simulation modeling. As we stated earlier, the classification of models into analytic models versus simulation models is merely for the convenience of organizing the chapters in this text.

Simulation models for computer systems can be further classified as either trace-driven simulation or self-driven simulation. A *trace* is a stream of major events observed in an operational system, recorded with the time of their occurrences. Like a benchmark program, a trace should be selected from a representative segment of the system workload. However, a benchmark is a program that is independent of the system in question, whereas a trace is a result of both the chosen program and the machine that executes the program.

In the self-driven simulation, we introduce the concept of a probabilistic sequence of resource demands presented by jobs. An advantage of the probabilistic model over the trace-driven model is that, since the event stream is generated artificially, it may be completely understood by the analyst; furthermore, the workload parameters are adjustable. In this sense, a probabilistic input model is to a trace-driven model as a synthetic job is to a benchmark. (Detailed discussions of these two different simulation methods will be presented in Section 4.2.2.) Self-driven (or probabilistic) simulation involves the use of random-number sequences, and in this regard it is similar to the Monte Carlo method: a numerical technique for solving a nonprobabilistic mathematical problem (for example, certain integral equations) by introducing a random variable whose mean or distribution corresponds to the solution of the original problem. In fact, these two numerical techniques have a great deal in common: The objective of probabilistic simulation can usually be formulated as a *mapping* from a random vector (a sequence of random-number variates) to a scalar value of some performance measure, as represented in Fig. 4.15 and Eq. (4.77). For this reason, many of the variance-reducing techniques developed in the Monte Carlo method are applicable to variance reductions in stochastic system simulations (see Section 4.9).

---

* The term hybrid is conventionally used for a technique that combines analog and digital techniques. Our use of the term here should not be confused with this convention.

Therefore, we sometimes use the term *Monte Carlo simulation* synonymously with self-driven or probabilistic simulation.

1.5.5   Measurement and Empirical Models

We can readily identify four different purposes or uses of measurement activities: (1) performance monitoring, (2) job accounting, (3) model input specifications, and (4) model verification. The first two items are more or less self-explanatory: Specific tools and methods for performance measurements will be discussed in Section 5.2. As for the third item, it is apparent that the accuracy of performance prediction is strongly influenced by the accuracies of the parameters and workloads used in the model, whether analytic or simulation. Specification of model parameters is just as important as the model solution technique. Section 5.4 discusses a number of graphical presentations of measured data that will reveal important information about the distributional form and other statistics.

The fourth item, the model verification based on measurement data, is an area that deserves our close attention. The accuracy of any predictive model can be validated only when it is checked against measured data in a real environment. Such data are scanty even with respect to systems that have been in operation for some years. Undoubtedly, many factors contribute to this deplorable situation. One prime reason, the author believes, is that any system-wide measurement activity requires a long-term commitment of system analysts who are knowledgeable about the system in question and its measurement tools, and who are also equipped with programming skills for data reduction and analysis. In addition, they must be sufficiently competent in statistical theory to draw sound and useful conclusions from a mass of collected data. Individuals or groups of individuals with such comprehensive skills are, at present, scarce human resources! Chapter 5 provides the reader with introductory materials related to statistical techniques.

Another use of measurement and analysis that is not listed above is (5) the construction of empirical models. By an empirical model we mean a statistical characterization of system performance based on data measured in a real system or simulator. The main idea of this approach is to capture the system behavior from a phenomenological viewpoint. Some might argue that since a computer is something that we scientists and engineers have created, with a completely logical structure, there should be nothing phenomenological about its behavior. But we should recall our earlier observation: The complexities of interactions among various system components and user programs have surpassed our ability to readily identify what system and algorithmic parameters are really significant ones, and in what functional form these variables are related to a chosen measure of performance. To answer these issues realistically, we must rely on empirical observations of an actual system or realistic simulator. Of course, the logical structure of the system in question should guide us in our search for an empirical model. Empirical characterization also often reveals unexpected system behaviors, close examination of which may lead to the detection of deficiencies in the system design or errors in the implementation.

Suppose we wish to make a performance comparison, based on system measurements, between several alternative parameter values (e.g., time-slice length, the maximum multiprogramming level), resource allocation policies (e.g., CPU dispatching algorithm, page replacement algorithm), or combinations thereof. We will be tempted to rank these alternatives merely on the basis of observed performance figures such as the CPU utilization, the number of page faults, or the mean response time of the jobs processed during the observation intervals. But how do we know that the difference between the observed figures is really due to the differences in the chosen system parameters or resource allocation policies? Can we be sure that the observed differences cannot be explained merely in terms of chance fluctuations of the workload? The theory of statistics provides us with a systematic procedure for assessing the degree of *uncertainty* inherent in any *statistical inference*. A measurement experiment should be carefully set up so as to minimize the degree of uncertainty in our statistical estimate. Such procedure is referred to by the general term "design of experiment," or "experimental design." Experimental design techniques guide us, for example, in dealing with an environment in which changes in the system workload during a measurement period may introduce some unrecognizable *biases* (as well as variances) into the observed performance values. They are also useful when the system in question contains multiple factors, such as the above-mentioned parameters and policies, which can be varied or adjusted. Some factors are quantitative (numeric) and some are qualitative (categorical). The effect of *levels**[*] of these factors on a chosen performance measure is generally not additive, and the different factors *interact*. As a result, the significance of each factor cannot be evaluated in isolation; rather, it is necessary to conduct experiments under various combinations of the values that the factors may take on. To exhaust all possible combinations of the experimental arrangements is certainly not

---

[*] The term level is used here to mean a specific choice of a factor, whether it be numeric or categorical. The LRU algorithm, for instance, is a level of the replacement algorithm factor.

practical, as the number of factors and the range of their levels increase. Chapter 5 discusses the fundamentals of statistical analysis applicable to the class of questions raised above.

DISCUSSIONS FOR FURTHER READING

As was stated in the preface, some familiarity with computer architecture and operating systems is a recommended prerequisite to this book. There are a number of textbooks on these subjects: Coffman and Denning (1973), Freeman (1975), Haberman (1975), Hansen (1973), Katzan (1973), Shaw (1974), Stone (1975), Tsichritzes and Bernstein (1974), Watson (1970), and Wilks (1968). Hellerman and Conroy (1973), Madnick and Donovan (1974), and the IBM Manual GR20-4260 give fairly comprehensive accounts of the virtual-storage technique implemented in the IBM System/370 and other computers. Those who desire to review the state of the art of storage technology are directed to Feth (1976), Matick (1975), and the *IEEE Proceedings*, a special issue of August 1975. The January 1978 issue of *Communications of the ACM* is a special issue on computer architecture, and Case and Padegs (1978) summarize the characteristics of IBM System/370 architecture. As for distributed systems and communication networks, the reader is referred to Cypser (1978) and Schwartz (1977). Cypser discusses in detail IBM's Systems Network Architecture; Schwartz focuses on communication network design and analysis methods.

The sources of materials discussed in Section 1.4 are Bucholz (1969), Calingaret (1967), Drummond (1973), Fuller (1975), Lucas (1971), and others. The notions of saturation and bottleneck are discussed by a number of authors: Scherr (1967), Kleinrock (1968), Buzen (1971), and Muntz (1975). The discussions on the structured modeling approach presented in Section 1.5.2 are influenced by a number of articles: in particular, Lynch (1972), Sekino (1972), Baskett and Muntz (1973), Browne et al. (1975), and Courtois (1975, 1977). Kobayashi (1978) gives an expository treatment on the subject.

REFERENCES

Abramson, N. (1973). "The ALOHA System." In N. Abramson and F. F. Kuo (eds.), *Computer-Communication Networks*, pp. 501–517. Englewood Cliffs, N.J.: Prentice-Hall.

ACM (1978). "Special Issues on Computer Architecture." *Communications of the Association for Computing Machinery* **21**(1): 3–96.

Baskett, F., and R. R. Muntz (1973). "Network of Queues." *Proceedings of the Seventh Annual Princeton Conference on Information Sciences and Systems* (March): 428–434.

Browne, J. C., K. M. Chandy, R. M. Brown, T. W. Keller, D. F. Towsley, and C. W. Dissly (1975). "Hierarchical Techniques for the Development of Realistic Models of Complex Computer Systems." *Proceedings of IEEE* 63(6): 966–975.

Bucholz, W. (1969). "A Synthetic Job for Measuring System Performance." *IBM Journal of Research and Development* 8(4): 309–318.

Buzen, J. P. (1971). "Analysis of System Bottlenecks Using a Queueing Network Model." *Proceedings of ACM-SIGOPS Workshop on System Performance Evaluation*, pp. 82–103. Cambridge, Mass.: Harvard University (April).

Calingaret, P. (1967). "System Performance Evaluation: Survey and Appraisal." *Communications of the Association for Computing Machinery* 10(1): 12–18.

Case, R. P., and A. Padegs (1978). "Architecture of the IBM System/370." *Communications of the Association for Computing Machinery* 21(1): 73–96.

Coffman, E. G., Jr., and P. J. Denning (1973). *Operating Systems Theory.* Englewood Cliffs, N.J.: Prentice-Hall.

Courtois, P. J. (1975). "Decomposability, Instability and Saturation in Multi-programming Systems." *Communications of the Association for Computing Machinery* 18(7): 371–376.

Courtois, P. J. (1977). *Decomposability: Queueing and Computer System Applications.* New York: Academic Press.

Cypser, R. J. (1978). *Architecture for Distributed Systems.* Reading, Mass.: Addison-Wesley.

Denning, P. J. (1968). "Thrashing: Its Causes and Preventions." *AFIPS Conference Proceedings, 1968 Fall Joint Computer Conference* 33 (Part 1): 915–922. Montvale, N.J.: AFIPS Press.

Denning, P. J. (1971). "Third Generation Computer Systems." *Computing Surveys* 3(4): 175–216.

Drummond, M. E., Jr. (1973). *Evaluation and Measurement Techniques for Digital Computer Systems.* Englewood Cliffs, N.J.: Prentice-Hall.

Feth, G. C. (1976). "Memories: Smaller, Faster, and Cheaper." *IEEE Spectrum* 13(6): 36–43.

Freeman, P. (1975). *Software Systems Principles.* Chicago: Science Research Associates.

Fuller, S. H. (1975). "Performance Evaluation." In H. S. Stone (ed.), *Introduction to Computer Architecture*, pp. 474–545. Chicago: Science Research Associates.

Haberman, A. N. (1975). *Operating System Principles.* Chicago: Science Research Associates.

Hansen, P. B. (1973). *Operating System Principles.* Englewood Cliffs, N.J.: Prentice-Hall.

Hellerman, H., and T. F. Conroy (1975). *Computer System Performance.* New York: McGraw-Hill.

IBM Corporation. "Introduction to Virtual Storage in System/370." No. GR20-4260. White Plains, N.Y.: IBM Corporation, Data Processing Division.

IEEE (1975). "Large Capacity Digital Storage Systems." *Proceedings of IEEE* **63**(8): 1092–1240.

Katzan, H. J., Jr. (1973). *Operating Systems: A Pragmatic Approach.* New York: Van Nostrand Reinhold.

Kleinrock, L. (1968). "Certain Analytic Results for Time-Shared Processors." *Proceedings of the International Federation for Information Processing Congress* (August): 838–845.

Kleinrock, L., and S. S. Lam (1975). "Packet Switching in a Multiaccess Broadcast Channel: Performance Evaluation." *IEEE Transactions on Communications* **COM-23**(4): 410–423.

Kobayashi, H. (1972). "Some Recent Progress in Analytic Studies of Systems Performance." *First USA-Japan Computer Conference Proceedings* (October): 130–138.

Kobayashi, H. (1978). "System Design and Performance Analysis Using Analytic Models." In K. M. Chandy and R. T. Yeh (eds.), *Current Trends in Programming Methodology, Vol. III: Software Modelling,* pp. 72–114. Englewood Cliffs, N.J.: Prentice-Hall.

Lassettre, E., and A. Scherr (1972). "Modeling the Performance of the OS/360 Time-Sharing Option (TSO)." In W. Freiberger (ed.), *Statistical Computer Performance Evaluation,* pp. 57–72. New York: Academic Press.

Lucas, H. (1971). "Performance Evaluation and Monitoring." *Computing Surveys* **3**(3): 79–91.

Lynch, W. C. (1972). "Operating System Performance." *Communications of the Association for Computing Machinery* **15**(7): 579–585.

Madnick, S. E., and J. J. Donovan (1974). *Operating Systems.* New York: McGraw-Hill.

Matick, R. E. (1975). "Memory and Storage." In H. S. Stone (ed.), *Introduction to Computer Architecture,* pp. 175–247. Chicago: Science Research Associates.

Muntz, R. R. (1975). "Analytic Models of Interactive Systems." *Proceedings of IEEE* **63**(6): 946–953.

Rosen, S. (1969). "Electronic Computers: A Historical Survey." *Computing Surveys* **1**(1): 7–36.

Scherr, A. L. (1967). *An Analysis of Time-Shared Computer Systems.* Cambridge, Mass.: MIT Press.

Schwartz, M. (1977). *Computer-Communication Network Design and Analysis.* Englewood Cliffs, N.J.: Prentice-Hall.

Sekino, A. (1972). "Performance Evaluation of Multiprogrammed Time-Shared Computer Systems." Ph.D. dissertation, Department of Electrical Engineering, MIT, Cambridge, Mass., June 1972.

Shaw, A. C. (1974). *The Logical Design of Operating Systems.* Englewood Cliffs, N.J.: Prentice-Hall.

Stone, H. (ed.) (1975). *Introduction to Computer Architecture.* Chicago: Science Research Associates.

Svobodova, L. (1977). *Computer Performance Measurement and Evaluation Methods: Analysis and Applications.* New York: Elsevier.

Tsichritzes, D. C., and P. A. Bernstein (1974). *Operating Systems.* New York: Academic Press.

Watson, R. W. (1970). *Time-Sharing System Design Concepts.* New York: McGraw-Hill.

Wilks, M. V. (1968). *Time-Sharing Computer Systems.* New York: American Elsevier.

2
Probability Theory

2.1 RANDOMNESS IN THE REAL WORLD

One way to approach the notion of probability is through the phenomenon of *statistical regularity*. There are many repeating situations in nature for which we can predict in advance from previous experiences *roughly* what will happen, but not *exactly* what will happen. We say in such cases that the occurrences are *random*. The reason that we cannot predict future events exactly may be that (1) we do not have enough data about the condition of the given problem, (2) the laws governing a progression of events may be so complicated that we cannot undertake a detailed analysis, or possibly (3) there is some basic indeterminacy in the physical world. Whatever the reason for the randomness, a definite average pattern of results may be observed in many situations leading to random occurrences when the situation is re-created a great number of times. For example, if a fair coin is flipped many times, it will turn up heads on about half the flips.

Another example of randomness is the response time of a transaction (or request) in an on-line interactive computing system. In a time-shared and multiprogrammed environment, the transaction will be processed together with other transactions. The total time that the transaction spends in the system depends not only on its processing demands, but also on the fraction of the system resources (e.g., CPU, main and secondary memory, channels, etc.) that it will be allocated. The delay due to contention for these resources is not exactly predictable, since the interactions between the system and the transactions are governed by a number of system variables and resource management policies. Thus, the response time that the user observes varies in a manner unpredictable in detail. We say that the response time varies *randomly*. Although we cannot predict exactly what the response time of a given transaction will be, we may find experimentally that certain *average* properties do exhibit a reasonable regularity. The response time of small transactions averaged over minutes will not vary greatly over an observation interval of several minutes; the response time averaged over a given day will not differ greatly from its value averaged over another day of similar system usage.

The tendency of repeated experiments to result in the convergence of the averages as more and more trials are made is called *statistical regularity*. This statistical regularity of averages is an experimentally verifiable phenomenon in many situations that involve randomly varying quantities. We are therefore motivated to construct a mathematical model adequate for the study of such phenomena. This is the domain of probability and statistics.

Random experiments and relative frequencies

We first introduce some terminology. By an *experiment*, we mean a measurement procedure in which all conditions are predetermined to the limit of our ability or interest. We use the word *trial* to mean the making of the measurement. An experiment is called *random* when the conditions of the measurement are not predetermined with sufficient accuracy and completeness to permit a precise prediction of the result of a trial. Whether an experiment should be considered random depends on the precision with which we wish to distinguish *possible outcomes*. If we desire or are able to look closely enough, in some sense any experiment is random.

We now discuss more precisely what we mean by statistical regularity. Let A denote one of the possible outcomes of some experiment, say, the "head" in coin tossing, and we repeat the experiment a large number of times (N) under uniform conditions. Denote by $N(A)$ the number of times that the outcome A occurs. The fraction

$$f_N(A) = \frac{N(A)}{N} \tag{2.1}$$

is called the *relative frequency* of outcome A. If there is a practical certainty that the measured relative frequency will tend to a limit as N increases without limit, we would like to say that the outcome A has a definite probability of occurrence, and take $P[A]$ to be that limit, i.e.,

$$f_N(A) \to P[A] \quad \text{as} \quad N \to \infty. \tag{2.2}$$

Unfortunately, this simple approach faces many difficulties. One obvious difficulty is that, strictly speaking, the limit may never be found, since an infinite number of repetitions of the experiment takes an infinite amount of time. Therefore, rather than defining a probability as the limit of a relative frequency, we will construct an abstract model of probability so that probabilities behave like the limits of relative frequencies. An important after-the-fact justification of this procedure is that it leads to the so-called *laws of large numbers,* according to which, in certain very general circumstances, the mathematical counterpart of an empirical relative frequency does converge to the appropriate probability. Hence an empirical relative frequency may be used to estimate a probability.

2.2 A MATHEMATICAL MODEL OF PROBABILITY THEORY

A mathematical model will prove useful in predicting the results of experiments in the real world, if the following two conditions are met. First, pertinent physical entities and their properties must be reflected in the model. Second, the properties of the model must be mathematically consistent and make analysis tractable. We begin by defining the following three abstract entities: *sample space, event,* and *probability measure.* We then develop a model by assigning to them mathematically consistent properties that reflect constraints in the real world.

2.2.1 Sample Space

The *sample space* is a mathematical abstraction of the collection of all possible experimental outcomes. We denote this collection by the symbol Ω. An object in Ω is called a *sample point* and denoted ω. Each sample point, therefore, corresponds to a possible outcome of a real-world experiment.

To illustrate this, consider the experiment of tossing two coins. If we are interested in whether each coin falls heads (h) or tails (t), then the possible outcomes are given by

$$\omega_1 = (h, h), \qquad \omega_2 = (h, t), \qquad \omega_3 = (t, h), \qquad \omega_4 = (t, t). \quad (2.3)$$

Every outcome of the experiment corresponds to exactly one member of the sample space

$$\Omega = \{\omega_1, \omega_2, \omega_3, \omega_4\}. \tag{2.4}$$

Another example is the experiment in which we measure the response time of a transaction in the time-shared system we discussed earlier. In theory, the system response time can be anywhere between 0 and plus infinity. Then Ω is the positive half-line:

$$\Omega = \{\omega : 0 \leq \omega < \infty\}. \tag{2.5}$$

2.2.2 Event

An *event* is a set of sample points. We usually denote events by capital letters, such as $A, B, \ldots$, or $A_1, A_2, \ldots$. An event is concisely defined by the expression

$$A = \{\omega : \text{certain conditions on } \omega \text{ are satisfied}\}, \tag{2.6}$$

which reads "Event A is the set of all ω such that certain conditions on ω are satisfied." Clearly an event is a subset of Ω. For example, consider again the experiment with two coins. If A is the subset

$$A = \{\omega_1, \omega_2, \omega_3\}, \tag{2.7}$$

then A is the event that there is at least one head. Similarly

$$B = \{\omega_1\} \tag{2.8}$$

is the event that there are two heads. Thus, an event may contain one or more sample points. An event like B, which contains only *one* sample point, is called a *simple event*.

In order to explain the significance of the notion of events, we may distinguish, in connection with a real-world experiment, between the terms *outcome* and *result*. By different outcomes we mean outcomes that are separately identifiable in an ultimate sense. On the other hand, by different results we mean sets of outcomes between which we choose to distinguish. Thus, *results* in the real world correspond to *events* in the mathematical model. For example, a result in our response-time experiment might be that the observed response time at the terminal is between 1.0 and 1.5 seconds. Such a result clearly embraces an infinite number of different possible response times or outcomes.

2.2.3 Probability Measure

A *probability measure* is an assignment of real numbers to the events defined on Ω. The probability of an event A is denoted by $P[A]$. The set of properties that the assignment must satisfy are sometimes called the *axioms for probability*, and will be discussed in the following section. The probability assigned to an event corresponds to that value at which we expect the relative frequency of the associated result to stabilize in an infinitely long sequence of independent trials of the real-world experiment.

Example 2.1. If the sample space Ω is the one defined by (2.3) and (2.4), a possible probability assignment to the simple events is

$$P[\{\omega_1\}] = \tfrac{1}{2}, \qquad P[\{\omega_2\}] = P[\{\omega_3\}] = \tfrac{1}{4}, \quad \text{and} \quad P[\{\omega_4\}] = 0.$$

However, this assignment is not the most useful to reflect the coin-tossing experiment.

Example 2.2. If Ω is the set of all response times given by (2.5) and we define the events E_t by $E_t = \{\omega : 0 \le \omega \le t\}$, a possible probability assignment is $P[E_t] = 1 - e^{-t}$.

2.2.4 Properties of a Probability Measure

Before we discuss the properties of the probability measure, we must know some elementary set theory, since the definition of a sample space Ω and events implies the existence of certain other identifiable sets of points.

1. The *complement* of event A, denoted A^c is the event containing all sample points that belong to Ω, but not to A:

$$A^c = \{\omega : \omega \text{ does not belong to } A\}. \qquad (2.9)$$

2. The *union* of A and B, denoted $A \cup B$, is the event containing all sample points that belong to at least one of the two sets A, B:

$$A \cup B = \{\omega : \omega \text{ belongs to } A \text{ or } B\}.^* \qquad (2.10)$$

3. The *intersection* of A and B, denoted by $A \cap B$, is the event containing all sample points in both A and B:

$$A \cap B = \{\omega : \omega \text{ belongs to both } A \text{ and } B\}. \qquad (2.11)$$

4. The event containing no sample points is called the *null event*, denoted $\emptyset$. For any event A, the intersection of A and A^c is the null event, i.e., $A \cap A^c = \emptyset$.

5. The event containing all points—that is, the sample space Ω—is called the *certain event* (an event that must occur). For any event A, the union of A and A^c is the certain event, that is, $A \cup A^c = \Omega$. It is clear that the null event and certain event are related by $\Omega^c = \emptyset$ and $\emptyset^c = \Omega$.

6. Two events A and B are called *disjoint* or *mutually exclusive* if they have no sample points in common, that is, if $A \cap B = \emptyset$.

---

* The word "or" is used in mathematics and logic in the inclusive sense. Thus, the statement "A or B" is the mathematical expression for "either A or B or both."

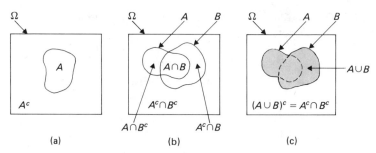

Fig. 2.1 Venn diagrams.

The relations between the operations (i.e., complement, union, and intersection) are easily visualized in the schematic diagrams of Fig. 2.1. Such drawings are called *Venn diagrams*. The symbols $\cup$ and $\cap$ are operations between any two sets just as $+$ and $\times$ are operations between any two numbers, and they obey similar laws:

Commutative law: $A \cup B = B \cup A$

$A \cap B = B \cap A$ (2.12)

Associative law: $(A \cup B) \cup C = A \cup (B \cup C)$

$(A \cap B) \cap C = A \cap (B \cap C)$ (2.13)

Distribution law: $A \cap (B \cup C) = (A \cap B) \cup (A \cap C)$

$A \cup (B \cap C) = (A \cup B) \cap (A \cup C)$ (2.14)

Finally, we note two very useful identities:

$$(A \cup B)^c = A^c \cap B^c, \qquad (2.15)$$

$$(A \cap B)^c = A^c \cup B^c, \qquad (2.16)$$

which are sometimes called *de Morgan's laws*. All of these laws can be readily verified by the Venn diagrams in Fig. 2.1.

Having extended the notion of an event, we will now consider certain properties that a probability measure should satisfy. In a long sequence of N independent trials of a real-world experiment, the observed relative frequency $\{f_N(A)\}$ of the result A meets certain conditions:

1. The relative frequency $f_N(A)$ is always nonnegative:

$$f_N(A) \geq 0.$$

2. Every trial of an experiment is certain to have a result. Hence,

$$f_N(\Omega) = 1.$$

3. If two results A and B are mutually exclusive, then

$$f_N(A \text{ or } B) = f_N(A) + f_N(B).$$

Since we are going to use probability theory to predict the results of real-world random experiments, it is reasonable that we impose similar conditions on corresponding entities in our mathematical model. We therefore require our assignment of probability measure $P[\ ]$ to satisfy the following properties (called the *axioms of probability*):

Property 1. $P[A] \geq 0$ for all events A in Ω.

Property 2. $P[\Omega] = 1$, that is, the probability of the certain event is unity.

Property 3. If A and B are mutually exclusive events—i.e., if $A \cap B = \emptyset$—then $P[A \cup B] = P[A] + P[B]$.

These properties, motivated from real-world considerations, are self-consistent and are adequate for a formal development of probability theory, whenever the totality of events on Ω is *finite*.

A consequence of Property 3 is that if $A_1, A_2, \ldots, A_M$ are M mutually exclusive events, then their union $A_1 \cup A_2 \cup \cdots \cup A_M$, which we denote $\bigcup_{m=1}^{M} A_m$, has the probability

$$P\left[\bigcup_{m=1}^{M} A_m\right] = \sum_{m=1}^{M} P[A_m]. \tag{2.17}$$

This is easily shown by successive applications of Property 3 or, more formally, by the method of mathematical induction (see Exercise 2.2.3). A consequence of Properties 2 and 3 is

$$P[A] \leq 1 \tag{2.18}$$

for any event A, since

$$P[A] + P[A^c] = P[\Omega] = 1 \tag{2.19}$$

and $P[A^c]$ is nonnegative. It also follows from Properties 2 and 3 that

$$P[\emptyset] = 1 - P[\Omega] = 0. \tag{2.20}$$

Since the event $A \cup B$ is decomposable into a set of mutually exclusive events $A \cap B$, $A^c \cap B$, and $A \cap B^c$ (see Fig. 2.1c), we have

$$\begin{aligned} P[A \cup B] &= P[A \cap B] + P[A^c \cap B] + P[A \cap B^c] \\ &= P[A \cap B] + P[B] - P[A \cap B] + P[A] - P[A \cap B] \\ &= P[A] + P[B] - P[A \cap B]. \end{aligned} \tag{2.21}$$

Hence

$$P[A \cup B] \le P[A] + P[B], \tag{2.22}$$

where the equality holds only when A and B are mutually exclusive.

If the total number of possible events is infinite, the above three properties alone are insufficient. It is necessary to extend Property 3 to include infinite unions of disjoint events.

Property 4. If $A_1, A_2 \ldots$ are mutually exclusive events, then their union $A_1 \cup A_2 \cup \cdots$, denoted $\bigcup_{m=1}^{\infty} A_m$, has the probability

$$P\left[\bigcup_{m=1}^{\infty} A_m \right] = \sum_{m=1}^{\infty} P[A_m].$$

Although (2.20) implies that the probability of the null event is zero, it does *not* imply that if the probability of an event is zero, it is the null event. The null event is the mathematical counterpart of an impossible outcome; probability theory assigns probability zero to anything impossible, but does not imply that if an event has probability zero it is impossible. It is entirely conceivable that there is an event A such that $f_N(A) \to 0$ even though $N(A)$ does not remain zero. For example, the probability that you observe the response time of exactly two seconds is zero, yet the response time of two seconds is a possible event.

Exercises

2.2.1 Prove the distribution laws (2.14) using Venn diagrams.

2.2.2 Show that $(A \cap B)^c = A^c \cup B^c$ (Eq. 2.16).

2.2.3 Derive Eq. (2.17) using mathematical induction. Show:
   a) The basis step: That Eq. (2.17) is true for $M = 2$.
   b) The induction step: That if Eq. (2.17) is true for $M = N (\ge 2)$, then it also holds for $M = N + 1$.

2.3 JOINT PROBABILITY, CONDITIONAL PROBABILITY, AND STATISTICAL INDEPENDENCE

2.3.1 Joint Probability and Conditional Probability

So far we have been concerned primarily with the outcomes of a single experiment. In real-world problems, however, we are often concerned with the outcomes of combined experiments. A joint experiment that consists of one experiment having the possible outcomes A_m's ($m = 1, 2, \ldots, M$) and another having the possible outcomes B_n's ($n = 1, 2, \ldots, N$) can be considered as a single experiment having the possible outcomes $(A_m \cap B_n)$'s. Probabilities relating to such a combined experiment are known as *joint probabilities*. The joint probability of events A and B is usually written as $P[A, B]$ instead of $P[A \cap B]$. From the axioms of the probability and related results discussed in the previous section, it follows that

$$0 \le P[A, B] \le 1. \tag{2.23}$$

If the M possible events A_m's and the N possible events B_n's are all mutually exclusive, we have

$$\sum_{m=1}^{M} \sum_{n=1}^{N} P[A_m, B_n] = 1. \tag{2.24}$$

Both (2.23) and (2.24) can be extended in obvious fashion to cases in which we deal with more than two basic experiments.

Suppose that the combined experiment is repeated N times, out of which the result A_m occurs $N(A_m)$ times, the result B_n occurs $N(B_n)$ times, and the compound result (A_m, B_n) occurs $N(A_m, B_n)$ times. Then the relative frequency of the compound result (A_m, B_n) is given by

$$f_N(A_m, B_n) = \frac{N(A_m, B_n)}{N}. \tag{2.25}$$

For the moment, let us focus our attention on those $N(A_m)$ trials in each of which the result A_m occurred. In each of these trials, one of the N possible results $\{B_n, 1 \le n \le N\}$ occurred; in particular, the result B_n occurred $N(A_m, B_n)$ times. Thus, the relative frequency of occurrence of the result B_n under the assumption that the result A_m also occurred is

$$f_N(B_n \mid A_m) = \frac{N(A_m, B_n)}{N(A_m)}. \tag{2.26}$$

This relative frequency is called the *conditional relative frequency* of B_n on the second experiment, given A_m on the first experiment. Alternatively, it may be expressed as

$$f_N(B_n \mid A_m) = \frac{f_N(A_m, B_n)}{f_N(A_m)}. \tag{2.27}$$

In accordance with (2.27), we define the *conditional probability* $P[B \mid A]$ of the event B given (the occurrence of) the event A by

$$P[B \mid A] = \frac{P[A, B]}{P[A]}, \tag{2.28}$$

provided that $P[A] > 0$. The conditional probability is undefined if $P[A] = 0$. We can rewrite (2.28) as

$$P[A, B] = P[B \mid A]P[A]. \tag{2.29}$$

Conditional probabilities possess essentially the same properties as the other probabilities already discussed. In particular, if the events B_n's form a set of N mutually exclusive events, and if these N events B_n's comprise the certain event Ω, then we obtain

$$\bigcup_{n=1}^{N} \{A \cap B_n\} = A, \tag{2.30}$$

and then

$$\sum_{n=1}^{N} P[A, B_n] = \sum_{n=1}^{N} P[A]P[B_n \mid A] = P[A]. \tag{2.31}$$

Thus by dividing both sides by $P[A] > 0$, we obtain

$$\sum_{n=1}^{N} P[B_n \mid A] = 1. \tag{2.32}$$

It follows that

$$0 \leq P[B_n \mid A] \leq 1. \tag{2.33}$$

We can also derive from the definition (2.28) that

$$P[B \mid A] \geq P[A, B] \tag{2.34}$$

and

$$P[A] \geq P[A, B]. \tag{2.35}$$

2.3.2 Statistical Independence

As interpreted above, $P[B \mid A]$ is the probability of occurrence of the event B assuming the occurrence of the event A. If this conditional probability is simply equal to the (unconditional) probability of occurrence of the event B, that is

$$P[B \mid A] = P[B], \tag{2.36}$$

or equivalently, if

$$P[A, B] = P[A]P[B], \tag{2.37}$$

then the events A and B are said to be *statistically independent*. Equations (2.36) and (2.37) are also equivalent to

$$P[A \mid B] = P[A]. \tag{2.38}$$

An interpretation of (2.36) and (2.38) is that if the pair of events A and B are statistically independent, a knowledge of the occurrence of one event tells us no more about the probability of occurrence of the other event than we knew without that knowledge.

When more than two events are to be considered, the situation becomes more complicated. A set of M events A_m's $(m = 1, 2, \ldots, M)$ is said to be statistically independent if and only if the probability of every intersection of M or fewer events equals the product of the probabilities of constituents. For example, three events A, B, C are statistically independent when

$$P[A, B] = P[A]P[B],$$
$$P[B, C] = P[B]P[C], \qquad (2.39)$$
$$P[A, C] = P[A]P[C],$$

and

$$P[A, B, C] = P[A]P[B]P[C]. \qquad (2.40)$$

No three of these relations necessarily implies the fourth. If only Eqs. (2.39) are satisfied, we say that the events are *pairwise independent.* Pairwise independence does not imply complete independence.

Example 2.3. Suppose that two true dice are thrown and that the dice are distinguishable. An outcome of this experiment is denoted by (m, n), where m and n are the faces of the dice. Let A and B be the following events of this experiment:

$$A = \{m + n = 11\},$$
$$B = \{n \neq 5\}.$$

Then we find

$$P[A] = P[(5, 6)] + P[(6, 5)]$$
$$= P[\{m = 5\}]P[\{n = 6\}] + P\{m = 6\}]P[\{n = 5\}] = \tfrac{1}{18},$$
$$P[B] = 1 - P[\{n = 5\}] = \tfrac{5}{6},$$

and

$$P[A, B] = P[\{m = 5\} \cap \{n = 6\}] = \tfrac{1}{36}.$$

Therefore

$$P[A, B] \neq P[A]P[B].$$

Thus, the events A and B are not statistically independent.

Example 2.4. (*Bernoulli trials*) Repeated independent trials are called *Bernoulli trials* if there are only two possible outcomes for each trial and their probabilities remain the same throughout the trials. It is usual to refer to the two possible outcomes as "success" and "failure." The sample space of each individual trial is

$$\Omega = \{s, f\},$$

where s stands for success and f for failure. If we denote the probability of the simple event $\{s\}$ by p, i.e.,

$$P[\{s\}] = p, \qquad 0 \le p \le 1$$

then the probability of the event $\{f\}$ is given by*

$$P[\{f\}] = 1 - p \triangleq q,$$

since the event $\{f\}$ is the complement of the event $\{s\}$.

The sample space for an experiment consisting of two Bernoulli trials is the Cartesian product of the sample space Ω with itself:

$$\Omega^2 = \Omega \times \Omega = \{\{ss\}, \{sf\}, \{fs\}, \{ff\}\}.$$

In general, the sample space for n Bernoulli trials is the nth-fold Cartesian product of Ω:

$$\Omega^n = \Omega \times \Omega \times \cdots \times \Omega = \{\{ss \ldots s\}, \{ss \ldots f\}, \ldots, \{ff \ldots s\}, \{ff \ldots f\}\}.$$

Each of the sample points is made up of a string of n symbols, s or f. Since the trials are independent, the probabilities multiply. For example, the probability of the outcome ssf ... fsf is given by ppq ... qpq. Suppose there are k successes and $n - k$ failures in a sequence of n Bernoulli trials. If the order in which the successes occur does not matter, then the number of sample points belonging to this event is equal to the number of *combinations* of n things taken k at a time. We denote this number as $\binom{n}{k}$ and it is given by

$$\binom{n}{k} = \frac{n!}{k!(n-k)!}.$$

Each of these sample points (simple events by themselves) has probability $p^k q^{n-k}$. Then the probability of k successes in n trials is given by

$$b(k; n, p) = \binom{n}{k} p^k q^{n-k}, \qquad k = 0, 1, 2, \ldots, n.$$

The set of probabilities $b(k; n, p)$ is called the *binomial* distribution.

---

* The notation $\triangleq$ is to be read "is defined as."

Exercises

2.3.1 Interpret Eq. (2.24) in terms of the relative frequencies of compound results (A_m, B_n).

2.3.2 Let A and B be two independent events such that with probability $\frac{1}{12}$ they will occur simultaneously, and with probability $\frac{1}{3}$ neither of them will occur. Obtain $P[A]$ and $P[B]$.

2.3.3 Consider a computer system that receives transactions from a large number of terminals. We assume that the transaction arrival mechanism is characterized by the following model: We divide the time axis into contiguous segments of Δ seconds, and Δ is chosen sufficiently small that the probability of receiving more than one transaction is negligibly small. We also assume that the arrivals in different segments are statistically independent events. Let p be the probability that a randomly chosen segment interval observes an arrival of transaction.

   a) Given an observation interval of $T = 5\Delta$ seconds, and let $p = 0.2$. What is the probability that at least two messages arrive during this observation interval?

   b) For any integer $n = 1, 2, 3, \ldots$, find the probability that $T = n\Delta$ will be the observation interval required to see the first arrival.

2.3.4 Suppose you are informed that there are k successes in n Bernoulli trials. Obtain the conditional probability that any particular trial resulted in a success.

2.3.5 *Bayes's formula.* Let B be an event in a sample space Ω. Suppose that events $A_1, A_2, \ldots, A_M$ are a set of mutually exclusive and *exhaustive* events in Ω, that is, $A_m \cap A_n = \emptyset$ for all m, n, and $\bigcup_{m=1}^{M} A_m = \Omega$. Show that

$$P[A_m \mid B] = \frac{P[B \mid A_m]P[A_m]}{\sum_{n=1}^{M} P[B \mid A_n]P[A_n]}.$$

2.4 RANDOM VARIABLES AND PROBABILITY DISTRIBUTION FUNCTIONS

2.4.1 Random Variables

In the preceding sections we defined a sample space, sample points, events, and a probability assignment to the events. Recall that an event is a set of sample points. Now we introduce the notion of a *random variable*. A real-valued function $X(\omega)$ defined on a sample space Ω of points ω is called a *random variable*. That is, the random variable is an association of a real number with each point in the sample space. Thus $X(\omega)$ may be regarded as a function that maps Ω into the real line: Given any sample point ω, the function $X(\bullet)$ specifies a finite real number $X(\omega)$. A simple example of such a mapping is illustrated in Fig. 2.2.

For example, in the coin-tossing experiment, Ω contains only two points, the head and the tail. Now we wish to associate one with the head

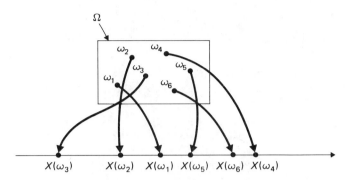

Fig. 2.2 A random variable $X(\omega)$ as mapping from Ω to the real line.

and zero with the tail. Then this mapping

$$X(\omega) = \begin{cases} 1 & \text{if} \quad \omega = \text{head} \\ 0 & \text{if} \quad \omega = \text{tail} \end{cases}$$

is clearly a random variable. In our earlier example of measuring the response time of a transaction, Ω itself is the real line (the positive half-line). Function $X(\omega) = \omega$ is clearly a legitimate random variable. So are $X(\omega) = 1/\omega$, $X(\omega) = \omega^2$, etc.

Since many readers may find this kind of mathematical abstraction unexciting at best, we hasten to point out that it is sufficient here to think of a random variable as a symbol for a number that is going to be produced by a random experiment. Once produced, the number is, of course, no longer random and is called a *realization* or *instance* of the random variable. The word random applies to the process that produces the number, rather than to the number itself. Hereafter, in referring to these functions, we often delete empty parentheses and simply write X to denote the function $X(\bullet)$.

A random variable X is characterized by its *probability distribution function* (or simply called the *distribution function*) $F_X(x)$:

$$F_X(x) = P[\{\omega : X(\omega) \le x\}] \tag{2.41}$$

or simply

$$F_X(x) = P[X \le x]. \tag{2.42}$$

The properties of distribution functions listed below follow directly from the definition (2.41) or (2.42).

Property 1. $F_X(x) \ge 0$, for $-\infty < x < \infty$ $\hspace{2em}$ (2.43)

Property 2. $F_X(-\infty) = 0$. $\hspace{9em}$ (2.44)

Property 3. $F_X(\infty) = 1.$ (2.45)

Property 4.   If $b > a$, $F_X(b) - F_X(a) = P[a < X \le b] \ge 0.$ (2.46)

The first three properties follow from the facts that $F_X(x)$ is a probability, $P[\emptyset] = 0$, and $P[\Omega] = 1$, respectively. Property 4 allows from the fact that

$$\{\omega : X(\omega) \le a\} \cap \{\omega : a < X(\omega) \le b\} = \emptyset$$

and

$$\{\omega : X(\omega) \le a\} \cup \{\omega : a < X(\omega) \le b\} = \{\omega : X(\omega) \le b\}.$$

(See Exercise 2.4.1).

Now we proceed to the case of two random variables. Given functions $X(\omega)$ and $Y(\omega)$ defined on the sample space Ω, we define the *joint probability distribution function* $F_{XY}(x, y)$ of the random variables X and Y by

$$F_{XY}(x, y) = P[\{\omega ; X(\omega) \le x, Y(\omega) \le y\}] = P[X \le x, Y \le y].$$
(2.47)

Thus $F_{XY}(x, y)$ is the probability assigned to the set of all points ω in Ω that are associated with the region of the two-dimensional Euclidean space that is shaded in Fig. 2.3.

The properties of joint distribution functions listed below follow directly from the definition (2.47).

Property 1. $F_{XY}(x, y) \ge 0$;   for $-\infty < x < \infty, -\infty < y < \infty$ (2.48)

Property 2. $F_{XY}(x, -\infty) = 0$;   for $-\infty < x < \infty$
$F_{XY}(-\infty, y) = 0$;   for $-\infty < \;\;\; < \infty$ (2.49)

Property 3. $F_{XY}(\infty, \infty) = 1$ (2.50)

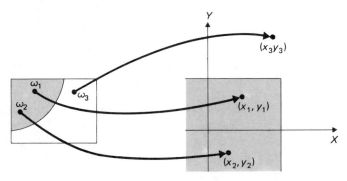

Fig. 2.3 A random variable $X(\omega)$, $Y(\omega)$ as a mapping from Ω to the two-dimensional Euclidean space.

Property 4. If $b > a$ and $d > c$,

$$F_{XY}(b, d) \geq F_{XY}(b, c) \geq F_{XY}(a, c) \tag{2.51}$$

Property 5. $F_{XY}(x, \infty) = F_X(x)$

$$F_{XY}(\infty, y) = F_Y(y). \tag{2.52}$$

Properties 1 through 4 are obvious extensions of the corresponding properties (2.43)–(2.46). Property 5 is a consequence of the fact that

$$\{\omega : X(\omega) \leq x\} \cap \{\omega : Y(\omega) < \infty\} = \{\omega : X(\omega) \leq x\} \cap \Omega$$

$$= \{\omega : X(\omega) \leq x\}.$$

Thus $F_{XY}(x, \infty)$ and $F_{XY}(\infty, y)$ are both ordinary one-variable distribution functions. They are, respectively, the distributions of X and Y alone as shown in Eq. (2.52) and are usually designated as the *marginal distribution functions*. In summary, $F_{XY}(x, y)$ is a nondecreasing function of both arguments and is always bounded by zero and one.

These definitions and results are extendable in a more or less obvious manner to the case of multidimensional random variables: Let $X_1, X_2, \ldots, X_m$ be random variables defined on Ω, and let $\mathbf{X}$ denote the m-tuple $(X_1, X_2, \ldots, X_m)$. We then define the m-dimensional joint probability distribution function $F_{\mathbf{X}}(\mathbf{x})$ as

$$F_{\mathbf{X}}(\mathbf{x}) = P[\{\omega : X_1(\omega) \leq x_1, X_2(\omega) \leq x_2, \ldots, X_m(\omega) \leq x_m\}]$$

$$= P[X_1 \leq x_1, X_2 \leq x_2, \ldots, X_m \leq x_m], \tag{2.53}$$

where $\mathbf{x} = (x_1, x_2, \ldots, x_m)$. We refer to $\mathbf{X}$ as an m-dimensional *vector* of random variables or, simply, as a *random vector*.

2.4.2 The Discrete Random Variable and the Probability Distribution

Random variable X is called a *discrete random variable* if the range of the function $X(\omega)$ consists of isolated points on the real line; that is, if X can take on only a finite or countably infinite number of values $\{x_1, x_2, x_3, \ldots\}$. For example, the number of heads appearing in N tosses of a coin is a discrete random variable. The complete set of probabilities $P[x_i]$'s associated with the possible values of x_i's of X is called the *probability distribution* of the discrete random variable X. The probability distribution and the probability distribution function defined by (2.41) are related according to

$$F_X(x) = \sum_{x_i \leq x} P[x_i]. \tag{2.54}$$

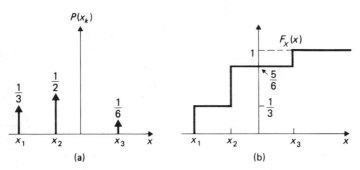

Fig. 2.4 (a) The probability distribution and (b) the probability distribution function of a discrete random variable.

Therefore, the probability distribution function is often referred to by the name of the *cumulative distribution function*. By letting x go to infinity,

$$F_X(\infty) = \sum_{\text{all } i} P[x_i] = 1. \tag{2.55}$$

An example of the probability distribution and the corresponding probability distribution function is shown in Fig. 2.4.

In a similar manner we define the *joint probability distribution* of two discrete random variables X and Y as the set of probabilities $P[x_i, y_j]$ for all possible values of the pair (x_i, y_j)'s. The corresponding joint probability distribution function defined by (2.47) is given by the expression

$$F_{XY}(x, y) = \sum_{x_i \leq x} \sum_{y_j \leq y} P[x_i, y_j]. \tag{2.56}$$

Therefore,

$$F_{XY}(\infty, \infty) = \sum_{\text{all } i} \sum_{\text{all } j} P[x_i, y_j] = 1. \tag{2.57}$$

An example of the joint probability distribution and the associated joint probability distribution function of two discrete variables is illustrated in Fig. 2.5.

The set of values that a discrete random variable (or a random vector) takes on can be regarded as the set of distinct sample points or distinct simple events. The various results obtained in Section 2.3 for a sample space and events are therefore directly translatable to the case of discrete random variables. Thus (2.57) follows directly from (2.24). The relations among the joint probability distribution, the conditional distribution, and the marginal distributions for discrete random variables are

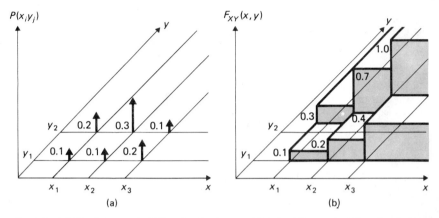

Fig. 2.5 (a) The joint probability distribution and (b) the joint probability distribution function.

now self-evident:

$$P[x_i, y_j] = P[x_i]P[y_j \mid x_i] = P[y_j]P[x_i \mid y_j], \qquad (2.58)$$

$$\sum_{\text{all } j} P[y_j \mid x_i] = \sum_{\text{all } i} P[x_i \mid y_j] = 1, \qquad (2.59)$$

$$P[x_i] = \sum_{\text{all } j} P[x_i, y_j] \quad \text{and} \quad P[y_j] = \sum_{\text{all } i} P[x_i, y_j], \qquad (2.60)$$

etc. The notion of *statistical independence* of two events is also directly applicable to two discrete random variables. We say that X and Y are *statistically independent random variables* if and only if

$$P[x_i, y_j] = P[x_i]P[y_j], \quad \text{for all values } (x_i, y_j) \qquad (2.61)$$

or, equivalently, if and only if

$$F_{XY}(x, y) = F_X(x)F_Y(y), \quad \text{for all values of } x \text{ and } y. \qquad (2.62)$$

Equivalence between (2.61) and (2.62) can be shown easily by using the relations (2.54) and (2.56). (See Exercise 2.4.2.)

Similarly, the discrete random variables $X, Y, \ldots, Z$ are said to be statistically independent random variables if and only if

$$P[x_k, y_\ell, \ldots, z_m] = P[x_k]P[y_\ell] \cdots P[z_m] \qquad (2.63)$$

is satisfied for all values $(x_k, y_\ell, \ldots, z_m)$ or, equivalently,

$$F_{XY\cdots Z}(x, y, \ldots, z) = F_X(x)F_Y(y) \cdots F_Z(z) \qquad (2.64)$$

for all values of $x, y, \ldots, z$. (See Exercise 2.4.2.)

2.4.3 The Continuous Random Variable and the Probability Density Function

Many random variables that we encounter in mathematical models of real-world problems are *continuous*. For example, the interarrival times of jobs or transactions from terminals to a central computer may assume *any* value between 0 and ∞. Similarly, the response time of a transaction may take on any positive value. A random variable is called a continuous random variable if its range is a continuum or, equivalently, if its probability distribution function is everywhere continuous.

For a given continuous random variable X, the probability that X lies in a small interval $(x, x + \Delta]$ is

$$P[x < X \le x+\Delta] = F_X(x + \Delta) - F_X(x) = \Delta\frac{[F_X(x + \Delta) - F_X(x)]}{\Delta}.$$
$$(2.65)$$

If Δ is small and $F_X(x)$ is differentiable everywhere except possibly a finite set of points, then the following approximation holds:

$$P[x < X \le x + \Delta] \cong \Delta F'_X(x), \qquad (2.66)$$

in which the prime denotes the derivative of F_X. Whenever it exists, the derivative of F_X is called the *probability density function* of X and is denoted by f_X. Thus,

$$f_X(x) = \frac{dF_X(x)}{dx}, \qquad (2.67)$$

or, in differential notation, we write formally

$$f_X(x)\, dx = dF_X(x) = P[x < X \le x + dx]. \qquad (2.68)$$

Therefore, given the probability density function X, its distribution function is computable as

$$F_X(x) = \int_{-\infty}^{x} f_X(u)\, du. \qquad (2.69)$$

Since the probability distribution function is a nondecreasing function, the probability density function is always nonnegative:

$$f_X(x) \ge 0. \qquad (2.70)$$

Figure 2.6 shows an example of the probability distribution function and the corresponding probability density function of a continuous random variable.

From (2.46) and (2.69) it follows that the probability $P[a < X \le b]$ is given by the integral of the probability density function over that

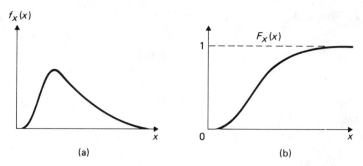

Fig. 2.6 (a) The probability density function and (b) the probability distribution function of continuous random variables.

interval:

$$P[a < X \le b] = \int_a^b f_X(x)\, dx. \tag{2.71}$$

In particular, when $a = -\infty$ and $b = \infty$, we obtain

$$\int_{-\infty}^{\infty} f_X(x)\, dx = 1. \tag{2.72}$$

This result simply reflects the fact that the probability of the certain event is unity (see Property 2 in Section 2.2.4).

2.4.4 The Joint Probability Density Function and the Conditional Probability Function

The various definitions and results given above can be extended to the case of two random variables X and Y. If the joint probability distribution $F_{XY}(x, y)$ is everywhere continuous and possesses a second partial derivative everywhere (except possibly on a finite set of curves), we define the joint probability density function by

$$f_{XY}(x, y) = \frac{\partial^2 F_{XY}(x, y)}{\partial x\, \partial y}. \tag{2.73}$$

Then

$$F_{XY}(x, y) = \int_{-\infty}^{x} \int_{-\infty}^{y} f_{XY}(u, v)\, du\, dv. \tag{2.74}$$

Thus $f_{XY}(x, y)\, dx\, dy$ may be interpreted as the probability that point (X, Y) falls in an incremental area $dx\, dy$ about the point (x, y) in a two-dimensional Euclidean space. Since the joint probability distribution is a nondecreasing function of its arguments, it follows that

$$f_{XY}(x, y) \ge 0. \tag{2.75}$$

By letting x and y both recede to infinity in (2.74), we obtain

$$\int_{-\infty}^{\infty} \int_{-\infty}^{\infty} f_{XY}(x, y) \, dx \, dy = 1. \tag{2.76}$$

If we instead let only one of the upper limits approach infinity, we obtain, on application of (2.52),

$$\int_{-\infty}^{x} \int_{-\infty}^{\infty} f_{XY}(u, v) \, du \, dv = F_X(x) \tag{2.77}$$

and

$$\int_{-\infty}^{\infty} \int_{-\infty}^{y} f_{XY}(u, v) \, du \, dv = F_Y(y). \tag{2.78}$$

By differentiating both sides of (2.77) and (2.78), we obtain

$$\int_{-\infty}^{\infty} f_{XY}(x, v) \, dv = f_X(x) \tag{2.79}$$

and

$$\int_{-\infty}^{\infty} f_{XY}(u, y) \, du = f_Y(y). \tag{2.80}$$

Let us consider now the probability that random variable Y is less than or equal to y, subject to the hypothesis that random variable X has a value falling in $(x, x + \Delta]$. It follows from the definition of conditional probability that

$$P[Y \le y \mid x < X \le x + \Delta] = \frac{P[x < X \le x + \Delta, \, Y \le y]}{P[x < X \le x + \Delta]}$$

$$= \frac{\displaystyle\int_{x}^{x+\Delta} \int_{-\infty}^{y} f_{XY}(u, v) \, du \, dv}{\displaystyle\int_{x}^{x+\Delta} f_X(u) \, du}. \tag{2.81}$$

The denominator can be replaced by $f_X(x)\Delta$ as $\Delta \to 0$. Thus we get

$$P[Y \le y \mid X = x] = F_{Y|X}(y \mid x)$$

$$= \frac{\displaystyle\int_{-\infty}^{y} f_{XY}(x, v) \, dv}{f_X(x)}, \tag{2.82}$$

which is the *conditional probability distribution function* of the random variable Y subject to the hypothesis $X = x$. Assuming that the usual continuity requirements are met for $F_{Y|X}(y \mid x)$, we may define the *conditional probability density function* $f_{Y|X}(y \mid x)$ to be the derivative of the conditional probability distribution function:

$$f_{Y|X}(y \mid x) = \frac{\partial F_{Y|X}(y \mid x)}{\partial y}. \tag{2.83}$$

Then

$$F_{Y|X}(y \mid x) = \int_{-\infty}^{y} f_{Y|X}(v \mid x) \, dv. \tag{2.84}$$

By differentiating (2.82) with respect to y, we obtain from (2.83)

$$f_{Y|X}(y \mid x) = \frac{f_{XY}(x, y)}{f_X(x)}, \tag{2.85}$$

which is the continuous version of (2.58).

As with all distribution functions, $F_{Y|X}(y \mid x)$ is a nondecreasing function of y; therefore, the conditional probability density function is nonnegative:

$$f_{Y|X}(y \mid x) \geq 0. \tag{2.86}$$

Similarly, we obtain

$$P[a < Y \leq b \mid X = x] = \int_{a}^{b} f_{Y|X}(y \mid x) \, dy \tag{2.87}$$

and

$$\int_{-\infty}^{\infty} f_{Y|X}(y \mid x) \, dy = 1, \tag{2.88}$$

which is a continuous analog of (2.59). The conditional probability density function $f_{X|Y}(x \mid y)$ may, of course, be defined in the same way, and corresponding properties can be derived in an obvious manner. Finally, if X and Y are statistically independent, we have the following product form expression

$$f_{XY}(x, y) = f_X(x) f_Y(y), \tag{2.89}$$

which is the continuous analog of (2.61).

Exercises

2.4.1 Derive Eq. (2.46). *Hint:* Use Property 3 in Section 2.2.

2.4.2 Show that Eqs. (2.61) and (2.62) are equivalent. Prove also the equivalence of Eqs. (2.63) and (2.64).

2.4.3 A sample space Ω consists of the four points

$$\Omega = \{\omega_1, \omega_2, \omega_3, \omega_4\}$$

and the probabilities of the simple events are

$$P[\{\omega_1\}] = \tfrac{1}{2}, \qquad P[\{\omega_2\}] = \tfrac{1}{4}, \qquad P[\{\omega_3\}] = \tfrac{1}{8}, \qquad P[\{\omega_4\}] = \tfrac{1}{8}.$$

Define random variables X and Y by

$$X(\omega_1) = 1, \; X(\omega_2) = 1, \; X(\omega_3) = 2, \; X(\omega_4) = 3;$$
$$Y(\omega_1) = 3, \; Y(\omega_2) = 3, \; Y(\omega_3) = 1, \; Y(\omega_4) = 1.$$

a) Find the probability distributions, and the distribution function of X. Do the same for Y.
b) Find the conditional probability $P[y_j \mid x_i]$ for all possible pairs $X = x_i$, $Y = y_j$.
c) Are the random variables X and Y statistically independent?

2.4.4 Consider a discrete random variable X whose range is the set of nonnegative integers. Let the probability distribution of X be of the form

$$p_i = P[X = i] = k\rho^i, \qquad i = 0, 1, 2, \ldots,$$

where ρ is a given parameter, $0 < \rho < 1$.

a) Determine the constant k.
b) Obtain the distribution function of X.

2.4.5 Consider a pair of continuous random variables (X, Y) that have the joint probability density function of the form

$$f_{XY}(x, y) = \begin{cases} k \exp\{-\lambda x - \mu y\}; & x \geq 0, y \geq 0 \\ 0; & \text{elsewhere} \end{cases}$$

where $\lambda > 0$, $\mu > 0$.

a) Obtain the joint distribution function $F_{XY}(x, y)$ and determine the normalization constant k.
b) Find the distributions $F_X(x)$ and $F_Y(y)$ and the conditional distribution function $F_{Y|X}(y \mid x)$.
c) Obtain the density functions $f_X(x)$, $f_Y(y)$, and $f_{Y|X}(y \mid x)$.

2.4.6 *Functions of random variables.* For a given random variable X, a function $Y = g(X)$ defines a new random variable Y. That is, the random variable Y is an association of real number $Y(\omega) = g(X(\omega))$ with each point ω in the sample space. The distribution function of Y is, from the definition, given by

$$F_Y(y) = P[g(X) \leq y] = P[X \in E_y],$$

where E_y denotes the set of points X for which $g(X) \leq y$.

a) Let X have a uniform distribution over $[-1, +1]$, and let $g(x) = x^2$. Find the distribution function and the density function of Y.

b) Let X have an exponential distribution

$$F_X(x) = \begin{cases} 1 - e^{-\lambda x}, & x \geq 0 \\ 0, & x < 0. \end{cases}$$

Let $g(x) = e^x$ and obtain the distribution and density functions of the random variable $Y = g(X)$.

2.5 EXPECTATION, MOMENTS, AND CHARACTERISTIC FUNCTION

2.5.1 Expectation of a Random Variable

Consider, for instance, an experiment in which we toss an ordinary die N times. Let X_t denote the result of the tth toss, $t = 1, 2, \ldots, N$. Clearly, X_t is a discrete random variable that takes on only integers between 1 and 6. The *empirical average* (also called the *sample mean*) of the N results, denoted by $\overline{X}$, is

$$\overline{X} = \frac{\sum_{t=1}^{N} X_t}{N}. \tag{2.90}$$

Let $N(i)$ denote the number of tosses that result in the integer i, $1 \leq i \leq 6$. Then the summation of (2.90) can be rewritten as

$$\overline{X} = \frac{\sum_{i=1}^{6} iN(i)}{N} = \sum_{i=1}^{6} i f_N(i), \tag{2.91}$$

where $f_N(i) = N(i)/N$ is the relative frequency of the outcome i.

Since the X_t's are random variables, so is their sample mean $\overline{X}$. But when N becomes sufficiently large, $f_N(i)$ will tend to the probability $P[i]$. Thus, for large N, we expect $\overline{X}$ to stabilize at the number $E[X]$ given by

$$E[X] = \sum_{i \leq i \leq 6} iP[i]. \tag{2.92}$$

We call $E[X]$ the *expectation* or the *mean* of the random variable X. We often write the expectation of X as μ_X for conciseness. In general, we define the expectation of a discrete random variable X as

$$\mu_X = E[X] = \sum_{\text{all } k} x_k P[x_k]. \tag{2.93}$$

Similarly, the expectation of a continuous random variable X, with the density function f_X, is

$$\mu_X = \int_{-\infty}^{\infty} x f_X(x) \, dx, \tag{2.94}$$

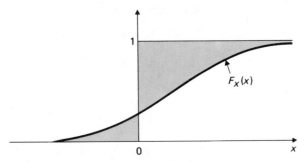

Fig. 2.7 The expectation of the random variable X is the difference of the shaded regions.

provided the integral exists. We may also write

$$\mu_X = \int_0^\infty x f_X(x)\, dx + \int_{-\infty}^0 x f_X(x)\, dx$$

$$= \int_0^\infty [1 - F_X(x)]\, dx - \int_{-\infty}^0 F_X(x)\, dx. \qquad (2.95)$$

The last expression was obtained (see Exercise 2.5.1) by applying the "integration by parts" and by assuming that $E[|X|] < \infty$.* The result (2.95) says that the mean value of the random variable X is equal to the difference of the right-hand and left-hand shaded areas in Fig. 2.7. If X is a nonnegative random variable, the second term of (2.95) disappears and we obtain the following formula:

$$\mu_X = \int_0^\infty F_X^c(x)\, dx, \qquad x \geq 0, \qquad (2.96)$$

where

$$F_X^c(x) = 1 - F_X(x) \qquad (2.97)$$

is called the *complementary distribution function* or the *survivor function* of the random variable X. The formulas (2.95) and (2.96) hold for a *discrete random variable* as well (see Exercise 2.5.2).

One of the most important properties of the expectation is that $E[\ ]$ is a linear operator. Therefore, the expectation of a weighted sum of many random variables is the weighted sum of their expectations:

$$E\left[\sum_i a_i X_i\right] = \sum_i a_i E[X_i]. \qquad (2.98)$$

This is true whether or not the X_i's are statistically independent.

---

* An example of a distribution that does not satisfy this condition is the Cauchy's distribution (see Section 5.5.3).

2.5.2 Moments of a Random Variable

If X is a random variable, so is its nth power X^n. The expectation of X^n,

$$E[X^n] = \int_{-\infty}^{\infty} x^n f_X(x)\, dx, \qquad \text{if } X \text{ is continuous,} \qquad (2.99a)$$

or

$$E[X^n] = \sum_{\text{all } k} x_k^n P[x_k], \qquad \text{if } X \text{ is discrete,} \qquad (2.99b)$$

is called the nth *moment* of X. The first moment is equal to the expectation μ_X.

The nth *central moment* of X is defined as

$$E[(X - \mu_X)^n] = \int_{-\infty}^{\infty} (x - \mu_X)^n f_X(x)\, dx \qquad (2.100a)$$

or

$$E[(X - \mu_X)^n] = \sum_{\text{all } k} (x_k - \mu_X)^n P[x_k]. \qquad (2.100b)$$

The second central moment is given the special name *variance* and is usually denoted σ_X^2:

$$\sigma_X^2 = E[(X - \mu_X)^2] = E[X^2 - 2\mu_X X + \mu_X^2]$$
$$= E[X^2] - \mu_X^2. \qquad (2.101)$$

The last expression is obtained by using the linear property (2.98) of $E[\ ]$. The square root of the variance, σ_X, is called the *standard deviation*.

If we think of a one-dimensional probability distribution $f_X(\bullet)$ as a mass distribution along a rod, the moments $E[X^n]$ have direct physical analogs. The expectation, μ_X, corresponds to the center of gravity; $E[X^2]$, to the moment of inertia around the origin; and σ_X^2, to the central moment of inertia. Another type of analogy is found in electrical circuits: If the random variable X represents a voltage or current, the mean μ_X gives the d-c component; the second moment $E[X^2]$ gives the average power carried by X and σ_X is the root-mean-square value of the a-c component.

We saw that the expression for the expectation μ_X is somewhat simplified when X is a nonnegative random variable. The expression for the second moment may also be simplified for a nonnegative random variable (see Exercise 2.5.3):

$$E[X^2] = 2 \int_0^{\infty} x F_X^c(x)\, dx, \qquad x \geq 0. \qquad (2.102)$$

Therefore, the variance of a positive random variable is given by

$$\sigma_X^2 = E[X^2] - \mu_X^2 = 2 \int_0^\infty x F_X^c(x)\, dx - \mu_X^2, \qquad x \geq 0. \quad (2.103)$$

Example 2.5. Consider a random variable X that has the distribution function

$$F_X(x) = \begin{cases} 1 - e^{-x/a}, & x \geq 0 \\ 0, & x < 0 \end{cases} \qquad (2.104)$$

and the density function

$$f_X(x) = \begin{cases} \dfrac{1}{a} e^{-x/a}, & x \geq 0 \\ 0, & x < 0. \end{cases} \qquad (2.105)$$

This distribution frequently appears in queueing systems. The distribution function (2.104) is called the exponential distribution function, and is shown in Fig. 2.8. Since X is a positive random variable with the complementary distribution $F_X^c(x) = e^{-x/a}$, we can use the formulas (2.96) and (2.103):

$$\mu_X = \int_0^\infty F_X^c(x)\, dx = \int_0^\infty e^{-x/a}\, dx = a \qquad (2.106)$$

and

$$\sigma_X^2 = 2 \int_0^\infty x e^{-x/a} - \mu_X^2$$
$$= 2a^2 - a^2 = a^2. \qquad (2.107)$$

Thus the standard deviation σ_X is the same as the mean μ_X when X is an exponentially distributed random variable.

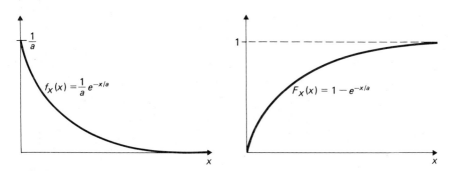

Fig. 2.8 The probability density and distribution functions of an exponential random variable.

The ratio of the standard deviation σ_X to the mean μ_X,

$$C_X = \frac{\sigma_X}{\mu_X}, \tag{2.108}$$

is called the *coefficient of variation* of the random variable X, and indicates in a rough way a departure from the exponential distribution, for which we know that $C_X = 1$ from (2.106) and (2.107).

2.5.3 Characteristic Functions

If X is a random variable and θ is a real parameter, $e^{i\theta X} = \cos(\theta X) + i \sin(\theta X)$ is a complex-valued random variable, where $i = \sqrt{-1}$. This interpretation requires that we extend our definition of random variable to include mappings from Ω into the complex plane. The expectation of $e^{i\theta X}$,

$$\phi_X(\theta) = E[e^{i\theta X}] = \int_{-\infty}^{\infty} e^{i\theta x} f_X(x)\, dx, \quad \text{if } X \text{ is continuous,}$$

$$\tag{2.109a}$$

or

$$\phi_X(\theta) = E[e^{i\theta X}] - \sum_k e^{i\theta x_k} P[x_k], \quad \text{if } X \text{ is discrete,} \tag{2.109b}$$

is called the *characteristic function* of a random variable X. It is continuous for all θ, and satisfies

$$|\phi_X(\theta)| \leq \phi_X(0) = 1. \tag{2.110}$$

The characteristic function of a continuous random variable X is equivalent to the Fourier transform of the probability density function of that random variable.* Therefore, we may use the inverse Fourier transformation

$$f_X(x) = \frac{1}{2\pi} \int_{-\infty}^{\infty} \phi_X(\theta) e^{-i\theta x}\, d\theta \tag{2.111}$$

to obtain the probability density function of X when we know its characteristic function. In fact, in many circumstances we derive the characteristic function first and then transform it to obtain the probability density function.

---

* In the Fourier transform, the sign of the exponent is usually minus, but this does not pose any essential difference.

2.5.4   Statistically Independent Random Variables and Convolution

Consider the problem of finding the density function of the sum of two statistically independent random variables, say, $Z = X + Y$. The characteristic function of Z is found to be

$$\phi_X(\theta) = E[e^{i\theta Z}] = E[e^{i\theta X}]E[e^{i\theta Y}] = \phi_X(\theta)\phi_Y(\theta), \qquad (2.112)$$

where we use the property that the expectation of the product of functions of independent random variables is equal to the product of the expectation of each function (see Exercise 2.5.5). Thus, by inverting the above result, we have

$$f_Z(z) = \frac{1}{2\pi} \int_{-\infty}^{\infty} \phi_X(\theta)\phi_Y(\theta)e^{-i\theta z}\, d\theta. \qquad (2.113)$$

On substituting for $\phi_X(\theta)$ from (2.109a) and rearranging the order of integration, we obtain

$$f_Z(z) = \int_{-\infty}^{\infty} f_X(x)\left\{\frac{1}{2\pi}\int_{-\infty}^{\infty} \phi_Y(\theta)e^{-i\theta(z-x)}\, d\theta\right\} dx. \qquad (2.114)$$

Hence, using (2.111),

$$f_Z(z) = \int_{-\infty}^{\infty} f_X(x)f_Y(z-x)\, dx. \qquad (2.115)$$

The latter equation is called the *convolution integral* (or simply *convolution*) of $f_X(\bullet)$ and $f_Y(\bullet)$. Using the symbol $\circledast$ to denote convolution, we can write

$$f_Z(z) = f_X(z) \circledast f_Y(z). \qquad (2.116)$$

By induction, we generalize the results (2.112) and (2.116) to many random variables. Let $\{X_k; k = 1, 2, \ldots, K\}$ be K statistically independent random variables with characteristic functions $\phi_k(\theta)$'s. Define the random variable Z to be the sum of X_k's:

$$Z = \sum_{k=1}^{K} X_k. \qquad (2.117)$$

Then the characteristic function of Z is given by the product of $\phi_k(\theta)$'s:

$$\phi_Z(\theta) = \prod_{k=1}^{K} \phi_k(\theta). \qquad (2.118)$$

Correspondingly, the probability density function of Z is given by the *K-fold convolution*:

$$f_Z(z) = f_1(z) \circledast f_2(z) \circledast \cdots \circledast f_K(z), \qquad (2.119)$$

where $f_k(\bullet)$ denotes the probability density function of X_k, $k = 1, 2, \ldots, K$.

2.5.5 Moment Generation

An important property of a characteristic function is its relation to the moments. By taking the nth derivative with respect to θ of the characteristic function (2.109),

$$\phi_X^{(n)}(\theta) = \int_{-\infty}^{\infty} (ix)^n e^{i\theta x} f_X(x) \, dx. \tag{2.120}$$

Evaluating (2.120) at $\theta = 0$, we find the following expression for the nth moment of X:

$$E[X^n] = (-i)^n \phi_X^{(n)}(0). \tag{2.121}$$

The differentiation required by this formula is sometimes much easier to carry out than the integration required by (2.99a).

Suppose that the Taylor-series expansion of the characteristic function exists throughout some interval in θ which contains the origin. We may then write

$$\phi_X(\theta) = \sum_{n=0}^{\infty} \frac{\phi_X^{(n)}(0)\theta^n}{n!}. \tag{2.122}$$

It then follows, using (2.121) and the property $i^2 = -1$, that

$$\phi_X(\theta) = \sum_{n=0}^{\infty} E[X^n] \frac{(i\theta)^n}{n!}. \tag{2.123}$$

Therefore, we see that if the characteristic function of a random variable has the Taylor-series expansion valid in some interval about the origin, it is uniquely determined in this interval by the moments of the random variable.

The logarithm of the characteristic function $\phi_X(\theta)$ is called the *cumulant generating function* and is denoted $\Psi_X(\theta)$:

$$\Psi_X(\theta) = \ln \phi_X(\theta). \tag{2.124}$$

We may also expand $\Psi_X(\theta)$ as follows:

$$\Psi_X(\theta) = \sum_{n=0}^{\infty} \kappa_n \frac{(i\theta)^n}{n!} \tag{2.125}$$

The quantities κ_n are called *cumulants*. Note that any cumulant κ_n is a polynomial in the moments, and vice versa. In particular, the first two cumulants are μ_X and σ_X^2, respectively:

$$\kappa_1 = (-i)\Psi_X^{(1)}(0) = \mu_X, \qquad (2.126)$$

$$\kappa_2 = (-i)^2\Psi_X^{(2)}(0) = \sigma_X^2. \qquad (2.127)$$

Example 2.6.   Consider the exponentially distributed random variable X discussed in Example 2.5. Its characteristic function is

$$\phi_X(\theta) = \int_0^\infty \frac{1}{a} e^{-x/a} e^{i\theta x} \, dx$$

$$= \frac{1}{1 - i\theta a}. \qquad (2.128)$$

The cumulant generating function is therefore given by

$$\Psi_X(\theta) = -\ln (1 - i\theta a). \qquad (2.129)$$

Therefore, by differentiating the above expression, we obtain

$$\mu_X = (-i)\Psi_X^{(1)}(0) = a, \qquad (2.130)$$

$$\sigma_X^2 = (-i)^2\Psi_X^{(2)}(0) = a^2. \qquad (2.131)$$

2.5.6 The Joint Characteristic Function

Suppose that $\mathbf{X} = [X_1, X_2, \ldots, X_m]$ is an m-dimensional random vector having the joint probability density function $f_\mathbf{X}(\mathbf{x})$. We define the (joint) characteristic function $\phi_\mathbf{X}(\boldsymbol{\theta})$:

$$\phi_\mathbf{X}(\boldsymbol{\theta}) = E[e^{i(\theta_1 X_1 + \theta_2 X_2 + \cdots + \theta_m X_m)}]$$

$$= \int_{-\infty}^\infty \int_{-\infty}^\infty \cdots \int_{-\infty}^\infty \exp \{i\langle \boldsymbol{\theta}, \mathbf{x}\rangle\} f_\mathbf{x}(\mathbf{x}) \, dx_1 \, dx_2 \cdots dx_m, \qquad (2.132)$$

where $\langle \boldsymbol{\theta}, \mathbf{x}\rangle$ represents the inner product (scalar product) of the two vectors. The joint characteristic function always exists, and it assumes its greatest magnitude (which is unity) at the origin $\boldsymbol{\theta} = \mathbf{0}$. The joint moment $E[X_1^{n_1} \cdots X_m^{n_m}]$, if it exists, can be obtained by differentiating the characteristic function n_1 times with respect to θ_1, n_2 times with respect to $\theta_2, \ldots, n_m$ times with respect to θ_m, and setting $\theta_1 = \theta_2 = \cdots = \theta_m = \theta$:

$$E[X_1^{n_1} \cdots X_m^{n_m}] = (-i)^{n_1 + \cdots + n_m} \left[\frac{\partial^{n_1 + \cdots + n_m}}{\partial \theta_1^{n_1} \cdots \partial \theta_m^{n_m}} \phi_\mathbf{X}(\boldsymbol{\theta}) \right]\Bigg|_{\boldsymbol{\theta}=0}. \qquad (2.133)$$

It should be observed that the joint characteristic function of any subset of the components of the random vector $\mathbf{X}$ is obtained by setting equal to zero those θ's that correspond to the random variables not included in the subset. For example, the characteristic function of the random vector $[X_1, X_2]$ is $\phi_X(\theta_1, \theta_2, 0, \ldots, 0)$.

The extension of the inverse transform (2.111) to the case of random vectors is straightforward and may be given as follows:

$$f_X(x) = \left(\frac{1}{2\pi}\right)^m \int_{-\infty}^{\infty} \int_{-\infty}^{\infty} \cdots \int_{-\infty}^{\infty} \exp\{-i\langle \theta, x\rangle\}\phi_X(\theta) \, d\theta_1 \, d\theta_2 \cdots d\theta_m.$$

$$(2.134)$$

Exercises

2.5.1 Show the derivation of Eq. (2.95). *Hint:* Use the following property: If the kth absolute moment of X is finite, then

$$\lim_{x\to\infty} x^k[1 - F_X(x)] = 0,$$

$$\lim_{x\to-\infty} x^k F_X(x) = 0.$$

2.5.2 Let X be a discrete random variable with probability distribution $p_i = P[X = i]$, $i = 0, \pm 1, \pm 2, \ldots$. Find expressions analogous to Eqs. (2.95) and (2.96).

2.5.3 Show that the second moment of a continuous random variable X is given by

$$E[X^2] = 2\int_0^{\infty} xF_X^c(x) \, dx - 2\int_{-\infty}^0 xF_X(x) \, dx.$$

2.5.4 Prove the inequality of Eq. (2.110).

2.5.5 Let X and Y be statistically independent random variables.

a) Show that $E[g(X)h(Y)] = E[g(X)]E[h(Y)]$ for arbitrary functions $g(\bullet)$ and $h(\bullet)$.

b) Show that the characteristic function of $Z = X + Y$ is given by (2.112).

2.5.6 a) Let X have the *geometric distribution* defined by

$$p_i = P[X = i] = (1 - \rho)\rho^i, \qquad i = 0, 1, 2, \ldots.$$

Evaluate the expectation and variance of X using the definitions (2.93) and (2.101).

b) Do the same for the *Poisson distribution* defined by

$$p_i = P[X = i] = \frac{\lambda^i}{i!} e^{-\lambda}, \qquad i = 0, 1, 2, \ldots.$$

c) Do the same for the *binomial distribution* defined by

$$b(i; n, p) = \binom{n}{i} p^i (1 - p)^{n-i}, \qquad i = 0, 1, 2, \ldots, n, \quad 0 < p < 1.$$

2.5.7 If the probability density function $f_X(x)$ is symmetric about $x = 0$, show that the characteristic function $\phi_X(\theta)$ takes on only real values.

2.5.8 A random variable X with the *standard normal distribution* is defined by the probability density function

$$f_X(x) = \frac{1}{\sqrt{2\pi}} e^{-x^2/2}$$

and its characteristic function is obtained (see Section 2.8) as

$$\phi_X(\theta) = e^{-\theta^2/2}.$$

Let $X_1, X_2, \ldots, X_K$ be independent random variables all having the unit normal distribution. Find the probability density function of the random variable $(1/\sqrt{K})(X_1 + X_2 + \cdots + X_K)$.

2.5.9 *Poisson distribution.* The Poisson distribution of parameter λ is defined by

$$p_k = \frac{\lambda^k}{k!} e^{-\lambda}, \qquad k = 0, 1, 2, \ldots.$$

a) Find the characteristic function of the distribution.
b) Compute the mean and variance.
c) Let X_i be independent random variables with Poisson distributions of parameters λ_i, $i = 1, 2, \ldots, n$. Find the distribution of the variable $Y = X_1 + X_2 + \cdots + X_n$.

2.5.10 *Geometric distribution.* Consider a sequence of Bernoulli trials with the probability of success p, and that of failure $q = 1 - p$. The number of trials that precede the first success is a discrete random variable, which we denote by X.

a) Show that the probability that $X = k$ is given by the *geometric* distribution

$$p_k = pq^k, \qquad k = 0, 1, 2, \ldots.$$

b) Find the mean and variance, using the characteristic function.

2.5.11 *Multinomial distribution.* Suppose that the outcome of a trial is one of m different events $E_1, E_2, \ldots, E_m$, which are mutually exclusive, and let the probability of event E_j be p_j, $1 \le j \le m$ with $\sum_{j=1}^{m} p_j = 1$. Suppose we make n independent trials.

a) Show that the probability E_1 will occur k_1 times, E_2, k_2 times, $\ldots$, E_m k_m times, where $k_1 + k_2 + \cdots + k_m = n$ is

$$p_{\mathbf{k}} = \frac{n!}{k_1! \, k_2! \cdots k_m!} p_1^{k_1} p_2^{k_2} \cdots p_m^{k_m},$$

where $\mathbf{k}$ stands for the vector $[k_1, k_2, \ldots, k_m]$. This distribution is called a *multinomial* distribution.

b) Find the joint characteristic function of the m-dimensional random vector $\mathbf{k} = [k_1, k_2, \ldots k_m]$.

c) Apply the moment generating formula (2.133) and find the mean and variance of k_i and the *covariance* of k_i and k_j defined by

$$\text{Cov}\,[k_i, k_j] = E[(k_i - E[k_i])(k_j - E[k_j])].$$

2.6 TRANSFORMS FOR NONNEGATIVE RANDOM VARIABLES

Many random variables that appear in mathematical models of computer systems assume values only on the nonnegative real line or nonnegative integers. Such random variables as the job service times, the waiting times, and the interarrival times are examples of nonnegative continuous random variables, whereas the number of arrivals or departures during a given interval, the queue length, etc., are nonnegative discrete random variables. For this class of random variables, it is often analytically more convenient to use other transforms than it is to use the corresponding characteristic functions. They are the *probability generating function* and the *Laplace transform*.

2.6.1 The Probability Generating Function

Consider a random variable X which assumes only values $0, 1, 2, \ldots$, with probabilities $p_0, p_1, p_2, \ldots$. We define the *probability generating function* (or simply the *generating function**) $G_X(z)$ as $E[z^X]$:

$$G_X(z) = E[z^X] = \sum_{k=0}^{\infty} p_k z^k, \qquad (2.135)$$

$G_X(z)$ is clearly a function of the "parameter" z only, since it is obtained by summing over the index k. But it is also a single quantity that represents the entire probabilities $p_0, p_1, p_2, \ldots$. We can recover (or generate) the values $p_0, p_1, p_2, \ldots$ from the function $G_X(z)$ assuming that the infinite sum in Eq. (2.135) exists for some values of z. The use of generating functions gives us an extremely powerful technique when we deal with certain operations involving the random variables or their probabilities.

---

*The notion of generating function can be more general than the treatment we give here. For a given sequence or vector $\{f(k); k = 0, \pm 1, \pm 2, \ldots\}$, the generating function is defined as a power series in z^k having as coefficients the value $f(k)$. In the field of system analysis, the name "z-transform" has gained wide acceptance in which usually a transformation based on power series in z^{-k} is used.

Example 2.7. Consider the *geometric distribution*

$$p_k = (1 - \rho)\rho^k, \qquad k \geq 0. \tag{2.136}$$

Using the formula for the sum of a geometric series,

$$G(z) = (1 - \rho) \sum_{k=0}^{\infty} (\rho z)^k = \frac{1 - \rho}{1 - \rho z}, \quad \text{for } |z| < \rho^{-1}. \tag{2.137}$$

The region $|z| \leq \rho^{-1}$ is called the region of convergence of (2.137), and the number ρ^{-1} is called the *radius of convergence*.

Example 2.8. The *Poisson distribution* with mean λ is defined by

$$p_k = \frac{\lambda^k}{k!} e^{-\lambda}, \qquad k \geq 0. \tag{2.138}$$

Using the formula

$$e^x = \sum_{k=0}^{\infty} \frac{x^k}{k!} \tag{2.139}$$

we obtain

$$G(z) = \sum_{k=0}^{\infty} \frac{(\lambda z)^k}{k!} e^{-\lambda}$$

$$= e^{\lambda(z-1)}, \quad \text{for } |z| < \infty. \tag{2.140}$$

Thus, the radius of convergence is infinite.

Example 2.9. Consider the *binomial distribution*

$$b(k; n, p) = \binom{n}{k} p^k q^{n-k}, \qquad k = 0, 1, 2, \ldots, n, \tag{2.141}$$

where $0 \leq p \leq 1$, and $q = 1 - p$. Then the generating function is given by

$$G(z) = \sum_{k=0}^{n} \binom{n}{k} (pz)^k q^{n-k}$$

$$= (pz + q)^n = \{1 + p(z - 1)\}^n, \quad \text{for } |z| < \infty. \tag{2.142}$$

The radius of convergence is again infinite.

Recall that the characteristic function $\phi_X(\theta)$ was used to generate the moments of X. Analogous results that we can obtain from the probability generating function are the following *factorial moments*. Taking the nth derivative with respect to z of (2.135) and setting z equal to 1, we find

$$G_X^{(n)}(1) = \sum_{k=0}^{\infty} k(k-1)\cdots(k-n+1)p_k$$

$$= E[X(X-1)\cdots(X-n+1)]. \tag{2.143}$$

In particular, for the first two moments, we have the following formulas:

$$G_X^{(1)}(1) = E[X] \tag{2.144}$$

$$G_X^{(2)}(1) = E[X(X-1)] = E[X^2] - E[X]. \tag{2.145}$$

Example 2.10. For the Poisson distribution, substituting (2.140) into the above formulas yields

$$E[X] = \lambda, \quad E[X^2] - E[X] = \lambda^2. \tag{2.146}$$

Therefore, the variance is given by

$$\sigma_X^2 = E[X^2] - E^2[X] = \lambda^2 + \lambda - \lambda^2 = \lambda. \tag{2.147}$$

Example 2.11. Similarly for the binomial distribution we obtain from (2.142)

$$E[X] = np,$$

$$E[X^2] - E[X] = n(n-1)p^2. \tag{2.148}$$

Thus

$$\sigma_X^2 = n(n-1)p^2 + np - (np)^2$$

$$= np(1-p) = npq. \tag{2.149}$$

In Section 2.5.4 we observed that the probability density function of the sum of two statistically independent, continuous random variables is given by the convolution integral of the individual density functions. We now consider the discrete analogue of the convolution formula (2.115). Let X and Y be independent random variables with probability distributions $\mathbf{p} = \{p_k; 0 \le k < \infty\}$ and $\mathbf{q} = \{q_k; 0 \le k < \infty\}$, respectively; let their generating functions be denoted by $G_X(z)$ and $G_Y(z)$, respectively. Then the sum

$$W = X + Y \tag{2.150}$$

has the generating function $G_W(z)$ that is the product of the individual generating functions

$$G_W(z) = E[z^W] = E[z^X]E[z^Y] = G_X(z)G_Y(z). \tag{2.151}$$

Let the probability distribution of the new random variable W be denoted by $\mathbf{r} = \{r_k; \ 0 \le k < \infty\}$. Then Eq. (2.151) can be written as

$$\sum_{k=0}^{\infty} r_k z^k = \left(\sum_{i=0}^{\infty} p_i z^i\right)\left(\sum_{j=0}^{\infty} q_j z^j\right). \tag{2.152}$$

By equating the coefficients of the terms z^k of both sides, we obtain

$$r_k = \sum_{i=0}^{k} p_i q_{k-i} \tag{2.153a}$$

or, equivalently,

$$r_k = \sum_{j=0}^{k} p_{k-j} q_j. \tag{2.153b}$$

Equation (2.153) is known as the *convolution summation* of the distributions $\{p_k\}$ and $\{q_k\}$. We may simply write the above relation, analogously to (2.116), as

$$\mathbf{r} = \mathbf{p} \circledast \mathbf{q}. \tag{2.154}$$

We can generalize the foregoing results to the case of many variables. Let X_N's, $(n = 1, 2, \ldots, N)$ be statistically independent nonnegative random variables with generating functions $G_n(z)$'s. A random variable W defined by

$$W = \sum_{n=1}^{N} X_n \tag{2.155}$$

has the generating function that is the product of the $G_n(z)$'s (see Exercise 2.6.3):

$$G_W(z) = \prod_{n=1}^{N} G_n(z). \tag{2.156}$$

The probability distribution $\mathbf{r}$ of W is given by the N-fold convolution summation:

$$\mathbf{r} = \mathbf{p}_1 \circledast \mathbf{p}_2 \circledast \cdots \circledast \mathbf{p}_N, \tag{2.157}$$

where $\mathbf{p}_n$ is the probability distribution of the variable X_n, $n = 1, 2, \ldots, N$.

2.6.2 The Inverse Transformation of Probability Generating Functions

A number of methods exist for finding the probability $\mathbf{p} = \{p_k\}$ given the generating function $G(z)$ in a specified region of convergence in the z-plane. An obvious inversion formula is to find by inspection the coefficient of each power term z^k of $G(z)$ or to obtain the Taylor series expansion of $G(z)$ around $z = 0$:

$$p_k = \frac{G^{(k)}(0)}{k!}. \tag{2.158}$$

In some cases, however, $G(z)$ is given in rather complicated form, and the inspection method or Taylor expansion method may be impractical. In such cases, one of the following two methods should be tried: (1) the partial fraction expansion method or (2) the recursion method.

The partial-fraction expansion method

One method of finding $\{p_k; k = 0, 1, 2, \ldots\}$ for a given rational function $G(z)$ is to carry out a partial-fraction expansion of $G(z)$. The partial-fraction expansion is a purely algebraic operation for expressing a rational function of z as sums of simple recognizable terms.

Consider $G(z)$, which is given as the ratio of two polynomials in z:

$$G(z) = \frac{N(z)}{D(z)} = \frac{a_n z^n + a_{n-1} z^{n-1} + \cdots + a_1 z + a_0}{b_d z^d + b_{d-1} z^{d-1} + \cdots + b_1 z + b_0}. \tag{2.159}$$

If $n > d$, we divide $N(z)$ by $D(z)$ until a remainder polynomial $N_1(z)$ that is of degree $d - 1$ or less is obtained:

$$G(z) = \sum_{k=0}^{n-d} c_{0k} z^k + \frac{N_1(z)}{D(z)}. \tag{2.160}$$

We then find the zeros $\{\alpha_i^{-1}; i = 1, 2, \ldots\}$ of $D(z)$ (that is, the poles of $G(z)$):

$$D(z) = \prod_{i=1}^{r} (1 - \alpha_i z)^{m_i}. \tag{2.161}$$

Equation (2.161) shows that the ith root $z = \alpha_i^{-1}$ occurs with multiplicity m_i. The set of m_i's must satisfy $\sum_{i=1}^{r} m_i = d$, which is the degree of $D(z)$. Then we can express $G(z)$ as

$$G(z) = \sum_{k=0}^{n-d} c_{0k} z^k + \sum_{i=1}^{r} \sum_{j=1}^{m_i} \frac{c_{ij}}{(1 - \alpha_i z)^j}. \tag{2.162}$$

The unknown coefficients $\{c_{ij}\}$ can be solved in the customary manner and are given by

$$c_{ij} = \frac{1}{(m_i - j)!(-\alpha_i)^{m_i - j}} \cdot \frac{d^{m_i - j}}{dz^{m_i - j}} \left[(1 - \alpha_i z)^{m_i} \frac{N_1(z)}{D(z)} \right]\Bigg|_{z = \alpha_i^{-1}} \tag{2.163}$$

where $i = 1, 2, \ldots, r$, and $j = 1, 2, \ldots, m_i$. Then by using the formula (see Exercise 2.6.4)

$$\sum_{k=0}^{\infty} \frac{(k + j - 1)(k + j - 2) \cdots (k + 1)}{(j - 1)!} \alpha^k z^k = \frac{1}{(1 - \alpha z)^j},$$

$$(2.164)$$

we obtain $\{p_k\}$:

$$p_k = c_{0k} + \sum_{i=1}^{r} \sum_{j=1}^{m_i} c_{ij} \frac{(k + j - 1)(k + j - 2) \cdots (k + 1)}{(j - 1)!} \alpha_i^k,$$

$$(2.165)$$

$$k = 0, 1, 2, \ldots,$$

where $c_{0k} = 0$ for $k > n - d$.

Example 2.12   Consider a probability generating function $G(z)$ given by

$$G(z) = \frac{66 - 69z + 3z^2 + 16z^3 - 4z^4}{12(18 - 33z + 20z^2 - 4z^3)}.$$

The numerator has a higher degree than the denominator; hence we divide $D(z)$ into $N(z)$, obtaining

$$G(z) = \frac{1 + z}{12} + \frac{24 - 27z + 8z^2}{6(18 - 33z + 20z^2 - 4z^3)}.$$

We find that $D(z) = 0$ has roots $\alpha_1^{-1} = 2$ and $\alpha_2^{-1} = \frac{3}{2}$ with $m_1 = 1$ and $m_2 = 2$. The expansion coefficients are given, from the formula (2.163), as

$$c_{00} = c_{01} = \tfrac{1}{12}, \quad c_{11} = \tfrac{1}{6}, \quad c_{21} = 0, \quad \text{and} \quad c_{22} = \tfrac{1}{18},$$

which lead to the result

$$G(z) = \frac{1}{12} + \frac{z}{12} + \frac{\frac{1}{6}}{(1 - (z/2))} + \frac{\frac{1}{18}}{(1 - \frac{2}{3}z)^2}.$$

Thus we obtain

$$p_k = \frac{\delta_{k,0}}{12} + \frac{\delta_{k,1}}{12} + \frac{1}{6}\left(\frac{1}{2}\right)^k + \frac{(k + 1)}{18}\left(\frac{2}{3}\right)^k,$$

where $\delta_{i,j}$ is the Kronecker's delta; that is, $\delta_{i,j} = 1$ for $i = j$ and $\delta_{i,j} = 0$

for $i \neq j$. The first few terms are calculated as

$$p_0 = \frac{1}{12} + \frac{1}{6} + \frac{1}{18} = \frac{11}{36},$$

$$p_1 = \frac{1}{12} + \frac{1}{12} + \frac{4}{54} = \frac{13}{54},$$

$$p_2 = \frac{1}{6}\left(\frac{1}{2}\right)^2 + \frac{3}{18}\left(\frac{2}{3}\right)^2 = \frac{25}{216}, \quad \text{etc.}$$

The recursion method

In the partial-fraction method, it is necessary to find the zeros of the denominator $D(z)$. This is not a simple task when the degree d is not small. An alternative technique is to return to the original equation (2.159):

$$\sum_{k=0}^{\infty} p_k z^k = \frac{\sum_{i=0}^{n} a_i z^i}{\sum_{j=0}^{d} b_j z^j}. \tag{2.166}$$

On multiplying the denominator on both sides, we obtain

$$\sum_{k=0}^{\infty} \sum_{j=0}^{d} p_k b_j z^{k+j} = \sum_{i=0}^{n} a_i z^i. \tag{2.167}$$

Comparison of the terms z^i on both sides leads to the following set of *linear difference equations:*

$$\sum_{j=0}^{\min\{d,i\}} p_{i-j} b_j = \begin{cases} a_i & \text{for} \quad i = 0, 1, \ldots, n \\ 0 & \text{for} \quad i > n. \end{cases} \tag{2.168}$$

We can then solve for $\{p_i;\ i = 0, 1, 2, \ldots\}$ in a recursive manner:

$$p_i = \frac{1}{b_0}\left[a_i - \sum_{j=1}^{\min\{d,i\}} b_j p_{i-j}\right], \quad i = 0, 1, 2, \ldots, \tag{2.169}$$

where $a_i = 0$ for $i > n$.

The recursion method is useful if the numerical evaluation is to be performed on a computer, since the above formula is extremely simple to program.

Exercises

2.6.1 Let $G(z)$ be the probability generating function of the probability distribution $\{p_k; \ k = 0, 1, 2, \ldots\}$. Show the following properties:

  a) $G(1) = 1$,
  b) $G(0) = p_0$.

2.6.2 Let $F(z)$ and $\{f_k; \ k = 0, 1, 2, \ldots\}$ form a z-transform pair defined by

$$F(z) = \sum_{k=0}^{\infty} f_k z^k.$$

Find $\{f_k\}$ for the following $F(z)$:

  a) $F(z) = \dfrac{1}{1 - \alpha z}$;

  b) $F(z) = \dfrac{1}{(1 - \alpha z)^2}$;

  c) $F(z) = \dfrac{\alpha z}{(1 - \alpha z)^2}$.

2.6.3 Show that the probability generating function of the sum of independent random variables is given by (2.156).

2.6.4 Prove the formula (2.164). What does this equation mean for the case $j = 1$?

2.6.5 *Final value theorem.* Refer to Exercise 2.6.2. Show that

$$\lim_{z \to 1} (1 - z)F(z) = \lim_{k \to \infty} f_k.$$

2.6.6 *Joint probability generating function.* Suppose $\mathbf{X} = [X_1, X_2, \ldots, X_m]$ is an m-dimensional discrete random vector with probability distribution $p_{\mathbf{k}} = P[\mathbf{X} = \mathbf{k}]$, where $\mathbf{k} = [k_1, k_2, \ldots, k_m]$. The *joint probability generating function* is defined by

$$G_{\mathbf{X}}(\mathbf{z}) = E[z_1^{X_1} z_2^{X_2} \cdots z_m^{X_m}] = \sum_{k_1} \sum_{k_2} \cdots \sum_{k_m} z_1^{k_1} z_2^{k_2} \cdots z_m^{k_m} p_{\mathbf{k}}.$$

  a) Show that the inversion formula is given by

$$p_{\mathbf{k}} = \frac{1}{k_1! k_2! \cdots k_m!} \frac{\partial^{k_1 + k_2 + \cdots + k_m}}{\partial z_1^{k_1} \partial z_2^{k_2} \cdots \partial z_m^{k_m}} G_{\mathbf{X}}(\mathbf{z}) \bigg|_{\mathbf{z} = \mathbf{0}}$$

where $\mathbf{0}$ is the vector whose components are all zeros.

  b) Find the joint generating function of the multinomial distribution defined in Exercise 2.5.11.

2.6.7 *Negative-binomial or Pascal distribution.* Consider a sequence of Bernoulli trials. Suppose the trials are performed until some fixed number n of successes are attained. We wish to determine the probability that exactly k trials must be made to accomplish this objective.

a) Show that the probability p_k that the nth success occurs at the kth trial is

$$p_k = \binom{k-1}{n-1} p^n q^{k-n}, \qquad k = n, n+1, n+2, \ldots.$$

This distribution is known as the *Pascal* or *negative-binomial* distribution.

b) In the Bernoulli trials, let $Y^{(i)}$ be the number of additional trials necessary to achieve the ith success, counting from the trial just after the $(i-1)$th success. Let X be the sum of the variables

$$X = Y^{(1)} + Y^{(2)} + \cdots + Y^{(n)}.$$

Show that the probability $X = k$ is equivalent to the Pascal distribution of part (a).

c) Calculate the mean and variance of the distribution.

2.6.8 *A derivation of the binomial distribution.* Derive the binomial distribution $b(k; n, p)$, the probability of observing k successes in n Bernoulli trials.

a) In order to obtain exactly k successes after n trials, either we must have already k successes after $(n-1)$ trials and then obtain a failure on the nth trial, or we must have $(k-1)$ successes after $(n-1)$ trials and then obtain a success on the nth trial. Based on this observation, find a linear difference equation for $b(k; n, p)$, $0 \le k \le n$.

b) Define the generating function $B(z; n)$ by

$$B(z; n, p) = \sum_{k=0}^{n} b(k; n, p) z^k.$$

Find a recursive equation which $\{B(z; n, p), n = 0, 1, \ldots\}$ must satisfy.

c) Define a two-dimensional generating function $C(z, w)$ by

$$C(z, w; p) = \sum_{n=0}^{\infty} B(z; n, p) w^n.$$

Find a closed form expression of $C(z, w; p)$ and then $B(z; n, p)$. Then obtain the binomial distribution $b(k; n, p)$.

2.6.9 Apply the recursion method to the problem discussed in Example 2.12 and obtain $\{p_0, p_1, p_2, \ldots\}$.

2.6.3 The Laplace Transform

For nonnegative continuous random variables, the Laplace transform plays a role similar to the one that the generating function does for discrete variables. Let X be a random variable assuming values only on the nonnegative real line, with the probability density function $f_X(x)$. We define the Laplace transform of f_X by

$$\Phi_X(s) = E[e^{-sX}] = \int_0^{\infty} f_X(x) e^{-sx} \, dx, \qquad (2.170)$$

where s is a complex parameter. It is not difficult to show that

$$|\Phi_X(s)| \leq \Phi_X(0) = 1 \quad \text{for} \quad Re\,(s) > 0 \qquad (2.171)$$

where $Re(s)$ means the real part of the complex-valued parameter s. Note the similarity between this transform and the characteristic function defined earlier. The latter exists for any probability density function, whereas the Laplace transform applies only to nonnegative random variables. We can compute moments of the variable X by differentiating $\Phi_X(s)$ in much the same way as we generated the moments from the characteristic function

$$E[X^n] = (-1)^n \Phi_X^{(n)}(0), \qquad (2.172)$$

which is quite similar to (2.121).

Example 2.13. Consider the exponentially distributed random variable X with the distribution function

$$F_X(x) = 1 - e^{-\lambda x} \qquad (2.173)$$

and the density function

$$f_X(x) = \lambda e^{-\lambda x}, \qquad (2.174)$$

respectively. The Laplace transform of f_X is thus evaluated as

$$\Phi_X(s) = \int_0^\infty \lambda e^{-\lambda x} e^{-sx}\, dx = \frac{\lambda}{s + \lambda}. \qquad (2.175)$$

On taking the natural logarithm* of $\Phi_X(s)$ and differentiating it with respect to s, we obtain

$$\frac{\Phi_X'(s)}{\Phi_X(s)} = -\frac{1}{s + \lambda}, \qquad (2.176)$$

which immediately leads to

$$E[X] = -\Phi_X'(0) = \frac{1}{\lambda} \Phi_X(0) = 1/\lambda. \qquad (2.177)$$

By differentiating (2.176) again and setting $s = 0$, we find

$$\Phi_X''(0) - (\Phi_X'(0))^2 = \frac{1}{\lambda^2}, \qquad (2.178)$$

---

* Direct differentiation of $\Phi_X(s)$ is straightforward in this case. If $\Phi_X(s)$ is a rational function of s, the logarithmic transformation significantly simplifies the computation.

which yields

$$E[X^2] = \Phi_X''(0) = \frac{2}{\lambda^2}. \tag{2.179}$$

Example 2.14. Consider random variable Y, which is also exponentially distributed, but with parameter μ:

$$f_Y(y) = \mu e^{-\mu y}. \tag{2.180}$$

Hence its Laplace transform is

$$\Phi_Y(s) = \frac{\mu}{s + \mu}. \tag{2.181}$$

Let us further assume that the variable X of Example 2.13 and Y are statistically independent, and consider their sum

$$W = X + Y. \tag{2.182}$$

The Laplace transform of the probability density function of the new variable W is then

$$\Phi_W(s) = E[e^{-sW}] = E[e^{-sX}]E[e^{-sY}]$$

$$= \Phi_X(s)\Phi_Y(s) = \frac{\lambda\mu}{(s + \lambda)(s + \mu)}. \tag{2.183}$$

By a simple algebraic manipulation we can write $\Phi_W(s)$ as

$$\Phi_W(s) = \frac{\lambda\mu}{(\mu - \lambda)} \left(\frac{1}{s + \lambda} - \frac{1}{s + \mu} \right). \tag{2.184}$$

Then by applying the formula (2.175), we find the probability density function:

$$f_W(x) = \frac{\lambda\mu}{\mu - \lambda} (e^{-\lambda x} - e^{-\mu x}). \tag{2.185}$$

2.6.4 The Inverse Laplace Transform

The Laplace transform of a real-valued function $f(t)$ (not necessarily a probability density function) is defined as

$$\Phi(s) = \int_0^\infty e^{-st} f(t) \, dt. \tag{2.186}$$

If $f(t)$ is a piecewise continuous function of exponential order α (i.e., $|f(t)| \leq M e^{\alpha t}$), the transform function $\Phi(s)$ is defined for $Re(s) > \alpha$. Here the parameter α is often called the *abscissa of convergence*.

Conversely, for a given function $\Phi(s)$ of the Laplacian variable s, the inverse transformation to obtain the corresponding $f(t)$ is given by the formula

$$f(t) = \frac{1}{2\pi i} \int_{c-i\infty}^{c+i\infty} e^{st}\Phi(s)\, ds, \tag{2.187}$$

where $i = \sqrt{-1}$ and c can be any real number greater than α. This integral formula is analogous to the inverse formula (2.111) for the characteristic function. In this section, we discuss two different methods of carrying out the inverse Laplace transform: (1) the partial-fraction method and (2) the numerical-inversion method.

A remark is in order concerning the Laplace transform of a probability density function. Although most of the results to be presented below apply to any piecewise continuous functions of exponential order, we are primarily interested in the case where $f(\bullet)$ is the probability density function of some nonnegative random variable. For this class of functions, the Laplace transform $\Phi(s)$ always exists for any positive value of α, since it is bounded according to

$$|\Phi(s)| \leq \int_{0^-}^{\infty} |e^{-sx}f(x)|\, dx \leq \int_{0^-}^{\infty} f(x)\, dx = 1 \quad \text{for} \quad Re\,(s) > 0. \tag{2.188}$$

In fact, the transform function could exist even for a negative value of α.

The partial-fraction expansion method

This method is a continuous counterpart of the partial-fraction expansion method discussed earlier for the z transform or the generating function. Let us assume that $\Phi(s)$ is a rational function of s:

$$\Phi(s) = \frac{N(s)}{D(s)} = \frac{a_n s^n + a_{n-1}s^{n-1} + \cdots + a_1 s + a_0}{b_d s^d + b_{d-1}s^{d-1} + \cdots + b_1 s + b_0}. \tag{2.189}$$

When $\Phi(s)$ is the Laplace transform of a probability density function, the degree of $N(s)$ cannot exceed that of $D(s)$ (see Exercise 2.6.14), that is,

$$n \leq d. \tag{2.190}$$

Furthermore, the property $\Phi(0) = 1$ immediately implies

$$a_0 = b_0. \tag{2.191}$$

If $n = d$, we divide $N(s)$ by $D(s)$ and obtain the expression

$$\Phi(s) = \frac{a_d}{b_d} + \frac{N_1(s)}{D(s)}, \tag{2.192}$$

where $N_1(s)$ is a polynomial of degree $d - 1$ or less. We then determine the zeros $\{-\lambda_i, i = 1, 2, \ldots, r\}$ of $D(s)$, obtaining an expression similar to (2.161):

$$D(s) = \prod_{i=1}^{r} (s + \lambda_i)^{m_i}, \tag{2.193}$$

which leads to the following partial-fraction expansion of $\Phi(s)$:

$$\Phi(s) = \frac{a_d}{b_d} + \sum_{i=1}^{r} \sum_{j=1}^{m_i} \frac{c_{ij}}{(s + \lambda_i)^j}, \tag{2.194}$$

where the coefficients $\{c_{ij}\}$ are given by

$$c_{ij} = \frac{1}{(m_i - j)!} \frac{d^{m_i - j}}{ds^{m_i - j}} \left[(s + \lambda_i)^{m_i} \frac{N_1(s)}{D(s)} \right] \Big|_{s = -\lambda_i} \tag{2.195}$$

Then by applying the formula (see also Exercise 2.6.10),

$$\int_0^\infty \frac{x^{j-1}}{(j-1)!} e^{-\lambda x} e^{-sx} \, dx = \frac{1}{(s + \lambda)^j}, \tag{2.196}$$

we obtain the probability density function

$$f(x) = \frac{a_d}{b_d} \delta(x) + \sum_{i=1}^{r} \sum_{j=1}^{m_i} \frac{c_{ij} x^{j-1}}{(j-1)!} e^{-\lambda_i x}, \tag{2.197}$$

where $\delta(x)$ is the unit-impulse function or Dirac δ function. The corresponding distribution function is

$$F(x) = \frac{a_d}{b_d} + \sum_{i=1}^{r} \sum_{j=1}^{m_i} \frac{c_{ij}}{\lambda_i^j} \left\{ 1 - e^{-\lambda_i x} \sum_{k=0}^{j-1} \frac{(\lambda_i x)^k}{k!} \right\}. \tag{2.198}$$

Example 2.15. Let $\Phi(s)$ be given by

$$\Phi(s) = \frac{s^3 + 8s^2 + 22s + 16}{4(s^3 + 5s^2 + 8s + 4)}.$$

The procedure given above leads to the partial-fraction expansion

$$\Phi(s) = \frac{1}{4} + \frac{1}{4(s + 1)} + \frac{1}{2(s + 2)} + \frac{1}{(s + 2)^2}.$$

The corresponding probability density function and the distribution function are therefore given by

$$f(x) = \frac{\delta(x)}{4} + \frac{e^{-x}}{4} + \frac{e^{-2x}}{2} + xe^{-2x}, \qquad 0 \le x < \infty$$

and

$$F(x) = \tfrac{1}{4} + \tfrac{1}{4}(1 - e^{-x}) + \tfrac{1}{4}(1 - e^{-2x}) + \tfrac{1}{4}\{1 - e^{-2x}(1 + 2x)\},$$
$$0 \le x < \infty.$$

The numerical-inversion method

Use of the partial-fraction method will become difficult when the degree of $D(s)$ becomes large. A computation program for finding the roots of a polynomial may be available in many scientific program libraries, but the computation of the coefficients $\{c_{ij}\}$ is a rather cumbersome task even if we are given a set of λ_i's. Another method frequently discussed in the literature is the evaluation of the integral by the Cauchy residue theorem. When calculating residues, however, one faces essentially the same type of difficulty as that pointed out for the partial-fraction method. An alternative approach is the *numerical-inversion method* to be discussed below.

By setting the complex variable s as

$$s = c + i\omega \tag{2.199}$$

where $i = \sqrt{-1}$, we can rewrite (2.187) in terms of the cosine transform:

$$f(t) = \frac{2e^{ct}}{\pi} \int_0^\infty \cos(\omega t) \, Re\,\{\Phi(c + i\omega)\} \, d\omega. \tag{2.200}$$

Here the constant c, as discussed earlier, is a number greater than α, the abscissa of convergence. In other words, all poles of the complex function $\Phi(s)$ must have their real parts strictly less than c. In the numerical evaluation of $f(t)$, however, choice of a suitable parameter c is an important consideration.

Suppose we wish to evaluate $f(t)$ over a finite range $0 \le t \le T$, and at $(N + 1)$ regularly spaced points $t = 0, \delta, 2\delta, \ldots, N\delta(= T)$. The value of $f(t)$ can be approximated by

$$f(t) \approx \frac{e^{ct}}{T}\left[\frac{1}{2} Re\,\{\Phi(c)\} + \sum_{k=1}^{\infty} Re\left\{\Phi\left(c + \frac{\pi i k}{2T}\right)\right\} \cos\frac{\pi k t}{2T}\right]. \tag{2.201}$$

The above summation formula is nothing more than a trapezoidal rule applied to the integral. Using the periodic property of the cosine function, the value of $f(t)$ at $t = j\delta = j(T/N)$ can be rewritten as

$$f(j\delta) \approx \frac{e^{cT}}{T}\left[\frac{1}{2} g_0 + \sum_{k=1}^{2N-1} g_k \cos\frac{\pi j k}{2N} + \frac{(-1)^j}{2} g_{2N}\right] \qquad j = 0, 1, \ldots, N \tag{2.202}$$

where

$$g_0 = Re\,\{\Phi(c)\} + 2 \sum_{m=0}^{\infty} Re\left\{\Phi\!\left(c + \frac{2\pi im}{\delta}\right)\right\} \qquad (2.203a)$$

and

$$g_k = \sum_{m=0}^{\infty} \left[Re\left\{\Phi\!\left(c + \frac{2\pi i}{\delta}\left(\frac{k}{4N} + m\right)\right)\right\} \right.$$
$$\left. + Re\left\{\Phi\!\left(c + \frac{2\pi i}{\delta}\left(1 - \frac{k}{4N} + m\right)\right)\right\} \right] \qquad k = 1, 2, \ldots, 2N.$$
$$(2.203b)$$

The above formula involves only $Re\,\{\Phi(s)\}$, hence it is easy to program on a digital computer.

An appropriate choice of the parameters c, N, and δ is a rather involved question. The interested reader is directed to the literature (see, for example, Dubner and Abate, 1968; Cooley, Lewis, and Welch, 1970; IBM, 1974) for the error analysis and further details of this numerical approximation method. It should be noted that the choice of $c = 0$ reduces the problem to the Fourier transform (or the characteristic function if $f(t)$ is a probability density function), and this selection may be quite acceptable provided the other parameters are appropriately specified.

Exercises

2.6.10 *Erlangian distribution.* Let $Y_1, Y_2, \ldots, Y_n$ be independent identically distributed (i.i.d.) random variables with the exponential distribution of mean $1/n\lambda$. Let X be a variable defined by

$$X = Y_1 + Y_2 + \cdots + Y_n.$$

a) Find the Laplace transform of the probability density function of X.
b) Show that the probability density function of X is given by

$$f_X(x) = \frac{n\lambda\,(n\lambda x)^{n-1}}{(n-1)!}\,e^{-n\lambda x}, \qquad x \geq 0,$$

which is called the n-stage *Erlangian* distribution.
c) Find the mean and variance of the above distribution.

2.6.11 *Convolution and the Laplace transform.* Let $f_1(x)$ and $f_2(x)$ be two probability density functions, and $g(x)$ their convolution of the form

$$g(x) = \int_0^{\infty} f_1(x - y)f_2(y)\,dy.$$

Find the Laplace transform of $g(x)$.

2.6.12 Given a probability density function $f(x)$ and the corresponding distribution function $F(x)$, let $\Phi(s)$ be the Laplace transform of $f(x)$. Show that

a) $\displaystyle\int_0^\infty e^{-sx} F(x)\, dx = \frac{\Phi(s)}{s}$;

b) $\displaystyle\int_0^\infty e^{-sx}\{1 - F(x)\}\, dx = \frac{1 - \Phi(s)}{s}$.

2.6.13 *The n-fold convolution of the uniform distribution.* Let X_i, $i = 1, 2, \ldots, n$, be i.i.d. random variables with the uniform distribution over the interval $[0, 1]$, that is,

$$F_X(x) = \begin{cases} 0, & x < 0 \\ x, & 0 \le x \le 1 \\ 1, & x > 1. \end{cases}$$

Let Y be their sum $Y = X_1 + X_2 + \cdots + X_n$. Show that the distribution of Y is given by

$$F_Y(y) = \frac{1}{n!} \sum_{k=0}^n (-1)^k \binom{n}{k} (y - k)_+^n$$

where

$$(x)_+ = \max\{x, 0\}.$$

Hint:

$$\int_0^\infty e^{-sx} \frac{(x - k)_+^{n-1}}{(n - 1)!}\, dx = s^{-n} e^{-ks}.$$

2.6.14 Show that the magnitude of the discontinuity of $F_X(x)$ at the origin $x = 0$ is obtained by

$$\lim_{x \to 0^+} F_X(x) = \lim_{s \to \infty} \Phi_X(s).$$

Generally, if $F_X(x)$ contains discontinuities of magnitudes p_k at points $x = x_k$, $\Phi_X(s)$ contains the corresponding terms $p_k \exp(-sx_k)$.

2.7 THE NORMAL DISTRIBUTION (GAUSSIAN DISTRIBUTION) AND THE CENTRAL LIMIT THEOREM

A real random variable X having the probability density function

$$f_X(x) = \frac{1}{\sqrt{2\pi\sigma^2}} \exp\left\{-\frac{(x - \mu)^2}{2\sigma^2}\right\} \tag{2.204}$$

is called a normal or Gaussian random variable with mean μ and variance σ^2. Often the distribution is referred to as the distribution $N(\mu, \sigma^2)$. Many random variables in physical situations are distributed in such a way as to have (at least approximately) the normal distribution. One reason for the prevalence of the normal distribution is contained in the *central limit theorem*, which states that, under very weak restrictions, the sum of a large number of random variables, properly scaled, tends to be normally distributed.

The most convenient form of the normal distribution for tabulation is the one that corresponds to a random variable Y defined by $Y = (X - \mu)/\sigma$. The distribution of Y

$$f_Y(y) = \frac{1}{\sqrt{2\pi}} \exp\left\{-\frac{y^2}{2}\right\} \tag{2.205}$$

is called the *standard* (or *unit*) *normal distribution*. The distribution function $F_Y(y)$ of the standard normal distribution

$$F_Y(y) = \frac{1}{\sqrt{2\pi}} \int_{-\infty}^{y} \exp\left\{-\frac{t^2}{2}\right\} dt \tag{2.206}$$

is widely tabulated. In Fig. 2.9 we show the density and distribution functions of the standard normal distribution function.

Since the density function of the standard normal distribution is an even function of y, the nth moment is zero for odd values of n:

$$E[Y^n] = 0 \quad (n \text{ odd}). \tag{2.207}$$

When $n \geq 2$ is even, we obtain

$$E[Y^n] = 1 \cdot 3 \cdot 5 \cdots (n - 1) \quad (n \text{ even}) \tag{2.208}$$

either by direct evaluation of the integral, or through the characteristic function (see Exercise 2.7.3). In particular,

$$E[Y] = 0 \quad \text{and} \quad \sigma_Y^2 = E[Y^2] = 1. \tag{2.209}$$

The original random variable

$$X = \sigma Y + \mu \tag{2.210}$$

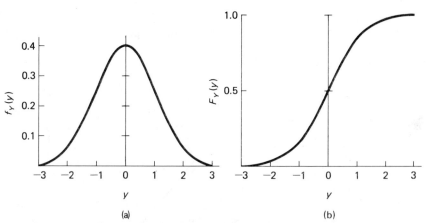

Fig. 2.9 The standard normal distribution: (a) the probability density function $f_Y(y)$; (b) the distribution function $F_Y(y)$.

with the density function (2.204) has the expectation and variance given by

$$E[X] = \mu \quad \text{and} \quad \sigma_X^2 = \sigma^2. \tag{2.211}$$

The characteristic function of the normal random variable Y is obtained as

$$\phi_Y(\theta) = e^{-\theta^2/2}. \tag{2.212}$$

The derivation of this result is not given here: It requires a contour integration of the theory of complex variables. We will often need to use the formula (2.212) in the analysis of normal random variables. The characteristic function of the random variable X can be obtained by using that of Y:

$$\phi_X(\theta) = E[e^{i\theta(\sigma Y + \mu)}]$$

$$= e^{i\theta\mu}\phi_Y(\theta\sigma) = \exp\left\{i\theta\mu - \frac{(\theta\sigma)^2}{2}\right\}. \tag{2.213}$$

The nth central moment of the random variable X is given by

$$E[(X - \mu)^n] = \sigma^n E[Y^n]. \tag{2.214}$$

It follows from (2.207) and (2.208) that

$$E[(X - \mu)^n] = \begin{cases} 0, & n \text{ odd} \\ \dfrac{n!\sigma^n}{2^{n/2}(n/2)!}, & n \text{ even.} \end{cases} \tag{2.215}$$

One important property of the normal variable is its reproductive property. Suppose X_i, $i = 1, 2, \ldots, N$, are independent random variables having distributions $N(\mu_i, \sigma_i^2)$, and let Z be a random variable defined by

$$Z = \sum_{i=1}^{N} c_i X_i, \tag{2.216}$$

where c_i are real constants. Then the distribution of Z is

$$N\left(\sum_{i=1}^{N} c_i\mu_i, \sum_{i=1}^{N} c_i^2\sigma_i^2\right)$$

(see Exercise 2.7.5).

Now we are ready to discuss the central limit theorem, which will explain why the normal distribution appears in many circumstances. Suppose that we have a population with an arbitrary distribution function $F(x)$, but with finite mean μ and variance σ^2. Let $\{X_i; 1 \le i \le n\}$ be any set of n independent samples from the population. Then we can make the following statement about the manner in which the distribution of the sample mean

$$\bar{X} = \frac{\sum_{i=1}^{n} X_i}{n} \tag{2.217}$$

behaves as $n \to \infty$.

Theorem 2.7.1 (The central limit theorem). If $\bar{X}$ is the mean of a sample of size n from a distribution having finite variance σ^2 and mean μ, then

$$\lim_{n \to \infty} P\left[\frac{\sqrt{n}}{\sigma}(\bar{X} - \mu) \leq x\right] = \frac{1}{\sqrt{2\pi}} \int_{-\infty}^{x} e^{-u^2/2} \, du. \tag{2.218}$$

We then say that $\bar{X}$ is *asymptotically* normally (or Gaussian) distributed according to $N(\mu, \sigma^2/n)$ for large n.

Proof. Let ϕ_n be the characteristic function of the random variable $n^{1/2}\sigma^{-1}(\bar{X} - \mu)$:

$$\begin{aligned}
\phi_n(\theta) &= E[e^{i\theta\sqrt{n}(\bar{X}-\mu)/\sigma}] \\
&= E\left[\exp\left\{i\theta \sum_{i=1}^{n} \frac{(X_i - \mu)}{\sqrt{n}\sigma}\right\}\right] \\
&= [\phi(\theta)]^n,
\end{aligned} \tag{2.219}$$

where ϕ is the characteristic function of $n^{-1/2}\sigma^{-1}(X - \mu)$ and where X represents the random variable of which $\{X_i\}$ are independent samples. From (2.123) we have

$$\phi_n(\theta) = 1 + iE\left[\frac{X - \mu}{\sqrt{n}\sigma}\right]\theta - \frac{1}{2}E\left[\left(\frac{X - \mu}{\sqrt{n}\sigma}\right)^2\right]\theta^2 + o\left(\frac{\theta^2}{n}\right). \tag{2.220}$$

Therefore, for any given θ, we have

$$\lim_{n \to \infty} \phi_n(\theta) = \lim_{n \to \infty} \left[1 - \frac{\theta^2}{2n} + o\left(\frac{\theta^2}{n}\right)\right]^n = e^{-\theta^2/2}. \tag{2.221}$$

We know from (2.212) that $e^{-\theta^2/2}$ is the characteristic function associated with the normal distribution $N(0, 1)$. Therefore, the distribution function of $n^{1/2}\sigma^{-1}(\bar{X} - \mu)$ converges to that of the distribution $N(0, 1)$ as $n \to \infty$. ■

The above stated theorem is known as the equal component case of the central limit theorem that holds under weaker restrictions. For extensive discussions of various forms of the central limit theorem, the reader is directed to Chung (1968) and Gnedenko and Kolmogorov (1964).

While the limiting distribution of the sample mean (2.217) is Gaussian, we sometimes find that the Gaussian limit gives a relatively poor approximation for the tail of the actual distribution of $\bar{X}$ when n is finite. See Feller (1968 Chapter 7) for further details. The well-known example of the probability distribution to which the central limit theorem does not apply is the Cauchy distribution defined by

$$f(x) = \frac{1}{\pi\alpha\left[1 + \dfrac{(x - \mu)^2}{\alpha^2}\right]}, \qquad -\infty < x < \infty. \qquad (2.222)$$

It is not difficult to show that the variance of the Cauchy distribution is infinite (see Exercise 2.7.6). In fact, the sum of any number of independent Cauchy random variables has the same distribution as any one of them; hence the average of n independent observations is no better than a single observation in this case.

Exercises

2.7.1 Show that for the distribution function of the standard normal distribution,

$$F_Y(-y) = 1 - F_Y(y).$$

2.7.2 For the standard normal distribution, show that for any $y > 0$,

$$\left(1 - \frac{1}{y^2}\right)\frac{e^{-y^2/2}}{\sqrt{2\pi}y} < 1 - F_Y(y) < \frac{e^{-y^2/2}}{y\sqrt{2\pi}}.$$

Hint: Use integration by parts.

2.7.3 Derive the moments (2.207) and (2.208) by making use of the characteristic function (2.212).

2.7.4 *The normal approximation to the binomial distribution.* Obtain the asymptotic form of the binomial distribution following the steps given below.

a) Let X be a variable that is distributed according to $P[X = k] = b(k; n, p)$. Find the characteristic function and the cumulant generating function of the variable

$$Y = \frac{X - \mu_X}{\sigma_X}.$$

b) Find the limit of the cumulant generating function of Y

$$\lim_{n \to \infty} \Psi_Y(\theta).$$

c) Show that the asymptotic distribution of Y (hence that of X also) is normal.

2.7.5 Show that the random variable Z defined by (2.216) is also a normal random variable.

2.7.6 Show that the Cauchy distribution defined by (2.222) does not have a finite variance.

2.8 RANDOM PROCESSES

So far we have not considered the possible time dependency of any of the probability functions. This omission was deliberate, since in many cases time has no particular bearing on the given problem. For example, in a coin-tossing experiment, information regarding the instants of trials is usually not relevant. However, there are many other cases in which the time dependency of the probability functions is important—for instance, the behavior of queue size in a certain servicing system. Such a process can be conveniently characterized by extending the notion of random variable as follows: Rather than a single number, we assign to each point ω in a sample space Ω a *real-time function*, say, $X(\omega, t)$. Imagine that we can observe this set of time functions $\{X(\omega, t); \ \omega \in \Omega\}$ at some instant $t = t_1$. Since each point ω of Ω has associated with it both the number $X(\omega, t_1)$ and its probability, the collection of numbers $\{X(\omega, t_1); \ \omega \in \Omega\}$ forms a random variable. By observing the time functions at a different time, say, t_2 we will have a different collection of numbers with a possibly different probability measure. Indeed, this set of time functions defines a separate random variable for each choice of observation instant.

A probability system, composed of a sample space, a set of real-time functions, and a probability measure, is called a *random process* (or *stochastic process*) and is usually denoted simply by a symbol such as $X(t)$. The individual time functions of the random process $X(t)$ are called *sample functions*, and the particular sample function associated with the point ω is denoted as $X(\omega, t)$. The set of all possible sample functions, together with a probability law, is called the *ensemble* of the sample functions. Naming a random process $X(t)$ and denoting the sample function associated with the point ω as $X(\omega, t)$ is consistent with our previous practice of naming a random variable X and denoting the sample value associated with the point ω as $X(\omega)$. By definition, a random process implies the existence of an infinite number of random variables, one for each t in the range $-\infty < t < \infty$. Thus, we may speak of the probability distribution function $F_{X(t_1)}(\bullet)$ and the probability density function $f_{X(t_1)}(\bullet)$ of the random variable $X(t_1)$ obtained by observing $X(t)$ at time t_1. Generally, for N time instants $\{t_i; i = 1, 2, \ldots, N\}$ we define the N random variables $X_i = X(t_i)$, $i = 1, 2, \ldots, N$. Then we can speak of the joint probability distribution function and the joint probability density function of $X_1, X_2, \ldots, X_N$.

Stationary random processes

In dealing with random processes in the real world, we often notice that statistical properties of interest are relatively independent of the time at which observation of the random process is begun. A *stationary random process* is defined as one for which all the distribution functions are *invariant* under a shift of the time origin. Thus a process $X(t)$ is said to be stationary if, for *every* finite set of time instants $\{t_i; i = 1, 2, \ldots, N\}$ and for every constant T, the joint probability functions of $X_i = X(t_i)$, $i = 1, 2, \ldots, N$ and those of $X_i' = X(t_i + T)$, $i = 1, 2, \ldots, N$ are identical:

$$F_{X_1 X_2 \cdots X_N}(x_1, x_2, \ldots, x_N) = F_{X_1' X_2' \cdots X_N'}(x_1, x_2, \ldots, x_N) \quad (2.223)$$

or, equivalently,

$$f_{X_1 X_2 \cdots X_N}(x_1, x_2, \ldots, x_N) = f_{X_1' X_2' \cdots X_N'}(x_1, x_2, \ldots, x_N) \quad (2.224)$$

if the joint probability density function exists.

    If the condition (2.223) is not met, then the random process is said to be nonstationary. The above condition for stationarity is often unnecessarily restrictive, and we define below a weaker form of stationarity. Random processes that satisfy the condition (2.223) are said to be *stationary in the strict sense.*

Wide-sense stationary processes

We extend the notions of mean (or expectation) and variance of a random variable, and define the following terms for random processes. We define the mean of a random process $X(t)$ by

$$\mu_X(t) = E[X(t)] \quad (2.225)$$

and the *autocorrelation function* of $X(t)$ by

$$R_X(t_1, t_2) = E[X(t_1)X(t_2)]. \quad (2.226)$$

If the joint density function exists, we can write

$$R_X(t_1, t_2) = \int_{-\infty}^{\infty} \int_{-\infty}^{\infty} x_1 x_2 f_{X(t_1)X(t_2)}(x_1, x_2) \, dx_1 \, dx_2. \quad (2.227)$$

    We say that process $X(t)$ is stationary *in the wide sense* (or stationary to the second order) if $\mu_X(t) = \mu_X$ for all $-\infty < t < \infty$, and its autocorrelation function satisfies

$$R_X(t_1, t_2) = R_X(0, t_2 - t_1); \quad (2.228)$$

that is, R_X is a function of the time difference $\tau = t_2 - t_1$ only. Hence we write the autocorrelation function of the wide-sense stationary process $X(t)$ as $R_X(\tau)$, indicating that it is a one-dimensional function.

It is not difficult to see that if a random process is stationary in the strict sense, then it must also be stationary in the wide sense. However, the converse does not hold true. We will apply the notion of the wide-sense stationarity in Section 4.8.

2.9 MARKOV CHAINS AND THEIR PROPERTIES

2.9.1 Markov Chains

In the preceding section, a random process was defined as an index collection of random variables $X(t)$. Often the time index t runs through the set of nonnegative integers, and in such a case we write $\{X_t\}$, where $t = 0, 1, 2, \ldots$. The random process $\{X_t\}$ of this type is frequently called a *random sequence* (or stochastic sequence, time series). The points in time may be equally spaced, or their spacing may depend on the behavior of the physical system in which the random process is *imbedded*—for example, the time between occurrences of some phenomenon of interest (see Section 3.11).

We assume that the values that X_t takes on are finite (or at most countably infinite); therefore, they can be labeled $0, 1, 2, \ldots, N$. We will often refer to "the *state* of the process (or of the underlying system) at time t" as being the value assumed by X_t.

Now we introduce an important random sequence called a *Markov chain*. A random sequence $\{X_t; t = 0, 1, 2, \ldots\}$ is said to possess a Markovian property or to be a *Markov chain*, if for every time t and all possible states of the X_t,

$$P[X_{t+1} = j \mid X_0 = a, X_1 = b, \ldots, X_t = i] = P[X_{t+1} = j \mid X_t = i].$$
$$(2.229)$$

This *Markovian property* means that the probability of any future state, given the entire past and present states, is *independent* of the past events and depends only on the present state of the process. The conditional probabilities $P[X_{t+1} = j \mid X_t = i]$ are called *transition probabilities* and are denoted by $q_{ij}(t)$.

We can write a simple recursion equation for the state probabilities of a Markov chain. Consider the probability $p_j(t + 1)$ that X_{t+1} takes on state j. Now at time t the system may be in any state i with probability $p_i(t), i = 1, 2, \ldots, N$. For each state i, there is a transition probability $q_{ij}(t)$ that the system will make the transition from this state to state j. Hence

$$p_j(t + 1) = \sum_{i=1}^{N} p_i(t)q_{ij}(t), \qquad j = 1, 2, \ldots, N \qquad (2.230)$$

or in matrix and vector representation

$$\mathbf{p}(t + 1) = \mathbf{p}(t)\mathbf{Q}(t), \tag{2.231}$$

where $\mathbf{p}(t)$ is an N-dimensional row vector with elements $p_j(t)$, $j = 1$, $2, \ldots, N$, and $\mathbf{Q}(t)$ is an $N \times N$ matrix with the elements $q_{ij}(t)$ and is called the (*Markov*) *transition probability matrix* at time t. If all $q_{ij}(t)$ are independent of t, we have

$$\mathbf{p}(t + 1) = \mathbf{p}(t)\mathbf{Q} \tag{2.232}$$

and the Markov chain is said to be *stationary* or *homogenous*.

A Markov chain can be represented graphically by the corresponding *state transition diagram*. It is a signal flow graph in which the nodes represent the states i and the directed arcs represent the transition probabilities q_{ij}. Figure 2.10 shows the state transition diagram of a stationary three-state Markov chain, whose transition probability matrix is given by

$$\mathbf{Q} = \begin{bmatrix} 0 & 1 & 0 \\ \frac{1}{4} & \frac{1}{4} & \frac{1}{2} \\ 0 & \frac{1}{2} & \frac{1}{2} \end{bmatrix}. \tag{2.233}$$

It is clear from the definition of conditional probabilities that the elements of the transition matrix $\mathbf{Q}$ must satisfy the following properties, whether the process is stationary or nonstationary:

$$q_{ij}(t) \geq 0 \quad \text{for all } i, j, \quad \text{and} \quad t = 0, 1, 2, \ldots \tag{2.234}$$

and

$$\sum_{j=1}^{N} q_{ij}(t) = 1 \quad \text{for all } i, \quad \text{and} \quad t = 0, 1, 2, \ldots. \tag{2.235}$$

Matrices satisfying (2.234) and (2.235) are called *stochastic*. Any stochastic matrix may serve as a transition probability matrix.

From (2.232) we find

$$\mathbf{p}(t) = \mathbf{p}(0)\mathbf{Q}(0)\mathbf{Q}(1) \cdots \mathbf{Q}(t - 1) \tag{2.236}$$

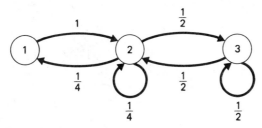

Fig. 2.10 An example of a state transition diagram.

if the process is nonstationary, and

$$\mathbf{p}(t) = \mathbf{p}(0)\mathbf{Q}^t \tag{2.237}$$

if the process is stationary. The latter equation shows that the state probabilities of a Markov chain are completely determined for all $t > 0$, if we know the transition probability matrix $\mathbf{Q}$ and the initial state probability vector $\mathbf{p}(0)$.

If we set $t = s + n$ in (2.237), we have

$$\mathbf{p}(s + n) = \mathbf{p}(0)\mathbf{Q}^s\mathbf{Q}^n = \mathbf{p}(s)\mathbf{Q}^n, \tag{2.238}$$

or letting the (i, j) element of the matrix $\mathbf{Q}^n$ be denoted $q_{ij}^{(n)}$, we have

$$p_j(s + n) = \sum_{i=1}^{N} p_i(s)q_{ij}^{(n)}. \tag{2.239}$$

Thus, $q_{ij}^{(n)}$ is the conditional probability that the process X_t, which is in state i at a given time, will be in state j after exactly n steps. Therefore, we call $\mathbf{Q}^n$ the n-step transition probability matrix.

The evaluation of (2.237) for large t is most conveniently done by the generating-function technique. If we let $\mathbf{P}(z)$ denote the vector (or multidimensional) generating function of the vector sequence $\{\mathbf{p}(t); t = 0, 1, 2, \ldots\}$, i.e.,

$$\mathbf{P}(z) = \sum_{t=0}^{\infty} \mathbf{p}(t)z^t, \tag{2.240}$$

then we have from (2.232)

$$\begin{aligned}
\mathbf{P}(z)\mathbf{Q} &= \sum_{t=0}^{\infty} \mathbf{p}(t + 1)z^t \\
&= z^{-1} \sum_{t=0}^{\infty} \mathbf{p}(t + 1)z^{t+1} \\
&= z^{-1}\mathbf{P}(z) - z^{-1}\mathbf{p}(0)
\end{aligned} \tag{2.241}$$

and hence

$$\mathbf{P}(z) = \mathbf{p}(0)[\mathbf{I} - \mathbf{Q}z]^{-1}, \tag{2.242}$$

where $\mathbf{I}$ is the $N \times N$ identity matrix.

Example 2.16. Consider the Markov chain whose transition probability matrix is defined by (2.233). The two-step transition probability matrix is given by

$$\mathbf{Q}^2 = \begin{bmatrix} 0 & 1 & 0 \\ \frac{1}{4} & \frac{1}{4} & \frac{1}{2} \\ 0 & \frac{1}{2} & \frac{1}{2} \end{bmatrix} \cdot \begin{bmatrix} 0 & 1 & 0 \\ \frac{1}{4} & \frac{1}{4} & \frac{1}{2} \\ 0 & \frac{1}{2} & \frac{1}{2} \end{bmatrix} = \begin{bmatrix} \frac{1}{4} & \frac{1}{4} & \frac{1}{2} \\ \frac{1}{16} & \frac{9}{16} & \frac{3}{8} \\ \frac{1}{8} & \frac{3}{8} & \frac{1}{2} \end{bmatrix}.$$

Similarly, the three-step transition probability matrix is calculated as

$$
\mathbf{Q}^3 = \begin{bmatrix} \frac{1}{4} & \frac{1}{4} & \frac{1}{2} \\ \frac{1}{16} & \frac{9}{16} & \frac{3}{8} \\ \frac{1}{8} & \frac{3}{8} & \frac{1}{2} \end{bmatrix} \cdot \begin{bmatrix} 0 & 1 & 0 \\ \frac{1}{4} & \frac{1}{4} & \frac{1}{2} \\ 0 & \frac{1}{2} & \frac{1}{2} \end{bmatrix} = \begin{bmatrix} \frac{1}{16} & \frac{9}{16} & \frac{3}{8} \\ \frac{9}{64} & \frac{25}{64} & \frac{15}{32} \\ \frac{3}{32} & \frac{15}{32} & \frac{7}{16} \end{bmatrix}.
$$

It can be shown that if $\mathbf{Q}^t$ is calculated successively for $t = 4, 5, 6, \ldots$, it converges to the following limit:

$$
\lim_{t \to \infty} \mathbf{Q}^t = \mathbf{Q}^\infty = \begin{bmatrix} \frac{1}{9} & \frac{4}{9} & \frac{4}{9} \\ \frac{1}{9} & \frac{4}{9} & \frac{4}{9} \\ \frac{1}{9} & \frac{4}{9} & \frac{4}{9} \end{bmatrix}.
$$

Namely, all rows become identical. By substituting the above result into (2.237), we obtain

$$
\lim_{t \to \infty} \mathbf{p}(t) = [p_1(0)p_2(0)p_3(0)]\mathbf{Q}^\infty = [\tfrac{1}{9} \ \tfrac{4}{9} \ \tfrac{4}{9}].
$$

That is, the probability of being in state j at time t approaches a certain definite value, independent of the initial state.

The same result can be obtained by using the formula (2.242). In this approach, we first need to compute the determinant of the matrix $\mathbf{I} - \mathbf{Q}z$.

$$
\det |\mathbf{I} - \mathbf{Q}z| = \det \begin{bmatrix} 1 & -z & 0 \\ -\dfrac{z}{4} & 1 - \dfrac{z}{4} & -\dfrac{z}{2} \\ 0 & -\dfrac{z}{2} & 1 - \dfrac{z}{2} \end{bmatrix}
$$

$$
= (1 - z)\left(1 + \frac{z}{4} - \frac{z^2}{8}\right) = \Delta.
$$

Hence

$$
[I - Qz]^{-1} = \frac{1}{\Delta} \begin{bmatrix} 1 - \dfrac{3z}{4} - \dfrac{z^2}{8} & z\left(1 - \dfrac{z}{2}\right) & \dfrac{z^2}{2} \\ \dfrac{z}{4}\left(1 - \dfrac{z}{2}\right) & 1 - \dfrac{z}{2} & \dfrac{z}{2} \\ \dfrac{z^2}{8} & \dfrac{z}{2} & 1 - \dfrac{z}{4} - \dfrac{z^2}{4} \end{bmatrix}.
$$

Then by substituting this expression and

$$
\mathbf{p}(0) = [p_1(0), p_2(0), p_3(0)]
$$

into (2.242), we obtain

$$\mathbf{P}(z) = [P_1(z), P_2(z), P_3(z)],$$

where

$$P_1(z) = \frac{1}{\Delta}\left[p_1(0)\left(1 - \frac{3z}{4} - \frac{z^2}{8}\right) + p_2(0)\frac{z}{4}\left(1 - \frac{z}{2}\right) + p_3(0)\frac{z^2}{8}\right],$$

$$P_2(z) = \frac{1}{\Delta}\left[p_1(0)z\left(1 - \frac{z}{2}\right) + p_2(0)\left(1 - \frac{z}{2}\right) + p_3(0)\frac{z}{2}\right],$$

and

$$P_3(z) = \frac{1}{\Delta}\left[p_1(0)\frac{z^2}{2} + p_2(0)\frac{z}{2} + p_3(0)\left(1 - \frac{z}{4} - \frac{z^2}{4}\right)\right].$$

By applying one of the inversion techniques discussed in Section 2.6.2, we can obtain the sequence of the probabilities $\{p_j(t); \ j = 1, 2, 3, \ t = 1, 2, \ldots\}$. The limiting probabilities $\{\lim_{t\to\infty} p_j(t)\}$ can be obtained, however, without going through the inversion of the probability generating functions. By applying the final value theorem (see Exercise 2.6.5), we have

$$\lim_{t\to\infty} p_1(t) = \lim_{z\to1} (1 - z)P_1(z) = \frac{1}{9}.$$

Similarly, we find

$$\lim_{t\to\infty} p_2(t) = \lim_{z\to1} (1 - z)P_2(z) = \frac{4}{9}$$

and

$$\lim_{t\to\infty} p_3(t) = \lim_{z\to1} (1 - z)P_3(z) = \frac{4}{9}.$$

Exercises

2.9.1 Consider a homogenous Markov chain whose transition matrix is given by

$$\mathbf{Q} = \begin{bmatrix} \frac{1}{2} & \frac{1}{2} & 0 \\ \frac{1}{3} & 0 & \frac{2}{3} \\ 0 & \frac{1}{5} & \frac{4}{5} \end{bmatrix}.$$

a) Draw the state transition diagram.
b) The system is initially at state 1, i.e.,

$$\mathbf{p}(0) = [1 \quad 0 \quad 0].$$

Find $\{\mathbf{p}(1), \mathbf{p}(2), \mathbf{p}(3), \ldots\}$.

c) Evaluate $\mathbf{p}(t)$ for arbitrary positive integer $t \geq 0$.

2.9.2 Consider the following simple queueing problem. Let X_t be the number of customers awaiting service or being served at time t. We make the following assumptions: (1) If the server is servicing a customer at time t, it will complete the customer before time $t + 1$ with probability β, and (2) between times t and $t + 1$, one customer will arrive with probability α, and with probability $1 - \alpha$ no customer will arrive. Show that $\{X_t\}$ is a Markov chain. Compute the transition probabilities.

2.9.2 Classification of States

Our primary interest here is in the asymptotic behavior of the n-step transition probabilities $\mathbf{Q}^n = [q_{ij}^{(n)}]$, as $n \rightarrow \infty$. An important classification of the states of a stationary Markov chain will be introduced.

Consider now an arbitrary but fixed pair of states (i, j) of a given Markov chain and suppose the system is initially in state i. We wish to make probabilistic statements about the number of transitions to be made by the process in going from state i to state j. This length of time (in terms of the number of transitions) is called the *first passage time* in going from state i to state j. When $j = i$, this time is just the number of transitions until the process returns to the initial state i, and it is called *recurrence time* for state i.

In general, the first passage times and recurrence times are random variables. Let $f_{ij}^{(n)}$ be the probability that the first passage time from state i to j is equal to n. The sum

$$f_{ij} = \sum_{n=1}^{\infty} f_{ij}^{(n)} \tag{2.243}$$

is the probability that starting from state i the system ever reaches state j. Thus if $f_{ij} < 1$, the process initially in state i may never reach state j. When $f_{ij} = 1$, $\{f_{ij}^{(n)}; n = 1, 2, \ldots\}$ can be considered as the probability distribution of the first passage time. In particular, for $j = i$ in (2.243), the sum

$$f_{ii} = \sum_{n=1}^{\infty} f_{ii}^{(n)} \tag{2.244}$$

is the probability that the system ever returns to the state i.

If $f_{ii} = 1$, the state i is called a *recurrent state** and if $f_{ii} < 1$, it is called a *transient state*.

For a recurrent state i, the recurrence time is a well-defined random variable; thus $\{f_{ii}^{(n)}; n = 1, 2, \ldots\}$ represents the probability distribution of the recurrence time.

---

* A recurrent state is sometimes called a persistent state (see Feller, 1968, p. 353).

Calculation of $f_{ij}^{(n)}$ for all n may be generally difficult, but it is relatively simple to obtain the expected first passage time from state i to state j. We define the expectation μ_{ij} by

$$\mu_{ij} = \begin{cases} \sum_{h=1}^{\infty} nf_{ij}^{(n)}, & \text{if} \quad f_{ij} = 1 \\ \infty, & \text{if} \quad f_{ij} < 1. \end{cases} \tag{2.245}$$

Then whenever $f_{ij} = 1$ for any two states i and j, the expected first passage time μ_{ij} satisfies uniquely the equation

$$\mu_{ij} = q_{ij} + \sum_{k \neq j} q_{ik}(\mu_{kj} + 1), \tag{2.246}$$

since the system in state i either goes to j in one step or else goes to intermediate step k and then eventually to j.

When $j = i$, the expected first passage time is called the *expected recurrence time*. A recurrent state i is called a *null-recurrent* state if the expected recurrence time μ_{ii} is infinite, and it is called a *positive-* (or *regular-*) *recurrent* state if $\mu_{ii} < \infty$. It is clear that in a finite Markov chain there are no null-recurrent states (that is, there are only positive-recurrent states and transient states).

A state i is said to be *periodic* with period t if $q_{ii}^{(n)} = 0$ whenever n is not divisible by t and t is the greatest integer (greater than 1) with this property; that is, if a return to state i is impossible except perhaps in t, $2t$, $3t, \ldots$ steps. A recurrent state that is neither null nor periodic is called an *ergodic state*. A state i is called an *absorbing state* if the (one-step) transition probability satisfies $q_{ii} = 1$. An absorbing state is a special case of a recurrent state since $q_{ii} = 1$ implies that $f_{ii} = f_{ii}^{(1)} = 1$. If a state is an absorbing state, the process will never leave it once it enters.

2.9.3 Irreducible Markov Chains

We say that state j is *reachable* from state i if there is an integer $n \geq 1$ such that $q_{ij}^{(n)} > 0$. If state i is reachable from state j and state j is reachable from state i, then the states i and j are said to *communicate*. If all the states in the chain communicate to each other, the chain is called *irreducible*.

It can be shown (see Rosenblatt, 1962) that the *states of an irreducible chain are either all recurrent or all transient. Furthermore, if one state in an irreducible chain is periodic with period t, all the states are periodic with period t.* The following theorem summarizes the above discussion.

Theorem 2.9.1. In an irreducible Markov chain all states belong to the same class: They are all transient states, all null recurrent states, or all positive recurrent states. Furthermore, the states are either all aperiodic or all periodic with the same period.

Positive recurrent states that are aperiodic are called ergodic states, as defined earlier. Several results related to the long-run behavior of finite-state Markov processes follow.

2.9.4 Steady-State Probabilities of an Ergodic Chain

In this section we restrict our discussion to aperiodic irreducible chains. An important question we want to address is that of *stability*. Does the system, regardless of its initial state, converge to some limiting distribution? Assume that the system is stable and let the limit of the probability distribution vector be π:

$$\lim_{t \to \infty} \mathbf{p}(t) = \pi. \tag{2.247}$$

Then by applying this limit to (2.232), we find that π must satisfy the equation

$$\pi = \pi \mathbf{Q}. \tag{2.248}$$

A probability distribution π satisfying (2.248) is called a *stationary distribution*. If the initial probability of being in state i is given by π_i for all i, that is, $\mathbf{p}(0) = \pi$, then the probability of finding the system in state i at time $t = 1, 2, \ldots$ is also given by π_i, that is, $\mathbf{p}(t) = \pi$. The next question we may ask will be "Does a solution of (2.248) result?"

Theorem 2.9.2. An irreducible aperiodic Markov chain has at most one stationary distribution, and one of the following two alternatives holds:

1. The states are all transient or all null states; in this case there exists no stationary distribution and, for all i, j,

$$\lim_{n \to \infty} q_{ij}^{(n)} = 0. \tag{2.249}$$

2. All states are ergodic; in this case there exists a unique stationary distribution (i.e., the solution of (2.248) is unique) and, for all i, j,

$$\lim_{n \to \infty} q_{ij}^{(n)} = \pi_j. \tag{2.250}$$

Furthermore, π_i is equal to the reciprocal of the mean recurrence time for state i, i.e.,

$$\pi_i = 1/\mu_{ii}; \qquad i = 1, 2, \ldots, N. \tag{2.251}$$

For the proof of this important theorem, the reader is referred to Feller (1968), Breiman (1969), and Rosenblatt (1962) (see also Exercise 2.9.8). The theorem assures us that (2.250) holds whenever the states are ergodic. Therefore, for any initial probability assignment $\{p_i(0); i = 1, 2, \ldots, N\}$, we have the following asymptotic result:

$$\lim_{n \to \infty} p_j(n) = \lim_{n \to \infty} \sum_{i=1}^{N} p_i(0)q_{ij}^{(n)}$$

$$= \sum_{i=1}^{N} p_i(0)\pi_j = \pi_j. \tag{2.252}$$

Thus, the stationary distribution is the steady-state distribution. The equation for the stationary distribution consists of (2.248) and the normalization condition:

$$\boldsymbol{\pi}\mathbf{1}' = 1, \tag{2.253}$$

where $'$ means transpose; hence $\mathbf{1}'$ is an N-dimensional column vector of all elements unity. By repeating (2.253) row-wise N times, we form the following matrix equation:

$$\boldsymbol{\pi}\mathbf{E} = \mathbf{1}, \tag{2.254}$$

where $\mathbf{E}$ is an $N \times N$ matrix with all entries unity, i.e., $\mathbf{E} = \mathbf{1}' \cdot \mathbf{1}$. By adding (2.248) and (2.254) we obtain

$$\boldsymbol{\pi}(\mathbf{Q} + \mathbf{E} - \mathbf{I}) = \mathbf{1}, \tag{2.255}$$

where $\mathbf{I}$ is the $N \times N$ identity matrix. Thus the stationary distribution vector is found as

$$\boldsymbol{\pi} = \mathbf{1}[\mathbf{Q} + \mathbf{E} - \mathbf{I}]^{-1}. \tag{2.256}$$

Exercises

2.9.3 Find stationary distributions of the following Markov chains using the formula (2.256).

a)

$$\mathbf{Q} = \begin{bmatrix} 0 & 1 & 0 \\ \frac{1}{4} & \frac{1}{4} & \frac{1}{2} \\ 0 & \frac{1}{2} & \frac{1}{2} \end{bmatrix}$$

b)

$$\mathbf{Q} = \begin{bmatrix} \frac{1}{2} & \frac{1}{2} & 0 \\ \frac{1}{3} & 0 & \frac{2}{3} \\ 0 & \frac{1}{5} & \frac{4}{5} \end{bmatrix}$$

2.9.4 Consider a Markov chain whose transition matrix is given by

$$\mathbf{Q} = \begin{bmatrix} \frac{2}{3} & \frac{1}{3} & 0 \\ \frac{1}{2} & 0 & \frac{1}{2} \\ 0 & 0 & 1 \end{bmatrix}.$$

a) Draw the state transition diagram of $\mathbf{Q}$ and classify the states.
b) Find the roots of the characteristic equation

$$\det |\mathbf{I} - z\mathbf{Q}| = 0.$$

c) Suppose that the system is in state 1 at $t = 0$. Find the probability vector $\mathbf{p}(t) = [p_1(t), p_2(t), p_3(t)]$ for $t = 0, 1, 2, \ldots$.

2.9.5 Consider a Markov chain with the transition matrix

$$\mathbf{Q} = \begin{bmatrix} 0 & 1 & 0 & 0 \\ \frac{1}{2} & 0 & \frac{1}{2} & 0 \\ 0 & \frac{1}{2} & 0 & \frac{1}{2} \\ 0 & 0 & 1 & 0 \end{bmatrix}.$$

a) Draw the state transition diagram of $\mathbf{Q}$.
b) Discuss the property of this chain.
c) Find the roots of the characteristic equation

$$\det |\mathbf{I} - z\mathbf{Q}| = 0$$

2.9.6 Answer the following questions regarding the roots of the characteristic equation

$$\det |\mathbf{I} - z\mathbf{Q}| = 0$$

of a Markov chain $\mathbf{Q}$.

a) Show that none of the roots may have a magnitude less than unity.
b) Show that at least one root is equal to unity. If there is more than one root equal to unity, what does this imply?
c) If the characteristic equation contains a factor $(z^k - 1)$, what does this mean?

2.9.7 Consider a Markov chain with the transition matrix

$$\mathbf{Q} = \begin{bmatrix} 1 & 0 & 0 & 0 \\ 0 & 1 & 0 & 0 \\ \frac{1}{2} & 0 & 0 & \frac{1}{2} \\ 0 & \frac{1}{2} & \frac{1}{2} & 0 \end{bmatrix}.$$

a) Draw the state transition diagram and classify the states.

b) Show that when n is an odd integer

$$\mathbf{Q}^n = \begin{bmatrix} 1 & 0 & 0 & 0 \\ 0 & 1 & 0 & 0 \\ * & * & 0 & \dfrac{1}{2^n} \\ * & * & \dfrac{1}{2^n} & 0 \end{bmatrix}.$$

c) Suppose the matrix $\mathbf{Q}$ is partitioned into the following form:

$$\mathbf{Q} = \begin{bmatrix} \mathbf{Q}_1 & \mathbf{0} & \mathbf{0} \\ \mathbf{0} & \mathbf{Q}_2 & \mathbf{0} \\ \mathbf{A} & \mathbf{B} & \mathbf{C} \end{bmatrix}.$$

What form does $\mathbf{Q}^n$ take?

2.9.8 *First-passage time matrix.* Consider an N-state Markov chain $\mathbf{Q}$. Let $\mathbf{M}$ be the matrix whose (i, j) component is the expected first passage time μ_{ij}, $1 \le i$, $j \le N$. Let $\mathbf{M}_{dg}$ be a matrix that has the same diagonal entries as $\mathbf{M}$ and zeros elsewhere.

a) Show that $\mathbf{M}$ satisfies the following matrix equation:

$$\mathbf{M} - \mathbf{E} + \mathbf{Q}(\mathbf{M} - \mathbf{M}_{dg}).$$

Hint: Start with Eq. (2.246).

b) Derive $\pi_i = 1/\mu_{ii}$, for all $i = 1, 2, \ldots, N$ (2.251).
   Hint: Multiply the equation of part (a) by π.

c) Find the first-passage time matrix of the two Markov chains defined in Exercise 2.9.3.

SUMMARY AND DISCUSSION

In this chapter we presented introductory probability theory based on the *axiomatic approach*, which is more rigorous than the relative frequency approach, although the latter has some appeal to our intuition. The notions of *statistical regularity* and the *law of large numbers* are central in the axiomatic approach and the relative frequency interpretation of probability. We introduced such concepts as the *sample space, events,* and *probability measure.* The rules of operations are based on set theory. Among various important notions included are *conditional probability* and *statistical independence.*

Informally speaking, a variable that eludes predictability in assuming its different values is called a *random variable.* More precisely, a random variable $X(\omega)$ is defined as a (real-valued) function that maps the sample space Ω into the real line. We express the probabilities associated with random variable X in terms of the *distribution function* $F_X(x)$. The probability distribution (or vector) $\{p_k\}$ and the probability density function $f_X(x)$ are used for characterizing *discrete* random variables and *continuous* random variables, respectively.

In the latter half of the chapter, we discussed various transformation methods related to probability distribution functions: *the characteristic function, the probability generating function, and the Laplace transform.* The transformation methods are quite powerful in computing the moments of a random variable, the convolution of two distribution functions, and other algebraic manipulations of probability functions. These techniques will be used extensively in Chapter 3.

The normal random variable discussed in Section 2.8 will be useful in the approximation models in Chapter 3. The normal distribution will play a central role in Chapter 5, in connection with statistical interpretation of simulation and measurement data.

The continuous-time analog of a Markov chain is a *Markov process*, which we did not cover in this chapter. The interested reader is referred to a number of textbooks on stochastic processes. In Chapter 3, however, we will study a special class of Markov processes, i.e., the Poisson process, the birth-and-death process, and its multidimensional analog.

REFERENCES

Bharucha-Reid, A. T. (1960). *Elements of the Theory of Markov Processes and Their Applications.* New York: McGraw-Hill.

Breiman, L. (1969). *Probability and Stochastic Processes with a View Toward Applications.* Boston: Houghton Mifflin.

Chung, K. L. (1968). *A Course in Probability Theory.* New York: Bruce & World.

Cox, D. R. (1962). *Renewal Theory.* New York: Halsted Press.

Cooley, J. W., P. A. W. Lewis, and P. D. Welch (1970). "The Fast Transform Algorithm: Programming Considerations in the Calculation of Sine, Cosine and Laplace Transforms." *Journal of Sound and Vibration* **12**(3): 315–337.

Davenport, W. B., and W. L. Root (1958). *An Introduction to the Theory of Random Signals and Noise.* New York: McGraw-Hill.

Doob, J. L. (1953). *Stochastic Processes.* New York: Wiley.

Dubner, H., and J. Abate (1968). "Numerical Inversion of Laplace Transforms by Relating Them to the Finite Fourier Cosine Transform." *Journal of the Association for Computing Machinery* **15**(1): 115–123.

Feller, W. (1968). *Introduction to Probability Theory and Its Applications,* 3rd ed., Vol. 1. New York: Wiley.

Freeman, H. (1965). *Discrete-Time Systems.* New York: Wiley.

Gaver, D. P., and G. L. Thompson (1973). *Programming and Probability Models in Operations Research*. Monterey, Calif.: Brooks/Cole.

Gnedenko, B. V., and N. Kolmogorov (1964). *Limit Distributions for Sums of Independent Random Variables*. Reading, Mass.: Addison-Wesley.

IBM (1974). "Inverse Laplace Transform." *IBM Subroutine Library—Mathematics, User's Guide*, 2nd ed., SH12-5300-1, pp. 490–492.

Johnson, N. L., and S. Kotz (1970). *Continuous Univariate Distributions*. Boston: Houghton Mifflin.

Papoulis, A. (1965). *Probability, Random Variables, and Stochastic Processes*. New York: McGraw-Hill.

Parzen, E. (1960). *Modern Probability Theory and Its Applications*. New York: Wiley.

Rosenblatt, M. (1962). *Random Processes*. New York: Oxford University Press.

Wilks, S. S. (1962). *Mathematical Statistics*. New York: Wiley.

3

Basic
Queueing
Analysis

3.1 QUEUEING THEORY AND COMPUTER SYSTEM MODELING

Queueing theory is a branch of probability theory that involves the mathematical study of queues.* The formation of queues is a common phenomenon that occurs whenever requests for a service facility exceed the current capacity of the facility. Decisions regarding the amount of service capacity to provide must be made in a variety of circumstances in industry and elsewhere: the number of checkout counters in a supermarket, the number of runways at an airport, and the number of telephone lines between switching centers, for example.

As we discussed in Chapter 1, queues for service of one kind or another arise in many hardware and software resources of a computer system: a queue of jobs waiting for main-memory allocation (the job scheduling queue); a queue of jobs that are allocated main memory, but are forced to wait for the central processing unit (CPU) service (the process scheduling queue); a queue of jobs waiting for service of some input output (I/O) device (the I/O scheduling queue), etc. In these examples, "customers" are those *jobs* (or what may appropriately be called *requests, transactions, tasks, processes,* or *programs*) that wait for some service to be given by such a "server" as main memory, the CPU, or an I/O device.

There are queueing situations in which customers are *not* jobs in the

---

*The term queue in computer science is often used simply to mean "list" or "ordered stack." In this chapter, however, we restrict its usage to designate a *waiting line* associated with some type of service facility.

usual sense of the word. Consider a multiprocessor system (i.e., a computer system that has more than one CPU). In order for a CPU to execute a job, it must fetch (or *read*) required instructions and data into its register. The instructions and data are stored in such storage devices as *main memory* and *cache memory*. The CPU must also store (or *write*) the executed result into main memory. Such *read/write operations* cannot be applied to the same *memory unit* or *memory module* simultaneously by more than one CPU. Therefore, while one CPU is reading from or writing into a memory unit, another CPU that needs to access to the same memory unit is forced to wait. This occasional conflict in accessing memory is referred to as *memory interference.* It is clear that in this circumstance the customers are the multiple CPU's and the servers are the memory units.

By the term server we do not necessarily mean such a physical device as the CPU, memory, or an I/O device. Consider a multiprocessor system again. In order for a job to be executed, a relevant portion of its program must be brought into main memory and one of the CPU's must be attached to that job. Those segments of the system program that involve possible changes in the related table entries should not allow a simultaneous use by more than one job or process. Such segments are often called *serially reusable programs,* whereas those segments of system programs that can be executed simultaneously by multiple processes are called *reentrant programs.* A process that finds a serially reusable program being used by another process is then *locked out* and must wait until that program is released. In terms of queueing theory, the processes are the customers and the serially reusable programs are the servers. To be "locked out" is nothing more than to "wait in the queue" for that server.

As is clear from the short description given above, queueing situations are found in a computer system in a variety of ways and at different levels. It is the main objective of this chapter to discuss queueing theory as a mathematical tool to analyze the effects of various queueing phenomena to be considered in the modeling and analysis of a computer system.

3.2 THE BASIC STRUCTURE OF A QUEUEING SYSTEM

The basic behavior assumed by most queueing systems can be broken down as shown in Fig. 3.1. The unit of the operational flow through a queueing system is called a customer or job. A sequence of *customers* arrives at some *server* (or *service center*). If an arriving customer finds the server busy, the customer joins the *queue* associated with that server and waits. At a certain point in time, the customer is selected for service

Fig. 3.1 The basic structure of a queueing system.

according to some rule known as the *service discipline.* The requested service is then performed for the customer by the server, and after the service completion the customer leaves the system. There are many alternative assumptions that can be made about such elements of a given queueing system as the *arrival pattern,* the *service mechanism,* and the *queue discipline.* These are discussed below.

3.2.1 The Arrival Pattern

A customer is drawn from the *population* or *input source.* One characteristic of the population is its *size,* that is, the total number of distinct potential customers. It may be either infinite or finite. Since the mathematical model tends to be more tractable for the infinite population, this assumption is often made even when the actual size is some relatively large finite number. The finite population model is more analytically involved, because the number of customers already in the queueing system at any point in time affects the number of potential customers actually remaining in the input source. In some cases we must make an explicit assumption of finite population, if the rate at which the input source generates customers is significantly affected by the number of customers in the queueing system.

Another characteristic of customer arrivals that we need to specify is the statistical pattern by which arriving customers are generated over time. The simplest arrivals one might think at first are the *regular arrivals:* Customers arrive at equally spaced instants, say, τ units of time apart. In this case, the arrival rate of customers is $\lambda = 1/\tau$ per unit time. The assumption of regular arrivals, however, is not only unrealistic in most actual applications, but is also not the easiest to deal with mathematically. The simplest and most useful model of arrival pattern is the *completely random arrival process,* which is usually referred to as the *Poisson arrival process* or, simply, the *Poisson process,* to be discussed in Section 3.3.

3.2.2 The Service Distribution and Service Capacity

The second component of a queueing system is a characterization of the amount of service required by an individual customer, which we call the *service demand,* or simply *work.**

---

* The terms *service* and *work* are somewhat abstract and may be the subject of argument. The unit we select to measure them can be arbitrary so long as it is consistent with that of *service rate* discussed below.

The unit of service or work varies depending on the nature of the server and its customers. If the server is a CPU and the customers are programs, an appropriate unit may be [instructions]. If the server is a transmission line and the customers are messages or data, the unit will be [bits] or [bytes]. In the great majority of cases, we assume that customer population is homogeneous, that is to say, the service demands of the customers are identically distributed with a common distribution, which we call the *service distribution*. In more complicated cases, the customers may be classified into several different types, each with its own distribution of service demand.

The arrival pattern and the service distribution are not sufficient to characterize the queueing system. We must also specify the capacity (or *processing rate*) of the server, that is, how fast the service facility processes the assigned work. We denote the service capacity as C, whose unit depends on the type of service. If the server is a CPU, the capacity C will have [instructions/sec] or [MIPS]* as its unit. If the server is a channel or transmission line, the capacity C should be counted in [bps (or bits per second)], [kbps (kilobits per second)], etc., and represents the *transfer rate* or *transmission rate*.

If the work demand of a customer is S [service units], and the corresponding server has the capacity C [service units/sec], then the ratio S/C [sec] is called the *service time*. Its expected value S/C [sec] is called the average service time, and its inverse

$$\mu = \frac{C}{S} \tag{3.1}$$

is called the *completion rate* or the *service rate*.† If C is constant, it is not essential to distinguish between the service demand and the service time, and we set C equal to 1 in such a case; that is, the service demand is measured in time. This convention is assumed throughout the chapter unless we state otherwise.

In some cases, the capacity is not constant but varies depending on the congestion level at the service station. Such an example is found in a multiserver queue, in which m parallel servers constitute a single service station and share a common waiting line, as shown in Fig. 3.2(a). We assume, for simplicity, a symmetric multiserver; that is, the capacities of the individual servers are all equal to, say, C. We then define the *state* of

---

* MIPS stands for "millions of instructions per second" and it is often used as a unit of speed of the CPU as discussed in Chapter 1.
† The symbol μ is used in this context in Chapter 3, whereas in Chapter 2, μ_X was the mean of random variable X.

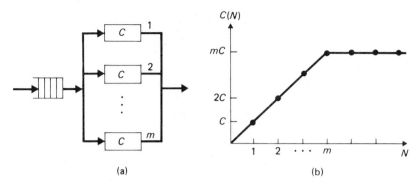

Fig. 3.2   (a) A service station with m parallel servers and (b) its capacity function.

the system by N, the number of customers currently in the station (either in service or in waiting line). Then the total capacity of the station is *state-dependent* and is given by $C(N) = \min\{N, m\}C$. In Fig. 3.2(b) we plot $C(N)$ versus N.

3.2.3   The Scheduling Discipline

We now consider how the customers are scheduled and served. Perhaps the most familiar scheduling rule or queueing discipline is the "first-come, first-served" (FCFS) discipline,* in which the customers are served to completion in the order of arrival. That the FCFS rule is not always desirable is easily seen: Invariably, some customers are more important than others, and therefore deserve better treatment than others. A procedure to differentiate among customers according to their importances is called a *priority scheduling* procedure, and such a queueing system is referred to as a *priority queue.* A priority assignment rule determines the order in which the waiting customers will be served. Classes of priority queueing disciplines can be divided into two types: *preemptive* and *nonpreemptive.* If a customer being served is interrupted from service and returned to the queue whenever a customer with a higher priority value appears in the system, then the scheduling discipline is said to be a preemptive priority discipline. If preemption is not allowed, the discipline is called nonpreemptive.

Even in the absence of externally assigned priority classes, the FCFS rule is not always appropriate. For example, consider the CPU service queue in an interactive computer system. Typically, the CPU service distribution has a long tail distribution, since there are some classes of jobs that, although small in number, require enormous amounts of CPU

---

* Sometimes called the "first-in, first-out" (FIFO) discipline.

time. Once such a large job enters the CPU, other jobs behind it will be forced to wait for an extraordinarily long period. In order to minimize the average waiting time, it is desirable to implement some kind of "shortest-in, first-out" rule. In reality, however, the scheduler may not be able to find a priori the exact service demands of waiting jobs. In such a case, the scheduler should predict the future service demands of jobs on their past behaviors and assign priorities accordingly. The round-robin (RR) scheduling and the foreground-background (FB) scheduling algorithms, which are often implemented in time-sharing computer systems, are typical examples of such dynamically assigned scheduling disciplines. See the section on Discussion and Further Reading for a further discussion of priority queueing disciplines.

Exercises

3.2.1 Consider an asymmetric two-server station in which the individual servers have the capacities C_1 and C_2 ($C_1 \neq C_2$). How should we define the "state" of the station? Obtain the state-dependent capacity for this station.

3.2.2 Suppose that data are transmitted over a communication link in the form of packets. A packet contains a variable number of bits. Assume that the distribution of packet length is approximated by an exponential distribution of mean 1000 bits, and that the communication link has the capacity of 50 kbps (kilobits per second). If we view the link as a server and the messages as customers, what is the service time distribution? What is the value of μ, the service completion rate?

3.3 THE POISSON PROCESS AND ITS PROPERTIES

3.3.1 The Poisson Process

In Section 3.2.1 we introduced the term Poisson process to designate a completely random arrival process. In this section, we discuss a formal definition of the Poisson process and its important properties.

Let us consider a finite time interval $(0, T)$ and find the probability distribution of the number of customers arriving in this period. To calculate this, we divide the period T into m subintervals, each of which has length $h = T/m$, as shown in Fig. 3.3. Let λ represent the average arrival rate of customers. For any subinterval, the probability that one customer arrives is $\lambda h + o(h)$, that two or more customers arrive is $o(h)$ and, therefore, that no customers arrive is $1 - \lambda h + o(h)$, where the

Fig. 3.3 Partitioning of the interval $(0, T)$ into m subintervals.

symbol $o(h)$ represents any quantity that approaches zero faster than h as $h \to 0$; that is, $o(h)/h \to 0$ as $h \to 0$.* When we say that the arrival process is completely random or Poisson, we mean that the following particular property holds: What we observe in any subinterval is statistically independent of what happens in any interval not overlapping this subinterval. Hence if we consider an arrival as a "success" of a Bernoulli trial, then the arrival pattern observed over the period of $T = mh$ can be regarded as the result of a sequence of m Bernoulli trials. Then the probability that exactly i customers arrive in the m subintervals can be approximated by the binomial distribution $b(i; m, \lambda h + o(h))$:

$$\binom{m}{i}[\lambda h + o(h)]^i[1 - \lambda h + o(h)]^{m-i}. \tag{3.2}$$

On taking the limits $h \to 0$ and $m \to \infty$ while keeping $mh = T$ constant, we find that $n(T)$, the number of customer arrivals in the period T, has the probability distribution

$$P[n(T) = i] = \frac{(\lambda T)^i}{i!} \lim_{m \to \infty} \frac{m!}{m^i(m - i)!} \lim_{m \to \infty} \left(1 - \frac{\lambda T}{m}\right)^{m-i}$$

$$= \frac{(\lambda T)^i}{i!} e^{-\lambda T}, \tag{3.3}$$

which is a *Poisson distribution*. Note that the distribution (3.3) has λT as the distribution parameter. The mean and variance of the random variable $n(T)$ are therefore both equal to λT. This implies that $E[n(T)/T] \to \lambda$, whereas $\text{Var}[n(T)/T] = \lambda/T \to 0$ as $T \to \infty$. Thus, $n(T)/T$ converges to λ as $T \to \infty$, justifying the name "arrival rate" for the parameter λ of the Poisson process. In Fig. 3.4 we plot the distribution (3, 3) for various values of λT.

    Another important property of the Poisson process is the distribution of intervals between arrivals. Let X be the interval from the time origin (arbitrarily chosen) to the first arrival. We can easily obtain the distribution of X by noting that no arrivals occur in $(0, x)$ if and only if $X > x$:

$$P[X > x] = P[n(x) = 0], \tag{3.4}$$

where $n(x)$ represents the number of arrivals during x time units. From (3.3) it is clear that $P[n(x) = 0] = e^{-\lambda x}$. Thus $F_X(x)$, the distribution

---

* For example,

$$o(h) = 2h^2, \qquad o(h) = \frac{h^2}{2!} + \frac{h^3}{3!} + \cdots.$$

It should also be clear that $o(h) + o(h) = o(h)$, $o(h) - o(h) = o(h)$, etc.

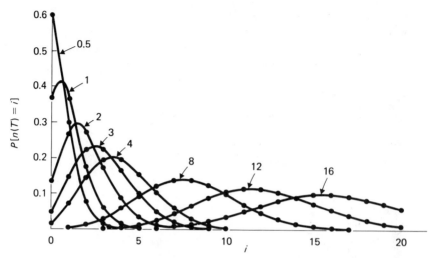

Fig. 3.4   The Poisson distribution with $\lambda\tau$ = 0.5, 1, 2, 3, 4, 8, 12, and 16.

function of X, and $f_X(x)$, the probability density function, are given by

$$F_X(x) = 1 - e^{-\lambda x}, \qquad x \geq 0 \qquad (3.5)$$

and by

$$f_X(x) = F'_X(x) = \lambda e^{-\lambda x}, \qquad x \geq 0, \qquad (3.6)$$

respectively. Thus, for the Poisson arrival process the interval X between an arbitrary instant and the time of the first arrival is *exponentially distributed* with mean $1/\lambda$. Note that the time origin was arbitrarily chosen. If we choose as the origin the instant of an arrival, then X represents the interarrival time. Thus we can conclude that the Poisson process has interarrival times that are exponentially distributed with mean $1/\lambda$.

The distribution function (3.5) can alternatively be obtained by the following argument: Choose the time origin at an arbitrary instant, and let $P_0(x)$ denote the probability that no customers arrive during $(0, x)$:

$$P_0(x) = P[n(x) = 0]. \qquad (3.7)$$

Then we have

$$
\begin{aligned}
P_0(x + dx) = \ & P[\text{no customers arrive during } (0, x) \\
& \text{nor during } (x, x + dx)] \\
= \ & P_0(x)\{1 - \lambda \, dx + o(dx)\} \qquad (3.8)
\end{aligned}
$$

using the statistical independence property of the Poisson arrival and the product law of probability for independent events. Then from (3.8) we obtain

$$\{P_0(x + dx) - P_0(x)\}/dx = P_0(x)\{-\lambda + o(dx)\} \qquad (3.9)$$

so that in the limit $dx \to 0$, we find

$$P_0'(x) = -\lambda P_0(x). \qquad (3.10)$$

It is not difficult to see that the solution for the above differential equation takes the form

$$P_0(x) = \alpha e^{-\lambda x}, \qquad (3.11)$$

where α is a constant. Since $P_0(0) = 1$ by definition, we can determine that $\alpha = 1$; therefore,

$$P_0(x) = e^{-\lambda x}. \qquad (3.12)$$

From (3.4), (3.7), and (3.12) we can obtain the distribution function $F_X(x)$ of (3.5). Other important properties of the Poisson process are discussed below.

3.3.2 Properties of the Poisson Process

1. Memoryless property. Let t_i be the time of the ith arrival and suppose that Y time units have elapsed before the arrival of the next customer, as shown in Fig. 3.5. We wish to find the probability that the next customer will arrive within r units of time: In other words, we want to compute $P[R \leq r \mid X \geq Y]$, where $R = X - Y$ represents the remaining time until the next arrival. By applying the definition of conditional probability, we can write

$$\frac{P[R \leq r, X \geq Y]}{P[X \geq Y]} = \frac{P[Y \leq X \leq Y + r]}{P[X \geq Y]}$$

$$= \frac{e^{-\lambda Y} - e^{-\lambda(Y+r)}}{e^{-\lambda Y}}$$

$$= 1 - e^{-\lambda r}. \qquad (3.13)$$

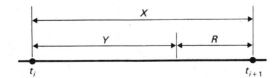

Fig. 3.5 The memoryless property of a Poisson process.

Thus the conditional distribution of R is independent of Y, and has the same distribution as the interarrival time. This result is, however, nothing more than a restatement of the property we discussed earlier in connection with (3.5). Thus the Poisson process is said to have the *memoryless* property in that in calculating the probability of the remaining time before the next arrival, we do not need to consider when the last arrival took place.

2. Superposition of Poisson processes. Consider m independent input sources that generate streams of customers, and assume that each stream is Poisson with rate λ_k, $k = 1, 2, \ldots, m$. If we combine these streams into a single stream as shown in Fig. 3.6, then we again have a Poisson process with the rate that is the sum of all components, that is, $\lambda = \lambda_1 + \lambda_2 + \cdots + \lambda_m$. This additivity of Poisson processes can easily be shown by using the probability generating function method. Consider an interval of length T. Then the number of arrivals from the kth source in this interval is Poisson-distributed with the parameter $\lambda_k T$, and its probability generating function, from (2.140), is given by

$$G_k(z) = e^{-\lambda_k T(1-z)}. \tag{3.14}$$

Therefore, the total number of arrivals from all the sources has the probability generating function

$$G(z) = \prod_{k=1}^{m} G_k(z) = e^{-\lambda T(1-z)} \tag{3.15}$$

with

$$\lambda = \sum_{k=1}^{m} \lambda_k, \tag{3.16}$$

where the product form of (3.14) is due to the statistical independence of the m sources. Thus the total number of arrivals in the merged stream is Poisson-distributed with mean λT; hence the combined stream forms a Poisson process with the rate λ. (See Exercise 3.3.2 for a different way of deriving this result.)

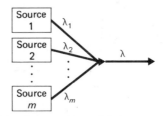

Fig. 3.6 The superposition of Poisson processes.

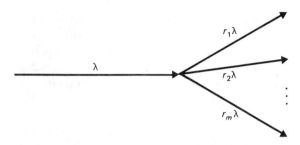

Fig. 3.7 The decomposition of a Poisson process.

3. Decomposition of a Poisson process.   Let us now consider the case in which a Poisson stream branches out into m output paths, as shown in Fig. 3.7. If the input rate is λ and the output path of each arrival is chosen independently with the probability r_k, then we will show that the kth output stream is a Poisson process with rate $r_k\lambda$, $k = 1, 2, \ldots, m$. Furthermore, these k streams are statistically independent.

   Let $n(T)$ denote, as before, the number of input arrivals in T time units and let $n_k(T)$ be the number of those that take the kth output path. Then the conditional joint distribution of $n_k(T)$ ($k = 1, 2, \ldots, m$), given $n(T) = n$, is the multinomial distribution (see Exercise 2.5.11):

$$P[n_1(T) = n_1, n_2(T) = n_2, \ldots, n_m(T) = n_m \mid n(T) = n]$$

$$= \frac{n!}{n_1!\, n_2! \cdots n_m!}\, r_1^{n_1} r_2^{n_2} \cdots r_m^{n_m}. \tag{3.17}$$

By multiplying the probability of the random variable n, which is the Poisson distribution with parameter $\lambda(T)$, we obtain

$$P[n_1, n_2, \ldots, n_m] = \frac{n!}{n_1!\, n_2! \cdots n_m!}\, r_1^{n_1} r_2^{n_2} \cdots r_m^{n_m} \frac{(\lambda T)^n}{n!}\, e^{-\lambda T}$$

$$= \prod_{k=1}^{m} \frac{(r_k \lambda T)^{n_k}}{n_k!}\, e^{-r_k \lambda T}. \tag{3.18}$$

Since the joint probability factors into m Poisson distributions, the random variables $n_1, n_2, \ldots, n_m$ are statistically independent for arbitrarily chosen interval T. Hence the output streams form independent Poisson processes.

3.3.3 General Independent Arrivals and Renewal Processes

A natural generalization of the Poisson arrival process is the following. Let X_k be the interarrival time between the kth and $(k - 1)$th arrivals.

The arrival process is called a *general independent* arrival process if the random variables X_k $(k = 1, 2, \ldots)$ are *independent and indentically distributed* (i.i.d.). The condition that the different intervals X_k are independent means, for example, that even if an interval time between two arrivals happens to be extraordinarily long or short, the distribution of the next interarrival time is still unaffected.

Suppose that a customer arrives at time $t = 0$. The first interarrival period terminates at time X_1, and the next interarrival period commences and terminates with the arrival of a customer at time $X_1 + X_2$, and so on. As soon as one interarrival period terminates, it is replaced by another. The situation is similar to that of renewing wornout (or failed) components (such as electric light bulbs). Thus, the general independent arrival process $\{X_k, \ k = 1, 2, \ldots\}$ is called a *renewal process*, or *regenerative process*, and X_k's are often called *failure times* of the components in the context of *renewal theory*. Renewal theory, as its name indicates, began as the study connected with the failure and replacements of some industrial articles. Recent work in the subject, however, is connected with a variety of mathematical problems of operations research, particularly with queueing theory. Needless to say, the Poisson process is a special case of a renewal process in that X_k's are i.i.d. with the exponential distribution.

Exercises

3.3.1 Obtain the Poisson distribution (3.3) through the following steps. Consider an observation period $(0, t]$, and let

$$P_i(t) = P[n(t) = i].$$

a) Show that $P_i(t)$ satisfies the following differential equation

$$P_i'(t) = -\lambda P_i(t) + \lambda P_{i-1}(t), \qquad i \geq 1$$

$$P_0'(t) = -\lambda P_0(t).$$

b) Solve first for $P_0(t)$. Insert this result into the differential equation for $i = 1$ and solve for $P_1(t)$. Continuing by induction, obtain $P_i(t)$ for all $i \geq 0$.

c) Alternatively, define the Laplace transforms

$$P_i^*(s) = \int_0^\infty P_i(t)e^{-st}\, dt.$$

Derive algebraic equations for $P_i^*(s)$ from the differential equations of part (a) and solve for $P_i^*(s)$ and then apply the inverse Laplace transform.

3.3.2 a) Let $\{X_j; j = 1, 2, \ldots m\}$ be a set of independent random variables, exponentially distributed with parameters λ_j, $j = 1, 2, \ldots, m$, respectively. Find the distribution of the random variable

$$Y = \min\{X_1, X_2, \ldots, X_m\}.$$

    b) Using the result of (a), show that the superposition of m independent Poisson processes with rates λ_j $(1 \leq j \leq m)$ generates a Poisson process with rate λ of (3.16).

3.3.3 Demonstrate the consistency of the definition that we have given for the Poisson process.

    a) Show from Eq. (3.3) that the probabilities of no arrival, of one arrival, and of multiple arrivals in a small interval h are given by $1 - \lambda h + o(h)$, $\lambda h + o(h)$, and $o(h)$, respectively.

    b) Derive the same set of probabilities as that given in part (a) from Eq. (3.5) alone.

3.3.4 a) Let $\{X_i\}$ be a sequence of independent identically distributed (i.i.d.) variables with the exponential distribution (3.5). Let $S_N = X_1 + X_2 + \cdots + X_N$, where N has the following geometric distribution:

$$P[N = n] = (1 - r)^{n-1}r, \qquad n = 1, 2, 3, \ldots,$$

where $0 < r < 1$. Show that S_N has an exponential distribution.

    b) Consider the problem of decomposing a Poisson stream into the m substreams, as discussed in the text. Using the result of part (a), show that each of these substreams is a Poisson process with rate λr_k, $k = 1, 2, \ldots, m$.

3.3.5 Refer again to the problem of decomposing a Poisson stream into m substreams: Rather than the independent selection, each substream receives every mth arrival; that is the 1st arrival, $(m + 1)$th arrival, $(2m + 1)$th arrival, $\ldots$, go to substream 1, the 2nd, $(m + 2)$th, $(2m + 2)$th, $\ldots$, arrivals go to substream 2, etc. Find the interarrival time distribution of the individual substreams.

3.4 SERVICE DISTRIBUTIONS

Although there are some theoretical results connected with queueing processes that can be carried through with a general service distribution, in practice it is useful to assume that the distribution is of some special type that can be characterized by a few parameters. The following is a brief description of distribution functions frequently used to represent service demands.

3.4.1 The Exponential Distribution

The mathematically simplest and one of the most appropriate in practice is the *exponential distribution* that was defined in Section 2.5.2 and plotted in Fig. 2.8. In queueing theory, it is customary to denote by $1/\mu$ the mean of this distribution:

$$F_S(t) = P[S \leq t] = 1 - e^{-\mu t}. \tag{3.19}$$

The corresponding probability density function is

$$f_S(t) = F'_S(t) = \mu e^{-\mu t}. \tag{3.20}$$

As we discussed in Section 2.5.2, the standard deviation of the exponential distribution is the same as the mean:

$$\bar{S} = E[S] = \frac{1}{\mu} \tag{3.21}$$

and

$$\sigma_S^2 = E[(S - \bar{S})^2] = \frac{1}{\mu^2}. \tag{3.22}$$

The server that provides service according to the exponential distribution with mean $1/\mu$ is often called an *exponential server* with service rate μ.

The most important property of the exponential service distribution is the *memoryless* property discussed in connection with the Poisson arrivals in the previous section. No matter how long the service Y that a customer has already received, the probability distribution of the residual life $R = S - Y$ is given by the same exponential distribution

$$P[R \leq r \mid S \geq Y] = 1 - e^{-\mu r}. \tag{3.23}$$

From this result comes also the *uniformity* of the service completion: The probability that the service of a customer will be completed in an interval Δt, given that the service has been in progress for Y time of units, is

$$P[0 \leq R \leq \Delta t \mid S \geq Y] = P[Y \leq S \leq Y + \Delta t]/P[S \geq Y]$$

$$= \{F_S(Y + \Delta t) - F_S(Y)\}/\{1 - F_S(Y)\}$$

$$= 1 - e^{-\mu \Delta t} = \mu \Delta t + o(\Delta t^2), \tag{3.24}$$

which is independent of Y. In other words, the probability that service is. completed in a small element of time is *constant*, independent of how much of service the customer has already received.

3.4.2 The Gamma and Erlangian Distributions

It is very common in applications to observe a unimodal distribution with the coefficient of variation (see (2.108)) substantially different from unity. In such circumstances, we often approximate the observed distribution by a *gamma distribution*

$$f_S(t) = \begin{cases} \dfrac{e^{-\alpha t}}{\Gamma(\beta)}\, \alpha(\alpha t)^{\beta-1}; & t \geq 0 \\ 0 \end{cases} \tag{3.25}$$

where α and β are both real and positive, and $\Gamma(\beta)$ is the gamma function

$$\Gamma(\beta) = \int_0^\infty y^{\beta-1} e^{-y}\, dy, \tag{3.26}$$

which is a generalization of the factorial. The mean and variance of the gamma distribution are

$$\bar{S} = \frac{\beta}{\alpha} \tag{3.27}$$

and

$$\sigma_S^2 = \frac{\beta}{\alpha^2}. \tag{3.28}$$

Note that when $\beta = 1$, the gamma distribution reduces to the exponential distribution with parameter α. Figure 3.8 shows how the gamma distribution of (3.25) looks, depending on whether β is greater or less than unity.

If $\beta = k$, a positive integer, then $\Gamma(k) = (k - 1)!$. If we write $1/\mu$ for the mean $\bar{S}$, that is,

$$\alpha = \beta\mu = k\mu, \tag{3.29}$$

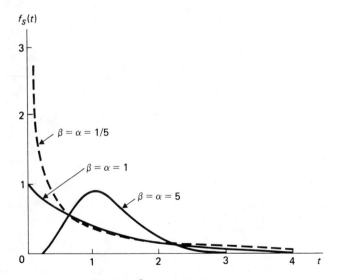

Fig. 3.8 Gamma distributions.

then the density function (3.25) and the corresponding distribution function become (see Exercise 3.4.3)

$$f_S(t) = \frac{k\mu(k\mu t)^{k-1}}{(k-1)!} e^{-k\mu t} \tag{3.30}$$

and

$$F_S(t) = 1 - e^{-k\mu t} \sum_{j=0}^{k-1} \frac{(k\mu t)^j}{j!}, \qquad t \geq 0, \tag{3.31}$$

respectively. This distribution is referred to as the *k-stage Erlangian distribution*. The Laplace transform of (3.30) is given by

$$\Phi_S(s) = \left[\frac{k\mu}{(k\mu + s)}\right]^k. \tag{3.32}$$

From (2.175), we see that the k-stage Erlangian distribution with mean $1/\mu$ is equivalent to the k-fold convolution of the exponential distribution with mean $1/k\mu$. Since the convolution of distribution functions corresponds to the sum of independent random variables, we can make the following interpretation of the k-stage Erlangian distribution. Consider the system shown in Fig. 3.9(a), in which the circle represents an exponential server with service rate $k\mu$. In this system, a customer entering the service facility (the square box) visits the exponential server k times before it departs from the facility. In each of the successive visits, the customer stays for an amount of time that is determined independently and randomly from the exponential distribution of mean $1/k\mu$.

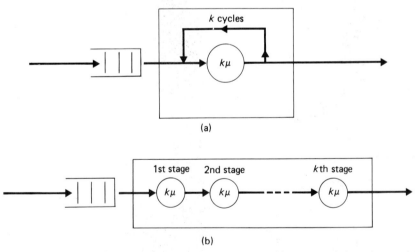

(a)

(b)

Fig. 3.9 The k-stage Erlangian distribution represented in terms of the exponential server.

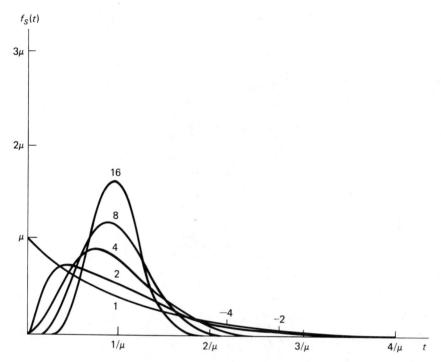

Fig. 3.10 The probability density functions of k-stage Erlangian distributions ($k = 1$, 2, 4, 8, 16).

Thus, the total time S that a customer spends in this service facility is the sum of the k independent identically distributed random variables, each chosen from the exponential distribution.

An equivalent and more commonly used representation of the k-stage Erlangian distribution is shown in Fig. 3.9(b). In this system, the service facility consists of k exponential servers in tandem, each of which has the service rate $k\mu$. In this representation, when a customer departs by exiting from the last (i.e., kth) stage, a new customer may enter and proceed one stage at a time. The total time that a customer spends in the k-stage facility is distributed according to the k-stage Erlangian distribution. In Fig. 3.10 we show the family of k-stage Erlangian probability density functions of (3.30) for $k = 1, 2, 4, 8, 16$. The mean is held constant at $1/\mu$, but the standard deviation is given by $1/\sqrt{k}\mu$. As k approaches infinity, the limit of this family of density functions approaches a unit impulse function at the point $t = 1/\mu$.

The distribution function (3.31) can, of course, be obtained by integrating the density function (3.30). But a simpler derivation is as

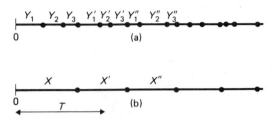

Fig. 3.11 (a) The Poisson arrivals and (b) the Erlangian arrivals.

follows. First let us consider a Poisson process with rate $k\mu$. If we select every kth arrival, then this forms an arrival process, in which interarrivals have the k-stage Erlangian distribution with mean $1/\mu$. Figure 3.11 illustrates the case in which $k = 3$.

In Fig. 3.11(b), the random variable T represents an arbitrarily chosen observation interval. The number of arrivals in the Poisson process during this interval is a random variable with the Poisson distribution of mean $\lambda = k\mu T$. From Fig. 3.11 it is clear that the probability that the random variable $X = Y_1 + Y_2 + \cdots + Y_k$ exceeds T is equal to the probability that there are at most $k - 1$ arrivals in the interval T. Therefore, by summing the Poisson distribution over $0, 1, 2, \ldots, k - 1$, we obtain

$$P[X > T] = \sum_{j=0}^{k-1} \frac{\lambda^j}{j!} e^{-\lambda}, \tag{3.33}$$

where $\lambda = k\mu T$. We then have

$$F_X(T) = 1 - e^{-k\mu T} \sum_{j=0}^{k-1} \frac{(k\mu T)^j}{j!}, \tag{3.34}$$

which is nothing but (3.31).

The Erlangian distribution is sometimes referred to as the hypoexponential distribution, as contrasted with the hyperexponential distribution to be described below. We should also note here that the k-stage Erlangian distribution is equivalent to the chi-square (χ^2) distribution with $2k$ degrees of freedom (see Section 5.5.2).

3.4.3 The Hyperexponential (Mixed Exponential) Distribution

Situations frequently arise in practice in which the service time distribution can be properly represented by a mixture of exponential distributions. Suppose that there are k types of customers, each type occurring with probability π_i, $i = 1, 2, \ldots, k$, and that a customer of type i has a service time exponentially distributed with mean $1/\mu_i$, $i = 1, 2, \ldots, k$.

Then the overall distribution of the service time is the following mixed exponential distribution:

$$F_S(x) = \sum_{i=1}^{k} \pi_i(1 - e^{-\mu_i x})$$

$$= 1 - \sum_{i=1}^{k} \pi_i e^{-\mu_i x} \tag{3.35}$$

and its density function

$$f_S(x) = \sum_{i=1}^{k} \pi_i \mu_i e^{-\mu_i x}. \tag{3.36}$$

This mixed exponential distribution is often referred to as the k-stage hyperexponential distribution. The mean and variance are found to be

$$\bar{S} = \sum_{i=1}^{k} \frac{\pi_i}{\mu_i} = \frac{1}{\mu} \tag{3.37}$$

and

$$\sigma_S^2 = \frac{1}{\mu^2} + \sum_{i=1}^{k}\sum_{j=1}^{k} \pi_i \pi_j \left(\frac{1}{\mu_i} - \frac{1}{\mu_j}\right)^2. \tag{3.38}$$

Therefore, the squared coefficient of variation is given as

$$C_S^2 = 1 + \mu^2 \sum_i \sum_j \pi_i \pi_j \left(\frac{1}{\mu_i} - \frac{1}{\mu_j}\right)^2 \geq 1 \tag{3.39}$$

where the equality holds if and only if $\mu_i = \mu$ for all i.

In Fig. 3.12 we plot an example of two-stage hyperexponential distribution, $F_S(t) = 1 - \pi_1 e^{-\mu_1 t} - \pi_2 e^{-\mu_2 t}$ and its probability density function, where $\pi_1 = 0.0526$, $\mu_1 = 0.1$, and $\mu_2 = 2.0$. The mean of the

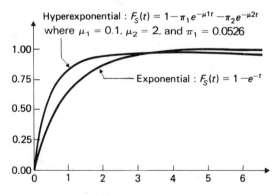

Fig. 3.12   A two-stage hyperexponential distribution with $\pi_\infty = 0.0526$, $\mu_\infty = 0.1$, and $\mu_\infty = 2.0$.

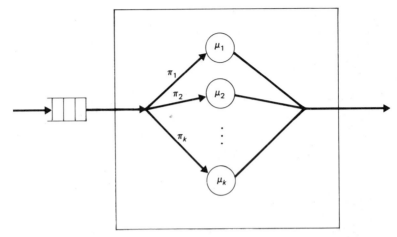

Fig. 3.13 The hyperexponential distribution represented in terms of exponential servers.

distribution is $1/\mu = \pi_1/\mu_1 + \pi_2/\mu_2 \cong 1.0$ and the squared coefficient of variation is $C_S^2 \cong 10.0$. A hyperexponential distribution is an appropriate model to apply to a situation in which the density function decreases monotone and has the coefficient of variation greater than unity.

  Although the gamma distribution with $\beta < 1$ can approximate a distribution that has the coefficient of variation greater than unity, the hyperexponential distribution is usually found to be more convenient because it allows the representation of the service facility in terms of parallel stages of the exponential servers as shown in Fig. 3.13. This should be compared with the serial stage representation (Fig. 3.9b) of the Erlangian distribution. Note that the system of Fig. 3.13 is different from a service station with k parallel servers: While a customer is in one of the k-stages, a new customer connot enter the facility. Thus, at any given time, at most one stage is actively servicing a customer. The Laplace transform of the distribution (3.36) is

$$\Phi_S(s) = \sum_{i=1}^{k} \frac{\pi_i\mu_i}{\mu_i + s}. \tag{3.40}$$

3.4.4 Shorthand Notation for Queueing Systems

In order to specify the type of a given queueing system, we often use the shorthand notation $A/B/m.$, where A and B describe the interarrival time distribution and the service time distribution, respectively, and m represents the number of parallel servers of the servicing system. The following is a list of the well-accepted symbols for frequently used distributions.

M Exponential distribution. The "memoryless" property of the exponential distribution is also referred to as the "Markovian" property.

D Deterministic variable, that is, interarrival times/service times are constant values.

E_k k-stage Erlangian distribution.

H_k k-stage hyperexponential distribution.

G General distribution.

GI General independent (interarrival time) distribution.

Thus, the system $M/M/1$ means a single server system with Poisson arrivals and exponential service times. Similarly, the system $GI/H_2/1$ is a single server system with a renewal arrival process and a two-stage mixed exponential service distribution.

Exercises

3.4.1 Consider the k-stage Erlangian distribution with mean $1/\mu$. Obtain the Laplace transform of the probability density function and obtain the limiting distribution as $k \to \infty$.

3.4.2 a) Find the mean and variance of a two-stage hyperexponential distribution.

b) Suppose we fix the ratio of the two exponential distribution parameters:

$$r = \frac{\mu_1}{\mu_2}.$$

What is, then, the maximum value of the coefficient of variation we can achieve using the two-stage hyperexponential distribution?

3.4.3 Derive the k-stage Erlangian distribution function (3.31) from the probability density function (3.30).

3.4.4 Find an alternative way of proving the inequality (3.39) by following these instructions:

a) Show that the second moment of S is given by

$$E[S^2] = 2 \sum_{i=1}^{k} \frac{\pi_i}{\mu_i^2}.$$

b) Prove that $C_S^2 \geq 1$ based on the well-known Cauchy-Schwartz inequality:

$$\left(\sum_i x_i y_i \right)^2 \leq \left(\sum_i x_i^2 \right)\left(\sum_i y_i^2 \right).$$

3.5 PERFORMANCE MEASURES OF A QUEUEING SYSTEM

When we construct a mathematical model of a system, the underlying motivation is to evaluate some *measure of performance*. If the system is a queueing system, then one of the relevant measures will be a measure of *congestion*. The simplest measure of congestion is the *traffic intensity*, or offered traffic. This is a dimensionless quantity,* defined as

$$\text{Traffic intensity} = \frac{\text{Mean service time}}{\text{Mean interarrival time}}. \tag{3.41}$$

Let us assume an infinite population model and denote the arrival rate by λ and the average service time by $1/\mu$. Then we can write

$$\text{Traffic intensity} = \text{Arrival rate} \times \text{Mean service time} = \frac{\lambda}{\mu}. \tag{3.42}$$

A traffic intensity greater than one indicates that customers are arriving faster than one server can handle. If there are m servers in parallel, each server receives λ/m customers per unit time. Therefore, the m-server system can handle the traffic intensity up to m.

A performance measure closely related to the traffic intensity is the *server utilization* or *utilization factor*. This quantity, which we denote by ρ, is also dimensionless and represents the fraction of time that a server is busy. Consider a sufficiently long interval T. In an m parallel server system we expect, on the average, $\lambda T/m$ customers to arrive per server, assuming that the traffic is evenly distributed among the m servers. Each customer requires a service of $1/\mu$ on the average, so that the total expected time that the server is busy is given by $\lambda T/m\mu$. Dividing this quantity by T, we obtain $\rho = \lambda/m\mu$. Since it is physically impossible for the server to be busy more than 100 percent of the time, the utilization factor cannot exceed unity. Thus the correct expression for the utilization factor of the m-server system is

$$\text{Utilization factor} = \rho = \min\left\{\frac{\lambda}{m\mu}, 1\right\}. \tag{3.43}$$

For a single server system, the server utilization is $\rho = \lambda/\mu$; thus the utilization factor and traffic intensity are the same if $\rho = \lambda/\mu < 1$.

The *throughput* (often written as *thruput* for shorthand notation) is a performance measure frequently used in the analysis of queueing models of computer systems. This quantity is defined as "the average number of customers completed per unit time." In the m-server system, there

---

* The traffic intensity is sometimes expressed using the unit [erlangs] in deference to A. K. Erlang for his pioneering work in queueing theory.

are $m\rho\mu$ customers to be completed every time unit; thus we find

$$\text{Throughput} = m\rho\mu = \min\{\lambda, m\mu\}. \qquad (3.44)$$

Thus, the throughput is equivalent to the arrival rate λ so far as λ is less than the maximum servicing rate $m\mu$, beyond which the throughput is saturated at the value $m\mu$.

Computation of the utilization and throughput becomes a less trivial problem in a finite population model, since the arrival rate is no longer constant, but is dependent on the state of the system. We will discuss this subject further in the section on queueing network models.

Perhaps the most important performance measure from the customers' viewpoint is the time that they must spend in the waiting line or in the system. We define the *waiting time* W_j of customer j to be the time that the customer spends in the queue, whereas the *response time** T_j is defined as the total time that the customer spends in the system. Thus, we have the following simple relation (by suppressing the subscript j):

$$\text{Response time } (T) = \text{Waiting time } (W) + \text{Service time } (S). \quad (3.45)$$

Both $\{W_j; j = 1, 2, \ldots\}$ and $\{T_j; j = 1, 2, \ldots\}$ are random processes, so we usually adopt their expected values $\overline{W}$ and $\overline{T}$ as measures of system performance. More frequently than not, the system performance specification is given in terms of percentile figures of the waiting time or the response time. For such a purpose, it is necessary to obtain their distribution functions $F_W(t)$ or $F_T(t)$.

Another measure of congestion that interests us is the *queue size*. Let random process $Q(t)$ represent the number of customers in the queue at time t. Similarly, we define $N(t)$ as the number of customers found at time t in the system, either in service or in the queue.† In an m-server system, they are related according to

$$Q(t) = \max\{0, N(t) - m\}. \qquad (3.46)$$

Information concerning the processes $Q(t)$ and $N(t)$ is useful in many situations. For example, if one wishes to evaluate the amount of buffer storage required to accommodate waiting customers, one must know the distribution of $Q(t)$ or $N(t)$ of the server.

The processes $Q(t)$ and $N(t)$ are integer-valued continuous-time *random processes*, whereas W_j and T_j are continuous-valued *random*

---

* In queueing theory literature, the term "queueing time" is often used rather than "response time."
† Sometimes the process $N(t)$ is called the queue size.

sequences. The following two sections discuss some fundamental relations by which these variables are tied together.

Exercises

3.5.1 Consider a single server queueing system with an infinite input source. The customers consist of two types: A type-1 customer requires, on the average, service time of 2 sec, and the average service time of type-2 customer is 5 sec. We assume that 80 percent of the customers are type 1, and 20 percent are type 2. What is the server utilization if the arrival rate is 15 customers per minute?

3.5.2 Consider a communication link over which data are transmitted from one end to the other in the form of packets. A packet contains a variable number of bits, and the mean packet size is 800 bits long. Assume that the communication link has a capacity of 50 kbps (kilobits per second). Suppose that we want to keep the line utilization below 50 percent in order to avoid an excessive queueing delay. What is the maximum allowable message rate that we can feed in?

3.6 LITTLE'S FORMULA: $L = \lambda W$

Probably the simplest and yet the most important formula that is used in queueing analysis is the formula $L = \lambda W$, known as *Little's formula* or *Little's theorem*, which in our notation should be rewritten as $\overline{Q} = \lambda \overline{W}$, where $\overline{Q}$ represents the average queue length, λ the mean arrival rate, and $\overline{W}$ the mean waiting time in queue. The proof of this formula was given by Little in 1961.

Consider a queueing system as shown in Fig. 3.14. Let $0 < t_1 < t_2 < \cdots$ be the arrival times of customers to the system numbered in the order of arrival. Let a *counting process* $A(t)$ represent, for each t, the cumulative number of arrivals up to time t:

$$A(t) = \text{number of } t_j \leq t. \tag{3.47}$$

This is a step function that increases by one at each time t_j, as shown in Fig. 3.15.

If we assume the FCFS queue discipline, then the order in which the customers leave the queue is the same as the order in which they arrive. In other words, if we denote by t'_j the departure time (from the queue) of the customer j, then

$$0 < t'_1 < t'_2 < \cdots. \tag{3.48}$$

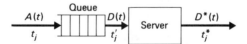

Fig. 3.14 A queueing system and its counting processes $A(t)$, $D(t)$, and $D^*(t)$.

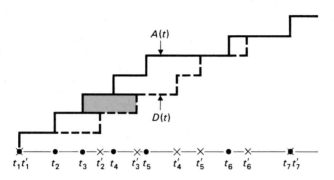

Fig. 3.15 Typical behavior of the counting processes $A(t)$ and $D(t)$.

Needless to say, the relation

$$t_j \leq t'_j \tag{3.49}$$

holds for all j, because the jth customer cannot leave the queue before its arrival. When a customer arrives at the system to find that the server is idle, then the customer enters service immediately, i.e., $t_j = t'_j$. We define another counting process

$$D(t) = \text{number of } t'_j \leq t, \tag{3.50}$$

that is, the cumulative number of customers who enter service by time t (Fig. 3.15). At any time t, $A(t) - D(t) = Q(t)$ represents the number of customers who have arrived since time 0 but have not yet left the queue. In other words, $Q(t)$ is the queue length at time t.

In the case of FCFS discipline, $t'_j - t_j$, the time that the jth customer spends in the queue, is equal to the horizontal distance (or equivalently the area of a horizontal strip) between the curves $A(t)$ and $D(t)$ at the level between $j - 1$ and j. In Fig. 3.15, the shaded area, for example, represents $t'_3 - t_3$. Choose the point of time reference (or the time origin) $t = 0$ for which $A(t) = D(t)$. In other words, the server is idle at $t = 0$. Then by choosing another instant τ such that $A(\tau) = D(\tau)$, we define the following variables:

$$n(\tau) = A(\tau) - A(0) = \text{the total number of arrivals}$$
$$\text{during the period } (0, \tau); \tag{3.51}$$

$$\lambda(\tau) = \frac{n(\tau)}{\tau} = \text{the mean arrival rate during } (0, \tau). \tag{3.52}$$

The entire shaded area of Fig. 3.16 can be decomposed into $n(\tau)$ separate horizontal strips of the type illustrated in Fig. 3.15. The average length of

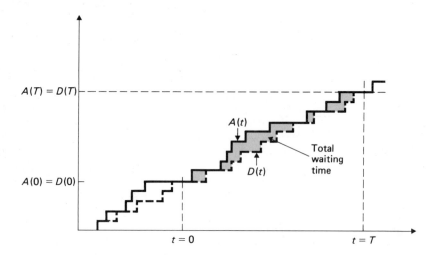

Fig. 3.16 The total waiting time.

the horizontal strip is

$$\overline{W}(\tau) = \frac{\sum_{j=1}^{n(\tau)} W_j}{n(\tau)} = \begin{array}{l}\text{the mean waiting time per}\\ \text{customer in the period } (0, \tau).\end{array} \quad (3.53)$$

Since the quantity $Q(t) = A(t) - D(t)$ represents the queue size function, its time average

$$\overline{Q}(\tau) = \frac{\int_0^\tau Q(t)\, dt}{\tau} \quad (3.54)$$

is the mean queue size over the peroid of $(0, \tau)$. Since each strip has the width of unity, the sum of the strip lengths is equal to the sum of the strip areas. Therefore, we have

$$\sum_{j=1}^{n(\tau)} W_j = \int_0^\tau Q(t)\, dt. \quad (3.55)$$

From (3.54) and (3.55) we have

$$\overline{Q}(\tau) = \frac{\sum_{j=1}^{n(\tau)} W_j}{\tau}. \quad (3.56)$$

By substituting the definitions of $\lambda(\tau)$ and $\overline{W}(\tau)$ into the right-hand side of (3.56), we find

$$\overline{Q}(\tau) = \lambda(\tau)\overline{W}(\tau). \quad (3.57)$$

If the limits

$$\lambda = \lim_{\tau \to \infty} \lambda(\tau) \quad (3.58)$$

and
$$\overline{W} = \lim_{\tau \to \infty} \overline{W}(\tau) \tag{3.59}$$

exist, then a limit for $\overline{Q}(\tau)$ also exists, defined by

$$\overline{Q} = \lim_{\tau \to \infty} \overline{Q}(\tau) \tag{3.60}$$

and the three limits must satisfy the relation

$$\overline{Q} = \lambda \overline{W}. \tag{3.61}$$

The relation (3.57) was derived under the assumptions that (1) the queue discipline is FCFS, and (2) $t = 0$ and $t = \tau$ are times at which the queue vanishes. First, we show that assumption (2) can be dropped easily. If the interval τ is sufficiently large, then the queue vanishes many times between $t = 0$ and $t = \tau$. Then any contribution to the total waiting time coming from the end conditions will become negligible in computing $\overline{Q}(\tau)$ and $\overline{W}(\tau)$, as τ tends to infinity.

If the queue discipline is not FCFS, the ordering relation (3.48) no longer holds. For example, under the "last-come, first-served" (LCFS) queue discipline, the times $\{t_j'\}$ will be like those shown in Fig. 3.17. By the time customer 1 is completed, customer 3 has arrived; therefore customer 3 rather than customer 2 enters service. By the time customer 3 is completed, customer 4 has been in queue, so again customer 2 misses the chance to enter service, and so forth. When customer 5 is completed, customer 2 is the only one in queue, and therefore finally enters service. Thus, in this example, we obtain the ordering relation $t_1' < t_3' < t_4' < t_5' < t_2' < t_6' < \cdots$. Then the total waiting time can be rewritten as

$$\sum_{j=1}^{n(\tau)} W_j = \sum_{j=1}^{n(\tau)} t_j' - \sum_{j=1}^{n(\tau)} t_j$$
$$= (t_1' - t_1) + (t_3' - t_2) + (t_4' - t_3) + (t_5' - t_4) + (t_2' - t_5) + \cdots, \tag{3.62}$$

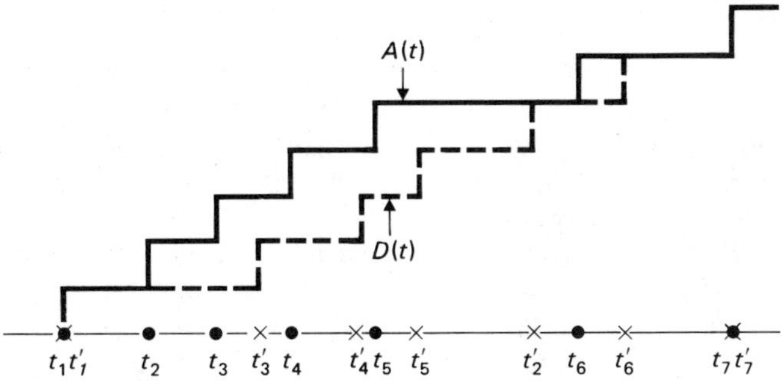

Fig. 3.17 $D(t)$ in the LCFS queue.

which is equivalent to the area surrounded by the arrivals $A(t)$ and $D(t)$, that is,

$$\sum_{j=1}^{n(\tau)} W_j = \int_0^\tau Q(t)\, dt. \tag{3.63}$$

The argument given above certainly holds for any ordering relation of the departure time sequence $\{t'_j\}$. Therefore, Little's formula is true not only for FCFS and LCFS, but also for any queue disciplines.

There are companion relations to (3.61) involving arrivals to and departures from the system (i.e., queue plus server). Let t_j^* be the time at which customer j departs from the system, as shown in Fig. 3.14. We define a counting process

$$D^*(t) = \text{number of } t_j^* \leq t, \tag{3.64}$$

that is, $D^*(t)$ is the cumulative number of customers who are given service and exit from the system by time t. Then the quantity

$$N(t) = A(t) - D^*(t) \tag{3.65}$$

represents the number of customers in the system at time t. The total area between the curves $A(t)$ and $D^*(t)$ is the *total response time* of customers served in this period, that is,

$$\int_0^\tau N(t)\, dt = \sum_{j=1}^{n(\tau)} T_j. \tag{3.66}$$

Then by proceeding exactly in the same manner as above, we obtain the formula

$$\bar{N} = \lambda \cdot \bar{T}, \tag{3.67}$$

where N refers to the average number of customers in the system, and $\bar{T}$ is the average response time (i.e., waiting time plus service time) per customer.

Exercises

3.6.1 Determine whether the following statements concerning the formula $L = \lambda W$ are true or false

   a) The formula $L = \lambda W$ holds only when the arrival process is a Poisson process with rate λ.
   b) It is not necessary to assume a Poisson arrival process, but interarrival times must be statistically independent variables.
   c) The formula $L = \lambda W$ is valid under any queueing discipline. Thus, the average queue length L is invariant under queue disciplines.
   d) The formula holds even when the arrival rate at a given time is dependent on the congestion state of the queueing system.

3.6.2 Suppose there are R types of jobs. The arrival rates are given by λ_r, $r = 1, 2, \ldots, R$. How do you generalize the formula $L = \lambda W$? If the queue discipline is FCFS, what can we say about the average queue sizes of different types?

3.6.3 Choose a sufficiently long observation interval $(0, \tau)$ such that $Q(t) = A(t) - D(t) = 0$ at both $t = 0$ and $t = \tau$. By the aid of the diagram $Q(t)$, show that the distribution of queue size seen by arriving customers is the same as that seen by departing customers.

3.7 WORK-CONSERVING QUEUE DISCIPLINES AND CONSERVATION LAWS

3.7.1 Work-Conserving Queue Disciplines

If the work or service demand of each customer is not affected by the queue discipline and if the server is not idle when there are customers waiting for service, a queue discipline is said to be *work-conserving*, where work is identified as the total time (or the total workload) required to serve the given group of customers. In the following, we discuss basic properties of work-conserving queues. In reality, however, there are many situations in which the total time required to serve a specified group of customers depends on the order of service or the frequency of interruptions.

To analyze work-conserving queues, it is useful to introduce the notion of *virtual waiting time* or *virtual delay*. The virtual waiting time at time t, $V(t)$, is the amount of time that a customer *would* have to spend in queue *if* the customer joined the queue at that instant, assuming the FCFS order of service. The virtual waiting time $V(t)$ can also be interpreted as the total amount of time needed to serve all the customers present in the system. Therefore, we may call $V(t)$ the *unfinished work* at time t. In Fig. 3.18, we plot the function $V(t)$ for a typical sequence of customer arrivals and their service times.

We see in this figure how *busy periods* alternate with *idle periods*—the busy periods are indicated by $B_1, B_2, B_3, \ldots$, and the idle periods by $I_1, I_2, \ldots$. Initially the system is empty and therefore the unfinished work is clearly zero. Thus, $V(t)$ makes a vertical jump of magnitude S_1 at $t = t_1$, and busy period B_1 starts. As time progresses, the server reduces the unfinished work at the rate of one unit of service per unit time so $V(t)$ decreases with slope equal to -1. At time t_2, customer 2 arrives at the system, and $V(t)$ makes a jump of magnitude S_2. The function $V(t)$ continues to decrease with the same rate as before until it reaches the instant when the server has completed all the work. This terminates the

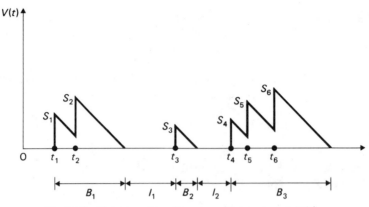

Fig. 3.18 Virtual waiting time or unfinished work $V(t)$.

busy period B_1 and initiates idle period I_1. The idle period I_1 is terminated at time t_3 when customer 3 enters, and so on.

From the point of view of the workload, a customer is merely a package of work, and the server is busy so long as there exists work to do. $V(t)$ depends solely on the arrival pattern of work and the elapsed time, and it is *independent of the queue discipline* insofar as the system is work-conserving. This simple observation has broad implications, one of which is a class of *conservation laws* that were originally derived by Kleinrock (1965).

3.7.2 Conservation Laws*

Let a process $A(t)$ represent, for each t, the cumulative amount of service demand that has arrived up to time t:

$$A_S(t) = \text{sum of } S_j \text{ such that } t_j \le t. \qquad (3.68)$$

This is a step function that jumps by the amount equal to S_j at the arrival epoch t_j of the jth customer, as shown in Fig. 3.19(a). Similarly, we define

$$D_S(t) = \text{sum of } S_j \text{ such that } t'_j \le t, \qquad (3.69)$$

or the function $D_S(t)$ is the cumulative amount of service demands that have entered service by time t. In Fig. 3.19(a), we draw $D_S(t)$ under the FCFS discipline. On the same graph, we draw a 45-degree straight line $B_S(t)$, which represents the total amount of time during which the server has been *busy*, that is, the total amount of work actually completed by time t. Then $A_S(t) - B_S(t)$ is equal to the unfinished work $V(t)$, which is

---

* The reader may choose to omit this section in the first reading.

sketched in Fig. 3.19(b). We now write

$$V(t) = V_Q(t) + V_R(t), \tag{3.70}$$

where

$$V_Q(t) = A_S(t) - D_S(t) \tag{3.71}$$

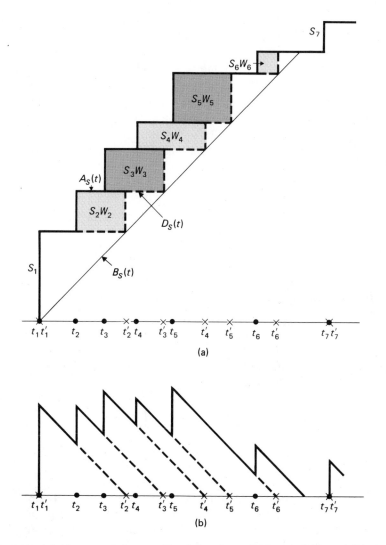

Fig. 3.19 (a) The cumulative workload functions $A_S(t)$ and $D_S(t)$ and (b) the unfinished work.

represents, at any time t, the total amount of backlog work waiting in the queue, and

$$V_R(t) = D_S(t) - B_S(t) \tag{3.72}$$

is the remaining service time (or the *residual life*) of the customer found in service at time t.

As before, we choose the time origin and a finite interval $(0, \tau)$ so that $A_S(t) = D_S(t)$ at $t = 0$ and $t = \tau$; hence $V_Q(t) = V_R(t) = 0$ at both $t = 0$ and $t = \tau$. Then by integrating (3.72), we obtain

$$\int_0^\tau V_R(t) \, dt = \frac{1}{2} \sum_{j=1}^{n(\tau)} S_j^2, \tag{3.73}$$

where S_j is the service time of the jth customer and the summation is taken over all the $n(\tau)$ customers that have arrived and completed during this period. The quantity of (3.73) is clearly independent of the service discipline insofar as it is work-conserving. By dividing (3.73) by τ and taking the limit, we obtain

$$\overline{V}_R = \lim_{\tau \to \infty} \frac{\int_0^\tau V_R(t) \, dt}{\tau}$$

$$= \frac{1}{2} \lim_{\tau \to \infty} \frac{n(\tau)}{\tau} \cdot \frac{\sum_{j=1}^{n(\tau)} S_j^2}{n(\tau)} = \frac{\lambda}{2} E[S^2]. \tag{3.74}$$

Similarly, for $V_Q(t)$ we can derive the following equality for any *nonpreemptive* discipline:

$$\int_0^\tau V_Q(t) \, dt = \sum_{j=1}^{n(\tau)} S_j W_j, \tag{3.75}$$

where W_j is the waiting time in queue of the jth customer. From (3.70) and (3.73), however, we can write

$$\int_0^\tau V_Q(t) \, dt = \int_0^\tau V(t) \, dt - \int_0^\tau V_R(t) \, dt$$

$$= \int_0^\tau V(t) \, dt - \frac{1}{2} \sum_{j=1}^{n(\tau)} S_j^2. \tag{3.76}$$

Since both $V(t)$ and $\sum_j S_j^2$ are independent of the queue discipline, it immediately follows from (3.75) that the *quantity* $\sum_j S_j W_j$ *is invariant under any queue discipline insofar as it is nonpreemptive.* This property represents one form of what Kleinrock (1965) aptly calls a conservation law.

Conservation law for $G/G/1$: For any finite period $(0, \tau)$ such that $V(t) = 0$ at $t = 0$ and $t = \tau$,

$$\sum_{j=1}^{n(\tau)} S_j W_j = \int_0^\tau V(t)\, dt - \frac{1}{2} \sum_{j=1}^{n(\tau)} S_j^2 \tag{3.77}$$

is invariant for any work-conserving and nonpreemptive queue disciplines. ∎

A simple interpretation of the conservation law is that if some customers are given preferential treatment, other customers suffer; thus the weighted sum $\sum_j S_j W_j$ remains constant, independent of the (non-preemptive) queue discipline.

The conservation law (3.77) stated above deals with the invariance of the weighted sum of the waiting times defined over a *given customer sequence* observed during any *finite* period of time. By dividing (3.75) by τ and letting τ approach infinity, we obtain

$$\overline{V}_Q = \lim_{\tau \to \infty} \frac{\int_0^\tau V_Q(t)\, dt}{\tau}$$

$$= \lim_{\tau \to \infty} \frac{n(\tau)}{\tau} \frac{\sum_{j=1}^{n(\tau)} S_j W_j}{n(\tau)}$$

$$= \lambda E[SW]. \tag{3.78}$$

Therefore, we can derive the following version of the conservation law, assuming that the queueing system $G/G/1$ is stable, and that the related random processes are all stationary.

Conservation law for a stationary $G/G/1$: If $\rho = \lambda \overline{S} < 1$, then

$$E[SW] = \frac{1}{\lambda} (\overline{V} - \overline{V}_R) \tag{3.79}$$

is invariant for any work-conserving and nonpreemptive queue discipline, where $\overline{V}$ and $\overline{V}_R$ are the expectations of the stationary processes $V(t)$ and $V_R(t)$, respectively. ∎

All the results obtained so far hold for a class of $G/G/1$ systems. If we specialize in an $M/G/1$ queue, we can show that the expected virtual waiting time $\overline{V}$ is equal to $\overline{W}_{\text{FCFS}}$, which is the expected waiting time under the FCFS discipline. Under the FCFS rule, the random variables W and S are independent, so that we obtain from (3.70), (3.74), and (3.78)

$$\overline{W}_{\text{FCFS}} = \overline{V}_Q + \overline{V}_R = \lambda \overline{S}\, \overline{W}_{\text{FCFS}} + \frac{\lambda}{2} E[S^2] \tag{3.80}$$

from which we solve for $\overline{W}_{\text{FCFS}}$:

$$\overline{W}_{\text{FCFS}} = \frac{\lambda E[S^2]}{2(1 - \rho)}, \tag{3.81}$$

where ρ is the utilization factor. Then by substituting the above result back into (3.78), we obtain the following.

Conservation law for an $M/G/1$: If $\rho < 1$, then

$$E[SW] = \frac{\rho E[S^2]}{2(1 - \rho)} \tag{3.82}$$

for any work-conserving and nonpreemptive queue discipline.   ■

Kleinrock (1976) extensively discusses applications of the conservation laws to various priority scheduling disciplines.

Exercises

3.7.1 Consider an $M/M/1$ system, that is, a queueing system with Poisson arrivals, the exponential service time distribution, and a single server.

a) Show that the mean waiting under the FCFS discipline is

$$\overline{W}_{\text{FCFS}} = \frac{\rho \bar{S}}{1 - \rho}.$$

b) Show that for any work-conserving (preemptive as well as nonpreemptive) queue discipline

$$E[SW] = \frac{\rho}{1 - \rho} \bar{S}^2.$$

3.7.2 Consider a single-server system with Poisson arrivals with rate $\lambda = 1$ [jobs/sec]. Consider the following three different types of service time distributions, having the same mean $E[S] = \frac{1}{2}$[sec]: (a) exponential distribution, (b) 2-stage Erlangian, (c) 2-stage hyperexponential distribution with the coefficient of variation equal to 2. Obtain $\overline{W}_{\text{FCFS}}$ for these three cases. Find also what form the conservation law takes.

3.7.3 Show that in an $M/G/1$ queueing system under the FCFS discipline, the average number of customers in the system (including one being served) is given by

$$\rho + \frac{\rho^2}{2(1 - \rho)}(1 + C_s^2),$$

where C_s is the coefficient of variation of the service time. (The above formula is often called the *Pollaczek-Khinchine* formula.)

3.8 BIRTH-AND-DEATH PROCESS MODELS

3.8.1 The Birth-and-Death Process

In this section we wish to study properties of the random process $N(t)$ (the number of customers found in the system at time t) for a special class of queueing models. Recall Fig. 3.14 and Eq. (3.65) in which $N(t)$ is written as

$$N(t) = A(t) - D^*(t), \tag{3.83}$$

where $A(t)$ is the arrival counting process and $D^*(t)$, the departure counting process. If we view $N(t)$ as the size of a *population*, then the process $A(t)$ is the total number of *births* up to time t, and the process $D^*(t)$ represents the total number of *deaths*. Thus $N(t)$ at each time t is the cumulative effect of births and deaths; therefore, we might appropriately call $N(t)$ a *birth-and-death process*. The formal definition of a birth-and-death process, however, is applied to the following special class of the random processes.

Definition. A random process $N(t)$ is called a *birth-and-death* process if the transition probabilities of $N(t)$

$$Q_{m,n}(h) = P[N(t + h) = n \mid N(t) = m] \tag{3.84}$$

are stationary (i.e., independent of t) and satisfy

1. $Q_{m,m+1}(h) = \lambda(m)h + o(h),$ (3.85)

2. $Q_{m,m-1}(h) = \mu(m)h + o(h),$ (3.86)

3. $Q_{m,m}(h) = 1 - \{\lambda(m) + \mu(m)\}h + o(h),$ (3.87)

and

4. $Q_{m,n}(h) = o(h)$ for $|m - n| > 1.$ (3.88)

The values $m = 0, 1, 2, \ldots$ that $N(t)$ takes on are called the *states of the system* that governs the birth-and-death process. The coefficients $\lambda(m)$ and $\mu(m)$ represent the *birth rate* and *death rate*, respectively, when population size is m (that is, when the system is in state m).

A birth-and-death process has the characteristics of Markov chains discussed in Chapter 2. Indeed, this process is a special case of a Markov process in which transitions from state m are permitted only to the neighboring states $m - 1$, m, and $m + 1$. Let $P_n(t)$ be the probability that the system is in state n at time t

$$P_n(t) = P[N(t) = n]. \tag{3.89}$$

To calculate $P_n(t + h)$ we note that the system can be in state n at time $t + h$ only if one of the following conditions is satisfied: (1) At time t, the system is in n and during $(t, t + h)$ no change occurs; (2) at time t the system is in $n - 1$ and a transition to n occurs; (3) at time t the system is in $n + 1$ and a transition to n occurs; (4) during $(t, t + h)$ two or more transitions occur. By our assumption, the probability of the last event is $o(h)$. The first three events are mutually exclusive, so that their probabilities add. Therefore,

$$P_n(t + h) = P_n(t)\{1 - \lambda(n)h - \mu(n)h + o(h)\}$$
$$+ P_{n-1}(t)\{\lambda(n - 1)h + o(h)\}$$
$$+ P_{n+1}(t)\{\mu(n + 1)h + o(h)\} + o(h). \qquad (3.90)$$

Let us subtract $P_n(t)$ from both sides and divide the equation by h; then by letting $h \to 0$, we obtain the following differential difference equations:

$$\frac{dP_n(t)}{dt} = -\{\lambda(n) + \mu(n)\}P_n(t) + \lambda(n - 1)P_{n-1}(t)$$
$$+ \mu(n + 1)P_{n+1}(t), \quad \text{for} \quad n = 1, 2, 3, \ldots, \qquad (3.91a)$$

and

$$\frac{dP_0(t)}{dt} = -\lambda(0)P_0(t) + \mu(1)P_1(t). \qquad (3.91b)$$

It is by no means trivial to show the existence and uniqueness of the solution to Eq. (3.91), and this question is beyond the scope of this book. The solution of the equation is manageable with certain restrictions imposed on the birth-and-death rates (Exercises 3.8.1–3.8.5). But the general time-dependent solution of (3.91) is difficult to come by, so we should content ourselves with the equilibrium state solution. Indeed in many applications, the equilibrium state solution is all we want.

We define an *equilibrium state* solution to be probability distribution p_n such that $P_n(t) = p_n$ specifies a (constant) solution to Eq. (3.91). If such a distribution exists, it is unique, and for each state n

$$\lim_{t \to \infty} P_n(t) = p_n. \qquad (3.92)$$

Since we are interested only in the statistical equilibrium properties of the system, we first take the limits as $t \to \infty$ throughout Eq. (3.91a), and set $\lim_{t \to \infty} (d/dt)P_n(t)$ equal to 0, thus obtaining the following linear difference equation:

$$\lambda(n)p_n - \mu(n + 1)p_{n+1} = \lambda(n - 1)p_{n-1} - \mu(n)p_n,$$
$$\text{for} \quad n = 1, 2, 3, \ldots. \qquad (3.93)$$

By rearranging this equation, we have

$$\lambda(n - 1)p_{n-1} - \mu(n)p_n = \text{constant}, \quad \text{for} \quad n = 1, 2, 3, \ldots. \tag{3.94}$$

From Eq. (3.91b) we find that

$$\lambda(0)p_0 - \mu(1)p_1 = 0. \tag{3.95}$$

So the constant in Eq. (3.94) must be zero, and we obtain the following *recurrence equation:*

$$\mu(n)p_n = \lambda(n - 1)p_{n-1}, \quad \text{for} \quad n = 1, 2, 3, \ldots. \tag{3.96}$$

The interpretation of (3.96) is as follows: The left-hand side represents the rate of transition from state n to state $n - 1$, and this quantity is balanced by the transition rate from state $n - 1$ to state n, which is given by the right-hand side of (3.96). These *balance equations* are shown schematically in Fig. 3.20.

The equilibrium state probabilities are then calculated by the recurrence equation

$$p_n = \frac{\lambda(n - 1)}{\mu(n)} p_{n-1} = \frac{\Lambda(n)}{M(n)} p_0, \tag{3.97}$$

where

$$\Lambda(n) = \prod_{i=1}^{n} \lambda(i - 1) \tag{3.98}$$

and

$$M(n) = \prod_{i=1}^{n} \mu(i). \tag{3.99}$$

The probability p_0 is uniquely determined by the condition that the probability distribution $\{p_n; n = 0, 1, 2, \ldots\}$ must add up to unity. That is to say, if the series

$$\mathscr{S} = 1 + \sum_{n=1}^{\infty} \frac{\Lambda(n)}{M(n)} = 1 + \sum_{n=1}^{\infty} \prod_{i=1}^{n} \frac{\lambda(i - 1)}{\mu(i)} \tag{3.100}$$

converges, then

$$p_0 = \mathscr{S}^{-1}. \tag{3.101}$$

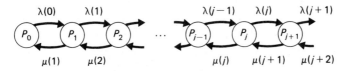

Fig. 3.20 A schematic diagram of the balance equation in the birth-and-death process.

Exercises

3.8.1 A birth-and-death process is called a *pure birth process* if $\lambda(n) = \lambda$ for all $n \geq 0$, and $\mu(n) = 0$ for all $n \geq 0$. Assuming $N(0) = 0$, solve the differential difference equations (3.91a) and (3.91b) for $P_n(t)$ of the pure birth process.

3.8.2 Set $\mu(n) = 0$ for all $n \geq 0$ as in the above problem but permit state-dependent birth rates $\lambda(n)$. Show that the solution for $P_n(t)$ satisfies

$$P_n(t) = e^{-\lambda(n)t} \left[\lambda(n-1) \int_0^t P_{n-1}(x) e^{\lambda(n)x} \, dx + P_n(0) \right].$$

3.8.3 Let us consider a pure death process, that is, $\lambda(n) = 0$ for all $n \geq 0$ and $\mu(n) = \mu$ for all $n \geq 1$. Let the initial population be $N(0) = N_0$. Show that the solution for $P_n(t)$ is given by

$$P_n(t) = \frac{(\mu t)^{N_0 - n}}{(N_0 - n)!} e^{-\mu t}, \quad \text{for} \quad 1 \leq n \leq N_0$$

and

$$P_0(t) = 1 - \sum_{i=0}^{N_0 - 1} \frac{(\mu t)^i}{i!} e^{-\mu t}.$$

3.8.4 *The time-dependent probability generating function.* We extend the notion of probability generating function discussed in Chapter 2 to the time-dependent probability distribution

$$G(z, t) = \sum_{n=0}^{\infty} P_n(t) z^n.$$

Solve the pure birth problem of Exercise 3.8.1 using this generating function.

3.8.5 Let $\lambda(n) = \lambda$ for all $n \geq 0$, and $\mu(n) = n\mu$ for all $n \geq 1$. Find the partial differential equation that $G(z, t)$ must satisfy. Show that the solution to this equation is

$$G(z, t) = \exp \left\{ \frac{\lambda}{\mu} (1 - e^{-\mu t})(z - 1) \right\}.$$

Obtain the solution for $P_n(t)$.

3.8.2 *M/M/1*: The Simple Queueing System

Consider an $M/M/1$ queueing system, that is, a single-server system with Poisson arrivals and exponentially distributed service times. As we studied in the previous section, a Poisson process with rate λ is a pure birth process with the birth rate λ (see Exercise 3.8.1). If we denote by $1/\mu$ the mean service time, the probability that a customer in service is completed within the next h [time units] is $1 - e^{-\mu h} = \mu h + o(h)$, regardless of the amount of time the server has already expended on this particular customer. Thus we can characterize $N(t)$, the number of customers in the $M|M|1$ system, by a birth-and-death process with

$$\lambda(n) = \lambda, \qquad n = 0, 1, 2, \ldots \tag{3.102}$$

and

$$\mu(n) = \mu, \qquad n = 1, 2, \ldots . \tag{3.103}$$

The recurrence relation (3.97) then becomes

$$p_n = \rho \, p_{n-1} = \rho^n p_0 \tag{3.104}$$

where

$$\rho = \frac{\lambda}{\mu} . \tag{3.105}$$

If $\rho < 1$, then the series (3.100) converges, and we obtain

$$p_0 = \left(1 + \sum_{n=1}^{\infty} \rho^n \right)^{-1}$$

$$= 1 - \rho. \tag{3.106}$$

Thus we have

$$p_n = (1 - \rho)\rho^n, \qquad n \geq 0 \tag{3.107}$$

which is the steady-state probability of finding n customers in the system. If $\rho > 1$, customers will arrive at the system faster than the server is able to handle them and therefore, in the long run, a queue will develop without bound.

The equilibrium distribution (3.107) is the geometric distribution that was studied in Chapter 2. The mean and variance of the number of customers in the system are readily obtainable as

$$\overline{N} = \sum_{n=0}^{\infty} n p_n = \frac{\rho}{1 - \rho} \tag{3.108}$$

and

$$\sigma_N^2 = \sum_{n=0}^{\infty} n^2 p_n - \overline{N}^2 = \frac{\rho}{(1 - \rho)^2} . \tag{3.109}$$

Figure 3.21 plots the mean $\overline{N}$ and the standard deviation σ_N as functions of ρ.

It is evident that as ρ approaches 1, the mean queue size grows without bound, giving rise to an infinitely long queue. Likewise, the standard deviation increases sharply with ρ. This explains the great

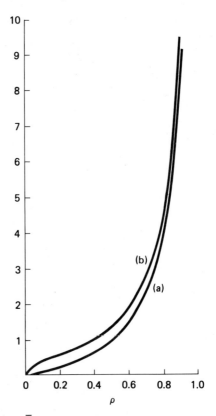

Fig. 3.21 (a) The mean $\bar{N}$ and (b) the standard deviation σ_N as functions of ρ in the $M/M/1$ queueing system.

variation of queue size we often observe in a highly utilized system. The average number of customers in the waiting line is given by

$$\bar{Q} = \sum_{n=1}^{\infty} (n-1)p_n = \frac{\rho^2}{1-\rho} \tag{3.110}$$

and its variance is

$$\sigma_Q^2 = \sum_{n=1}^{\infty} (n-1)^2 p_n - \bar{Q}^2 = \frac{\rho^2(1+\rho-\rho^2)}{(1-\rho)^2}. \tag{3.111}$$

Note that (3.108) and (3.110) give

$$\bar{N} = \bar{Q} + \rho. \tag{3.112}$$

This is not unexpected: The server utilization ρ can be interpreted as the expected number of customers found in the server.

Now let us turn our attention to the waiting and response times. The mean waiting time $\overline{W}$ and the mean response time $\overline{T}$ can be calculated from $\overline{N}$ and $\overline{Q}$ by using Little's formula (3.61) or (3.67):

$$\overline{W} = \frac{\overline{Q}}{\lambda} = \frac{\rho}{\mu(1 - \rho)} \qquad (3.113)$$

and

$$\overline{T} = \frac{\overline{N}}{\lambda} = \frac{1}{\mu(1 - \rho)}. \qquad (3.114)$$

It should be noted that we did not make any specific assumption concerning the scheduling discipline. Indeed all the results obtained thus far in the present section hold for any work-conserving queue disciplines, including preemptive disciplines.

Let us proceed to the derivation of the waiting-time and response-time distributions. Suppose that a new customer arrives to the system and finds n customers ahead of him—that is, the system is in state n. We define the conditional probability distribution function

$F_W(x \mid n) = P[$the customer's waiting time $W \le x \mid n$ customers are
                 found in the system upon arrival].   (3.115)

If we assume the FCFS discipline, the waiting time of this new customer is the sum of the remaining service time, R_1, of the customer currently in service plus the total time to serve the $n - 1$ customers in the queue:

$$W = R_1 + S_2 + \cdots + S_n. \qquad (3.116)$$

Recall the fundamental property of the exponential distribution that the *remaining service time* also has the exponential distribution with mean $1/\mu$. Therefore, the conditional distribution is the n-stage Erlangian distribution with mean n/μ:

$$F_W(x \mid n) = 1 - e^{-\mu x} \sum_{j=0}^{n-1} \frac{(\mu x)^j}{j!}, \qquad x \ge 0 \qquad (3.117)$$

and its density function is given by

$$f_W(x \mid n) = \frac{(\mu x)^{n-1}}{(n - 1)!} \mu e^{-\mu x}, \qquad x \ge 0. \qquad (3.118)$$

We can show (Exercise 3.8.7) that when the arrival process is Poisson, the queue size distribution observed by arriving customers is the same as the long-run time average distribution: The parameter n in the above equation is a random variable with the distribution $\{p_n\}$ of (3.107). The distribution function of the waiting time is thus given by the weighted sum of the conditional distribution:

$$F_W(x) = \sum_{n=0}^{\infty} p_n F_W(x \mid n).$$ (3.119)

Here $F_W(x \mid 0)$ is the waiting-time distribution for a customer who finds, upon arrival, the empty system:

$$F_W(x \mid 0) = \begin{cases} 1, & x \geq 0 \\ 0, & x < 0. \end{cases}$$ (3.120)

Therefore,

$$F_W(x) = 1 - \rho + (1 - \rho) \sum_{n=1}^{\infty} \rho^n \left\{ 1 - e^{-\mu x} \sum_{j=0}^{n-1} \frac{(\mu x)^j}{j!} \right\}, \qquad x \geq 0.$$ (3.121)

By rearranging the double summation of the second term, and with some algebraic manipulation (see Exercise 3.8.8), we finally obtain

$$F_W(x) = 1 - \rho e^{-\mu(1-\rho)x}, \qquad x \geq 0.$$ (3.122)

We plot $F_W(x)$ versus μx in Fig. 3.22 for the case $\rho = 0.8$. Thus the probability that a customer must wait longer than x time units is

$$F_W^c(x) = P[W > x] = \rho e^{-\mu(1-\rho)x}, \qquad x \geq 0.$$ (3.123)

By using the formula (2.96), we obtain the mean waiting time as

$$\overline{W} = \int_0^{\infty} F_W^c(x)\, dx = \frac{\rho}{(1 - \rho)\mu};$$ (3.124)

this, of course, agrees with (3.113), which was obtained under the less restrictive assumption on the scheduling discipline.

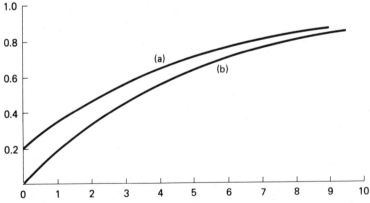

Fig. 3.22 (a) The waiting-time distribution function and (b) the response-time distribution function in the $M/M/1$ queueing system ($\rho = 0.8$).

The response time or delay time is by definition $T = W + S$, where S is the service time of the arriving customer. For the FCFS discipline, the variables W and S are independent; thus the distribution function of T can be obtained by convolving the distribution function of W and the density function of S:

$$F_T(x) = \int_0^\infty F_W(x - y) f_S(y) \, dy$$

$$= \int_0^\infty [1 - \rho e^{-\mu(1-\rho)(x-y)}] \mu e^{-\mu y} \, dy$$

$$= 1 - e^{-\mu(1-\rho)x}, \qquad x \geq 0. \tag{3.125}$$

Thus, the response time T has simply the exponential distribution with mean $1/\mu(1 - \rho)$. We plot the curve $F_T(x)$ versus μx also in Fig. 3.22.

Exercises

3.8.6 Consider the $M/M/1$ system discussed above.

a) Obtain the balance equation and its schematic diagram (state-transition-rate diagram).
b) Find the probability generating function $G(z)$ from the balance equation.
c) Find $\{p_n\}$.

3.8.7 Consider an $M/M/1$ queueing system and let $\{p_n\}$ be the probability distribution of the number of customers found in the system at a randomly chosen time. It should also be equivalent to the long-run time average distribution. If we choose a sufficiently long interval $(0, T)$, the portion of time that the system contains n customers is, on the average, $p_n T$.

a) Assume a Poisson arrival process with rate λ. What is the expected number of arriving customers during the interval $(0, T)$ who find exactly n customers in the system? Show then that $\{a_n\}$, the probability distribution seen by an arriving customer, is equal to $\{p_n\}$.
b) What can you say about the relation between $\{p_n\}$ and $\{d_n\}$, the distribution seen by a departing customer?
c) If the arrival process is not Poisson, the above result is no longer true in general. Find some examples to illustrate this fact.

3.8.8 Show the derivation of Eq. (3.122).

3.8.9 Obtain the waiting- and response-time probability density distributions of the $M/M/1$ system through the Laplace transform method. *Hint:* What is the Laplace transform of $f_W(x \mid n)$ of (3.118)?

3.8.10 Calculate $P[N > n]$ for the $M/M/1$ system.

3.8.3   Arrival and Processing Rates Dependent on Queue Length

We now preceed to more general situations, in which the arrival rate and/or the service rate may depend on the size of the queue. Thus, we shall suppose that transition $n \to n - 1$ is associated with rate $\mu(n)$. We continue to make the Markovian assumption, namely, the probabilities referring to transitions in $(t, t + h)$ depend only on $N(t)$, the state of the system at time t, but not on what happened before t. Then the queue of this system forms a birth-and-death process, and the equilibrium state distribution of $N(t)$ is the general solution given by (3.97).

$M/M/\infty$: Service facility with ample servers

We assume as before that customers arrive according to the Poisson process with rate λ, and that service demands have the negative exponential distribution with mean $\bar{S}$. Suppose now that whenever a new customer arrives, there is always a server of processing rate C immediately available to the customer. Thus, when there are n customers in the system, n servers will work; hence there is no queue to build up. This means that the service capacity of the facility is a function of n: $C(n) = nC$. Since the number n can become arbitrarily large, the facility must have, in theory, infinitely many servers with capacity C. Hence we denote such a queueing system by $M/M/\infty$. Then, the birth and death rates that govern the process $N(t)$ of the $M/M/\infty$ system are given by

$$\lambda(n) = \lambda, \qquad n = 0, 1, 2, \ldots \tag{3.126}$$

and

$$\mu(n) = \frac{C(n)}{\bar{S}} = n \cdot \mu, \qquad n = 1, 2, 3, \ldots, \tag{3.127}$$

where μ is the completion rate defined by (3.1). The substitution of the above results into (3.100) leads to

$$\mathscr{S} = 1 + \frac{\lambda}{\mu} + \frac{1}{2!} \left(\frac{\lambda}{\mu} \right)^2 + \cdots + \frac{1}{n!} \left(\frac{\lambda}{\mu} \right)^n + \cdots$$

$$= e^{\lambda/\mu}. \tag{3.128}$$

Therefore from (3.97) and (3.101), we obtain the equilibrium-state probability distribution of the number of customers in $M/M/\infty$:

$$p_n = \frac{(\lambda/\mu)^n}{n!} e^{-\lambda/\mu}, \qquad n = 0, 1, 2, \ldots, \tag{3.129}$$

which is a Poisson distribution with mean λ/μ. Hence the number of busy servers is, on the average, λ/μ. The queueing system $M/M/\infty$ is one of the few systems for which the nonequilibrium solution is easily obtainable (see Exercise 3.8.5).

$M/M/m$: Service facility with m servers

We now consider a modification of the previous example by imposing an upper limit m on the number of servers that can be made available. Let $N(t)$ be the number of customers found at time t in this service facility consisting of m parallel servers. If $N(t) = n \le m$, then the n customers are simultaneously served by n separate servers. On the other hand, if $N(t) = n > m$, then there develops a queue of $n - m$ waiting customers. For this setup we have the following birth-and-death process model:

$$\lambda(n) = \lambda, \qquad 0, 1, 2, \ldots, \tag{3.130}$$

$$\mu(n) = \min\{n, m\}\mu. \tag{3.131}$$

We define the traffic intensity by

$$a = \frac{\lambda}{\mu}. \tag{3.132}$$

If $a < m$, then the series $\mathscr{S}$ of (3.100) converges, yielding

$$\mathscr{S} = \sum_{n=0}^{m-1} \frac{(m\rho)^n}{n!} + \frac{(m\rho)^m}{m!} \frac{1}{1-\rho}, \tag{3.133}$$

where

$$\rho = \frac{a}{m} = \frac{\lambda}{m\mu} < 1 \tag{3.134}$$

is the utilization factor. Thus

$$p_0 = \mathscr{S}^{-1}, \tag{3.135a}$$

$$p_n = \frac{a^n}{n!} p_0, \qquad n = 1, 2, \ldots, m, \tag{3.135b}$$

and

$$p_n = \rho^{n-m} p_m, \qquad n > m. \tag{3.135c}$$

It will be interesting to observe that the distribution in the region $0 \le n \le m$ takes the form of a Poisson distribution (just as in the $M/M/\infty$ system), whereas in the range $n > m$ it is a geometric distribution with parameter ρ (just as in the $M/M/1$ system). These two distribution functions are concatenated at $n = m$.

Now we wish to obtain the waiting-time distribution in the $M/M/m$ queue. Using the same reasoning that we applied to the analysis of the $M/M/1$, we find that the probability that an arriving customer finds n customers waiting in the queue is given by p_{m+n}. Thus, the probability that a customer will not receive service immediately is

$$F_W^c(0) = P[W > 0] = \sum_{n=0}^{\infty} p_{m+n} = \frac{p_m}{1 - \rho}$$

$$= \frac{\dfrac{a^m}{m!(1 - \rho)}}{\sum_{k=0}^{m-1} \dfrac{a^k}{k!} + \dfrac{a^m}{m!(1 - \rho)}}. \qquad (3.136)$$

The last expression of (3.136) is often referred to as the Erlang delay formula or Erlang's second formula. We define the complement of the conditional distribution function of the waiting time:

$F_W^c(x \mid m + n) = P[$the customer's waiting time $W > x \mid (m + n)$
customers found in the system upon arrival].

$$(3.137)$$

Then we obtain the following expression:

$$F_W^c(x) = P\{W > x\} = \sum_{n=0}^{\infty} p_{m+n} F_W^c(x \mid m + n)$$

$$= F_W^c(0)(1 - \rho) \sum_{n=0}^{\infty} \rho^n F_W^c(x \mid m + n). \qquad (3.138)$$

Note that the results (3.137) and (3.138) hold for any work-conserving queue discipline. Now we focus on the FCFS discipline. Let T_1' be the interval between the arrival of the customer in question and the first service completion that takes place in the system. Similarly, let T_i be the interval between the $(i - 1)$th service completion and the ith completion, $i = 2, 3, \ldots, n + 1$, as illustrated in Fig. 3.23. Then we can see (Exercise 3.8.12) that $T_1', T_2, \ldots, T_{n+1}$ are independent and identically

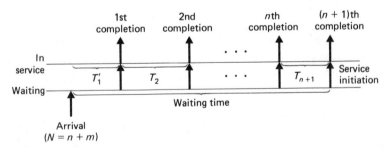

Fig. 3.23 The relationship between the waiting-time variable W and service completion intervals in the $M/M/m$ queue.

distributed random variables with the exponential distribution of mean $1/m\mu$. Then the waiting time of the customer under consideration is $T_1' + T_2 + \cdots + T_{n+1}$. Then by following the arguments that led us to (3.117), we obtain

$$F_W(x \mid m + n) = 1 - e^{-m\mu x} \sum_{j=0}^{n} \frac{(m\mu x)^j}{j!} \qquad (3.139)$$

which is an Erlangian distribution with parameter n and mean $n/m\mu$. Substitution of (3.139) into (3.138) gives the result

$$F_W^c(x) = F_W^c(0)e^{-m\mu x}(1 - \rho) \sum_{n=0}^{\infty} \rho^n \sum_{j=0}^{n} \frac{(m\mu x)^j}{j!} . \qquad (3.140)$$

By interchanging the order of summation and using the formula for a geometric series, we obtain the result (Exercise 3.8.13)

$$F_W^c(x) = F_W^c(0)e^{-m\mu(1-\rho)x} \qquad (3.141)$$

or, equivalently,

$$F_W(x) = 1 - F_W^c(0)e^{-m\mu(1-\rho)x}. \qquad (3.142)$$

For $m = 1$, the latter result indeed reduces to (3.121), the waiting-time distribution for the $M/M/1$ queue.

3.8.4   A Queueing System with Finite Storage and a Two-Stage Cyclic Queueing System

Consider a single-server queue with Poisson arrivals and exponential service times as before, but now suppose that there is no room for more than K customers to queue (including the one being served). In this situation, customers who arrive and find no waiting room leave without being served. The behavior of this system can also be characterized by a birth-and-death process. The birth-and-death rates are given by

$$\lambda(n) = \begin{cases} \lambda; & n < K \\ 0; & n \geq K \end{cases} \qquad (3.143)$$

$$\mu(n) = \mu; \qquad n = 1, 2, \ldots. \qquad (3.144)$$

Then $\mathscr{S}$ of (3.100) is the finite sum

$$\mathscr{S} = 1 + \frac{\lambda}{\mu} + \left(\frac{\lambda}{\mu}\right)^2 + \cdots + \left(\frac{\lambda}{\mu}\right)^K = \frac{1 - \left(\frac{\lambda}{\mu}\right)^{K+1}}{1 - \frac{\lambda}{\mu}}. \qquad (3.145)$$

We then have the following equilibrium distribution for the number of customers in the system:

$$p_n = \frac{\left(1 - \frac{\lambda}{\mu}\right)\left(\frac{\lambda}{\mu}\right)^n}{1 - \left(\frac{\lambda}{\mu}\right)^{K+1}}, \qquad 0 \le n \le K, \qquad (3.146)$$

which is a *truncated* geometric distribution. The distribution (3.146) reduces to (3.107) as $K \to \infty$, if $\lambda/\mu < 1$.

It is interesting and important to note that the same analysis and results hold for an entirely different queueing system. Consider a two-stage cyclic queue as shown in Fig. 3.24(a). We assume that the system is *closed:* By this we mean that there is no arrival from nor departure to the outside. The two servers are both exponential servers with the completion rates λ and μ, respectively. Suppose that there are K customers in this closed system and let $N(t)$ represent the number of jobs at server 2 at time t; thus the number of customers at server 1 is $K - N(t)$. Then the process $N(t)$ is a birth-and-death process governed by (3.143) and (3.144). So long as server 1 is busy (i.e., $N(t) < K$), its departure process is a Poisson process with rate λ, and once $N(t)$ becomes K, server 1 becomes idle. This is, in effect, equivalent to blocking additional arrivals to server 2. Therefore, the two-stage cyclic queueing system of Fig. 3.24(a) is equivalent to the system of Fig. 3.24(b) insofar as the behavior of $N(t)$ is concerned.

The equivalence between the two queueing systems holds under a more general assumption. For example, $\mu(n)$ can be explicitly dependent on n. In Section 3.11.5 we will discuss the case in which service times at server 2 are random variables drawn from a general distribution. In this case, of course, $N(t)$ is no longer a birth-and-death process.

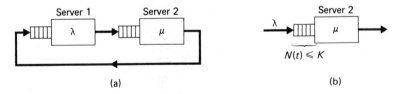

(a)   (b)

Fig. 3.24 (a) A two-stage cyclic queueing system and (b) its equivalent single-server system.

Exercises

3.8.11 Calculate the probability generating function of the queue size Q in the $M/M/m$ system. Then show that the average queue size is given by

$$\bar{Q} = \frac{p_0 a^m \rho}{m!(1-\rho)^2}.$$

Calculate the variance of Q.

3.8.12 Let the random variables $T_1', T_2, \ldots, T_{n+1}$ be those defined in the text and illustrated in Fig. 3.23. Show that $T_1', T_2, \ldots, T_{n+1}$ are independent and identically distributed according to the exponential distribution of mean $1/m\mu$.

3.8.13 Show the derivation step from (3.140) to (3.141).

3.8.14 Obtain $F_W(x)$ of (3.142) through the Laplace transform method (see Exercise 3.8.9). Also obtain $F_T(x)$, the response-time distribution.

3.8.15 *Discouraged arrivals: Kleinrock* (1975). Let us choose the birth-and-death rate coefficients as follows:

$$\lambda(n) = \frac{\lambda}{n+1}, \qquad n = 0, 1, 2, \ldots;$$

$$\mu(n) = \mu, \qquad n = 1, 2, \ldots.$$

Show that the distribution $\{p_n\}$ takes the same form as that of $M/M/\infty$.

3.8.16 *Pressured server and discouraged arrivals: Hillier and Lieberman* (1967). Let us generalize the $M/M/\infty$ and the system with the discouraged arrivals (Exercise 3.8.15), choosing the following birth-and-death coefficients:

$$\lambda(n) = \frac{\lambda}{(n+1)^b}, \qquad n = 0, 1, 2, \ldots;$$

$$\mu(n) = n^c \mu, \qquad n = 1, 2, 3, \ldots,$$

where c is the "pressure coefficient"—a constant that indicates the degree to which the service rate of the system is affected by the system state. Similarly b is a constant that might be called the "discouraging coefficient." Obtain the steady-state distribution $\{p_n\}$ for this birth-and-death process model. What is the distribution when $b + c = 1$?

3.8.17 Consider the queueing system with finite storage discussed in the text.

a) Obtain the balance equation and its schematic diagram (state-transition-rate diagram).
b) Find the probability generating function $G(z)$ of the distribution $\{p_n\}$.
c) Find $\{p_n\}$.

3.8.18 Consider the two-stage cyclic queueing system of Fig. 3.24(a).

a) Obtain expressions for the expected values of the numbers of customers found in servers 1 and 2, respectively.

b) Obtain their limits as $K \to \infty$. (*Hint:* Consider three different cases: $\lambda > \mu$, $\lambda = \mu$, and $\lambda < \mu$.)

c) Sketch the mean values obtained above as functions of K.

3.8.19 Consider an $M/M/m$ queueing system with storage capacity m. If a customer arrives when all the m servers are busy, the customer will be lost.

a) Specify the birth-and-death rate coefficients and draw the state-transition-rate diagram.

b) Obtain the equilibrium state distribution $\{p_n\}$.

c) How many arrivals will be lost, on the average, per unit time?

3.9 A QUEUEING SYSTEM WITH FINITE POPULATION: A MODEL FOR A MULTIACCESS SYSTEM

In this section, we consider a queueing system in which requests for service are generated by a finite input source as schematically shown in Fig. 3.25. This queueing model is known in queueing theory literature as the *machine servicing* model (Feller, 1966) or the *machine interference* model (Cox and Smith, 1961) in which a server (or a team of servers) is assigned the responsibility of maintaining a group of K machines. Each machine is in one of two states: either "up" (running) or "down" (requiring repair service). When a machine breaks down, it joins the queue for repair. If one of the servers is free, the server immediately begins to service the machine. If all of the servers are busy, the machine must wait for service.

We are interested in this model, since it can be viewed as a general model of a multiaccess system. In such a case the group of K machines corresponds to a set of K terminal users, and the server corresponds to a multiaccess system such as a time-sharing computer system or a

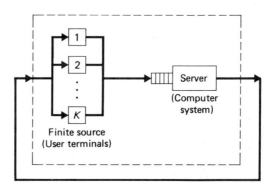

Fig. 3.25 A queueing system with finite input source.

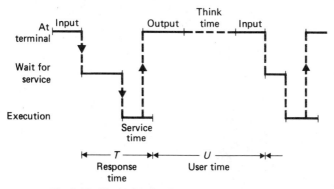

Fig. 3.26 Typical behavior of user transactions.

multiaccess communication channel. In this section we consider the former example, that is, an interactive time-sharing system. Figure 3.26 shows a typical sequence of operations at a user terminal and the corresponding processing performed by the computer system.

Each user sends from the terminal a request for processing. This "input" operation is usually completed by a carriage return. The system (or the server) puts this request into the system queue. When the particular request is selected for processing, the program associated with it is executed. The execution usually results in an "output," which is sent to the user's terminal. In practice, the program execution may not be performed in one stretch, but may be interleaved with processing of other users' programs. Such interleaving is usually accomplished by the multiprogramming technique. An explicit treatment of such multiprogramming is deferred until Section 3.10.5.

The user response time, U, is defined here as a random variable that represents the interval of time that a user spends from the moment of service completion of the last request until the generation of the next request. We define the system response time, T, of a request as the time interval between the instant when the input to the system is completed and the instant when its processing by the system is completed. Therefore, the user response time and the system response time together constitute one cycle of interaction.

3.9.1 General Properties and Asymptotic Behavior

With the definitions stated above, the parameters in the model of Fig. 3.25 are now well specified. Before we proceed to solve a specific model, we will derive several important properties that hold in a very general setting. Let λ be the throughput of the system, in other words, the number of requests completed by the system per unit time. Then the rate of arrivals to (and that of departures from) the box surrounded by the dotted line in Fig. 3.25 is λ. Then by applying the formula $\lambda W = L$ we obtain the relation

$$\lambda(\overline{T} + \overline{U}) = K. \tag{3.147}$$

Note that this equation holds under any scheduling discipline: It need not be even work-conserving. We assume neither statistical independence of user response times, U's, nor their distributional form. All that we require is that the equilibrium state of the system exists.

Let p_0 be the probability that the system is idle, and $\overline{S}$ be the average service time of a request. Then the server can process, on the average, as many as $(1 - p_0)/\overline{S}$ requests per unit time:

$$\lambda = \frac{1 - p_0}{\overline{S}}. \tag{3.148}$$

This equation is also valid under a very general condition: The only restriction is that the queue discipline is work-conserving in that the service times, S's, of individual requests are not affected by the queue discipline. From the last two equations we readily obtain the following expression for the average response time:

$$\overline{T} = \frac{K\overline{S}}{1 - p_0} - \overline{U}. \tag{3.149}$$

We define the system service rate μ and the request generation rate ν by

$$\mu = \frac{1}{\overline{S}} \tag{3.150}$$

and by

$$\nu = \frac{1}{\overline{U}}, \tag{3.151}$$

respectively. We denote their ratio by r, that is,

$$r = \frac{\mu}{\nu} = \frac{\text{mean user response time}}{\text{mean service time}}. \tag{3.152}$$

Then the normalized mean response time (i.e., $\overline{T}/\overline{S}$) is

$$\mu\overline{T} = \frac{K}{1 - p_0} - r. \tag{3.153}$$

Note that we made no specific assumptions in deriving the last formula.

The formula holds, practically speaking, under almost any conditions: The distributions of U and S can be arbitrary, and the queue discipline can be anything so long as it is work-conserving. Furthermore, the user times, U's, and service times, S's, need not be homogeneous nor independent sequences. This statement is not meant to imply, however, that the mean response time is invariant to these system parameters. The probability p_0 will generally depend on the distributional forms of U's and S's and on the service discipline. The important point here is the extreme simplicity and generality of the above formula.

The probability p_0 approaches zero as K increases to infinity. Thus, if we plot $\mu \bar{T}$ versus K, we will obtain a curve such as the one shown in Fig. 3.27(a). The two asymptotes are

$$\mu \bar{T} \approx K - r \quad \text{for large} \quad K, \tag{3.154}$$

and

$$\lim_{K \to 1} \mu \bar{T} = 1. \tag{3.155}$$

The latter result is quite obvious: If there is only one terminal user, the waiting time is zero; therefore, the system response time is always equal to the service time. From this and from Eq. (3.153), we also obtain a general property

$$\lim_{K \to 1} p_0 = \frac{\mu}{\mu + \nu} = \frac{r}{r + 1}, \tag{3.156}$$

which could be directly derived (see Exercise 3.9.2). The value of K for which the two asymptotes (3.154) and (3.155) intersect each other is

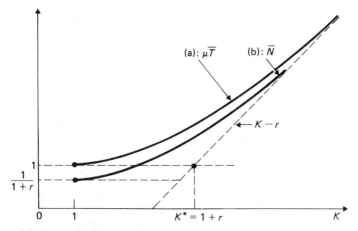

Fig. 3.27 (a) The normalized mean response time and (b) the mean queue size versus the population size K.

given by

$$K^* = 1 + r. \tag{3.157}$$

The value K^* is called the *saturation point* (Kleinrock, 1969).

The mean queue size $\bar{N}$ (the number of requests either in service or in waiting queue) is obtained by use of Little's formula

$$\bar{N} = \lambda\bar{T}, \tag{3.158}$$

which can be written, using (3.148) and (3.149), as

$$\bar{N} = K - (1 - p_0)r \tag{3.159}$$

and has the asymptotes

$$\bar{N} \approx K - r \quad \text{for large } K \tag{3.160}$$

and

$$\lim_{K \to 1} \bar{N} = \frac{\nu}{\mu + \nu} = \frac{1}{1 + r}. \tag{3.161}$$

Curve (b) of Fig. 3.27 is a plot of $\bar{N}$ versus K. The curves of Fig. 3.27 illustrate an important characteristic of a finite source model: Both the response time and queue size first gradually increase as the system load K increases, and beyond the saturation point K^*, they rise almost linearly with the load. Each additional user causes the system queue size to increase almost by one and the system response to be delayed for additional $\bar{S}$ time units.

Exercises

3.9.1 In Fig. 3.25, move the boundary of the box of dotted lines so that the server lies outside the box: It contains the K terminals and the waiting line of the server. Apply the formula $L = \lambda W$ to this subsystem, and then derive an expression for the *normalized mean waiting time*, that is, $\bar{W}/\bar{S}$.

3.9.2 Obtain the result of (3.156) directly.

3.9.3 Suppose that the user response time is a constant $1/\nu$, and the service time of each request is a constant $1/\mu$. Furthermore, their ratio $r = \mu/\nu$ is an integer. Plot the mean response time versus K. What is the distribution of the response time?

3.9.2 The Quasi-Random Input Model

The particular kind of finite source input that we will consider here is often called a quasi-random input (as opposed to a completely random or Poisson input). We say that a finite number K of sources generate quasi-random input if (1) the probability that any particular source generates a request in an interval $(t, t + h)$ is $vh + o(h)$ when the source is eligible to generate a new request at time t, and (2) all sources act independently of the states of any other sources. It follows from this definition that if a particular source is eligible at time t, the distribution of the interval from t until the source generates a job is exponential with mean v^{-1}. Then it is not difficult to show (Exercise 3.9.4) that the merged traffic from the K independent sources is a birth process with rate

$$\lambda(n) = \begin{cases} (K - n)v, & 0 \leq n \leq K \\ 0, & n > K. \end{cases} \qquad (3.162)$$

We assume a single server and the service time S is exponentially distributed with mean $1/\mu$. Then the number of jobs, $N(t)$, found in the server at time t is a birth-and-death process with the birth rate (3.162) and the death rate

$$\mu(n) = \mu, \qquad n \geq 1. \qquad (3.163)$$

The quantity $\mathcal{S}$ of (3.100) is, in this case, a finite sum of $K + 1$ terms. For later convenience we write the explicit dependency of $\mathcal{S}$ and p_n on the population size K, thus denoting them as $\mathcal{S}(K)$ and $p_n(K)$, respectively:

$$p_0^{-1}(K) = \mathcal{S}(K) = \sum_{n=0}^{K} \frac{K!}{(K - n)!r^n} \qquad (3.164)$$

and

$$p_n(K) = \frac{K!}{(K - n)!r^n} p_0(K), \qquad 0 \leq n \leq K, \qquad (3.165)$$

where r is defined by (3.152). By defining the function $F(x, n)$ by

$$F(x, n) = 1 + nx + n(n - 1)x^2 + \cdots + n!x^n, \qquad (3.166)$$

we can write $p_0^{-1}(K)$ as

$$p_0^{-1}(K) = F(r^{-1}, K). \qquad (3.167)$$

The function $F(x, n)$ is easily computed from the recursive relation

$$F(x, 0) = 1, \qquad (3.168)$$

$$F(x, n) = 1 + nxF(x, n - 1). \qquad (3.169)$$

We derive below an alternative expression for $p_0(K)$, which is suited for the numerical calculation when we use a Poisson distribution table. Let $P(k; \lambda)$ denote the Poisson distribution with mean λ, and let $Q(k; \lambda)$

be its cumulative distribution:

$$P(k;\lambda) = \frac{\lambda^k}{k!} e^{-\lambda}, \qquad 0 \le k < \infty; \tag{3.170}$$

$$Q(k;\lambda) = \sum_{i=0}^{k} P(i;\lambda), \qquad 0 \le k < \infty. \tag{3.171}$$

The Poisson distribution plotted in Fig. 3.4 corresponds to a group of distributions $P(k;\lambda)$ for $\lambda = 0.5, 1, 2, 3, 4, 8, 12,$ and 16. Figure 3.28 shows the curves $Q(k;\lambda)$ for the same set of parameter values λ. Then by rearranging (3.165), we obtain the following formula:

$$p_n(K) = \frac{P(K - n; r)}{Q(K; r)}, \qquad 0 \le n \le K. \tag{3.172}$$

The last result shows that the number of eligible sources (or the number of terminals in the user-response-time phase), $j = K - n$, has a *truncated Poisson distribution.*

The utilization factor and throughput of the server are (see Exercise 3.9.5)

$$\rho(K) = \text{utilization} = 1 - p_0(K) = \frac{Q(K - 1; r)}{Q(K; r)} \tag{3.173}$$

and

$$\lambda_t(K) = \text{throughput} = \mu\rho(K). \tag{3.174}$$

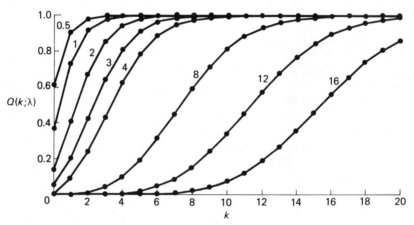

Fig. 3.28   The cumulative distribution $Q(k, \lambda)$ of the Poisson distributions for $\lambda = 0.5,$ 1, 2, 3, 4, 8, 12, and 16.

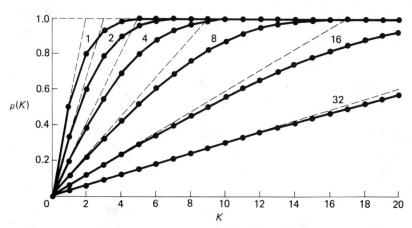

Fig. 3.29   The server utilization $\rho(K)$ versus the population size K for $r = 1, 2, 4, 8, 16,$ and 32.

Figure 3.29 illustrates the utilization $\rho(K)$ versus K for different values of the parameter r. The measure of performance perceived by the individual terminal users is the system response time. By denoting the normalized response time of (3.153) by $Y(K)$, we have

$$Y(K) = \frac{K}{1 - p_0(K)} - r. \tag{3.175}$$

A substitution of $p_0(K)$ of (3.172) into the last equation yields

$$Y(K) = \frac{K}{1 - \dfrac{P(K;r)}{Q(K;r)}} - r = \frac{KQ(K;r)}{Q(K-1;r)} - r. \tag{3.176}$$

We can also derive the following recurrence equation for $Y(K)$ (see Exercise 3.9.6):

$$Y(1) = 1; \tag{3.177a}$$

$$Y(K) = K - \frac{r(K-1)}{Y(K-1) + r}. \tag{3.177b}$$

Figure 3.30 plots $Y(K)$ versus K for different values of the parameter r. From the (normalized) mean response time of (3.176) and the throughput (3.174), we can obtain the following simple expression for the expected number of jobs found in the system:

$$\bar{N} = \lambda_t(K) \cdot \frac{Y(K)}{\mu} = K - \frac{rQ(K-1;r)}{Q(K;r)}. \tag{3.178}$$

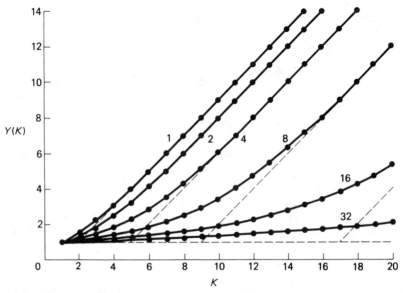

Fig. 3.30 The normalized mean response time $Y(K)$ versus the population size K for $r = 1, 2, 4, 8, 16$, and 32.

The last expression could, of course, be obtained from the probability distribution (3.172) (see Exercise 3.9.9).

Now let us turn our attention to the derivation of the waiting-time distribution function $F_W(x)$. The queue size distribution of direct relevance to this purpose is not the time-average distribution $\{p_n\}$ (3.172) but the distribution $\{a_n\}$ seen by arriving requests. Recall that in a Poisson input model, these two distributions are identical (see Exercise 3.8.7). This property no longer holds for the quasi-random input. Fortunately, however, a simple relation can be found between the distributions $\{p_n\}$ and $\{a_n\}$, as we shall see below. Over a long time interval $(t, t + \tau)$ throughout which statistical equilibrium is to prevail, the average number of requests that arrive when the system is in state n (that is, when n requests are waiting for service or in service and $K - n$ terminals are in the user-response-time phase) is given by $\lambda(n)\tau p_n(K)$. As $\tau \to \infty$, the proportion of arriving jobs that find the system in state n is, therefore, given by

$$a_n(K) = \frac{\lambda(n)\tau p_n(K)}{\sum_{i=0}^{K} \lambda(i)\tau p_i(K)}$$

$$= \frac{\lambda(n)p_n(K)}{\sum_{i=0}^{K} \lambda(i)p_i(K)}, \qquad 0 \le n \le K - 1. \qquad (3.179)$$

Note that the last expression holds for any queueing system with state-dependent birth (or arrival) process, not just for the model under discussion. A simple substitution of (3.162) into (3.179) yields

$$a_n(K) = \frac{(K - n)p_n(K)}{\sum_{i=0}^{K} (K - i)p_i(K)}, \qquad 0 \le n \le K - 1. \qquad (3.180)$$

By substituting (3.165) or (3.172) into (3.180), we obtain a surprisingly simple result (Exercise 3.9.7):

$$a_n(K) = p_n(K - 1), \qquad 0 \le n \le K - 1. \qquad (3.181)$$

The last result may be interpreted as follows. The state distribution seen by arriving requests is the same as the distribution that would be observed at a *randomly chosen instant* if that particular source were not contributing to the system load. To calculate the waiting-time distribution $F_W(X)$, we write its complement as

$$F_W^c(x) = P[W > x] = \sum_{n=1}^{K-1} a_n(K)F_W^c(x \mid n)$$

$$= \sum_{n=1}^{K-1} p_n(K - 1)F_W^c(x \mid n), \qquad (3.182)$$

where $F_W^c(x \mid n)$ is the complementary distribution function of waiting time given that $(n - 1)$ requests are waiting in queue and one request is in service (see (3.117)).

$$F_W^c(x \mid n) = P[W > x \mid n]$$

$$= e^{-\mu x} \sum_{i=0}^{n-1} \frac{(\mu x)^i}{i!}$$

$$= Q(n - 1; \mu x), \qquad (3.183)$$

where the Q function is defined by (3.171). On substituting (3.172) and (3.183) into (3.182), we have the following expression for the waiting-time distribution function:

$$F_W(x) = 1 - \frac{1}{Q(K - 1; r)} \sum_{i=0}^{K-2} P(K - 2 - i; r)Q(i; \mu x)$$

$$= 1 - \frac{Q(K - 2; r + \mu x)}{Q(K - 1; r)}, \qquad x \ge 0 \qquad (3.184)$$

where we used the following formula that holds between $P(k; \lambda)$ and $Q(k; \lambda)$ (Exercise 3.9.8):

$$\sum_{k'=0}^{k} P(k - k'; \lambda_1)Q(k'; \lambda_2) = Q(k; \lambda_1 + \lambda_2). \qquad (3.185)$$

Formula (3.184) shows that the waiting-time distribution can be numerically obtained from a Poisson distribution table. Note that the cumulative Poisson distribution can be expressed as (see Exercise 3.9.8):

$$Q(k : \lambda) = \sum_{i=0}^{k} \frac{\lambda^i}{i!} e^{-\lambda} = \frac{1}{k!} \int_{\lambda}^{\infty} e^{-y} y^k \, dy$$

$$= \int_{\lambda}^{\infty} P(k : y) \, dy. \tag{3.186}$$

In order to obtain the distribution function of the system response time T, we merely need to convolve $F_W(x)$ and $f_S(x)$ (or $f_W(x)$ and $F_S(x)$), and we find, after some algebraic manipulation,

$$F_T(x) = F_W(x) \circledast f_S(x)$$

$$= 1 - \frac{Q(K - 1; r + \mu x)}{Q(K - 1; r)}, \qquad x \geq 0. \tag{3.187}$$

The probability density function of the response time is therefore given by

$$f_T(x) = \frac{\mu P(K - 1; r + \mu x)}{Q(K - 1; r)}, \qquad x \geq 0. \tag{3.188}$$

Exercises

3.9.4 Based on the definition of the quasi-random input, show that the merged traffic from the K independent sources is a birth process with rate given by Eq. (3.162).

3.9.5 Let $p_0(K)$ be defined by (3.164). Show that $p_0(K)$ can be obtained by the recursive relation

$$p_0(0) = 1;$$

$$p_0^{-1}(K) = 1 + \frac{K}{r} p_0^{-1}(K - 1), \qquad K \geq 1.$$

Then derive the expressions for the server utilization as given in Eq. (3.174).

3.9.6 Derive the recursive relation for the normalized response time $Y(K)$ given by (3.177).

3.9.7 For $\lambda(n) = (K - n)\nu$, derive the formula (3.181):

$$a_n(K) = p_n(K - 1), \qquad 0 \leq n \leq K - 1.$$

Let the birth rate be now given by

$$\lambda(n) = f(K - n)$$

where $f(\bullet)$ is an arbitrary function. What can you say about the relationship between a_n and p_n?

3.9.8 Show the following properties of $Q(k : \lambda)$.

a) $\displaystyle\sum_{k'=0}^{k} P(k - k'; \lambda_1)Q(k'; \lambda_2) = Q(k; \lambda_1 + \lambda_2)$

b) $\displaystyle Q(k; \lambda) = \int_{\lambda}^{\infty} P(k; y)\, dy$

c) $\displaystyle Q(k; \lambda) = \frac{\lambda Q(k - 1; \lambda)}{k + \lambda + 1} + \frac{(k + 1)Q(k + 1; \lambda)}{k + \lambda + 1}$

d) $\displaystyle\sum_{j=0}^{k-1} Q(j; \lambda) = kQ(k; \lambda) - \lambda Q(k - 1; \lambda)$

e) $\displaystyle\int_{\lambda}^{\infty} Q(k - 1; y)\, dy = kQ(k; \lambda) - \lambda Q(k - 1; \lambda)$

3.9.9 Derive $\bar{N}$ of (3.178) from the probability distribution (3.172). *Hint:* Use the property that the mean value of a nonnegative discrete random variable is

$$\sum_{n=0}^{\infty} (1 - F_n),$$

where F_n is the cumulative distribution.

3.9.10 Show that $F_W(x)$ is also given as

$$F_W(x) = 1 - \frac{p_0(K)}{\rho(K)} \frac{Q(K - 2; \mu x + r)}{P(K; r)}.$$

3.9.11 Show the derivation of the system response time distribution (3.187).

3.9.12 *Multiserver station.* Replace the single server of rate μ by m-parallel servers, each of which has completion rate μ, that is,

$$\mu(n) = \min\{n, m\}\mu; \qquad 0 \le n \le K.$$

a) Show that the probability $p_0(K)$ that all of the m servers are idle is given by

$$p_0^{-1}(K) = \sum_{n=0}^{m-1} \frac{K!}{(K - n)!n!r^n} + \sum_{n=m}^{K} \frac{K!}{(K - n)!m!m^{n-m}r^n}$$

$$= \sum_{n=0}^{m-1} \frac{\binom{K}{n}}{r^n} + \frac{\binom{K}{m}}{r^m} F\left(\frac{1}{mr}, K - m\right),$$

where $F(x, n)$ is defined by (3.166). Show then that $p_0(K)$ satisfies the recurrence formula

$$p_0^{-1}(K) = 1 + \frac{K}{mr} p_0^{-1}(K - 1) + \frac{K}{r} \sum_{i=0}^{m-1} \frac{\binom{K - 1}{i}}{r^i} \left[\frac{1}{i + 1} - \frac{1}{m}\right].$$

b) Show that the distribution of the number of jobs in the m-parallel server is

$$
p_n(K) = \begin{cases}
\binom{K}{n} r^{-n} p_0(K), & 0 \le n \le m \\[2mm]
\dfrac{P(K - n; mr)}{P(K; mr)} \dfrac{m^m}{m!} p_0(K), & m \le n \le K \\[2mm]
0, & n > K.
\end{cases}
$$

c) Show that the complementary waiting-time distribution is given by

$$
F_W^c(x) = \sum_{n=0}^{K-m-1} p_{m+n}(K - 1) F_W^c(x \mid m + n),
$$

where

$$
F_W^c(x \mid m + n) = e^{-m\mu x} \sum_{i=0}^{n} \frac{(m\mu x)^i}{i!}
$$

$$
= Q(n; m\mu x).
$$

d) Show that the distribution function and probability density function of waiting time are given by

$$
F_W(x) = 1 - \frac{m^m}{m!} p_0(K - 1) \frac{Q\!\left(K - m - 1; m\mu\!\left(x + \dfrac{1}{\nu}\right)\right)}{P(K - 1; mr)}
$$

and

$$
f_W(x) = F_W(0)\delta(x) + \frac{m^m \mu}{(m - 1)!} p_0(K - 1) \frac{P\!\left(K - m - 1; m\mu\!\left(x + \dfrac{1}{\nu}\right)\right)}{P(K - 1; mr)}.
$$

e) Derive the distribution function and probability density function of response time.

3.9.3 Approximate Analysis and Graphical Interpretations

The main results of the previous section are Eqs. (3.172), (3.184), and (3.187): (1) The number of customers in the service station is distributed according to a truncated Poisson distribution, and (2) the distribution functions of waiting time and response time can be expressed in terms of the cumulative Poisson distribution. The numerical evaluation of these solutions is rather straightforward and does not pose any computational problem. In this section, however, we derive approximation expressions for these solutions, which will provide us with additional insights as to how the system behaves for given values of K, μ, and ν. We will also introduce simple graphical analysis methods based on the concept of *fluid approximation*. We begin with discussions on relations between the Poisson distribution and the normal distribution.

The normal approximation of a Poisson distribution

In Chapter 2 we saw that the normal distribution may be used as an approximation to the binomial distribution (see Exercise 2.7.4). Recall also how the Poisson distribution was derived as a limiting case of the binomial distribution. It then follows that when the value of λ is large, the Poisson distribution may be approximated by the normal distribution with mean λ and variance λ. This means that the probability distribution $P(x; \lambda)$ and the cumulative distribution function $Q(x; \lambda)$ may be written as

$$P(x; \lambda) = \frac{\lambda^x}{x!} e^{-\lambda} \simeq \frac{1}{\sqrt{2\pi\lambda}} \exp\left\{\frac{(x + \frac{1}{2} - \lambda)^2}{2\lambda}\right\} \qquad (3.189)$$

and

$$Q(x; \lambda) = e^{-\lambda} \sum_{i=0}^{x} \frac{\lambda^i}{i!} \simeq \Phi\left(\frac{x + \frac{1}{2} - \lambda}{\sqrt{\lambda}}\right), \qquad (3.190)$$

where Φ is the cumulative distribution of the standard normal distribution:

$$\Phi(x) = \frac{1}{\sqrt{2\pi}} \int_{-\infty}^{x} \exp\left\{\frac{-t^2}{2}\right\} dt. \qquad (3.191)$$

The term $\frac{1}{2}$ in (3.189) is added in view of the fact that $P(x; \lambda)$ takes its maximum value approximately at $X = \lambda - \frac{1}{2}$.

Let us assume that $r \gg 1$ and $K - r \gg 1$, where r is the ratio of the mean user response time to mean service time as defined in (3.152). Then $Q(K - 1; r) \simeq 1$ and the distribution (3.172) may be written as

$$p_n(K) \simeq \frac{1}{\sqrt{2\pi r}} \exp\left\{-\frac{[n - (K - r + \frac{1}{2})]^2}{2r}\right\}, \qquad 0 \le n \le K, \qquad (3.192)$$

which shows that the number of customers in the service station is approximately normally distributed with mean $K - r$ and variance r. In Fig. 3.31 we plot both the exact solution (3.172)—the set of discrete arrows—and the approximate solution (3.192)—the dashed curve—for the case with $r = 8$ and $K = 20$.

The approximation formula (3.190) could be also applied to the distribution function of waiting time given by Eq. (3.184). The resulting approximation result is rather uninviting. We adopt, instead, a different approximation formula: If x is approximately normally distributed with

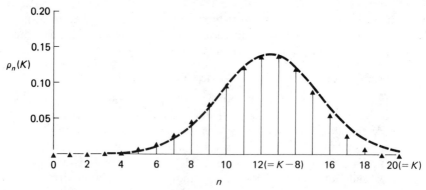

Fig. 3.31 The exact solution (3.172)—the set of discrete probabilities shown by the arrows—and the approximate solution (3.192)—the continuous probability density function shown by the dashed curve—of the queue size distribution when $r = 8$ and $K = 20$.

mean λ and variance λ, $y = 2\sqrt{x}$ is also approximately normally distributed with mean $2\sqrt{\lambda}$ and variance 1. It follows that the cumulative distribution function may be approximated by

$$Q(x; \lambda) \simeq \Phi(2(\sqrt{x + \tfrac{1}{2}} - \sqrt{\lambda})), \qquad (3.193)$$

so that from (3.184) we obtain

$$F_W(x) = 1 - \frac{Q(K - 2; r + \mu x)}{Q(K - 1; r)}$$

$$\simeq 1 - \Phi(2(\sqrt{K - 2 + \tfrac{1}{2}} - \sqrt{r + \mu x}))$$

$$= \Phi(2(\sqrt{r + \mu x} - \sqrt{K - 2 + \tfrac{1}{2}})). \qquad (3.194)$$

In Fig. 3.32, we plot the function (3.194) (dashed curves) for the case of $K = 20$ and $r = 1, 2, 4, 8$, and 16. Also shown are the exact solutions (3.184) (solid curves). An approximate expression for the response-time distribution can be obtained by substituting the formula (3.193) into (3.187).

The fluid approximation

The mean number of customers in the server is approximately $K - r$, since the normal distribution is symmetric around its center. If we were interested only in the approximate mean value, we could have obtained the same result more directly via a *fluid approximation model:* We approximate the flow of customers by a flow of fluid, which is tantamount to ignoring the random fluctuation in the arrival and departure processes.

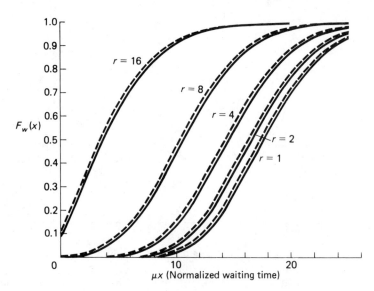

Fig. 3.32 The exact solution (3.184) (solid curves) and the approximate solution (3.194) (dashed curves) of the normalized waiting-time distribution function when $K = 20$ and $r = 1, 2, 4, 8,$ and 16.

The number of customers, $\cdot n$, in the service station is now viewed as the amount of fluid volume, x, contained in some reservoir. The rate of *flow in* corresponds to the arrival rate $\lambda(x)$, and the rate of *flow out* is given by the departure rate $\mu(x)$, which are given, from (3.162) and (3.163), as

$$\lambda(x) = \max\{(K - x)\nu, 0\}, \qquad 0 \le x < \infty \tag{3.195}$$

and

$$\mu(x) = \max\{x, \mu\}, \qquad 0 \le x < \infty. \tag{3.196}$$

We plot these two curves in Fig. 3.33, and find that the intersection point $P = (K - r, \mu)$ is a *stable point*. If $x < K - r$, the inflow rate exceeds the outflow rate; thus x tends to increase. On the other hand, if $x > K - r$, the outflow dominates and x will decrease. Therefore, these exists some force of self-regulating *central-restoring tendency* toward the center P. This force makes P a stable operating point of the system.

    The approximate value of the mean response time $\bar{T}$ is also easily obtained from the diagram. The mean flow rate at the operating point P is μ; thus Little's formula takes the form

$$\mu\bar{T} = \bar{x} \tag{3.197}$$

from which we derive the following graphical solution for $\bar{T}$. Draw a line from the origin to the point P. Let Q be the intersection point of the line

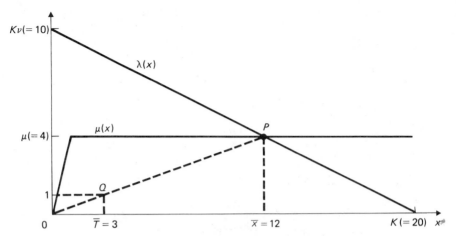

Fig. 3.33 The graphical analysis based on the fluid approximation.

OP and a horizontal line of height unity. The abscissa value of Q corresponds to $\bar{T}$. Needless to say, the unit of the time and that of the flow rate must be consistent in this analysis. In Fig. 3.33, we illustrate the case in which $K = 20$, $\mu = 4 \, [\text{sec}^{-1}]$, and $\nu = 0.5 \, [\text{sec}^{-1}]$. The approximate solutions are then $\bar{x} = 20 - (4/0.5) = 12$ and $\bar{T} = 3 \, [\text{sec}]$.

The fluid approximation presented above may be called a first-order approximation model, since we used only the first-order statistics (i.e., the mean values). If we wish to take into account the effects of the second-order statistics (i.e., the variances of interarrival times and interdeparture times), we must construct a second-order approximation model. A diffusion approximation model serves such a purpose (see the section on Discussion and Further Reading).

Exercises

3.9.13 Refer to the example of the fluid approximation analysis discussed in conjunction with Fig. 3.33. Obtain exact solutions of $\bar{N}$ and $\bar{T}$. How will the accuracy of the fluid approximation change, as K and r change?

3.10 MULTIPLE RESOURCE MODELS: NETWORKS OF QUEUES

Most of the queueing models discussed thus far have dealt with a single service station.* Many of the systems that we wish to model in practical

---

* We distinguish between the terms "server" and "service station" (or "service center"): A station may have multiple servers, but possesses a single queue (or waiting line). The $M/M/m$ and $M/M/\infty$ systems, for example, are single service stations with multiple servers.

applications are *multiple resource systems,* in which different stations operate asynchronously and concurrently. Such an example is a multi-programmed computer system in which CPU's and I/O processors (or channels) run in parallel. A *queueing network* (or network of queues) representation provides us with a basic mathematical framework in dealing with resource allocation/contention problems in such systems.

3.10.1   An Open Queueing Network with Exponential Servers

Let us assume that a queueing network consists of M separate service stations, labeled $1, 2, \ldots, M$, each of which has its own queue. The *network topology* we assume here is quite general: We can view a *closed queueing network* (such as that shown in Fig. 3.34a) as a *graph $G = (V, E)$*, where $V = \{1, 2, \ldots, M\}$ is the set of vertices (or nodes) representing the M service stations (including the corresponding queues), and $E = V \times V$ is the set of edges (or arcs) that link the stations.* We define the multidimensional (or vector) process

$$\mathbf{N}(t) = [N_1(t), N_2(t), \ldots, N_i(t), \ldots, N_M(t)], \qquad (3.198)$$

where $N_i(t)$ represents the number of customers (waiting or in service) at station i at time t. In a closed network there are no external arrivals or departures; thus the population size

$$N = \|\mathbf{N}(t)\| = \sum_{i=1}^{M} N_i(t) \qquad (3.199)$$

is a constant.

    An *open queueing network,* on the other hand, is a network with a "source" of infinite population and a "sink" (or "destination") which absorbs all the customers who are departing from the network proper, as illustrated in Fig. 3.34(b). We make the following set of assumptions.

    1. The stream of customers generated at the source node is a birth process with rate $\lambda(N)$, when $\|\mathbf{N}(t)\| = N$. An arriving customer goes first to station i with probability q_{si}, $1 \le i \le M$. Then, generalizing property 3 of the Poisson process discussed in Section 3.3, we find that the substreams into the individual stations are statistically independent birth processes (or queue-dependent Poisson processes) with rates $\lambda(N)q_{si}$, $1 \le i \le M$.

    2. The service demand of a customer at station i is drawn from the exponential distribution of mean $\bar{S}_i$, $1 \le i \le M$. The processing capacity

---

* $E = V \times V$ (the Cartesian product of V with itself) is the set of all ordered pairs of the form $\langle i, j \rangle$ where $i \in V$ and $j \in V$. The element $\langle i, j \rangle$ represents the path from station i to station j.

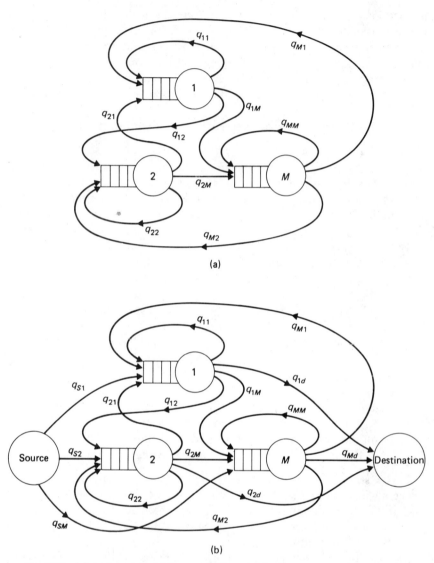

Fig. 3.34 (a) A closed queueing network and (b) an open queueing network.

of station i can be dependent on the queue size $n_i = N_i(t)$ found in this station at a given time, and we denote its functional form by $C_i(n_i)$, $1 \leq i \leq M$. Then the completion rate at station i is also queue-dependent and is given by

$$\mu_i(n_i) = \frac{C_i(n_i)}{\bar{S}_i}. \tag{3.200}$$

3. The queue discipline at each station can be any work-conserving one.

4. The routing of a customer is governed by a first-order Markov chain: The probability that a customer departing station i goes next to station j is given by q_{ij}, $j = 1, 2, \ldots, M$ and d (d = destination). We assume that the Markov chain is irreducible.

Then the vector process $\mathbf{N}(t)$ can be viewed as a multidimensional analog of the birth-and-death process and we can define $\mathbf{N}(t)$ as the *state* of the network at time t. Let $P(\mathbf{n}; t)$ be the probability that the system is in state $\mathbf{n} = [n_1, n_2, \ldots, n_M]$ at time t:

$$P(\mathbf{n}; t) = P[\mathbf{N}(t) = \mathbf{n}]. \tag{3.201}$$

By following exactly the same sequence of steps as that developed in Section 3.8.1, we find that the steady-state distribution

$$P[\mathbf{n}] = \lim_{t \to \infty} P(\mathbf{n}; t) \tag{3.202}$$

is unique, and must satisfy the following set of linear difference equations (see Exercise 3.10.1):

$$\lambda(N)P[\mathbf{n}] - \sum_{j=1}^{M} q_{jd}\mu_j(n_j + 1)P[\mathbf{n} + \mathbf{1}_j]$$

$$= \lambda(N - 1) \sum_{i=1}^{M} q_{si}P[\mathbf{n} - \mathbf{1}_i] - \sum_{i=1}^{M} \mu_i(n_i)P[\mathbf{n}]$$

$$+ \sum_{i=1}^{M} \sum_{j=1}^{M} q_{ji}\mu_j(n_j + 1 - \delta_{ij})P[\mathbf{n} + \mathbf{1}_j - \mathbf{1}_i] \tag{3.203}$$

and

$$\lambda(0)P[\mathbf{0}] - \sum_{j=1}^{M} q_{jd}\mu_j(1)P[\mathbf{1}_j] = 0, \tag{3.204}$$

where the random variable N is the total population size found in the open network, that is, $N = \sum_{i=1}^{M} n_i$; δ_{ij} is Kronecker's delta ($\delta_{ij} = 1$ when $i = j$ and $\delta_{ij} = 0$ otherwise); $\mathbf{0}$ is the vector of all components being zero; $\mathbf{1}_j$ is the jth unit vector:

$$\mathbf{1}_j = [0, \ldots, 0, \overset{j\text{th}}{1}, 0, \ldots, 0]. \tag{3.205}$$

Note that Eq. (3.203) must hold for all *feasible* values of the state vector $\mathbf{n} = [n_1, n_2, \ldots, n_M]$. This equation is a multidimensional analog of the balance equation (3.93). Similarly, Eq. (3.204) corresponds to (3.95). The balance equation (3.203) is too complex for us to derive the solution for $P[\mathbf{n}]$ directly. Thus, we seek a way to break up (3.203) and obtain a set of simpler relations similar to the recurrence equation (3.96). To that end, we introduce the quantities $\{e_i\}$ that are the solutions for the following linear equations:

$$e_i = q_{si} + \sum_{j=1}^{M} e_j q_{ji}, \qquad 1 \le i \le M \tag{3.206}$$

or, equivalently,

$$q_{si} = e_i - \sum_{j=1}^{M} e_j q_{ji}, \qquad 1 \le i \le M. \tag{3.207}$$

By substituting the latter expression into the term q_{si} on the right-hand side of expression (3.203), we find that the balance equation now takes the form (see Exercise 3.10.2):

$$\mathscr{A}(\mathbf{n}) = \sum_{i=1}^{M} \left\{ \mathscr{B}_i(\mathbf{n}) - \sum_{j=1}^{M} q_{ji} \mathscr{B}_j(\mathbf{n} + \mathbf{1}_j - \mathbf{1}_i) \right\} \tag{3.208}$$

where

$$\mathscr{A}(\mathbf{n}) = \lambda(N)P[\mathbf{n}] - \sum_{j-1}^{M} q_{jd} \mu_j(n_j + 1)P[\mathbf{n} + \mathbf{1}_j] \tag{3.209}$$

and

$$\mathscr{B}_i(\mathbf{n}) = \lambda(N-1)e_i P[\mathbf{n} - \mathbf{1}_i] - \mu_i(n)P[\mathbf{n}], \qquad 1 \le i \le M. \tag{3.210}$$

By inspection it is not difficult to see that

$$\mathscr{B}_i(\mathbf{n}) = 0 \quad \text{for all} \quad \mathbf{n} \quad \text{and} \quad 1 \le i \le M \tag{3.211}$$

is a multidimensional analog of the recurrence equation (3.96). We are thus tempted to *conjecture* that Eq. (3.211) holds. If this is indeed the case, it implies that (see Exercise 3.10.2):

$$\mathscr{A}(\mathbf{n}) = 0 \quad \text{for all} \quad \mathbf{n}. \tag{3.212}$$

As a consequence, the balance equation (3.208) is also met! Thus, we see that the recurrence equation (3.211) is a *sufficient* (but not necessary) condition for the balance equation (3.208) (hence, (3.203) as well) to hold. The reader is urged to examine the implications of Eqs. (3.208), (3.211), and (3.212) (see Exercise 3.10.3).

Equation (3.211) can be written as

$$\mu_i(n_i)P[\mathbf{n}] = e_i \lambda(N-1)P[\mathbf{n} - \mathbf{1}_i] \quad \text{for all} \quad \mathbf{n} \quad \text{and} \quad 1 \le i \le M, \tag{3.213}$$

from which we immediately obtain the solution

$$P[\mathbf{n}] = P[\mathbf{0}]\Lambda(N) \prod_{i=1}^{M} \frac{e_i^{n_i}}{M_i(n_i)} \qquad (3.214)$$

where

$$N = \|\mathbf{n}\| = \sum_{i=1}^{M} n_i. \qquad (3.215)$$

The functions $\Lambda(\bullet)$ and $M_i(\bullet)$ are the same as those of (3.98) and (3.99):

$$\Lambda(N) = \prod_{n=1}^{N} \lambda(n-1); \qquad (3.216)$$

$$M_i(n_i) = \prod_{n=1}^{n_i} \mu_i(n), \qquad 1 \leq i \leq M. \qquad (3.217)$$

By substituting the defining relation (3.200), we have an alternative expression for $P[\mathbf{n}]$:

$$P[\mathbf{n}] = P[\mathbf{0}]\Lambda(N) \prod_{i=1}^{M} \frac{\overline{W}_i^{n_i}}{\Gamma_i(n_i)}, \qquad (3.218)$$

where the new parameter $\overline{W}_i$ is defined by*

$$\overline{W}_i = e_i \overline{S}_i \qquad (3.219)$$

and

$$\Gamma_i(n_i) = \prod_{n=1}^{n_i} C_i(n). \qquad (3.220)$$

Now a few remarks concerning the solution (3.218) and some observations are in order. In Section 2.9, we studied the properties of an ergodic Markov chain: One of the important results was the uniqueness of a steady-state solution (if it exists). The process $\mathbf{N}(t)$ of (3.198) is a continuous-time and multidimensional version of a Markov sequence, and it is called an *ergodic Markov process* if $P[\mathbf{0}]$ is nonzero (that is, the system occasionally empties), or, equivalently, if the following sum converges:

$$\mathcal{G} = \sum_{\mathbf{n}} \Lambda(N) \prod_{i=1}^{M} \frac{\overline{W}_i^{n_i}}{\Gamma_i(n_i)} < \infty, \qquad (3.221)$$

which is a generalization of (3.100) and the sum is taken over all feasible states $\mathbf{n}$. Since the steady state of an ergodic Markov process is unique,

---

* $\overline{W}_i$ here has no relation with waiting time W defined earlier.

the probability distribution (3.214) is indeed the unique solution of the original balance equations (3.203) and (3.204).

One of the key steps in the discussions leading to the solution (3.214) was the introduction of the parameters e_i's defined by (3.206). From the inspection of (3.206) it is not difficult to find that

e_i = Expected number of visits that a customer makes to station i during
the customer's lifetime in the network.   (3.222)

We can also recognize $e_i\lambda(N)$ as the total arrival rate to station i when the network population is N, out of which $q_{si}\lambda(N)$ is the contribution due to external arrivals, and $e_j q_{ji}\lambda(N)$ is the arrival rate of those customers who come from station j, $1 \le j \le M$. We can then interpret the parameters $\overline{W}_i$ of (3.219) as follows:

$\overline{W}_i$ = Expected *total* work (service demand) that a customer places on
server i during the customer's lifetime in the network.   (3.223)

Note that the transition probabilities $\{q_{ij}\}$ do not explicitly appear in the solution expression (3.218); the only workload parameters that appear are the set of $\overline{W}_i$'s. In fact we can remove assumption (4) made at the beginning of this section. That is, we can assume a Markov chain of *arbitrary order* for the job routing behavior, and yet we obtain the same solution as (3.219). For further details, the reader is referred to Kobayashi and Reiser (1975) and Kobayashi (1978).

Let us consider a special case in which the arrival rate is independent of the network population:

$$\lambda(N) = \lambda \quad \text{for all} \quad N = \|\mathbf{n}\| \ge 0.^* \qquad (3.224)$$

Then

$$\Lambda(N) = \lambda^N = \prod_{i=1}^{M} \lambda^{n_i}. \qquad (3.225)$$

The substitution of the last expression into (3.214) or (3.218) leads to the following simple product form (see Exercise 3.10.4):

$$P[\mathbf{n}] = \prod_{i=1}^{M} p_i(n_i), \qquad (3.226)$$

where $p_i(n_i)$ is the marginal distribution of the variable n_i:

$$p_i(n_i) = \frac{(\lambda e_i)^{n_i}}{M_i(n_i)} p_i(0), \qquad (3.227)$$

---

* $\|\mathbf{n}\|$ is, as defined in Eq. (3.199), the sum of all the elements of the vector $\mathbf{n}$, i.e., $\|\mathbf{n}\| = \sum_{i=1}^{M} n_i$.

$$p_i^{-1}(0) = \sum_{n=0}^{\infty} \frac{(\lambda e_i)^n}{M_i(n)}. \qquad (3.228)$$

The result (3.226) is often referred to as *Jackson's decomposition theorem* since it was first shown by J. R. Jackson (1963) that the joint distribution is decomposable into the product of the M marginal distributions. This result suggests that the individual stations behave as if they were separate Markovian queueing systems with Poisson inputs with rates λe_i and queue-dependent processing rates $\mu_i(n_i)$, $1 \le i \le M$.

Exercises

3.10.1 Derive the balance equation (3.203) following the steps indicated in the text. Also show that a rearrangement of Eq. (3.203) can be interpreted as

The rate of transitions *out of* state **n**
                    = the rate of transition into state **n** for all state **n**.

3.10.2 Show the equivalency of Eqs. (3.203) and (3.208).

3.10.3 Figure 3.35 shows the state-transition-rate diagram in which the *i*th and

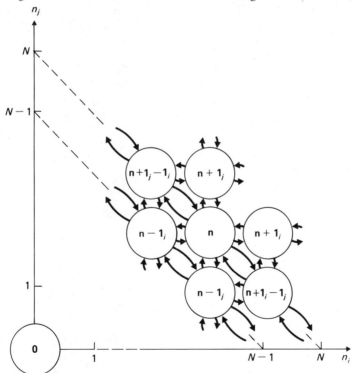

Fig. 3.35 The state-transition-rate diagram.

jth components of the state vector $\mathbf{n}$ are in the x-axis and y-axis, respectively. All states on any of $-45°$ lines correspond to the same network population size; that is, $\|\mathbf{n}\|$ = constant. Give interpretations of Eqs. (3.211) and (3.212) using this state-transition-rate diagram.

3.10.4 Show that when the arrival rate is independent of the network population, the joint distribution of $\mathbf{n}$ is given by (3.226). What is the value of $\mathscr{S}$ of (3.221) in this case?

3.10.2   A Closed Queueing Network

In many problems of practical interest, an infinite population model is inadequate or unrealistic. Thus we often deal with a closed network of queues in which the total number of jobs $N = \|\mathbf{n}\|$ remains constant. The time-sharing system model discussed in Section 3.9 is an example of a closed network. In that model, the set of user terminals can be viewed as a station with ample parallel servers; thus the system of Fig. 3.25 can be modeled as a closed queueing network with *two* stations. In this and the following sections, we maintain the same set of assumptions as assumptions 2, 3, and 4 made in Section 3.10.1. Of course we drop assumption 1, since we now have no external arrivals or departures. The system balance equation of (3.203) now takes the following simple form:

$$\sum_{i=1}^{M} \sum_{j=1}^{M} q_{ji}\mu_j(n_i + 1 - \delta_{ij})P[\mathbf{n} + \mathbf{1}_j - \mathbf{1}_i] - \sum_{i=1}^{M} \mu_i(n_i)P[\mathbf{n}] = 0. \quad (3.229)$$

Equation (3.206) now becomes

$$e_i = \sum_{j=1}^{M} e_j q_{ji} \quad (3.230)$$

or, equivalently,

$$1 = \sum_{j=1}^{M} \frac{e_j}{e_i} q_{ji}, \quad i = 1, 2, \ldots, M. \quad (3.231)$$

Now let us multiply (3.231) and $\mu_i(n_i)$ of (3.229), $i = 1, 2, \ldots, M$, obtaining

$$\sum_{i=1}^{M} \sum_{j=1}^{M} q_{ji}\left\{\mu_j(n_i + 1 - \delta_{ij})P[\mathbf{n} + \mathbf{1}_j - \mathbf{1}_i] - \frac{e_j}{e_i}\mu_i(n_i)P[\mathbf{n}]\right\} = 0. \quad (3.232)$$

Thus it is clear that if the recurrence equation

$$\mu_j(n_j + 1 - \delta_{ij})P[\mathbf{n} + \mathbf{1}_j - \mathbf{1}_i] = \frac{e_j}{e_i}\mu_i(n_i)P[\mathbf{n}] \quad (3.233)$$

holds for all $\mathbf{n}$ and $i, j = 1, 2, \ldots, M$, then the balance equation (3.232) is certainly satisfied. We can solve for $P[\mathbf{n}]$ from (3.233) (see Exercise

3.10.5) and obtain

$$P[\mathbf{n}] = \frac{1}{\mathscr{S}(N, M)} \prod_{i=1}^{M} \frac{e_i^{n_i}}{M_i(n_i)} \tag{3.234}$$

or, equivalently,

$$P[\mathbf{n}] = \frac{1}{\mathscr{S}(N, M)} \prod_{i=1}^{M} \frac{\overline{W}_i^{n_i}}{\Gamma_i(n_i)}, \tag{3.235}$$

where $\overline{W}_i$ and $\Gamma_i(n_i)$ were defined earlier by (3.219) and (3.220), respectively. The term $\mathscr{S}(N, M)$ is a normalization constant and is similar to $\mathscr{S}$ of (3.221):

$$\mathscr{S}(N, M) = \sum_{\mathbf{n} \in \mathscr{F}(N)} \prod_{i=1}^{M} \frac{\overline{W}_i^{n_i}}{\Gamma_i(n_i)}, \tag{3.236}$$

where the sum is taken over the set of feasible states defined by

$$\mathscr{F}(N) = \left\{ \mathbf{n} \mid n_i \geq 0 \quad \text{for all} \quad i = 1, 2, \ldots, M \quad \text{and} \quad \sum_{i=1}^{M} n_i = N \right\}. \tag{3.237}$$

Efficient methods for computing the sum (3.236) and related quantities will be discussed in the following section.

The parameters $\{e_i\}$ of (3.230) require an interpretation different from (3.222). The vector

$$\mathbf{e} = [e_1, e_2, \ldots, e_M] \tag{3.238}$$

is now the left eigenvector of the $M \times M$ Markov transition matrix $\mathbf{Q} = [q_{ij}]$ associated with the eigenvalue of unity:

$$\mathbf{e}\mathbf{Q} = \mathbf{e}. \tag{3.239}$$

Thus the solution for $\mathbf{e}$ is unique only to within a multiplicative constant. If we introduce an additional constraint

$$\sum_{i=1}^{M} e_i = 1, \tag{3.240}$$

then $\mathbf{e}$ represents the stationary distribution of the Markov chain and is given (see Eq. (2.257)) by

$$\mathbf{e} = \mathbf{1}[\mathbf{Q} + \mathbf{E} - \mathbf{I}]^{-1}. \tag{3.241}$$

Of course, by choosing a constraint different from (3.240), we can attach a different physical interpretation to the set of parameters e_i's and $\overline{W}_i$'s (see Exercise 3.10.6).

3.10.3   Computational Algorithms for Queueing Networks

The normalization constant

The number of terms to be summed for the evaluation of $\mathcal{S}(N, M)$ of (3.236) is given by

$$|\mathcal{F}(N)| = \binom{N + M - 1}{M - 1}$$

(see Exercise 3.10.7), which is too large to handle even for moderate values of M and N. Thus we should be interested in seeking an efficient way of computing the normalization factor $\mathcal{S}(N, M)$. Let us define the generating function (or the z-transform) of the sequence $\{1/\Gamma_i(n); \ n = 1, 2, 3, \ldots\}$ by

$$R_i(z) = \sum_{n=0}^{\infty} \frac{z^n}{\Gamma_i(n)}, \qquad 1 \le i \le M. \tag{3.242}$$

We then define $S_m(z)$ as the product of the m functions $R_i(\overline{W}_i z)$, $1 \le i \le m$:

$$S_m(z) = \prod_{i=1}^{m} R_i(\overline{W}_i z). \tag{3.243}$$

Define $\mathcal{S}(n, m)$ as the coefficient of the term z^n in $S_m(z)$:

$$\mathcal{S}(n, m) = \frac{1}{n!} \left[\frac{\partial^n}{\partial z^n} S_m(z) \right]_{z=0}. \tag{3.244}$$

It is not difficult to show that $\mathcal{S}(N, M)$ of (3.236) is, in fact, the value of $\mathcal{S}(n, m)$ of (3.244) evaluated for $n = N$ and $m = M$. By writing $S_m(z)$ as

$$S_m(z) = S_{m-1}(z) R_m(\overline{W}_m z) \tag{3.245}$$

and substituting this expression into (3.244), we obtain

$$\mathcal{S}(n, m) = \sum_{k=0}^{n} \mathcal{S}(n - k, m - 1) \frac{\overline{W}_m^k}{\Gamma_m(k)}. \tag{3.246}$$

This is a recurrence equation of the two-dimensional array $\mathcal{S}(n, m)$. The boundary conditions are

$$\mathcal{S}(0, m) = 1 \quad \text{for all} \quad m \ge 0 \tag{3.247a}$$

and

$$\mathcal{S}(n, 0) = \delta_{n,0} = \begin{cases} 1, & n = 0 \\ 0, & n > 0. \end{cases} \tag{3.247b}$$

We can show (Exercise 3.10.9) that the number of computations involved in the recursive formula (3.246) is substantially less than the computation efforts required in a brute-force enumeration.

The computational step (3.246) at $m = i$ will be further simplified if the processing rate of server i is independent of its queue size, that is,

$$C_i(n_i) = C_i \quad \text{for all} \quad n_i > 0. \tag{3.248}$$

Under this condition we have

$$\mathscr{S}(n, i) = \mathscr{S}(n, i - 1) + \tau_i \mathscr{S}(n - 1, i), \tag{3.249}$$

where the parameter τ_i is defined by

$$\tau_i = \frac{\overline{W}_i}{C_i} = \frac{e_i}{\mu_i}. \tag{3.250}$$

If all the M stations have constant processing rates (but not necessarily common), the evaluation of $\mathscr{S}(N, M)$ requires, in total, $(M - 1)N$ multiplications and additions.

The marginal distributions

We define the joint probability generating function of (3.235) by

$$
\begin{aligned}
Q(\mathbf{z}) &= E[z_1^{n_1} z_2^{n_2} \dots z_M^{n_M}] \\
&= \frac{1}{\mathscr{S}(N, M)} \sum_{\mathbf{n} \in \mathscr{F}(N)} \prod_{i=1}^{M} \frac{(\overline{W}_i z_i)^{n_i}}{\Gamma_i(n_i)} \\
&= \frac{1}{\mathscr{S}(N, M)} \frac{1}{N!} \left[\frac{\partial^N}{\partial \theta^N} \prod_{i=1}^{M} R_i(\overline{W}_i z_i \theta) \right]_{\theta=0}.
\end{aligned}
\tag{3.251}
$$

The last expression is obtained by recognizing that the set of coefficients of the terms θ^N correspond to the set $\mathscr{F}(N)$ of (3.237). In order to obtain the marginal distributions, we begin by considering the marginal distribution at the Mth station. We set $z_i = 1$, $1 \le i \le M - 1$, and $z_M = z$ in the above equation (Exercise 3.10.10):

$$
\begin{aligned}
Q_M(z) &= E[z^{n_M}] \\
&= \frac{1}{\mathscr{S}(N, M)} \frac{1}{N!} \left[\frac{\partial^N}{\partial \theta^N} \{ S_{M-1}(\theta) R_M(\overline{W}_M z \theta) \} \right]_{\theta=0} \tag{3.252} \\
&= \frac{1}{\mathscr{S}(N, M)} \sum_{n=0}^{N} \mathscr{S}(N - n, M - 1) \frac{(\overline{W}_M z)^n}{\Gamma_M(n)}.
\end{aligned}
$$

By inverting the probability generating function $Q_M(z)$ of (3.252), we obtain the marginal distribution of the number of customers in station M:

$$p_M(n) = \frac{\mathscr{S}(N - n, M - 1)}{\mathscr{S}(N, M)} \frac{\overline{W}_M^n}{\Gamma_M(n)}, \quad 0 \le n \le N. \tag{3.253}$$

Note that the values of $\mathscr{S}(N - n, M - 1)$ for $0 \le n \le N$ will be available by the time $\mathscr{S}(N, M)$ is to be computed by the recurrence formula (3.246). The marginal distribution at any other station can be obtained by relabeling the station numbers so that the service station of interest is designated as the Mth station, and by applying the computational algorithm to the renumbered network. If the service rate of station i is independent of the queue size, we can obtain an alternative expression, using the relation (3.249) as

$$p_i(n) = \frac{\{\mathscr{S}(N - n, M) - \tau_i \mathscr{S}(N - n - 1, M)\} \tau_i^n}{\mathscr{S}(N, M)}, \qquad 0 \le n \le N \quad (3.254)$$

for all $i = 1, 2, \ldots, M$. This is substantially simpler than the algorithm of (3.253).

Utilization and throughput

The utilization of station M is, by definition,

$$\rho_M = 1 - p_M(0) = 1 - \frac{\mathscr{S}(N, M - 1)}{\mathscr{S}(N, M)}. \qquad (3.255)$$

The utilization of any other station can be computed in a similar fashion merely by relabeling the station numbers as pointed out above. If the station i has a constant service rate, we obtain from (3.254) the following simple expression:

$$\rho_i = \tau_i \frac{\mathscr{S}(N - 1, M)}{\mathscr{S}(N, M)}, \qquad i = 1, 2, \ldots, M. \qquad (3.256)$$

The *throughput* λ_M of station M is, by definition, the average number of customers served at this station per unit time. It is thus given by

$$\lambda_M = \sum_{n=0}^{N} p_M(n) \mu_M(n). \qquad (3.257)$$

A substitution of (3.253) into the above expression yields (Exercise 3.10.11)

$$\lambda_M = \frac{\mathscr{S}(N - 1, M) e_M}{\mathscr{S}(N, M)}. \qquad (3.258)$$

Since the second argument of the $\mathscr{S}$ functions in both denominator and numerator is M, the above formula carries over directly to any station i:

$$\lambda_i = \frac{\mathscr{S}(N - 1, M) e_i}{\mathscr{S}(N, M)}, \qquad i = 1, 2, \ldots, M, \qquad (3.259)$$

which could have been obtained directly from (3.256). Note that the results (3.256) and (3.259) do not require, unlike the formula (3.254), the assumption of constant service rate. It is not surprising that the through-put λ_i's are proportional to the parameters e_i's, $1 \le i \le M$.

Moments of the number of customers

The kth moment of the number of customers at station i is straightfor-ward to obtain, once the distribution $p_i(n)$ of (3.253) or (3.254) is computed:

$$E[n_i^k] = \sum_{n=0}^{N} n^k p_i(n), \qquad i = 1, 2, \ldots, M. \tag{3.260}$$

However, if we are interested only in some of the moments of the random variable n_M, not in the distribution, a more economical computation procedure is possible. By substituting the marginal distribution (3.253) into the above expression, we have

$$E[n_M^k] = \frac{\mathscr{S}^{(k)}(N, M)}{\mathscr{S}(N, M)} \tag{3.261}$$

where $\mathscr{S}^{(k)}(N, M)$ is defined by

$$\mathscr{S}^{(k)}(N, M) = \sum_{n=0}^{N} \mathscr{S}(N - n, M - 1) \frac{n^k \overline{W}_M^n}{\Gamma_M(n)}. \tag{3.262}$$

From (3.246) and (3.262) we find that $\mathscr{S}^{(k)}(N, M)$ is what $\mathscr{S}(N, M)$ would be, if we should substitute $n^k/\Gamma_M(n)$ for $1/\Gamma_M(n)$. When the station M has a constant service rate—that is, $\Gamma_M(n) = C_M^n$—then we have an alterna-tive expression for the kth moment. By substituting the relation (3.249) and (3.250) into (3.262), we have

$$\mathscr{S}^{(k)}(N, M) = \sum_{n=0}^{N} [\mathscr{S}(N - n, M) - \tau_M \mathscr{S}(N - n - 1, M)] n^k \tau_M^n$$

$$\tag{3.263}$$

$$= \sum_{n=1}^{N} \mathscr{S}(N - n, M)[n^k - (n - 1)^k] \tau_M^n.$$

We can readily see that the kth moment of any station i that has a constant service rate is given by

$$E[n_i^k] = \frac{1}{\mathscr{S}(N, M)} \sum_{n=1}^{N} \mathscr{S}(N - n, M)[n^k - (n - 1)^k] \tau_i^n \tag{3.264}$$

regardless of whether the other $(M - 1)$ stations have queue-dependent service rates or not. Of particular importance among the various moments is the first moment, or the average, of n_i:

$$\bar{n}_i = \frac{1}{\mathscr{S}(N, M)} \sum_{n=1}^{N} \mathscr{S}(N - n, M)\tau_i^n. \tag{3.265}$$

The mean response time at station i (that is, the expected amount of time that a customer must spend each time the customer visits station i) can be obtained from Little's formula: $\bar{T}_i = \bar{n}_i / \lambda_i$, $i = 1, 2, \ldots, M$. The mean waiting time and the mean queue size are also easily obtainable (Exercise 3.10.13).

Exercises

3.10.5 Show that the solution for the recurrence equation (3.233) is given by (3.234).

3.10.6 Let us choose a multiplication constant for the solution $\{e_i\}$ of (3.239) so that $e_1 = 1$. What interpretation can be given to quantities e_i and $\bar{W}_i = e_i \bar{S}_i$, $1 \le i \le M$?

3.10.7 Show that the size of set $\mathscr{F}(N)$, the set of all feasible values that $\mathbf{n}$ can take on in a closed network, is given by

$$\binom{N + M - 1}{M - 1}.$$

3.10.8 Derive the recursive formula (3.249) when the condition (3.248) is given. *Hint:* Obtain the corresponding relation in the z-domain.

3.10.9 Find the number of multiplications and additions required for computing $\mathscr{S}(N, M)$ by the formula (3.246).

3.10.10 Show the derivation step from (3.251) to (3.252).

3.10.11 Derive (3.258), the expression for the throughput at station M via (3.257).

3.10.12 Assume that the service rate at station i is constant.

a) Show that the probability that there are at least n customers in the station i is given by

$$\tau_i^n \frac{\mathscr{S}(N - n, M)}{\mathscr{S}(N, M)}.$$

b) Derive (3.265) using the above result (see Exercise 2.5.2).

3.10.13 Obtain expressions for the mean waiting time and mean queue size at station i.

3.10.4 Computational Algorithms via the Pólya Theory of Enumeration

In this section we introduce another computational algorithm for evaluating the normalization constant $\mathscr{S}(n, m)$. This algorithm is restricted to a network with exponential servers, all of which have fixed service rates, that is, the case where Eq. (3.248) holds for all $i = 1, 2, \ldots, M$. Then certainly we could use the recursive formula throughout the entire step, starting with the boundary condition (3.247). The evaluation $\{\mathscr{S}(n, m);$ $1 \leq n \leq N, 1 \leq m \leq N\}$ would require only $(M - 1)N$ multiplications and additions. However, the computational formula to be discussed below is sometimes more convenient, especially when N is small.

The method is based on the Pólya theory of enumeration, an application of theory of groups to combinatorial problems. The reader unfamiliar with the related mathematics may wish to skip the derivation step and just use the computational formula presented in Formula (3.278). For the definitions of those words that are italicized, the reader is directed to texts on combinatorial mathematics (Liu, 1968) or mathematics for discrete structures (Stone, 1973; Preparata and Yeh, 1973).

The assumption of the constant service rates

$$C_i(n) = C_i \quad \text{for all} \quad n \geq 1, \quad i = 1, 2, \ldots, M \quad (3.266)$$

allows us to write $\mathscr{S}(N, M)$ of (3.236) as

$$\mathscr{S}(N, M) = \sum_{\mathbf{n} \in \mathscr{F}(N)} \prod_{i=1}^{M} \tau_i^{n_i}, \quad (3.267)$$

where τ_i was defined by (3.250). Let us define the following two sets: the set of M stations

$$\mathscr{M} = \{1, 2, \ldots, M\} \quad (3.268)$$

and the set of N customers

$$\mathscr{N} = \{1, 2, \ldots, N\}. \quad (3.269)$$

Consider then a set of *functions* that have $\mathscr{N}$ and $\mathscr{M}$ as their domain and range, respectively:

$$F = \{f \mid f : \mathscr{N} \to \mathscr{M}\}. \quad (3.270)$$

A function f in the set F represents a way of placing the N customers at the M service stations of the closed network. In order to be explicit about the mapping, we write, for example,

$$f(j) = i, \quad j \in \mathscr{N}, \quad i \in \mathscr{M} \quad (3.271)$$

which implies that customer j is placed in station i.

Now we consider a permutation π defined over $\mathscr{N}$—that is, a bijection (one-to-one and onto mapping) from $\mathscr{N}$ onto $\mathscr{N}$—and let S_N be the set of all such permutations defined over $\mathscr{N}$:

$$S_N = \{\pi \mid \pi : \mathscr{N} \to \mathscr{N}\}. \quad (3.272)$$

It is known that the elements of S_N form a group called the *symmetric group* of degree N. For a given function $f_1 \in F$ and permutation $\pi \in S_N$, we can define another function f_2 by

$$f_2(j) = f_1(\pi(j)), \qquad j \in \mathcal{N}. \tag{3.273}$$

Clearly, the function f_2 is also a member of F. However, the functions f_1 and f_2 correspond to the same queue size vector $\mathbf{n}$ in the network:

$$\mathbf{n} = [n_1, n_2, \ldots, n_M]. \tag{3.274}$$

Therefore, we say that the functions f_1 and f_2 are *indistinguishable* or *equivalent* relative to the permutation group S_N. It is also clear that distinct values of $\mathbf{n} \in \mathcal{F}(N)$ correspond to distinct *equivalence classes*.

We now interpret the parameter τ_i of (3.250) as the *weight* of element i in the set $\mathcal{M}$, and thus

$$\sum_{i \in \mathcal{M}} \tau_i \tag{3.275}$$

represents the *inventory* of the set $\mathcal{M}$. If a function f belongs to the equivalence class $\mathbf{n}$ of (3.274), then the *weight* $W(f)$ of the function f is

$$W(f) = \prod_{i \in \mathcal{M}} \tau_i^{n_i}, \quad \text{for all} \quad f \in \mathbf{n}, \tag{3.276}$$

which is called the *weight of the equivalence class* $\mathbf{n}$. Then the *pattern inventory* of F—the sum of weights of distinct equivalence classes relative to the permutation group S_N—is

$$\sum_{\mathbf{n} \in \mathcal{F}(N)} W(f), \tag{3.277}$$

which is nothing but $\mathcal{S}(N, M)$ of (3.267)! This observation immediately calls our attention to the celebrated Pólya theorem.

Pólya theorem. The pattern inventory $\mathcal{S}(N, M)$ of the set of the equivalence classes of functions from the domain $\mathcal{N}$ to the range $\mathcal{M}$ is

$$\mathcal{S}(N, M) = Z_{S_N}\left(\sum_{i \in \mathcal{M}} \tau_i, \sum_{i \in \mathcal{M}} \tau_i^2, \ldots, \sum_{i \in \mathcal{M}} \tau_i^N\right), \tag{3.278}$$

where $Z_{S_N}(x_1, x_2, \ldots, x_N)$ is the *cyclic index polynomial* of the permutation group S_N.

Therefore, our problem reduces to that of finding the cyclic index polynomial of S_N. It is directly given from *Cauchy's formula*:

$$Z_{S_N}(x_1, x_2, \ldots, x_N) = \sum \frac{x_1^{\mu_1} x_2^{\mu_2} \ldots x_N^{\mu_N}}{\mu_1! \, 2^{\mu_2} \mu_2! \ldots N^{\mu_N} \mu_N!}, \tag{3.279}$$

TABLE 3.1   CYCLE INDEX POLYNOMIALS OF SYMMETRIC GROUPS

N	Z_{S_N}
1	x_1
2	$\frac{1}{2}(x_1^2 + x_2)$
3	$\frac{1}{6}(x_1^3 + 3x_1x_2 + 2x_3)$
4	$\frac{1}{24}(x_1^4 + 6x_1^2x_2 + 3x_2^2 + 8x_1x_3 + 6x_4)$
5	$\frac{1}{120}(x_1^5 + 10x_1^3x_2 + 15x_1x_2^2 + 20x_1^2x_3 + 20x_2x_3 + 30x_1x_4 + 24x_5)$

where the sum is taken over the set of distinct N tuples, $\langle \mu_j; j = 1, 2, \ldots, N \rangle$ such that

$$\sum_{j \in N} j\mu_j = N. \tag{3.280}$$

Table 3.1 tabulates (3.279) for $N = 1, 2, \ldots, 5$. The number of terms in Z_{S_N} is not so large for the moderate size of N. Thus for small values of N, we compute the set of values

$$x_k = \sum_{i \in M} \tau_i^k, \qquad k = 1, 2, \ldots, \tag{3.281}$$

and substitute them into the polynomial Z_{S_N}. Even for $N \geq 6$ it is not difficult to calculate the polynomial from the formula (3.279).

As an alternative method, we can develop a recursive algorithm for computing $\mathcal{S}(n, m)$, $1 \leq n \leq N$, $1 \leq m \leq M$. We can derive the following equation for the cycle index polynomials of the symmetric group S_n, $n = 1, 2, 3, \ldots$

$$Z_{S_n}(x_1, x_2, \ldots, x_n) = \begin{cases} \dfrac{1}{n} \displaystyle\sum_{k=0}^{n-1} x_{n-k} Z_{S_k}(x_1, x_2, \ldots, x_k) & \text{for } n \geq 1 \\[2mm] 1, & \text{for } n = 1 \end{cases} \tag{3.282}$$

which, in turn, leads to the recurrence relation of the sequence $\mathcal{S}(n, M)$, $n = 1, 2, 3, \ldots$

$$\mathcal{S}(n, M) = \frac{1}{n} \sum_{k=0}^{n-1} x_{n-k} \mathcal{S}(k, M) \tag{3.283}$$

$$= \frac{1}{n} \sum_{k=1}^{n} x_k \mathcal{S}(n - k, M)$$

with the initial condition

$$\mathcal{S}(0, M) = 1, \qquad M \geq 1. \tag{3.284}$$

It will be instructive to show that the formula (3.283) can be derived also from (3.265). By summing $\bar{n}_i$ of (3.265) over all $i = 1, 2, \ldots, M$, we obtain

$$N = \sum_{i=1}^{M} \bar{n}_i = \frac{1}{\mathscr{S}(N, M)} \sum_{n=1}^{N} \mathscr{S}(N - n, M) \left(\sum_{i=1}^{M} \tau_i^n \right) \qquad (3.285)$$

from which Eq. (3.283) is immediately obtainable.

The computation formula (3.278) is extremely simple, since it can be evaluated by just using the polynomial formulas (see Table 3.1). The number of computations required in the algorithm (3.283) is in the order of N^2, if the effort of evaluating x_k's is negligible. If many of the service centers are identical in both service rates and the mean service times, then the corresponding parameters τ_i's are identical, and the evaluation of x_k's is rather trivial. Thus, when $M > N$, the algorithm (3.283) is preferable to (3.249), whose computation effort is in the order of MN.

3.10.5 An Application Example: Modeling an Interactive System with Multiprogramming in Virtual Storage

We will now apply the various results obtained in the preceding sections to a case study concerning the performance analysis of computer systems. We will cite numerical values, wherever possible, to provide the reader with a better appreciation of the theoretical results presented thus far. It is also an objective of this section to clarify the limitations of the analytic techniques currently available to us. These discussions will motivate us to study advanced materials to be found in later chapters, and will also reveal some of the current research problems that require further investigations.

Many contemporary computer systems are built on *virtual storage* operating systems, as discussed in Chapter 1. The essential feature of a virtual storage system lies in its memory management policy, called *paging*. The paging technique has been implemented, for example, in TSS/360, CP-67, MULTICS, VM370, and VS/370. The reader is directed to many books and articles for detailed discussions of virtual storage systems. In this section, we will discuss a multiprogrammed time-shared system built on a virtual storage system. This example follows closely a study reported by Boyse and Warn (1975). Our modeling approach is not exactly the same as that taken by the original authors, but the numerical values are cited from their article.

The system description

The system is a virtual storage system in which demand paging is used to move required portions of a user's address space into main storage. The system supports a number of graphic terminals, which place a heavy computational workload on the system and access a large data base. The data base is contained in this address space; thus, no explicit I/O is done by application programs. A page fault occurs if the referenced data are not in main storage. The external page storage devices consist of drums with nine logical sectors and several disk storage on two separate channels. Page reads receive priority over page writes.

In this multiprogrammed system, the scheduling and resource allocation are performed in *two levels*. First, a job from a user terminal is placed in the *job scheduling queue* and waits until it is multiprogrammed, that is, until the user's address space is swapped into the virtual storage space. What happens physically at this moment is that some of the pages of that user program are loaded from the external page storage into main storage. After this preloading is done, the program is now in the "ready" state, joins the *CPU scheduling queue*, and contends with other ready jobs for the usage of the CPU. The ready job must wait if the CPU is currently occupied by some other job in the multiprogramming mix. Once the CPU is dispatched for this job, it will execute until the job is completed or until an I/O operation is required. Usually the time-slicing technique is adopted to avoid excessive queueing delays that might be incurred otherwise by huge CPU-bound jobs. In this case, the CPU execution of a job will be temporarily suspended when the allocated time slice expires. Recall that in this virtual storage system essentially all the events are I/O due to paging, and whenever a page fault occurs, the required page must be read into main storage. A page read requires typically 20 to 100 msec. The CPU execution time interval between page faults is comparable to or less than the I/O execution time. Thus, the CPU is relinquished to another ready job, while a page read is performed. Page writes, on the other hand, are normally overlapped with CPU use.

The model

From the system description given above, it is evident that we must formulate the two levels of queues: at a higher level the job scheduling queue, and at a lower level the CPU scheduling queue and the I/O scheduling queue. Therefore, we structure the model as shown in Fig. 3.36. This two-level hierarchical model is a simple example that illustrates how a complex system should be decomposed into subsystem models. The notion of decomposition was discussed in Section 1.5.2 in a more general framework. The outer model (the higher-level model) is a finite-input source model, which was extensively discussed in Section 3.9. The inner model is a rather simple queueing network; it can be viewed as a

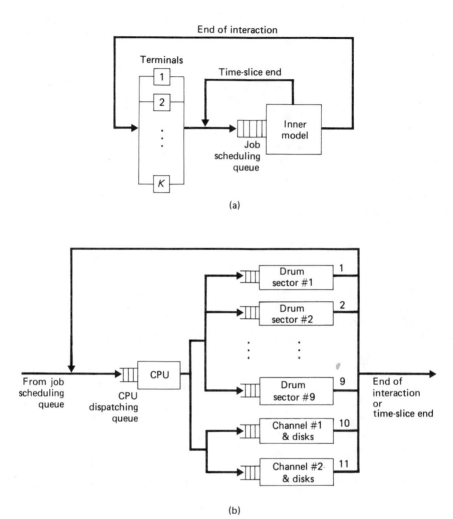

Fig. 3.36 A hierarchical model of the interactive system with multiprogramming in virtual storage: (a) the outer model (a time-shared system model) and (b) the inner model (a central server model).

generalization of the cyclic queueing model discussed in Section 3.8.4. However, this type of model is usually referred to as a *central server model* (Buzen, 1971); the CPU corresponds to the central server. The inner model and the outer model are coupled through the job scheduling queue. A job becomes a customer of the inner model when the job's address space is swapped into virtual storage. The job departs from this inner model either (1) when the interaction is completed, or (2) when the time slice allocated to the job is terminated and the job is swapped out and returns to the job scheduling queue.

The multiprogramming level, N (which corresponds to the number of jobs found in the central server model), varies as time changes. Usually the value N is controlled through the job scheduler in order to maintain high throughput. In the system under consideration, the multiprogramming level is limited to three, that is, $N \leq 3$. For a given value of N, we can model the inner model of Fig. 3.36(b) as a closed network of queues, in which we label the paging I/O devices as stations 1–11 and the CPU as station 12 ($= M$). Each I/O station corresponds to an independent access path of drum/disk storage devices. If we assume that the CPU execution time and page read time can be approximated by random variables with exponential distributions, we can directly apply the results of Sections 3.10.2 and 3.10.3. The implications of the exponential assumption will be discussed later.

Measurement data and the model parameters

The initial hardware configuration consists of a single CPU with 1.5 megabytes of core memory, with IBM 2301 drums and 2314 disks as external page storage. The page size is 4K ($= 4096$) bytes. The following data were recorded during a period of heavy workload:

Number of active terminals	$K = 10$
Average user time	$\bar{U} = 4 \text{ sec}$
Degree of multiprogramming	$N = 3$
Total observation period	$T_0 = 1800 \text{ sec}$
Total job CPU time	$T_P = 613 \text{ sec}$
Total system CPU time	$T_S = 827 \text{ sec}$
Number of interactions processed	$I = 720$
Total page reads	$R_{pg} = 75600$
Total 2301 drum reads	$R_{drm} = 60480$
Total 2314 disk reads	$R_{dsk} = 15120$

The system CPU time is the time that the CPU spends in the supervisor state (e.g., the time used for page fault handling, job scheduling, etc.).

Analysis of the inner model

From the measurement data presented above, we can derive the following parameter values:

Average CPU work per interaction
$$\overline{W}_{CPU} = \overline{W}_{12} = \frac{T_P + T_S}{I} = 2.0 \text{ sec}$$

Average number of page reads per interaction
$$e_{12} = \frac{R_{pg}}{I} = 105$$

Average CPU execution interval between page faults
$$\overline{S}_{12} = \frac{\overline{W}_{12}}{e_{12}} = \frac{T_P + T_S}{R_{pg}} = 19 \text{ msec}$$

Average number of 2301 drum reads per interaction
$$e_1 + e_2 + \cdots + e_9 = \frac{R_{drm}}{I} = 84$$

Average number of 2304 disk reads per interaction
$$e_{10} + e_{11} = \frac{R_{dsk}}{I} = 21$$

The parameters $\{e_i\}$ are those defined in (3.230) and the proportionality constant is chosen so that e_i represents the average number of calls to station i during one interaction. The average service time for a page read operation (i.e., paging I/O time) can be computed as the sum of the average *seek time*, the average *latency time* (one half revolution), and the *transfer time* for the page (four kilobytes per page). Table 3.2 summarizes the average service time for IBM 2314 and 3330 disks and 2301 and 2305 drums. Therefore, we obtain the following additional parameters of the inner model:

Average service time at stations 1–9 $\overline{S}_1 = \overline{S}_2 = \cdots = \overline{S}_9$

$$= 21.5 \text{ msec}$$

Average service time at stations 10 and 11 $\overline{S}_{10} = \overline{S}_{11} = 104 \text{ msec}$

In the absence of measurement data concerning how these drum reads and disk reads are distributed among the separate access paths, we

TABLE 3.2

Device	Seek	Latency	Page transfer	Average paging I/O time
2314	75 msec	12.5 msec	16.66 msec	104 msec
3330	30 msec	8.4 msec	5.6 msec	44 msec
2301	—	17.5 msec	4.0 msec	21.5 msec
2305	—	5.0 msec	3.33 msec	8.33 msec

assume the uniform distributions:

$$e_1 = e_2 = \cdots = e_9 = \frac{84}{9} = 9.33 \,[\text{reads/interaction}];$$

$$e_{10} = e_{11} = 10.5 \,[\text{reads/interaction}];$$

$$\overline{W}_1 = \overline{W}_2 = \cdots = \overline{W}_9 = \frac{84}{9} \times 21.5 \,[\text{msec}] = 0.2006 \text{ sec};$$

$$\overline{W}_{10} = \overline{W}_{11} = 10.5 \times 104 \,[\text{msec}] = 1.092 \text{ sec}.$$

Since the service (or work) $\{\bar{S}_i\}$ is represented in time, the processing rate $\{C_i\}$ should be set to unity, $1 \leq i \leq 12$. Hence the parameters $\{\tau_i\}$ of (3.250) are the same as $\{\overline{W}_i\}$:

$$\tau_1 = \tau_2 = \cdots = \tau_9 = 0.2006 \text{ sec};$$

$$\tau_{10} = \tau_{11} = 1.092 \text{ sec};$$

$$\tau_{12} = 2.0 \text{ sec}.$$

Then the recurrence formula (3.249) can be used to compute $\mathscr{S}(1, 12)$, $\mathscr{S}(2, 12)$, and $\mathscr{S}(3, 12)$. However, the formula (3.278) is more suitable in this case, since N is small and many of the parameters τ_i's are identical to each other. Thus, we compute the parameters x_i's of (3.281):

$$x_1 = 0.2006 \times 9 + 1.092 \times 2 + 2.0 = 5.989 \text{ sec};$$

$$x_2 = 0.2006^2 \times 9 + 1.092^2 \times 2 + 2.0^2 = 6.747 \text{ sec}^2;$$

$$x_3 = 0.2006^3 \times 9 + 1.092^3 \times 2 + 2.0^3 = 10.677 \text{ sec}^3.$$

Then from Formula (3.278) and the polynomials of Table 3.1, we obtain

$$\mathscr{S}(1, 12) = 5.989 \text{ sec};$$

$$\mathscr{S}(2, 12) = 21.30 \text{ sec}^2;$$

$$\mathscr{S}(3, 12) = 59.56 \text{ sec}^3.$$

Hence the predicted values, $\hat{\rho}_{\text{CPU}}(N)$, for CPU utilization for the degree of multiprogramming $N = 1, 2, 3$ are obtained from Formula (3.256) as

$$\hat{\rho}_{\text{CPU}}(1) = \frac{\overline{W}_{\text{CPU}}}{\mathscr{S}(1, 12)} = 0.33;$$

$$\hat{\rho}_{\text{CPU}}(2) = \overline{W}_{\text{CPU}} \frac{\mathscr{S}(1, 12)}{\mathscr{S}(2, 12)} = 0.56;$$

$$\hat{\rho}_{\text{CPU}}(3) = \overline{W}_{\text{CPU}} \frac{\mathscr{S}(2, 12)}{\mathscr{S}(3, 12)} = 0.72.$$

The actual utilization factor from the 30-minute measurement data, during which the degree of multiprogramming was always 3, is directly obtainable as

$$\rho_{\text{CPU}}(3) = \frac{T_P + T_S}{T_0} = \frac{613 + 827}{1800} = 0.80.$$

There is a relative error of approximately 10 percent between the values $\hat{\rho}_{\text{CPU}}(3) = 0.72$ and $\rho_{\text{CPU}}(3) = 0.80$. We will postpone discussions on this discrepancy, and go on to the analysis of the outer model.

Analysis of the outer model

The outer model can be formulated as the machine servicing model discussed in Section 3.9, where the server corresponds to the inner model box—the combination of the CPU and the storage devices. The servicing rate of this server is not constant, but depends on the number of multiprogrammed jobs:

$$\mu(1) = \frac{\hat{\rho}_{\text{CPU}}(1)}{\overline{W}_{\text{CPU}}} = 0.165 \text{ interactions/sec;}$$

$$\mu(2) = \frac{\hat{\rho}_{\text{CPU}}(2)}{\overline{W}_{\text{CPU}}} = 0.28 \text{ interactions/sec;}$$

and

$$\mu(n) = \frac{\hat{\rho}_{\text{CPU}}(3)}{\overline{W}_{\text{CPU}}} = 0.36 \text{ interactions/sec} \quad \text{for} \quad n \geq 3,$$

where the argument n of the function $\mu(n)$ represents the number of user jobs that are multiprogrammed plus those waiting in the job scheduling queue.

The average user time is, from the table on p. 181, estimated as

$$\overline{U} = 4 \text{ sec.}$$

Thus, the job generation rate at a user terminal is

$$\nu = 0.25 \text{ sec}^{-1}.$$

Figure 3.37 plots the $\mu(n)$ obtained above and the job arrival rate $\lambda(n)$ given by (3.162) for $K = 10$. We can observe from this figure that the server is quite congested: On the average, the server has more than eight jobs. This means that the multiprogramming level is almost always at its maximum value (that is, $N = 3$) and an additional five or more jobs are waiting in the job scheduling queue. Therefore, the probability of $n = 1$ or $n = 2$ is negligibly small (see Exercise 3.10.14). This argument is

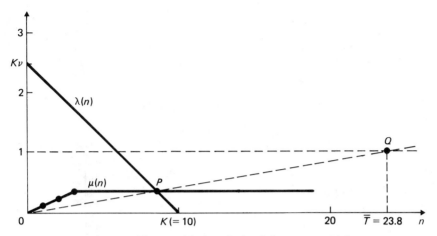

Fig. 3.37 The graphical analysis of the outer model.

consistent with the actual observation, namely, that the multiprogramming level was three throughout the total observation period of $T_0 = 1800$ seconds. Thus, we now approximate the processing rate function of the server as

$$\mu(n) = \mu = 0.36 \, [\text{interactions/sec}], \quad \text{for all} \quad n \geq 1.$$

Then the results of Section 3.9.2 are directly applicable here. The parameter r of (3.152) takes

$$r = \frac{\mu}{\nu} = 1.44.$$

From Fig. 3.29, we see that for this value of r the server utilization is, practically speaking, equal to 100 percent. Then from (3.153) or (3.176) the normalized mean response time is obtained as

$$Y(10) = K - r = 8.56,$$

which also represents the mean value of the number of jobs in the server. In Fig. 3.37, it corresponds to the abscissa of point P. Then by multiplying this by $1/\mu$, the average time that a job resides in main storage per interaction, we obtain the following predicted value of the mean response time:

$$\hat{T} = \frac{Y(10)}{\mu} = 23.8 \text{ sec.}$$

This value can also be obtained as the abscissa of point Q in Fig. 3.37.

The actual mean response time during the monitored period can be calculated from the measurement data: The throughput rate λ in the

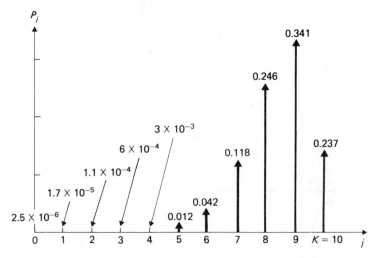

Fig. 3.38 The distribution of the number of jobs in the multiprogramming mix plus the job scheduling queue.

interval of $T_0 = 1800$ sec is

$$\lambda = \frac{I}{T_0} = \frac{720}{1800} = 0.4 \text{ interactions/sec.}$$

Hence from (3.147) we obtain

$$\overline{T} = \frac{K}{\lambda} - \overline{U} = \frac{10}{0.4} - 4 = 21.0 \text{ [sec]}.$$

The error between the predicted value and actual value is 2.8 sec, which is approximately 14 percent in terms of the relative error.

As a final step in this case study, let us proceed to the calculation of the distributions of queue size. The queue distribution is given as a truncated Poisson distribution of (3.172), but for $K = 10$ and $r = 1.44$, the denominator is almost equal to unity:

$$Q(10; 1.44) \simeq 1.$$

Hence the distribution of the number of jobs, j, is obtained along the horizontal axis by reversing the Poisson distribution of mean $r = 1.44$, as shown in Fig. 3.38.

Discussion

A few remarks are in order to qualify some of the assumptions made in our model. One of the approximations enforced in the analysis was the assumption regarding the paging devices. The service times at these devices are known to have distributions more regular than the exponential distribution. Furthermore, the scheduling discipline used in drums and disks is generally not FIFO; it takes into account the locations of pending requests relative to the current position of the head, and schedules these requests so that the latency time and seek time will be minimized. Such a discipline does not belong to the class of work-conserving queue disciplines defined in Section 3.7. The lack of such detailed considerations, however, seems to have an insignificant effect on the results of the overall analysis here. As we have seen, the system is heavily CPU-bound, so that queues will rarely be formed at the disks or drums (Exercise 3.10.4). If we ignore the device queues completely and assume that all requests are immediately served, then we can approximate the central server model of Fig. 3.34(b) by the machine servicing model (Exercise 3.10.19), which is indeed the model adopted in the study by Boyse and Warn (1975). It is known that in the machine servicing model we can drop the exponential assumption of the up time, since the queue distribution depends on the up-time distribution only through its mean. This robustness in the machine servicing model is intricately related to the fact that the queue distribution in an $M/G/\infty$ system is the same as that of an $M/M/\infty$ system with the same mean service time (see, for example, Mirasol, 1963).

Now a few remarks concerning the *outer* model. The total amount of time that a job resides in the inner model is known to have, more often than not, skewed distribution with a long tail, a type of distribution that would be nicely fitted by a hyperexponential or gamma distribution ($\beta < 1$). However, the use of the *time-slicing* technique in the job scheduling rule eliminates effects of the distributional form on the performance; the queue distribution of the outer model should depend, practically speaking, only on $1/\mu$, the expected time that a job resides in main storage, if the time-slicing technique is properly used. Hence the results obtained under the exponential assumption should hold under much weaker conditions. A more formal argument to support this robustness is based on the equivalence between the $M/M/1$ and the $M/G/1$ system with the *processor-sharing* (PS) scheduling. The PS discipline is a mathematical idealization of the time-slicing technique (see Kleinrock, 1976; O'Donovan, 1974; Baskett et al., 1975; Kobayashi, 1978; and the section on Discussion and Further Reading).

Thus, we may safely conclude that the various simplifying assumptions made in our model are well justified, insofar as we are interested only in the average response time, utilization, throughput, etc. The distribution of response time, however, will certainly be dependent on the distributional forms.

Exercises

3.10.14 Refer to the inner model (the central server model) discussed in the text. Calculate the following quantities, when the multiprogramming level is three.

    a) The throughput rates of the CPU and the devices
    b) The average number of jobs at the CPU queue and at the device queues
    c) The probability distribution of the number of jobs at the CPU

3.10.15 Based on the model discussed in the text, evaluate the probability that the multiprogramming level is equal to one or two.

3.10.16 Suppose that you replace IBM/2314 disks with 3330 disks, and 2301 drums with 2305 drums. What kind of performance improvement will you expect? Discuss this in terms of CPU utilization, average response time, and response-time distribution.

3.10.17 In the analysis of the outer model discussed in the text, treat the multiprogrammed computer (i.e., the inner model) as a service station with *three parallel servers* (rather than the queue-dependent single server as treated in the text). Use the result of Exercise 3.9.12 and compute the distribution of the number of jobs in the multiprogramming mix plus those in the job scheduling queue. How does this result compare with Fig. 3.38?

3.10.18 Using the three-server model described in Exercise 3.10.17, obtain the *waiting-time distribution* and *response-time distribution* that a terminal user experiences.

3.10.19 (*Boyse and Warn, 1975*). Assume that the effect of queueing at the paging drums and disks in Fig. 3.36(b) is negligibly small. Show that the inner model can then be formulated as a machine servicing model. What is the number of machines? Conduct the performance analysis (i.e., the CPU utilization, average response time, etc.) based on this model.

3.11 QUEUEING MODELS WITH NONEXPONENTIAL SERVICE DISTRIBUTION

In Sections 3.8–3.10 we consistently (except in Section 3.9.1) assumed that the interarrival times and service times are all exponential. This exponential assumption greatly simplified the system analysis, since $N(t)$, the number of jobs in the system (or the vector $\mathbf{N}(t)$ in a queueing network), forms a Markov process. Recall that a Markov process has the memoryless property; in other words, how the system has reached the present state $N(t)$ is irrelevant to the future behavior of the process.

    In this section we will discuss how to analyze a queueing system with a nonexponential service-time distribution.

3.11.1 The Generalized Method of Stages

One approach to dealing with nonexponential service-time distributions is the so-called method of stages and its generalization. In Section 3.4.2 we

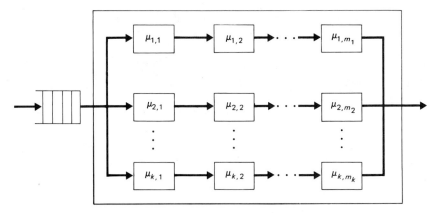

Fig. 3.39 A serial-parallel stage representation of a general service distribution.

showed that a server with k-stage Erlangian service distribution is equivalent to the k stages of fictitious exponential servers in cascade. Similarly, a service facility with hyperexponential (or mixed-exponential) service-time distribution is representable in terms of parallel stages of fictitious exponential servers (Section 3.4.3). By generalizing the above argument, we can combine serial and parallel stages as shown in Fig. 3.39, and represent a rather complex service-time distribution:

$$\Phi_S(s) = \sum_{i=1}^{k} \pi_i \prod_{j=1}^{m_i} \frac{\mu_{ij}}{s + \mu_{ij}}. \tag{3.286}$$

Conversely, for a given distribution $F_S(t)$, we can approximate its Laplace transform in the form of (3.286), and represent the server by a serial and parallel combination of exponential servers. If the arrival is a Poisson process, then the system can be described by a Markov process in a suitably defined state space. Here we can represent the system state by a triplet (n, i, j), where n represents the number of customers in the queue, and i and j are the row and column numbers of the state in which a customer in service finds himself. Note that within the service facility only one of the stages may be occupied at any moment. Such representation and solution techniques are called the *generalized method of stages*. In principle, the technique can be extended to a broader class of queueing systems including non-Poisson arrivals and queueing network models. The problem is, however, that the dimension of the state space rises rather sharply as the system complexity grows.

The Laplace transform $\Phi_S(s)$ of (3.286) has all its poles on the negative real axis. If we choose an arbitrary probability density function, $f_S(t)$, of a nonnegative random variable, its Laplace transform may have complex poles. Cox (1955) showed that the method of stages can be extended to such a case. Consider, for instance,

$$f_S(t) = ab^{-2}(a^2 + b^2)e^{-at}(1 - \cos bt) \qquad t > 0 \qquad (3.287)$$

whose Laplace transform is given by

$$\Phi_S(s) = \frac{a(a^2 + b^2)}{(a + s)[(a + s)^2 + b^2]} \qquad (3.288)$$

so that we have poles in a conjugate pair. This property must hold generally since $\Phi_S(s)$ is real for real s. We also note that the real parts of the poles are negative; otherwise $f_S(t)$ would diverge as $t \to \infty$.

Consider a general form of rational function $\Phi_S(s)$:

$$\Phi_S(s) = \frac{N(s)}{D(s)}, \qquad (3.289)$$

where $D(s)$ is a polynomial of degree d; thus, $N(s)$ is a polynomial of degree at most d. If the zeros of the denominator are at $-\mu_j$ ($j = 1, 2, \ldots, d$), we can expand $\Phi_S(s)$ using one of the partial-fraction methods. When the μ_j's are all distinct, one way is to apply the ordinary partial-fraction method discussed in Section 2.6.4:

$$\Phi_S(s) = \pi_0 + \sum_{j=1}^{d} \pi_j \frac{\mu_j}{s + \mu_j}, \qquad (3.290)$$

where $\sum_{j=0}^{d} \pi_j = 1$. This representation is analogous to the parallel stage structure of the hyperexponential distribution. Another type of expansion is

$$\Phi_S(s) = b_0 + \sum_{j=1}^{d} a_0 \ldots a_{j-1} b_j \prod_{i=1}^{j} \frac{\mu_i}{s + \mu_i}, \qquad (3.291)$$

where $a_i + b_i = 1$, for $i = 0, 1, \ldots, d - 1$, and $b_d = 1$. In this expansion we do not require that the μ_i's be different. Thus it is more general than the expansion (3.290). Figure 3.40 shows this decomposition as a serial stage of d exponential servers with complex service completion rates μ_i,

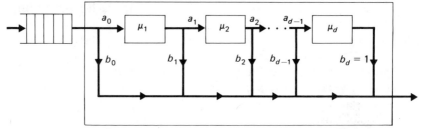

Fig. 3.40   Cox's representation of a general service distribution.

$1 \leq i \leq d$. We recognize that the expansion (3.291) is a generalization of the serial stage representation for Erlangian distribution.

The notion of the generalized method of stages is an important device for numerical analyses of complex queueing systems. For further discussions and applications of the method, the reader is directed to Kleinrock (1975) and Wallace and Rosenberg (1966). The Cox's representation (3.291) was used by Baskett et al. (1975) as a mathematical device in dealing with general distribution in a network of queues.

Exercises

3.11.1 Consider an $M/E_2/1$ system, that is, a queueing system with Poisson arrivals and the two-stage Erlangian service distribution.

   a) Define a set of system states over which the behavior of the queueing system defines a Markov process.
   b) Draw a system transition diagram and find a set of balance equations.
   c) Apply the z-transform method to the balance equation, and show that the probability generating function of the number of customers in the system is given by

$$P(z) = \frac{4(1 - \rho)}{\rho^2 z^2 - (4 + \rho)\rho z + 4}.$$

   d) Obtain the distribution when $\rho = 0.25$.

3.11.2 Consider an $M/H_2/1$ queueing system with service distribution

$$F_S(t) = 1 - \pi_1 \exp(-\mu_1 t) - \pi_2 \exp(-\mu_2 t),$$

where $\pi_1 + \pi_2 = 1$.

   a) Compute the Laplace transform of $f_S(t) = (d/dt)F_S(t)$ and find its representation of the form (3.291) and Fig. 3.40.
   b) Using the representation obtained above, define the system state and write down the balance equation.
   c) Obtain the distribution of the number of customers in the $M/H_2/1$ system.

3.11.2   The Imbedded Markov Chain Technique and M/G/1 Queueing System

In Section 3.11.1 we showed that our $M/G/1$ queueing system can be analyzed by transforming the general service-time distribution into stages of exponential servers. Over a suitably chosen state space, the system behavior was characterized by a Markov process. Note, however, that the process $N(t)$, the number of customers in the system at time t, is not a Markov process in the $M/G/1$ system.

The second approach to the $M/G/1$ system under the FCFS discipline is the method of the *imbedded Markov chain*. This method depends on examining the system at suitably selected points in time. We showed earlier that for the $M/G/1$ system, the distribution of the number of customers found by arriving customers is equivalent to the long-run time average distribution. We also found that this distribution is the same as that seen by departing customers (Exercises 3.8.7 and 3.6.3). Let N_k be the number of customers found in the system just after the service completion of the kth customer, and let X_k be the number of customers who arrive while the kth customer is served. Clearly, $X_1, X_2, \ldots$ are independent and identically distributed. Furthermore, under the FCFS discipline X_k is independent of $N_1, N_2, \ldots, N_{k-1}$. However, the quantities N_k and X_k are not independent random variables and we find the following recursive equation:

$$N_k = \begin{cases} X_k, & \text{if} \quad N_{k-1} = 0 \\[2mm] N_{k-1} + X_k - 1, & \text{if} \quad N_{k-1} > 0. \end{cases} \tag{3.292}$$

The first line is obtained from the following reasoning: If $N_{k-1} = 0$, then the kth customer finds the system empty, and on departure the customer leaves behind those who have arrived during the customer's service. The second line of (3.292) says that the queue left behind by the kth customer consists of the previous queue N_{k-1}, decreased by one (the kth customer) and augmented by new arrivals during the customer's service. By defining the function $U(\cdot)$ by

$$U(x) = \begin{cases} 1, & x > 0 \\[2mm] 0, & x \le 0 \end{cases} \tag{3.293}$$

we may combine the two equations for N_k and write

$$N_k = N_{k-1} - U(N_{k-1}) + X_k. \tag{3.294}$$

From the last expression it is clear that the sequence $\{N_k\}$ is a Markov chain. We call this sequence the Markov chain *imbedded* in the time-continuous (non-Markov) process $N(t)$. Because the distribution of the variable N_k (for arbitrary k) and that of the variable $N(t)$ (for arbitrary time t) are the same (Exercise 3.8.7), we choose to analyze the sequence $\{N_k\}$ instead of the process $N(t)$. In order to find the probability distribution $\{p_n\}$ of the variable N_k (in the limit $k \to \infty$), we first obtain its probability generating function:

$$P(z) = \sum_{n=0}^{\infty} p_n z^n = E[z^{N_k}]. \tag{3.295}$$

Then, substituting (3.294) into the above equation and using the fact that X_k and N_{k-1} are independent, we find

$$P(z) = E[z^{X_k}]E[z^{N_{k-1}-U(N_{k-1})}] = A(z)\left[p_0 + \sum_{n=1}^{\infty} p_n z^{n-1}\right]$$

$$= A(z)[p_0 + z^{-1}(P(z) - p_0)], \tag{3.296}$$

where $A(z)$ is the probability generating function of the discrete random variable X_k. If the service time of customer k is t, then X_k has a Poisson distribution of mean λt:

$$P[X_k = i \mid S_k = t] = \frac{e^{-\lambda t}(\lambda t)^i}{i!}. \tag{3.297}$$

By denoting the probability density function of the service time by $f_S(t)$, we have

$$a_i = P[X_k = i] = \int_0^{\infty} \frac{e^{-\lambda t}(\lambda t)^i}{i!} f_S(t)\, dt. \tag{3.298}$$

The probability generating function of X_k is then given by

$$A(z) = E[z^{X_k}] = \sum_{i=0}^{\infty} \int_0^{\infty} \frac{e^{-\lambda t}(\lambda t z)^i}{i!} f_S(t)\, dt$$

$$= \int_0^{\infty} e^{-\lambda t} e^{\lambda t z} f_S(t)\, dt = \Phi_S(\lambda - \lambda z), \tag{3.299}$$

where $\Phi_S(\bullet)$ is the Laplace transform of $f_S(t)$. From (3.296) and (3.299), we obtain

$$P(z) = p_0 \frac{\Phi_S(\lambda - \lambda z)(z - 1)}{z - \Phi_S(\lambda - \lambda z)}. \tag{3.300}$$

The constant p_0 is obtained by setting $z \to 1$ in the last equation and applying l'Hôpital's rule:

$$1 = p_0 \frac{\Phi_S(0)}{1 + \lambda \Phi_S'(0)} = \frac{p_0}{1 - \lambda \bar{S}}. \tag{3.301}$$

Hence we find

$$p_0 = 1 - \lambda \bar{S} = 1 - \rho \tag{3.302}$$

which is not unexpected. By substituting (3.302) into (3.300), we finally have

$$P(z) = \frac{(1 - \rho)(z - 1)\Phi_S(\lambda - \lambda z)}{z - \Phi_S(\lambda - \lambda z)}. \tag{3.303}$$

Example 3.1 ($M/H_2/1$).   Consider the case in which $F_S(t)$ is a two-phase hyperexponential distribution

$$F_S(t) = 1 - \pi_1 e^{-\mu_1 t} - \pi_2 e^{-\mu_2 t} \tag{3.304}$$

where $\pi_1 + \pi_2 = 1$ and $1/\mu = \pi_1/\mu_1 + \pi_2/\mu_2$ is the mean service time. The Laplace transform of the density function $f_S(t) = (d/dt)F_S(t)$ is given by

$$\Phi_S(s) = \frac{\pi_1 \mu_1}{\mu_1 + s} + \frac{\pi_2 \mu_2}{\mu_2 + s}. \tag{3.305}$$

Then from (3.288), we have

$$A(z) = \Phi_S(\lambda - \lambda z) = \frac{\pi_1}{1 + \rho_1(1 - z)} + \frac{\pi_2}{1 + \rho_2(1 - z)}, \tag{3.306}$$

where

$$\rho_i = \lambda/\mu_i, \quad i = 1, 2. \tag{3.307}$$

Therefore

$$P(z) = \frac{(1 - \rho)[1 + (\rho_1 + \rho_2 - \rho)(1 - z)]}{\rho_1 \rho_2 z^2 - (\rho_1 \rho_2 + \rho_1 \rho_2)z + 1 + \rho_1 + \rho_2 - \rho}. \tag{3.308}$$

The probability distribution $\{p_n\}$ is obtained, for example, through the partial-fraction expansion of $P(z)$. This requires us to solve the characteristic equation:

$$\rho_1 \rho_2 z^2 - (\rho_1 + \rho_2 + \rho_1 \rho_2)z + 1 + \rho_1 + \rho_2 - \rho = 0. \tag{3.309}$$

If z_1 and z_2 are the characteristic roots, $P(z)$ has the following partial-fraction representation:

$$P(z) = \frac{C_1 z_1}{z_1 - z} + \frac{C_2 z_2}{z_2 - z} \tag{3.310}$$

where C_1 and C_2 are determined by setting $z = 0$ and $z = 1$ in the last equation and by using the following property of the generating function:

$$P(1) = \sum_{i=0}^{\infty} p_i = 1 \tag{3.311}$$

and

$$P(0) = p_0 = 1 - \rho. \tag{3.312}$$

Thus, we determine the coefficients

$$C_1 = \frac{(z_1 - 1)(1 - \rho z_2)}{z_1 - z_2} \tag{3.313}$$

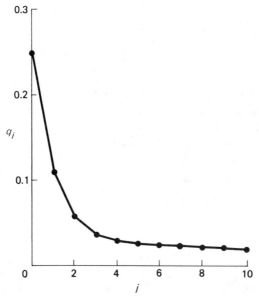

Fig. 3.41   An example of the distribution $p(n)$ in $M/H_2/1$ queue.

and

$$C_2 = \frac{(z_2 - 1)(1 - \rho z_1)}{z_2 - z_1}. \tag{3.314}$$

Finally we obtain

$$p_n = C_1 z_1^{-n} + C_2 z_2^{-n}. \tag{3.315}$$

Alternatively we can derive a recurrence formula to compute the sequence p_n starting with the initial condition $p_0 = 1 - \rho$ (see Exercise 3.11.3). As a numerical example, consider the case in which the Poisson arrival rate is $\lambda = 0.75$ and the parameters of the two-stage hyperexponential service time are $\pi_1 = 0.0576$, $\mu_1 = 0.1$, and $\mu_2 = 2$ (see Fig. 3.12). Figure 3.41 is a plot of the distribution p_n.

Example 3.2 ($M/E_k/1$).   Let us now consider the k-stage Erlangian distribution of the mean service time $1/\mu$. Then the Laplace transform of the density function is given, from (3.32), by

$$\Phi_S(s) = \left(1 + \frac{s}{k\mu}\right)^{-k}. \tag{3.316}$$

Thus we readily obtain

$$A(z) = \Phi_S(\lambda - \lambda z) = \left[1 + \frac{\rho(1 - z)}{k}\right]^{-k} \tag{3.317}$$

and

$$P(z) = \frac{(1 - \rho)(z - 1)}{z\left[1 + \frac{\rho(1 - z)}{k}\right]^k - 1}. \tag{3.318}$$

For a small value of k, the generating function $P(z)$ can be inverted by the partial-fraction method. The recursion method discussed in Section 2.6.2 is applicable to the function $P(z)$ even for large k (Exercise 3.11.6). We shall obtain below, instead, a closed form expression for the probability distribution p_n's. By defining the dimensionless parameters

$$R = 1 + \frac{\rho}{k} \tag{3.319}$$

and

$$r = \frac{\rho}{k + \rho} = 1 - R^{-1}, \tag{3.320}$$

we can rewrite $P(z)$ as

$$P(z) = \frac{(1 - \rho)(1 - z)}{1 - z[R(1 - rz)]^k} \tag{3.321}$$

$$= (1 - \rho)(1 - z) \sum_{j=0}^{\infty} z^j R^{kj}(1 - rz)^{kj}.$$

By equating the coefficients of the terms z^n in both sides of the equation, we find

$$p_n = (1 - \rho) \sum_{j=0}^{n} (-1)^{n-j} r^{n-j-1} R^{kj} \left[\binom{kj}{n-j} r + \binom{kj}{n-j-1}\right]. \tag{3.322}$$

In Fig. 3.42, we plot the distributions $\{p_n\}$ for the cases $k = 1$, 2, and 4 with the traffic intensity $\rho = 0.75$. By letting k approach infinity, we will obtain the solution for the $M/D/1$ system. In the next example, we will obtain a closed form expression to which the solution (3.322) should converge as $k \to \infty$.

Example 3.3 ($M/D/1$). Suppose that the service times of all customers are a constant $1/\mu$. If we define the unit step function $u(x)$ by

$$u(x) = \begin{cases} 1, & x \geq 0 \\ 0, & x < 0 \end{cases} \tag{3.323}$$

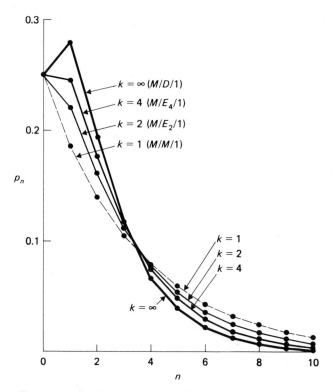

Fig. 3.42   The queue distribution of the $M/E_k/1$ queueing system (Example 3.2).

then the distribution function of the service time can be written as

$$F_S(x) = u\left(x - \frac{1}{\mu}\right). \tag{3.324}$$

This function is not differentiable at $x = 1/\mu$, but we symbolically write the derivative of $u(x)$ as $\delta(x)$, which is usually referred to as the unit impulse function or Dirac delta function. Hence we write

$$f_S(x) = \frac{d}{dx} F_S(x) = \delta\left(x - \frac{1}{\mu}\right). \tag{3.325}$$

The function $\delta(x)$ can be regarded as a highly concentrated pulse with a unit area. For any function $g(x)$ that is continuous at $x = x_0$, the product $g(x)\delta(x - x_0)$ represents a pulse of the area $g(x_0)$. Therefore

$$\int_{-\infty}^{\infty} g(x)\delta(x - x_0)\, dx = g(x_0). \tag{3.326}$$

Indeed we can consider (3.326) as the definition of the notation $\delta(x - x_0)$. The Laplace transform of $f_S(x)$ of (3.325) is therefore

$$\Phi_S(s) = \int_0^\infty e^{-sx}\delta\left(x - \frac{1}{\mu}\right) dx = e^{-s/\mu}. \tag{3.327}$$

Then by substituting the above result into (3.303), we obtain

$$P(z) = \frac{(1 - \rho)(1 - z)}{1 - ze^{\rho(1-z)}}. \tag{3.328}$$

It will be worth noting that this result could have been derived from (3.321) by taking the limit $k \to \infty$ (see also Exercise 3.4.1). The Taylor series expansion of (3.328) gives

$$P(z) = (1 - \rho)(1 - z) \sum_{j=0}^\infty z^j e^{j\rho} e^{-j\rho z}. \tag{3.329}$$

By equating the coefficients of z^n terms, we obtain

$$p_n = (1 - \rho) \sum_{j=0}^n (-1)^{n-j} \frac{(j\rho)^{n-j-1}(j\rho + n - j)e^{j\rho}}{(n - j)!}. \tag{3.330}$$

In Fig. 3.41, we plot the distribution (3.330) to which the solution for the $M/E_k/1$ system converges as $k \to \infty$.

By differentiating (3.303) with respect to z and setting $z \to 1$, we obtain the average number of customers in the $M/G/1$ systems (Exercise 3.11.4):

$$\bar{N} = P'(1) = \rho + \frac{\lambda^2 E[S^2]}{2(1 - \rho)}$$

$$= \rho + \frac{\rho^2(1 + C_S^2)}{2(1 - \rho)}, \tag{3.331}$$

where C_S is the coefficient of variation of the service time. The last formula is called the *Pollaczek-Khinchine* formula, and there are other ways of deriving this result (see Exercises 3.7.3 and 3.11.5). If the service-time distribution is exponential, then $C_S = 1$ and (3.331) reduces to

$$\bar{N} = \frac{\rho}{1 - \rho}. \tag{3.332}$$

On the other hand, if service time is constant, then $C_S = 0$ and

$$\bar{N} = \frac{\rho\left(1 - \dfrac{\rho}{2}\right)}{1 - \rho}. \tag{3.333}$$

Thus, under the heavy traffic condition ($\rho \cong 1$), the ratio of the mean queue size of an $M/M/1$ queue to that of an $M/D/1$ queue is two to one.

Since the utilization factor ρ of a single-server system can be interpreted as the mean number of customers in service, we can write $\bar{N}$ as the sum of ρ and the mean number $\bar{Q}$ of customers waiting in the queue. Thus

$$\bar{N} = \rho + \bar{Q}. \tag{3.334}$$

From (3.333) and (3.334) we have

$$\bar{Q} = \frac{\lambda^2 E[S^2]}{2(1 - \rho)}. \tag{3.335}$$

The mean waiting time under the FCFS queue discipline is now readily obtainable using Little's formula:

$$\bar{W}_{\text{FCFS}} = \frac{\bar{Q}}{\lambda} = \frac{\lambda E[S^2]}{2(1 - \rho)}, \tag{3.336}$$

which, of course, agrees with the earlier result (3.81). Similarly, we find the mean response time under the FCFS discipline:

$$\bar{T}_{\text{FCFS}} = \frac{\bar{N}}{\lambda} = \bar{S}\left[1 + \frac{\rho(1 + C_S^2)}{2(1 - \rho)} \right]$$

$$= \bar{S} + \bar{W}_{\text{FCFS}}. \tag{3.337}$$

Now we turn our attention to the distribution of the response time and waiting time. In the FCFS queue discipline, the number of customers, N_k, left behind by the kth departing customer is equivalent to the number of arrivals during the response time of customer k. Then the relation of $P(z)$ to the response-time distribution $F_T(t)$ is exactly analogous to the relation we found between $A(z)$ and the service-time distribution $F_S(t)$ (Exercise 3.11.7). Therefore, the relation (3.299) implies

$$P(z) = \Phi_T(\lambda - \lambda z), \tag{3.338}$$

where $\Phi_T(\cdot)$ is the Laplace transform of the probability density function $f_T(t) = (d/dt)F_T(t)$, which we want to obtain. By equating (3.303) and (3.338) and setting $s = \lambda - \lambda z$, we find

$$\Phi_T(s) = \frac{(1 - \rho)s\Phi_S(s)}{s - \lambda + \lambda\Phi_S(s)}. \tag{3.339}$$

Let us denote by W_k the waiting time of customer k. Then

$$T_k = W_k + S_k, \tag{3.340}$$

where S_k is the service time of customer k. Since W_k and S_k are independent random variables, the following relation must hold:

$$\Phi_T(s) = \Phi_W(s)\Phi_S(s), \tag{3.341}$$

where $\Phi_W(s)$ is the Laplace transform of the density function $f_W(t)$ of the waiting time. Then from (3.339) and (3.341), it follows that

$$\Phi_W(s) = \frac{(1 - \rho)s}{s - \lambda + \lambda\Phi_S(s)}. \tag{3.342}$$

The methods used to invert formulas such as (3.339) and (3.342) were discussed in Chapter 2.

Example 3.4 ($M/M/1$).   Consider the exponential service time with rate μ. Then $\Phi_S(s) = \mu/(s + \mu)$ and we obtain from (3.341) and (3.342)

$$\Phi_T(s) = \frac{\mu(1 - \rho)}{s + \mu(1 - \rho)} \tag{3.343}$$

and

$$\Phi_W(s) = \frac{(1 - \rho)(s + \mu)}{s + \mu(1 - \rho)} = (1 - \rho) + \frac{\rho\mu(1 - \rho)}{s + \mu(1 - \rho)} \tag{3.344}$$

so that the corresponding probability density functions are given by

$$f_T(t) = \mu e^{-\mu(1-\rho)t}, \qquad t \geq 0 \tag{3.345}$$

and by

$$f_W(t) = (1 - \rho)\delta(t) + \rho\mu(1 - \rho)e^{-\mu(1-\rho)t}, \qquad t \geq 0. \tag{3.346}$$

By integrating them, we obtain the distribution functions

$$F_T(t) = 1 - e^{-\mu(1-\rho)t}, \qquad t \geq 0 \tag{3.347}$$

and

$$F_W(t) = 1 - \rho e^{-\mu(1-\rho)t}, \qquad t > 0 \tag{3.348}$$

which agree with the results obtained earlier (see (3.122) and (3.125)).

Exercises

3.11.3 Refer to Example 3.1 on the $M/H_2/1$ queue. Compute the probability distribution $\{p_n\}$ using the recursion formula discussed in Section 2.6.2.

3.11.4 Show the derivation steps from (3.303) to (3.331).

3.11.5 Derive the Pollaczek-Khinchine formula as instructed below.

    a) Take the expectation of (3.294) and find the probability that the server is busy in the equilibrium state.

b) Square both sides of (3.294) and then take the expectation. Derive the formula (3.331).

3.11.6 Show how $P(z)$ of (3.318) can be inverted by the recursion method.

3.11.7 Discuss the relation between $P(z)$ and $F_T(t)$ and derive the expression of (3.338).

3.11.8 *The response-time distribution of the $M/H_2/1$.* Show that the response-time distribution $F_T(t)$ of an $M/H_2/1$ system is also a two-stage hyperexponential distribution. Plot the curve assuming the set of parameters given in Example 3.1.

3.11.3   *M/G/1* System with Finite Storage

In this section we will discuss the single-server queue with a Poisson input, general service-time distribution, and a finite number, $K - 1$, of waiting rooms as shown in Fig. 3.43(a). The maximum number of customers that can be accommodated in the system at a given time is K. If a customer arrives when all waiting positions are occupied, the customer will be rejected or, equivalently, the customer will depart from the system without receiving any service. The model is the same as the one discussed in Section 3.8.4 except that the service-time distribution is now assumed to be general.

The $M/G/1$ queue with finite storage (or waiting rooms) is an important mathematical model in its own right, but the model has an additional importance because of its equivalence to a two-stage cyclic queue with general and exponential servers. Consider the cyclic queueing system of Fig. 3.43(b) with a fixed number K of customers circulating in the system, where server 2 has exponentially distributed service times $\{\tau\}$ with mean λ^{-1}, that is, $P[\tau \le t] = 1 - e^{-\lambda t}$. Then we can observe the following equivalency between the cyclic queueing system of Fig. 3.43(b) and the $M/G/1$ queue with finite storage of Fig. 3.43(a). Customers arrive at server 1 according to a Poisson stream with rate λ while server 2 is serving. If server 2 becomes idle (that is, $n_2 = 0$), then all K customers are in server 1, and there will be no arrivals at server 1. This situation corresponds exactly to the case in which the equivalent $M/G/1$ queue has

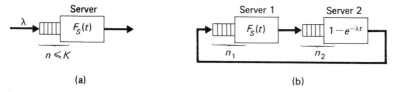

(a)   (b)

Fig. 3.43   (a) The system $M/G/1$ with finite waiting rooms and (b) a cyclic queueing system with a general server.

all the waiting rooms full. Note that this relationship was used earlier in Section 3.8.4 in establishing the equivalency between the $M/M/1$ with finite storage and the two-stage cyclic queue with exponential servers. It is based on the memoryless property of the exponential server and the corresponding Poisson process. Let the joint probability distribution of the system of Fig. 3.43(b) be

$$p(n_1, n_2) = P[n_1 \text{ customers in server 1, } n_2 \text{ customers in server 2}],$$
(3.349)

where $n_1 + n_2 = K$. Then because of the equivalence relation, we have

$$p(n, K - n) = p_k(n),$$ (3.350)

where $p_K(n)$ is the distribution of the number of customers in the $M/G/1$ system with capacity K. Now we wish to calculate this distribution. We again use the imbedded Markov chain technique.

Let N_k^* be the number of customers found in the system of Fig. 3.43(a) just after the service completion of customer k. Then the random variable N_k^* takes on integer values $0, 1, 2, \ldots, K - 1$. (Note that N_k^* cannot be K, because when a customer leaves the server, the customer cannot leave behind a completely full system; at least one waiting position must be empty.) Let X_k be the total number of arrivals (including those rejected because of the full waiting room) during the kth service period. Then analogously to (3.294) we have

$$N_k^* = \min \{N_{k-1}^* - U(N_{k-1}^*) + X_k, \quad K - 1\}.$$ (3.351)

Thus, the sequence N_k^* is again a Markov chain. Let p_n^* ($n = 0, 1, 2, \ldots, K - 1$) be the equilibrium probability that the sequence N_k^* takes on value n. We write $P^*(z)$ for the probability generating function of the random variable N_k^* in the equilibrium:

$$P^*(z) = \lim_{k \to \infty} E[z^{N_k^*}]$$

(3.352)

$$= \sum_{n=0}^{K-1} \sum_{i=0}^{\infty} p_n^* a_i z^{\min \{n - U(n) + i, K - 1\}},$$

where $\{a_i\}$ is the probability distribution of the random variable X and is given by (3.298). By comparing the coefficients of z^j of (3.352), we obtain the following equations for $\{p_j^*\}$:

$$p_j^* = p_0^* a_j + \sum_{n=1}^{j+1} p_n^* a_{j-n+1}, \quad \text{for} \quad 0 \le j \le K - 2$$ (3.353)

and

$$p_{K-1}^* = p_0^* \sum_{i=K-1}^{\infty} a_i + \sum_{n=1}^{K-1} p_n^* \left(\sum_{k=K-n}^{\infty} a_i \right). \qquad (3.354)$$

The distribution $\{p_j^*\}$ we obtained above is the probability that a customer leaves j customers behind when departing from the system. This distribution is equivalent to the distribution of the number of customers in the system found by a customer who arrives at the system when it is not full. This equivalency between the distributions at arrival and departure time periods was discussed earlier (Exercise 3.6.3), and is based on the simple observation that the upward transitions $j \to j + 1$ of the system state should balance with the downward transitions $j + 1 \to j$.

What we want to calculate, however, is the distribution $\{q_j: 0 \le j \le K\}$ of the number of customers found by a random outside observer or, equivalently, the time average distribution of the population size in system. Before we seek this solution, let us investigate the relation between $\{p_j^*\}$ and $\{p_j\}$, the solution obtained in Section 3.11.2 under no storage constraint (i.e., $K = \infty$).

If we just write down the coefficients of the terms z^j of both sides in (3.296) we have

$$p_j = p_0 a_j + \sum_{n=1}^{j+1} p_n a_{j-n+1}, \quad \text{for all} \quad j \ge 0. \qquad (3.355)$$

This expression is essentially the same as (3.353), which can be written in the following recurrence form:

$$p_{j+1}^* = \frac{p_j^* - a_j p_0^* - \sum_{n=1}^{j} a_{j-n+1} p_n^*}{a_0}, \quad \text{for} \quad 0 \le j \le K - 2. \qquad (3.356)$$

Similarly, from (3.355),

$$p_{j+1} = \frac{p_j - a_j p_0 - \sum_{n=1}^{j} a_{j-n+1} p_n}{a_0}, \quad \text{for all} \quad j \ge 0. \qquad (3.357)$$

Therefore, if we take the first K terms $p_0, p_1, \ldots, p_{K-1}$ of the solution $\{p_j: j \ge 0\}$ of (3.355), the set of equations

$$p_j^* = c p_j, \qquad 0 \le j \le K - 1 \qquad (3.358)$$

should satisfy (3.356) for any scalar c. The constant c should be determined uniquely so that (3.354) is met; this is equivalent to

$$\sum_{j=0}^{K-1} p_j^* = 1. \qquad (3.359)$$

Thus we have

$$c = \frac{1}{\sum_{j=0}^{K-1} p_j}. \tag{3.360}$$

Therefore, the probability $\{p_j^*\}$ can be obtained by simply truncating and scaling the solution of the $M/G/1$ queue with infinite storage.

Suppose we observe the system with finite storage over an interval of T and let $A_j(T)$ be the total number of customers who find, upon arrival, that there are j customers in the system, $0 \le j \le K$. Clearly, $A_K(T)$ is the number of arrivals who are rejected due to the full storage. Then letting

$$A(T) = \sum_{j=0}^{K} A_j(T) \tag{3.361}$$

$$A^*(T) = \sum_{j=0}^{K-1} A_j(T) = A(T) - A_K(T) \tag{3.362}$$

we can write the distributions $\{p_j^*\}$ and $\{q_j\}$ as

$$p_j^* = \lim_{T \to \infty} \frac{A_j(T)}{A^*(T)}, \quad 0 \le j \le K - 1 \tag{3.363}$$

and

$$q_j = \lim_{T \to \infty} \frac{A_j(T)}{A(T)}, \quad 0 \le j \le K. \tag{3.364}$$

Therefore, the distributions $\{q_j\}$ and $\{p_j^*\}$ are proportional in the range $0 \le j \le K - 1$:

$$q_j = dp_j^*, \quad 0 \le j \le K - 1 \tag{3.365}$$

where d is a scalar constant. Then from this and (3.358) it follows that

$$q_j = fp_j, \quad 0 \le j \le K - 1 \tag{3.366}$$

where $f = cd$ is a scaling constant to be determined below.

The probability q_K and the scalar constant f are calculated as follows. Divide (3.362) by T:

$$\frac{A^*(T)}{T} = \frac{A(T)}{T}\left(1 - \frac{A_K(T)}{A(T)}\right). \tag{3.367}$$

Since $A^*(T)$ is the total number of arrivals accepted for service, the expected total work placed on the server is $A^*(T)\bar{S}$. The server is busy, on the average, over the period of $(1 - q_0)T$ to meet the service requirement. Therefore, for sufficiently large T, we have

$$A^*(T)\bar{S} \cong (1 - q_0)T. \tag{3.368}$$

Then in the limit $T \to \infty$, we find

$$\lim_{T \to \infty} \frac{A^*(T)}{T} = \frac{1 - q_0}{\bar{S}}. \tag{3.369}$$

The right-hand side of (3.367) should converge to $\lambda(1 - q_K)$ as $T \to \infty$. This leads to the following result:

$$\frac{1 - q_0}{\bar{S}} = \lambda(1 - q_K). \tag{3.370}$$

The last equation simply says that the departure rate is equal to the accepted arrival rate in Fig. 3.43(a). For the cyclic queue system of Fig. 3.42(b), the equation means that the departure rate from server 1 is equal to that from server 2. Note that $1 - q_K$ represents the probability that server 2 is busy. We can rewrite (3.370) as

$$1 - q_0 = \lambda \bar{S}(1 - q_K). \tag{3.371}$$

Then from (3.366), (3.371), and the constraint

$$\sum_{j=0}^{K} q_j = 1 \tag{3.372}$$

we find the distribution of the number of customers for finite storage capacity in terms of the probabilities for the ordinary $M/G/1$ queue:

$$q_n = f p_n, \quad \text{for} \quad 0 \le n \le K - 1 \tag{3.373a}$$

and

$$q_K = 1 - \frac{1 - f p_0}{\lambda \bar{S}} \tag{3.373b}$$

where

$$f = \frac{1}{p_0 + \lambda \bar{S} \sum_{n=0}^{K-1} p_n}. \tag{3.374}$$

The equilibrium distribution $\{p_n\}$ exists under the condition $\lambda \bar{S} < 1$. When $\lambda \bar{S} > 1$, the equilibrium distribution $\{p_n\}$ does not exist, but we can obtain, within a proportionality constant, a finite term $\{p_n : 0 \le n \le K - 1\}$ from the recursive formula (3.357).

Example 3.5 ($M/H_2/1$ with finite storage).   Consider the $M/H_2/1$ system studied in Example 3.1. We maintain the same set of parameter values; that is, the Poisson arrival rate of Fig. 3.43(a) (or, equivalently, the service rate of server 2 of Fig. 3.42b) is $\lambda = 0.75$, the service distribution is $F_S(t) = 1 - \pi_1 e^{-\mu_1 t} - \pi_2 e^{-\mu_2 t}$ where $\pi_1 = 0.0526$, $\mu_1 = 0.1$, and $\mu_2 = 2$, and the mean service time is

$$\frac{1}{\mu} = \frac{\pi_1}{\mu_1} + \frac{\pi_2}{\mu_2} \cong 1.0.$$

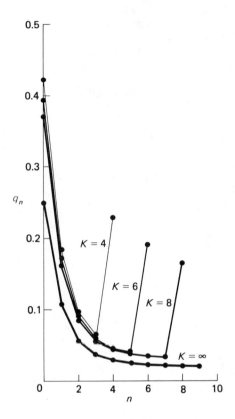

Fig. 3.44 The queue distribution of the $M/H_2/1$ queueing system with K units of storage capacity (Example 3.5).

The distribution of the number of customers in the system without storage constraint (i.e., $K = \infty$) was given by $\{p_n\}$ of (3.315), which is a mixed geometric distribution.

Figure 3.44 plots the distribution $\{q_n\}$ of (3.373) for the storage size $k = 4$, 6, 8, and ∞. The curve for $k = \infty$ is, of course, the same as that of Fig. 3.41. Note that for finite K the probability q_K is much larger than q_{K-1}. This is quite a contrast to what we observed for the case of exponential service time in Section 3.8.4. It explains that the throughput of the system with a skewed service-time distribution is low; the throughput is given by $\lambda(1 - q_K)$.

Example 3.6 ($M/D/1$ with finite storage). Refer to the $M/D/1$ system of Example 3.3, in which the service time is a constant, $1/\mu = 1.0$, and the arrival rate $\lambda = 0.75$; hence $\rho = 0.75$. The queue distribution without storage constraint is given by $\{p_n\}$ of (3.330) and is shown in Fig. 3.42. A family of the distributions, $\{q_n\}$, with the storage capacity $K = 4, 6$, and 8 is plotted in solid curves in Fig. 3.45. We also plot, in dashed curves, the distributions of the $M/M/1$ with finite storage to illustrate the effect of service-time distribution. This group of curves is the truncated geometric distribution of (3.146) with the same mean values, that is, $\lambda/\mu = 0.75$. It is important to note that for the $M/D/1$ with finite storage, the probability q_K is lower than the $M/M/1$ case. This contrasts even more sharply with the hyperexponential case of the previous example, and it is a manifestation of a general property of a queueing system; the more regular the service time is, the higher the throughput $\lambda(1 - q_K)$ becomes.

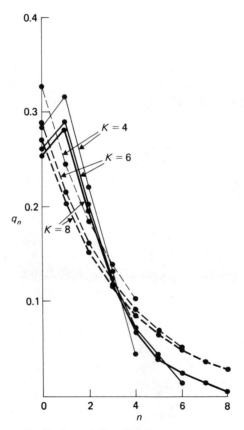

Fig. 3.45 The queue distribution of the $M/D/1$ queueing system with K units of storage capacity (Example 3.6).

DISCUSSION AND FURTHER READING

Most of the results given in this chapter are based on the Markov process representation of queueing systems: the Poisson process, the exponential service distribution, the birth-and-death process, queueing networks with exponential servers, and the method of stage representation of general service times; they are all ingredients that render a model of a mathematically tractable Markovian system.

Formula $L = \lambda W$ of Section 3.6 and the conservation laws of Section 3.7 are of particular importance, since they hold for a large class of stable queueing systems. A rigorous proof of $L = \lambda W$ is given by Stidham (1974). The notion of work-conserving queue discipline was introduced by Kleinrock (1965) and the results of Section 3.7 are primarily due to Kleinrock (1965, 1976), Wolff (1970b), and Schrage (1970).

The birth-and-death process model of Section 3.8 is discussed in many books on queueing theory: Cooper (1972), Feller (1966), Kleinrock (1975), Syski (1960), among many others. The machine servicing model (or finite source model) of Section 3.9 is discussed also by Cox and Smith (1961), Syski (1960), and Kleinrock (1969, 1975). Our treatment, however, emphasizes the numerical computation algorithms. Many of the formulas in Section 3.9.2 and the approximate analysis of Section 3.9.3, to the best of the author's knowledge, are not discussed elsewhere. An application of the machine servicing model to a time-sharing system was first discussed by Scherr (1967) in the performance analysis of MIT-CTSS and later by Lassettre and Scherr (1972) in the development of OS/360 Time Sharing Option (TSO). Boyse and Warn (1975) discuss its application to a multiprogramming system analysis, as referenced in Section 3.10.5. These authors assume the exponential model in their studies, but as we claim in Section 3.10.5, the results are, in many cases, robust with respect to the distributional forms.

The queueing network models of Section 3.10 are essentially multidimensional analogs of the birth-and-death process model. The results of Sections 3.10.1–3.10.2 are based on the classical work by Jackson (1963) and Gordon and Newell (1967). C. G. Moore (1971) and Buzen (1971) were among the first to recognize the use of queueing network models in the performance analysis of multiprogramming computer systems. Giammo (1976) gives some discussions of the validation of queueing network models.

The recurrence equation derived from the system balance condition in its equilibrium is often called the *local balance* equation (Chandy, 1972) or *individual balance* equation (Whittle, 1965). The class of queueing network models for which the product form is found has been enlarged recently by Chandy (1972), Baskett et al. (1975), Kobayashi and Reiser (1975), Kelly (1975, 1976), Barbour (1976), and Chandy, Howard, and Towsley (1977). The reader is also referred to Kleinrock (1975, 1976) and review articles by Disney (1975), Kobayashi and Konheim (1977), and Lemoine (1977). The computational algorithms of Section 3.10.3 follow the work by Buzen (1973) and Reiser and Kobayashi (1975). The algorithm presented in Section 3.10.4 is due to Kobayashi (1976). A closed form solution for the queueing network model becomes extremely difficult to obtain once *blocking* due to the finite capacity constraint is introduced. Konheim and Reiser (1977) and Pittel (1976) address this problem. All of the results discussed in queueing network models are concerned with queue-size distributions rather than waiting- or response-time distributions. Exceptions are the expressions (3.184) and (3.187) of the machine servicing model, which is a special case of a closed queueing network model. Chow (1977a, 1977b) obtained algebraic expressions for the cycle time distribution for the cyclic queue model and central server model. Yu (1977) discusses the Laplace transform method to compute the passage-time distribution in a queueing network model.

The method of stage representation of Section 3.11.1 is due to Cox (1955) and can be regarded as extensions of the concept associated with the Erlangian distribution. Bux and Herzog (1977) discuss how to obtain such representation from empirical data. Wallace and Rosenberg (1966) discuss applications of this representation to a general network of queues. The imbedded Markov chain approach discussed in Section 3.11.2 was originally introduced by Kendall (1951, 1953) to the system $M/G/1$ and to $GI/M/m$. Lindley (1952) carried out the imbedded Markov chain analysis of waiting time of $GI/G/1$ and his work was continued by Smith (1953). For further discussions on this subject, the reader is referred to Kleinrock (1975), Cooper (1972), and Konheim (1975).

Gaver (1967) and Smith (1967) formulated a multiprogramming system as a two-stage cyclic queueing system. Shedler (1970) discussed an embedded Markov chain analysis of the cyclic queueing system. Adiri (1972) gives a full account of this class of queueing models. The $M/G/1$ with finite storage is discussed by Cooper (1972) and Keilson (1965). The closed form expressions of queue distributions for $M/E_k/1$ and $M/D/1$ (for example, Eqs. (3.322) and (3.330)) were due to Reiser and Kobayashi (1974b).

One important topic that was excluded from this chapter is a discussion of *priority queues*. Priority queues treated in the conventional queueing theory literature (see Cobham, 1954; Jaiswal, 1968; Conway, Maxwell, and Miller, 1967; Kleinrock, 1976) usually adopt the notion of *external priority*. That is, the priority level or value of a customer is determined externally and before the customer enters the system. There are two classes of scheduling rules in priority systems: *preemptive* and *nonpreemptive* (see Section 3.2.3). The solutions for the waiting-time distributions in the $M/G/1$ system with multiclass customers are usually expressed in the Laplace transforms. (So is the general solution of an ordinary $M/G/1$ queue discussed in Section 3.11.2.) The numerical inversion method of Section 2.6.4 allows us to obtain the time-domain expressions.

Other types of priority are defined in terms of what we sometimes call the *running time* or *dynamic* priority: A customer increments or decrements his priority level as a function of elapsed time since entry into the system. The CPU scheduling of a time-shared system (and often in a batch-type multiprogrammed system as well) adopts some kind of running time priority and corresponding scheduling rule—for instance, RR (round-robin), PS (processor-sharing), FB (foreground-background) scheduling algorithms, and variants on these. The notion of PS scheduling was initially introduced by Kleinrock (1967) as the limiting case of RR scheduling in which the time quantum (or time slice) is allowed to approach zero. Under this discipline, when there are n customers at the service facility, each customer receives service at the rate C/n [work-units/sec], where C is the total capacity of the server.

If the input (or arrival) process is Poisson, and if then the output process is also Poisson, we say that the system has the $M \Rightarrow M$ property. The $M \Rightarrow M$ property of an $M/G/\infty$ was shown by Doob (1953) and Mirasol (1963), and that of $M/G/1$ under PS by Muntz (1972). The $M \Rightarrow M$ property of these queueing systems has an interesting relation to the class of queueing networks discussed in Section 3.10 and the extended class reported by Chandy (1972), Baskett et al. (1975), and Reiser and Kobayashi (1975). If we are given an arbitrary set of service stations connected in an arbitrary topology, the joint probability distribution of queue sizes in equilibrium is given in a product form (that is, Eqs. (3.218) and (3.235)), provided each service station satisfies the $M \Rightarrow M$ property. Furthermore, as shown by Kobayashi and Reiser (1975), the distribution depends on the service-time distribution and customers' routing behavior *only through* the mean total work parameters $\{\overline{W}_i\}$ defined by (3.223), insofar as the routing behavior is representable by an hth order Markov chain (where h can be arbitrarily large). See Kobayashi (1978) for related discussions.

Other priority queueing systems—preemptive and nonpreemptive systems with external priority, and the systems with dynamic priorities such as RR, FB, SPT (shortest-processing-time-first), SRPT (shortest-remaining-processing-time-first), etc.—have been solved only in the context of the $M/G/1$ system (with multiclass customers in case of external priority), and the solutions are given in terms of the mean response (or waiting) time for a given service time; that is, $T(x) = E[T | S = x]$ (or $W(x) = E[W | S = x]$). Since these queueing disciplines do not possess the $M \Rightarrow M$ property in the $M/G/1$ situation, they cannot be incorporated in multiple resource models. We should note, however, that both RR and FB are work-conserving queue disciplines (assuming that job switching at the end of each time slice is done without imposing additional work on the server*); hence, use of these disciplines does not change the queue distribution in the multiple resource models of Section 3.10 if the service demand variables at the corresponding stations are drawn from (single class) exponential distributions. For further details, the reader is directed to McKinney (1969), Wolff (1970a), Coffman and Denning (1973), and Kleinrock (1973, 1976) who discuss various processor scheduling disciplines in the $M/G/1$ setting.

Before we close this chapter, we make a few remarks on other important subjects not treated in this text, such as approximation and bounding techniques. In Sections 3.9.3 and 3.10.5 we introduced fluid approximation and related graphical analysis. Kleinrock and Lam (1975) discuss the *stability* problem of the ALOHA multiaccess communication channel based upon the fluid approximation approach. Courtois (1975) gives discussions of the stability and control problems in a virtual-storage multiprogrammed system using the fluid approximation approach. See also Kobayashi (1978) for an expository treatment of the subject. The fluid approximation model is often called a first-order approximation model, since only mean values are considered in the model. The *diffusion approximation* model is a second-order model, since it can incorporate statistical fluctuations of model variables—the variance of interarrival time, the variance of service times or delay parameters. A *diffusion process* is a *continuous-time continuous-state Markov process,* and does not possess jumps or discontinuities that appear in queueing processes such as $N(t)$ (the number of customers in the system) and $V(t)$ (unfinished work). The behavior of a diffusion equation is characterized by a partial-differential equation called the *diffusion equation* or *Kolmogorov's equation.* Our problem is, therefore, reduced to that of solving the diffusion equation with appropriate *initial* and *boundary conditions* and such mathematical procedure is often (but not always) easier to deal with than the underlying system equation that characterizes jump processes. The idea of approximating a discrete-state process (e.g., a random walk)

---

* The degradation or overhead due to job switching can be indirectly incorporated by the suitable choice of the queue-dependent server capacity function $C(n)$.

by a diffusion process with continuous path is not new (see Feller, 1966, and references therein). Applications to congestion theory have recently been reported by Kingman (1962, 1965), Cox and Miller (1965), Iglehart (1968), and Newell (1971). Gaver (1968, 1971) applied the diffusion approximation method to the waiting time in an $M/G/1$ queue and to the analysis of delays and the backlogs at remote terminals.

Gaver and Shedler (1973) proposed an approximate method to evaluate the CPU utilization of a multiprogrammed system represented by a cyclic queueing model. Kobayashi (1974a, 1974b) considered the multidimensional diffusion approximation as a technique for treating the general queueing network. Reiser and Kobayashi (1974a) report numerical results on the accuracy of the approximate model proposed by Kobayashi (1974a). See also Gelenbe (1975) and Gelenbe and Pujolle (1976) on related subjects and applications to a packet-switching network. Kobayashi, Onozato, and Huynh (1977) discuss a diffusion approximation model of the ALOHA system.

Chandy, Herzog, and Woo (1975a) proposed an iterative method for the approximate analysis of a queueing network with general service-time distributions. For a given network of queues, they consider a "near-equivalent" network of exponential servers. One of the remaining research tasks in both the iterative approximation and the diffusion approximation is to establish some general formula that allows us to assess the accuracies of the approximate solutions. See also Courtois (1977), Disney and Cherry (1974), and Sevcik et al. (1977) for discussions on decomposition and approximations of a queueing network model.

In connection with approximate methods, *bounds* for waiting-time distributions or other quantities offer problems for research of both mathematical depth and practical importance. Kingman (1970) established upper and lower bounds on the tail of the waiting-time distribution in the $G/G/1$ system. Ross (1974) improved on Kingman's upper bound; Kobayashi (1974c) applied to the $G/G/1$ queue Kolmogorov's inequality for submartingale and obtained an upper bound on $P[W_n > x]$, where W_n is the waiting time of the nth customer in a busy period. In the limit $n \to \infty$, his bound converges to Kingman's bound. Marshall (1968), Kingman (1970), Brumelle (1971), Calo (1976), and Wolff (1977) discuss bounds on the *mean* response time in the $G/G/1$ and $G/G/m$ queues.

The problem of buffer overflow analysis is important to many communication-related issues: estimation of the buffer capacity required in multiplexors, message switching processors, etc. Many of the buffer behavior problems can be formulated in a form that is mathematically equivalent to the waiting-time problem in $G/G/1$ queues. Based on this analogy, Kobayashi and Konheim (1977) derived an upper bound on the probability of buffer overflow as a function of the buffer capacity. See also Wyner (1974) on related subjects. Kleinrock (1976) gives a full account of the diffusion approximation and bounds with a comprehensive list of references up to 1974.

REFERENCES

Adiri, I. (1972). "Queueing Models for Multiprogrammed Computers." *Proceedings of the International Symposium on Computer-Communication Networks and Teletraffic*, pp. 441–448. Brooklyn, N.Y.: Polytech Press.

Allen, A. O. (1978). *Probability, Statistics, and Queueing Theory with Computer Science Applications*. Washington, D.C.: Academic Press.

Avi-Itzhak, B., and D. P. Heyman (1973). "Approximate Queueing Models for Multiprogramming Computer Systems." *Operations Research* **21**(6): 1212–1230.

Barbour, A. O. (1976). "Networks of Queues and the Method of Stages." *Advances in Applied Probability* **8**: 584–591.

Baskett, F., K. M. Chandy, R. R. Muntz, and F. G. Palacios (1975). "Open, Closed and Mixed Networks of Queues with Different Classes of Customers." *Journal of the Association for Computing Machinery* **22**(2): 248–260.

Boyse, J. H., and D. R. Warn (1975). "A Straightforward Model for Computer Performance Prediction." *Computing Surveys* **7**(2): 73–93. (Copyright 1975, Association for Computing Machinery, Inc. Reprinted by permission.)

Brumelle, S. L. (1971). "Some Inequalities for Parallel-Server Queues." *Operations Research* **19**(2): 402–413.

Burke, P. J. (1956). "The Output of a Queueing System." *Operations Research* **4** (December): 699–704.

Burke, P. J. (1972). "Output Processes and Tandem Queues." *Proceedings of the 22nd International Symposium on Computer-Communication Networks and Teletraffic*, pp. 419–428. Brooklyn, N.Y.: Polytech Institute of Brooklyn.

Bux, W., and U. Herzog (1977). "The Phase Concept: Approximation of Measured Data and Performance Analysis." In K. M. Chandy and M. Reiser (eds.), *Proceedings of the International Symposium on Computer Performance Modeling, Measurement, and Evaluation*, pp. 23–37. Amsterdam: North-Holland.

Buzen, J. P. (1971). "Queueing Network Models of Multiprogramming." Ph.D. thesis, Division of Engineering and Applied Sciences, Harvard University, Cambridge, Mass.

Buzen, J. P. (1973). "Computational Algorithms for Closed Queueing Networks with Exponential Servers." *Communications of the Association for Computing Machinery* **16**(9): 527–531.

Calo, S. R. (1976). "Bounds and Approximations for Moments of Queueing Processes." Ph.D. dissertation, Department of Electrical Engineering, Princeton University (April 1976).

Chandy, K. M. (1972). "The Analysis and Solutions for General Queueing Networks." *Proceedings of the Sixth Annual Princeton Conference on Information Sciences and Systems*, pp. 224–228. Princeton, N.J.: Princeton University.

Chandy, K. M., U. Herzog, and L. Woo (1975a). "Approximate Analysis of General Queueing Networks." *IBM Journal of Research and Development* **19**(1): 43–49.

Chandy, K. M., U. Herzog, and L. Woo (1975b). "Parametric Analysis of Queueing Networks." *IBM Journal of Research and Development* **19**(1): 36–42.

Chandy, K. M., J. H. Howard, and D. F. Towsley (1977). "Product Form and Local Balance in Queueing Networks." *Journal of the Association for Computer Machinery* **24**(2): 250–263.

Chiu, W., D. Dumont, and R. Wood (1975). "Performance Analysis of a Multiprogrammed Computer System." *IBM Journal of Research and Development* **19**(3): 263–271.

Chow, W-M. (1975). "Central Server Model for Multiprogrammed Computer Systems with Different Classes of Jobs." *IBM Journal of Research and Development* **19**(3): 314–320.

Chow, W-M. (1977a). "The Cycle Time Distribution of Exponential Cyclic Queues." IBM Research Report RC-6484, Yorktown Heights, N.Y. (April).

Chow. W-M. (1977b). "The Cycle Time Distribution of Exponential Central Server Queues." IBM Research Report RC-6765, Yorktown Heights, N.Y. (September).

Chu, W. W., and A. G. Konheim (1972). "On the Analysis and Modeling of a Class of Computer Communication Systems." *IEEE Transactions on Communications* **COM-20**(6), Part II, pp. 645–660.

Cinlar, E. (1975). *Introduction to Stochastic Processes*. Engelwood Cliffs, N.J.: Prentice-Hall.

Cobham, A. (1954). "Priority Assignment in Waiting Line Problems." *Operations Research* **2**(1): 70–76.

Coffman, E. G., Jr., and P. J. Denning (1973). *Operating System Theory*. Englewood Cliffs, N.J.: Prentice-Hall.

Cohen, J. W. (1969). *The Single Server Queue*. New York: American Elsevier.

Cohen, J. W. (1976). *On Regenerative Processes in Queueing Theory*. New York: Springer-Verlag.

Conway, R. W., W. L. Maxwell, and L. W. Miller (1967). *Theory of Scheduling*. Reading, Mass.: Addison-Wesley.

Cooper, R. B. (1972). *Introduction to Queueing Theory*. New York: MacMillan.

Courtois, P. J. (1975). "Decomposability, Instability, and Saturation in Multiprogramming Systems." *Communications of the Association for Computing Machinery* **18**(7): 371–376.

Courtois, P. J. (1977). *Decomposability: Queueing and Computer System Applications.* New York: Academic Press.

Cox, D. R. (1955). "A Use of Complex Probabilities in Theory of Stochastic Processes." *Proceedings of Cambridge Philosophical Society* **51:** 313–319.

Cox, D. R., and H. D. Miller (1965). *The Theory of Stochastic Processes.* New York: John Wiley.

Cox, D. R., and W. L. Smith (1961). *Queues.* London: Methuen.

Disney, R. L. (1975). "Random Flow in Queueing Networks: A Review and Critique." *AIIE (American Institute of Industrial Engineers) Transactions* **7**(3): 268–288.

Disney, R. L., and W. P. Cherry (1974). "Some Topics in Queueing Network Theory." In A. B. Clarke (ed.), *Mathematical Methods in Queueing Theory.* Berlin: Springer-Verlag.

Doob, J. L. (1953). *Stochastic Processes.* New York: John Wiley.

Eilon, S. (1969). "A Simpler Proof of $L = \lambda W$." *Operations Research* **17**(5): 915–916.

Feller, W. (1966). *An Introduction to Probability and Its Applications,* Vol. II. New York: John Wiley.

Gaver, D. P. (1967). "Probability Models for Multiprogramming Computer Systems." *Journal of the Association for Computing Machinery* **14**(3): 423–438.

Gaver, D. P. (1968). "Diffusion Approximations and Models for Certain Congestion Problems." *Journal of Applied Probability* **5:** 607–623.

Gaver, D. P. (1971). "Analysis of Remote Terminal Backlogs Under Heavy Demand Conditions." *Journal of the Association for Computing Machinery* **18**(3): 405–415.

Gaver, D. P., and G. S. Shedler (1973). "Processor Utilization in Multiprogramming Systems via Diffusion Approximations." *Operations Research* **21**(2): 569–576.

Gelenbe, E. (1975). "On Approximate Computer System Models." *Journal of the Association for Computing Machinery* **22**(2): 261–269.

Gelenbe, E., and G. Pujolle (1976). "The Behavior of a Single Queue in a General Queueing Network." *Acta Informatica* **7**(2): 123–136.

Giammo, T. (1976). "Validation of a Computer Performance Model of the Exponential Queueing Network Family." *Acta Informatica* **7**(2): 137–152.

Gordon, W. L., and G. F. Newell (1967). "Closed Queueing Systems with Exponential Servers." *Operations Research* **15**(2): 254–265.

Gross, D., and C. M. Harris (1974). *Fundamentals of Queueing Theory.* New York: Wiley.

Hillier, F. S., and G. J. Lieberman (1967). *Introduction to Operations Research.* San Francisco: Holden-Day.

Iglehart, D. L. (1968). "Diffusion Approximations in Applied Probability." In G.

Dantzig and A. Veinott (eds.), *Mathematics of the Decision Sciences, Part 2.* Providence, R.I.: American Mathematical Society.

IBM Corporation. *Analysis of Some Queueing Models in Real-Time Systems, IBM Data Processing Techniques Manual,* F20-0007-1. White Plains. New York.

Jackson, J. R. (1963). "Job Shop-Like Queueing Systems." *Management Sciences* **10**(1): 131–142.

Jaiswal, N. (1968). *Priority Queues.* New York: Academic Press. .

Keilson, J. (1965). *Green's Function Methods in Probability Theory,* pp. 147–172. New York: Hafner.

Kelly, F. P. (1975). "Networks of Queues with Customers of Different Types." *Journal of Applied Probability* **12:** 542–554.

Kelly, F. P. (1976). "Networks of Queues." *Advances in Applied Probability* **8:** 416–432.

Kendall, D. G. (1951). "Some Problems in the Theory of Queues." *Journal of the Royal Statistical Society* Series B **13**(2): 151–185.

Kendall, D. G. (1953). "Stochastic Processes Occurring in the Theory of Queues and Their Analysis by the Method of Imbedded Markov Chains." *Annals of Mathematical Statistics* **24:** 338–354.

Kingman, J. F. C. (1962). "On Queues in Heavy Traffic." *Journal of the Royal Statistical Society* Series B **24**(2): 383–392.

Kingman, J. F. C. (1965). "The Heavy Traffic Approximation in the Theory of Queues." In W. L. Smith and W. E. Wilkinson (eds.), *The Proceedings of the Symposium on Congestion Theory,* pp. 137–159. Chapel Hill: University of North Carolina Press.

Kingman, J. F. C. (1970). "Inequalities in the Theory of Queues." *Journal of the Royal Statistical Society Series B* **32**(1): 102–110.

Kleinrock, L. (1965). "A Conservation Law for a Wide Class of Queueing Disciplines." *Naval Research Logistics Quarterly* **12:** 181–192.

Kleinrock, L. (1967). "Time-Shared Systems: A Theoretical Treatment." *Journal of the Association for Computing Machinery* **14**(2): 242–261.

Kleinrock, L. (1968). "Certain Analytic Results for Time-Shared Processor." *Proceedings of the International Federation for Information Processing Congress,* pp. 838–845. New York: North-Holland.

Kleinrock, L. (1973). "Scheduling, Queueing and Delays in Time-Shared Systems and Computer Networks." In N. Abramson and F. F. Kuo (eds.), *Computer-Communication Networks,* pp. 95–141. Englewood Cliffs, N.J.: Prentice-Hall.

Kleinrock, L. (1975). *Queueing Systems, Volume I: Theory.* New York: John Wiley.

Kleinrock, L. (1976). *Queueing Systems, Volume II: Computer Applications.* New York: John Wiley.

Kleinrock, L., and S. S. Lam (1975). "Packet Switching in Multiaccess Broadcast

Channel: Performance Evaluation." *IEEE Transactions on Communications* **COM-23**(4): 410–423.

Kobayashi, H. (1974a). "Application of Diffusion Approximation to Queueing Networks, Part I." *Journal of the Association for Computing Machinery* **21**(2): 316–328.

Kobayashi, H. (1974b). "Application of Diffusion Approximation to Queueing Networks, Part II." *Journal of the Association for Computing Machinery* **21**(3): 459–469.

Kobayashi, H. (1974c), "Bounds for the Waiting Time in Queueing Systems." In E. Gelenbe and R. Mahl (eds.), *Computer Architecture and Networks*, pp. 263–274. New York: North-Holland/American Elsevier.

Kobayashi, H. (1976). "A Computational Algorithm for Queue Distribution via Polya Theory of Enumeration." IBM Research Report RC-6154, IBM T. J. Watson Research Center, Yorktown Heights, New York (August).

Kobayashi, H. (1978). "System Design and Performance Analysis Using Analytic Models." In K. M. Chandy and R. T. Yeh (eds.), *Current Trends in Programming Methodology, Vol. III: Software Modelling*, pp. 72–114. Englewood Cliffs, N.J.: Prentice-Hall.

Kobayashi, H., and A. G. Konheim (1977). "Queueing Models for Computer Communications System Analysis." *IEEE Transactions on Communications* **COM-25**(1): 2–29.

Kobayashi, H., Y. Onozato, and D. Huynh (1977). "An Approximate Method for Design and Analysis of an ALOHA System." *IEEE Transactions on Communications* **COM-25**(1): 148–157.

Kobayashi, H., and M. Reiser (1975). "On Generalization of Job Routing Behavior in a Queueing Network Model." IBM Research Report RC-5252, IBM T. J. Watson Research Center, Yorktown Heights, New York (February).

Konheim, A. G. (1975). "An Elementary Solution of the Queueing System *G/G/*1." *SIAM Journal on Computing* **4**(4): 540–545.

Konheim, A. G., and M. Reiser (1976). "A Queueing Model with Finite Waiting Room and Blocking." *Journal of the Association for Computer Machinery* **23**(2): 328–341.

Lam, S. S. (1977). "Queueing Networks with Lost and Triggered Arrivals." *IBM Journal of Research and Development* **21**(4): 370–378.

Lassettre, E. R., and A. L. Scherr (1972). "Modelling the Performance of the OS/360 Time-Shared Option." In W. Freiberger (ed.), *Statistical Computer Performance Evaluation*, pp. 57–72. New York: Academic Press.

Lemoine, A. J. (1977). "Networks of Queues—A Survey of Equilibrium Analysis." *Management Science* **24**(4): 464–481.

Lindley, D. V. (1952). "The Theory of Queues with a Single Server." *Proceedings of Cambridge Philosophical Society* **48:** 277–289.

Little, J. D. C. (1961). "A Proof of the Queueing Formula $L = \lambda W$." *Operations Research* **9**(3): 383–387.

Liu, C. L. (1968). *Introduction to Combinatorial Mathematics.* New York: McGraw-Hill.

Marshall, K. T. (1968). "Bounds for Some Generalizations for the $GI/G/1$ Queue." *Operations Research* **16**(4): 841–848.

McKinney, J. M. (1969). "A Survey of Analytical Time-Sharing Models." *Computing Surveys* **1**(2): 105–116.

Mirasol, N. M. (1963). "The Output of an $M/G/\infty$ is Poisson." *Operations Research* **11**(2): 282–284.

Moore, C. G., III (1971). "Network Models for Large-Scale Time-Sharing Systems." Technical Report No. 71-1, Department of Industrial Engineering, University of Michigan, Ann Arbor, Michigan (April).

Moore, F. R. (1972). "Computational Model of a Closed Queueing Networks with Exponential Servers." *IBM Journal of Research and Development* **16**(6): 567–572.

Muntz, R. R. (1972). "Poisson Departure Processes and Queueing Networks." IBM Research Report RC-4145, IBM T. J. Watson Research Center, Yorktown Heights, New York (December).

Muntz, R. R. (1975). "Analytic Modeling of Interactive Systems." *Proceedings of IEEE* **63**(6): 946–953.

Newell, G. F. (1971). *Applications of Queueing Theory.* London: Chapman and Hall.

O'Donovan, T. M. (1974). "Direct Solution of $M/G/1$ Processor-Sharing Models." *Operations Research* **22**(6): 1232–1235.

Pittel, B. (1976). "Closed Exponential Networks of Queues with Blocking." IBM Research Report RC-6174, Yorktown Heights, New York.

Preparata, F. P., and R. T. Yeh (1973). *Introduction to Discrete Structures for Computer Science and Engineering.* Reading, Mass.: Addison-Wesley.

Reich, E. (1957). "Waiting Times When Queues are in Tandem." *Annals of Mathematical Statistics* **28**: 768–773.

Reiser, M., and H. Kobayashi (1974a). "Accuracy of the Diffusion Approximation for Some Queueing Systems." *IBM Journal of Research and Development* **18**(2): 110–124.

Reiser, M., and H. Kobayashi (1974b). "The Effects of Service Time Distributions on System Performance." *Proceedings of the International Federation for Information Processing Congress*, pp. 230–234. New York: North-Holland.

Reiser, M., and H. Kobayashi (1975). "Queueing Networks with Multiple Closed Chains: Theory and Computational Algorithms." *IBM Journal of Research and Development* **19**(May): 282–294.

Rosenshine, M. (1975). "Queueing Theory: The-State-of-the-Art." *AIIE* (*American Institute of Industrial Engineers*) *Transactions* **7**(3): 257–267.

Ross, S. M. (1974). "Bounds on the Delay Distribution in $GI/G/1$ Queues." *Journal of Applied Probability* **11**: 417–421.

Sauer, C. H., and K. M. Chandy (1975). "Approximate Analysis of Central Server Models." *IBM Journal of Research and Development* **19**(3): 301–313.

Scherr, A. L. (1967). *An Analysis of Time-Shared Computer Systems.* Cambridge, Mass.: MIT Press.

Schrage, L. (1970). "An Alternative Proof of a Conservation Law for the Queue $G/G/1$." *Operations Research* **18**(1): 185–187.

Sevcik, K. C., A. I. Levy, S. K. Tripathi, and J. L. Zahorjan (1977). "Improving Approximations of Aggregated Queueing Network Subsystems." In K. M. Chandy and M. Reiser (eds.), *Proceedings of the International Symposium on Computer Performance Modeling, Measurement and Evaluation,* pp. 1–22. Amsterdam: North-Holland.

Shedler, G. S. (1970). "A Cyclic-Queue Model of a Paging Machine." IBM Research Report RJ-2814, Yorktown Heights, New York.

Smith, J. L. (1967). "Multiprogramming under a Page on Demand Strategy." *Communications of the Association for Computing Machinery* **10**(10): 636–646.

Smith W. L. (1953). "On the Distribution of Queueing Times." *Proceedings of Cambridge Philosophical Society* **49**: 449–461.

Stidham, S. (1974). "A Last Word on $L = \lambda W$." *Operations Research* **22**(2): 417–421.

Stone, H. (1973). *Discrete Mathematical Structures and Their Applications.* Chicago: Science Research Associates.

Syski, R. (1960). *Introduction to Congestion Theory in Telephone Systems.* London: Oliver and Boyd.

Takacs, L. (1962). *Introduction to the Theory of Queues.* New York: Oxford University Press.

Wallace, V. L., and R. S. Rosenberg (1966). "Markovian Models and Numerical Analysis of Computer System Behavior." *Proceedings of AFIPS Spring Joint Computer Conference,* pp. 141–148.

Whittle, P. (1965). "Equilibrium Distributions for an Open Migration Process." *Journal of Applied Probability* **5**: 561–567.

Wolff, R. W. (1970a). "Time Sharing with Priorities." *SIAM Journal on Applied Mathematics* **19**(3): 566–574.

Wolff, R. W. (1970b). "Work-Conserving Priorities." *Journal of Applied Probability* **7**: 327–337.

Wolff, R. W. (1977). "An Upper Bound for Multi-Channel Queues." *Journal of Applied Probability* 14 (4).

Wyner, A. D. (1974). "On the Probability of Buffer Overflow Under an Arbitrary Bounded Input-Output Distribution." *SIAM Journal on Applied Mathematics* **27**(4): 544–570.

Yu, P. S. (1977). "Passage Time Distributions for a Class of Queueing Networks: Closed, Open, or Mixed, with Different Classes of Customers with Applications to Computer System Modeling." Technical Report No. 135, Digital Systems Laboratory, Stanford University (March).

4

The
Simulation
Method

4.1 SIMULATION FOR SYSTEM MODELING

The use of a digital computer to perform simulated experiments on a numerical model of some system has long been a popular technique in many disciplines. Simulation makes possible the systematic study of problems when analytic solutions are not available and experiment on the actual system is impossible or impractical. The simulation method has been an important means of determining the performance differences between alternative configurations (both hardware and software) of a computing system, whether it be in its design stage, its installation stage, or its tuning stage.

The simulation model describes the operation of the system in terms of individual events of the individual elements in the system. The interrelationships among the elements are also built into the model. Then the model allows the computing device to capture the effect of the elements' *actions* on each other as a dynamic process.

After being constructed, the simulation model is driven either by generating input data (probabilistic or Monte-Carlo simulation) or by feeding some representative input data (deterministic or trace-driven simulation) and then simulates the actual dynamic behavior of the system. By repeating this process for various alternative system configurations and parameters, and comparing their performances, one may identify an optimal system structure. Therefore, simulation is essentially the technique of conducting sampling experiments on the model of the system. Thus, simulated experiments should be regarded as ordinary physical experiments, and should be based on sound statistical techniques.

It is quite often found, however, that a simulation model takes much longer to construct, requires much more computer time to execute, and yet provides much less information than the model writer expected. Therefore, simulation should generally be considered a technique of last resort. Yet, many problems associated with design and configuration changes of computing systems are so complex that an analytical approach is often unable to characterize the real system in a form amenable to solution. Consequently, despite its difficulties and the costs and time required, simulation is often the only practical solution to a real problem.

There are several phases in solving a problem by a simulation method:

1. Formulation of a simulation model;
2. Implementation of the model;
3. Design of the simulation experiments;
4. Validation of the simulation model; and
5. Execution of the simulation experiment and analysis of simulation data.

Most simulation projects seem completely dominated by phases 1 and 2. Large and complex programs involved in constructing a simulation model are so demanding of time and effort that many investigators have little time left for validating the simulator, planning the efficient execution of the simulator, and correctly interpreting the simulation data. Yet these problems are at least as important as construction of the simulator.

4.2 TYPES OF COMPUTER SYSTEM SIMULATIONS

4.2.1 Level of Simulation

When we plan to perform some system analysis via simulation, we must first carefully determine at what level of detail the simulator should be constructed. The right level of detail depends on the purpose of the performance evaluation task, the degree of understanding of the system to be modeled and its environment, and the output statistics required. At one extreme we may design a model that simulates the CPU execution of instructions. Such detailed, or microscopic, simulation may be necessary when we are interested in, for example, CPU hardware design and the effect of memory interference. At the other extreme, a simulation model may represent an entire computing system as a single entity. Such global, or macroscopic, representation is sufficient when the objective of simulation study is, for instance, the design of a computer network in which the allocation of processing power and communication links may be major issues to be investigated.

There are, of course, a number of different levels between these two extreme cases, and the choice of a particular level is by no means a trivial matter. Suppose we are interested in studying the major components of an operating system, such as the job scheduling algorithm, the CPU dispatching algorithm, and the store management algorithm. If the system in question is a virtual-storage system, there are at least three different levels of detail to choose from. If the focus of the investigation regarding the store management is on the allocation of memory space to individual processes and not on the page replacement rule, then we may adequately represent the program behavior in terms of a sequence $\{X_i\}$, where X_i represents the CPU execution interval from the instant of the $(i-1)$th page fault until the ith page fault of a given program. If the system analyst has some reason to believe that the page replacement algorithm is an important consideration, the sequence $\{X_i\}$ is not an adequate level for representing the program behavior. Rather, the analyst must have page reference patterns $\{r_k\}$ to drive the simulator, where r_k is the name of the page in the kth reference. Even the page reference stream will not be detailed enough, if the capacity of cache (buffer memory) and/or its management (for example, buffer replacement algorithm) are among the design issues to be considered. For this level of detail, some representation of block reference patterns or address stream (that is, the executed sequence of storage addresses) must be available to conduct the simulation study at the right level.

In cases such as those cited above, it is not easy to select *a priori* the right level of simulation. The interactions of system components (both hardware and software) are so complex that we cannot always foresee how significant the design choice of a particular component may be in terms of the overall performance consideration. A solution to cope with such uncertainties is to *modularize* the structure of the simulator as much as possible. By this we mean that the simulation model should be structured in such a way that some change in subsystem component should not affect the entire simulator. This has much to do, of course, with the structure of the system in question. As we discussed in Chapter 1, the model, whether it be analytic or simulative, should be structured in a hierarchical form. In the case study of Section 3.10.5 we modeled the virtual-storage interactive system on a two-level structure (the inner model and the outer model). Both models were solved analytically owing to several simplifications and approximations that we introduced. If some of these restrictions were judged to be inadequate, we should have recourse to a simulation effort. The hierarchical structure introduced in that model formulation is of great value in the simulation environment as well: We might convert only one of the models (say, the inner model) to a simulation model, whereas we could retain the analytic solution technique for the outer model. These two models should be interfaced, in this particular case, via a set of the CPU utilization figures $\rho_{CPU}(n)$ obtained for a suitable range of n, the multiprogramming level.

The example cited above is one of the few clear cases in which the hierarchical decomposition of a total system is easily specified. Generally such decomposition and the corresponding set of variables that interface the submodels may not be clearly determined *a priori*; an adequate model construction may be achieved only through a sequence of model changes and the performance analysis steps. Nevertheless, a persistent attempt for the modular approach should facilitate the iterative process required of model construction.

4.2.2 Self-Driven Simulation vs. Trace-Driven Simulation

We will now discuss two distinct approaches to simulating a computer system: self-driven simulation and trace-driven simulation. Let us consider, for illustration, a single-server queueing model rather than a computer system model. A simple queueing system, as discussed in Chapter 3, consists of a collection of jobs to be processed and a mechanism for processing them. To specify the system we must know (1) the arrival mechanism, or the description of the pattern of job arrivals at the server; (2) the service mechanism, or the description of the service time for a job; and (3) the queue discipline, or the procedure by which jobs are selected from any extant queue for service.

The service time (e.g., the CPU processing time if the server in question is the CPU) is usually variable and it is natural to describe the variabillty in terms of a probability distribution of the service time. In the absence of definite evidence that one service can affect the next, independence is ordinarily assumed and the set of service times S_i's is taken as samples of independent items from the service-time distribution, $F_s(s) = P[S_i \leq s]$. This assumes that the jobs constitute a homogeneous set. To be more realistic, we often *classify* jobs into several classes and assign different service-time distributions to different classes. The arrival times of jobs to the queue do not usually form a regular sequence, that is, the interarrival periods X_i's vary in unpredictable fashion. Again, the probability distribution, $F_X(x) = P[X_i \leq x]$, provides a most convenient characterization of the varying intervals. Once these distributions are prescribed we can write a program that generates sequences of service and arrival time variates according to the procedure to be discussed in Section 4.4. We can then drive the simulator with these random sequences. We call

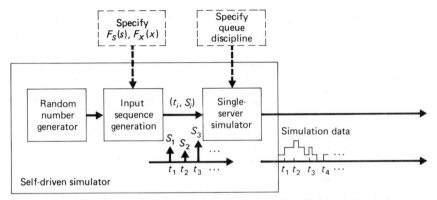

Fig. 4.1 Simulation of a single-server system with self-driven simulation.

this type of simulation model a *self-driven* simulator. Figure 4.1 illustrates the conceptual structure of the self-driven simulation of this single-server model, where the arrival time t_i is determined by adding the interarrival time X_i to the previous arrival time, that is, $t_i = t_{i-1} + X_i$.

Ideally, the parametric representation of system workload in terms of the distribution functions $F_X(x)$ and $F_S(s)$ should be based on real data. One must also carefully test whether the random sequences (that is, the interarrival times and service times) are stationary or nonstationary, and whether they are serially correlated or independent. But such an empirical characterization is usually not a simple matter. Since we find these statistical tests and estimations difficult or cumbersome, we often resort to another simulation approach, that is, what we call *trace-driven simulation*. Figure 4.2 shows the structure of the trace-driven simulation of the same

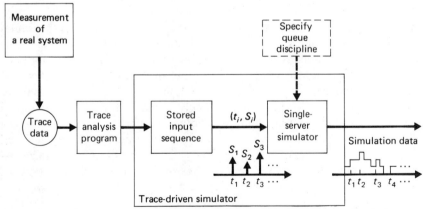

Fig. 4.2 Simulation of a single-server system with trace-driven simulation.

single-server model. In this type of simulation, the model is driven by input sequences derived from trace data (rather than from a random-number generator). The trace data is a profile of job execution steps actually observed in a running system, which is called the *base* system. Trace data is usually obtained by a *tracing program*, which monitors activities of the system and jobs that are pertinent to the planned simulation. For example, in the IBM System/360 and System/370, one of the service aids programs, called GTF (Generalized Trace Facility), is capable of tracing all supervisor call events (SVC's) and I/O interrupts. The recorded trace data is then edited by a *trace analysis* program, which translates the data into a form suitable as simulator input. This input data defines specific sequences of resource demands, which are then inter-preted by the simulator in a *deterministic* manner. This is the determining characteristic of the trace-driven simulation. Were the trace data to be reduced to statistical distribution and then used to specify a probabilistic driving mechanism, the simulation would be self-driven.

The primary requirement for the trace-driven simulation is the instrumentation of a tracing program capable of recording at an appropriate level the activities of the base system and jobs running on it. The types of activities and events to be traced largely depend on the scope and level of detail in the planned simulation, ranging from the fairly gross accounting log level to the instruction trace level (Schatzoff and Tillman, 1975). For instance, if the primary purpose of a trace-driven simulation is to investigate various paging and dispatching algorithms in a virtual-storage system, the trace should contain page reference information, instruction counts, and I/O data. The simulator may then generate step-by-step reports of all major system events such as page exceptions, I/O starts and completions, and dispatching decisions, as well as summary data on hardware utilization and response times.

As we stated earlier, the main advantage of the trace-driven simula-tion approach is that we need not obtain statistical characterization of the job or program behavior. Using self-driven simulation, we normally characterize the job behavior process only in terms of first-order statis-tics: independent, identically distributed interarrival times and service times, a first-order Markov chain model for job routing, etc. Of course, we ought to generate a nonstationary autocorrelated sequence if there is a clear evidence of such behavior and if we suspect that the selected measure of performance will be critically dependent on these characteris-tics of the model input. In trace data the correlation and interrelations of the job's and the system's behavior are preserved, even though we may not explicitly recognize them. This property often makes the trace-driven method appear more direct, realistic, and hence more appealing than the self-driven approach.

When the modeled system is different from the base system, the *trace analysis* program must adjust for the effects of their differences. Some of the required adjustments, such as time scaling due to channel speed differences, may be rather straightforward. If the trace is used to simulate a different CPU, then the CPU execution times must be adjusted according to the execution speed of the simulated CPU. In many cases, however, this adjustment cannot be done by a single scaling, since certain instructions may be executed faster or slower than other types of instructions on a different CPU. Such *transformations* or adjustments of the trace-derived data are even more difficult for some system components; it is not easy, for example, to account for a change in memory capacity and/or allocation algorithm in a trace-driven model of a virtual-storage system, if the raw trace is at the level of page faults. The time (or the number of instructions executed) between page faults critically depends on the amount of memory space allocated to each job, and hence on the degree of multiprogramming as well. Another possible criticism of the trace-driven simulation study is the issue of the "representativeness of traced data." Without a quantitative characterization of the system workload, there is no scientific way of ascertaining that a particular finite set of trace data is representative of the given application environment. After all, one trace-data sequence is one *realization* (that is, one sample point) from the *ensemble* (or the sample space) of all possible trace sequences.

Perhaps the strongest point of the trace-driven simulation is the relative ease of model verification efforts. While trace data is collected, any performance measures can be gathered simultaneously at little extra programming or computing costs. The availability of trace data and performance data obtained in the same operational period allows us to calibrate the credibility of the simulation model.

We may safely say that the use of a trace-driven simulation is most appropriate when we want to analyze the effects of moderate modifications in a currently running system. The validity of the trace becomes more questionable when the system under modeling and the base system become appreciably different. Despite all the drawbacks raised and the laborious efforts required, the trace-driven modeling approach will remain an important technique until the day that some more realistic representation of system workload is obtained in compact parametric form. For further references on trace-driven modeling, the reader is referred to Noetzel and Herring (1976), review articles by Sherman and Browne (1973) and Sherman (1976), and references therein.

4.3   FORMULATION OF A SIMULATION MODEL

4.3.1   Time Control in a Simulator

We now return to the problem of simulating the queue system of Fig. 4.1. To summarize the physical operation of the system: arriving jobs enter the queue, wait for the service, eventually receive the service, and then leave. Thus the model must describe and synchronize the arrival of jobs and servicing of jobs. The two methods for handling such synchronization in a digital computer are called *synchronous timing* (or *unit-time advance*) and *asynchronous timing* (or *event advance*) (Hillier and Lieberman, 1968).

With synchronous timing, the time of the simulation model is *advanced* by an appropriately chosen unit time Δt. The system state is then *updated* by determining what events occurred during this elapsed time unit, and these two steps (advancing and updating) are repeated for as many time units as desired. If Δt is chosen relatively small, the probability of two or more arrivals or departures during a time unit will be negligible. Thus, the only two possible *events* that need to be observed during a time unit Δt are the arrival of a job and the completion of a job in service, if any. Each of these events has a known probability. For example, if the arrival is Poisson, that is, $F_X(t) = 1 - e^{-\lambda t}$, the probability that a job will arrive during an elapsed time unit is $\lambda \Delta t$ *regardless* of the instance when the last arrival took place. Suppose that $\lambda \Delta t = 0.02$. The computer would need to generate one of the 100 possible two-digit numbers $(00, 01, \ldots, 99)$ at random. By associating two of the possible numbers (say, 00 and 01) with the arrival event and the remaining with nonarrival, the random number generated determines whether a simulated arrival occurs in that time unit. If the arrival mechanism is not Poisson, the situation is not as simple as this (see Exercise 4.3.1). In general, it is necessary to store information concerning the number of time units that have elapsed since the last arrival, and change accordingly the rule of associating the generated random number with the arrival event. If a job is in the process of being served, this same method is used to determine whether a service completion occurs or not during the elapsed time unit. Again this probability is constant only when the service-time distribution is exponential. If no job is being served, the simulator automatically decides that no service completion has occurred during the elapsed time unit. To implement this, the simulator uses an *indicator* that records whether the server is busy or idle. Similarly, a *counter* is used to record the current number of jobs waiting in the queue. Thus, updating the system amounts to updating the indicator and counter after each time advance. At the same time, the simulator should record the desired information about the aggregate behavior of the system—for example, the number of jobs in the queue and the response time of any job that just completed the service. If it is required only to obtain the mean values rather than the probability distributions of the queue size and response time, the simulator merely counts cumulative sums of these observed quantities, and the sample averages are obtained after the simulation run is completed.

Asynchronous timing (or event advance) differs from synchronous timing in that the *simulator clock* is advanced by a variable amount rather than by a fixed amount each time. Conceptually, this timing procedure is to keep the system running until an *event* occurs, at which point the simulator pauses momentarily to record the change in the system. To implement this concept, the simulator actually proceeds by keeping track of the *event list* or *calendar*. In the simple example under consideration, the event list consists of only two future events, namely, when the next job will arrive and when the server will finish servicing the current job in service, if any. In the self-driven simulation these event times are obtained by taking a random sample from $F_X(x)$ and $F_S(s)$, respectively.

In the case of trace-driven simulation, the event list is taken from an event trace, that is, the time-ordered sequence of events that is provided to the simulator as an input. Whether the simulator is trace-driven or self-driven, each time an arrival or service completion occurs, the simulator first determines how long it will be until the next time that this class of event will occur, and then adds this to the current clock time. This sum is then stored in the event list. To determine which event will occur next, the simulator merely finds the minimum of the scheduled times in the event list or calendar. Figure 4.3 illustrates this example. This

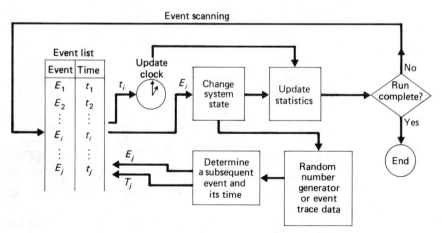

Fig. 4.3 An example of a simulator with asynchronous timing.

implementation method is often called the *event-scheduling approach.* We should note, however, that the event-scheduling approach is not the only scheme to implement the asynchronous-timing concept.

The synchronous-timing method may have an advantage over asynchronous timing, if the system under study contains highly periodic or synchronous activities (for example, simulation of a hardware at a highly detailed level in which the machine cycle should be chosen as the unit time Δt). In most situations, however, the asynchronous-timing approach is found more efficient in program execution, and perhaps easier to program. Most simulation programming languages adopt this method.

4.3.2 Data Structures in a Simulator

In a simulation program, system changes occur when an event takes place. The system state is represented as a collection of related objects, such as jobs in a queueing system. The relationships between objects are usually described by a data structure such as a *list, queue,* or *table.* The event list of Fig. 4.3 is a typical example encountered in a simulation program. Consider the example of the simulation of a single-server system cited in Section 4.3.1. If all jobs belong to a single class, there are only two types of events: arrivals and departures. Suppose that the service discipline is FIFO, and that we are interested only in the queue size behavior, and not in the individual job's behavior. Then the state of the system at time t is specified simply by $N(t)$, the number of jobs in the system. In order to keep the simulator running, it suffices to have at most two future events in the event list at any time: the next departure (if the server is currently serving) and the next arrival. Thus the size of the calendar generally can be kept rather small. Alternatively, however, we may wish to put all the arrivals in the event list, either by reading in all such data from the edited trace in a trace-driven simulation, or by generating internally a sequence of arrival times at once. These procedures will certainly require more memory space, but may also shorten the computer time required for reading data from external storage, or the time for calling the subroutine of arrival time generation.

The event list will become larger and more complex as we introduce more classes of jobs and/or increase the number of servers in the model. In these circumstances the structure of lists or queues becomes an important consideration not only with respect to space utilization, but also in terms of the computer time consumed in scanning and updating the event list.

The system-related performance statistics—throughput, utilization, queue distribution—can be easily collected by invoking a *statistics*

	1	2	3	4 ——▶ J
	Job number	Job class	Arrival time	Service time
1	113	1	1205	105
2	114	2	1218	112
3	115	1	1282	12
4	116	1	1291	58

I

(a)

	1	2	3	4 ——▶ J
	Job number	Job class	Arrival time	Service time
1	115	1	1282	12
2	116	1	1291	58
3	114	2	1218	112
4				

I

(b)

Fig. 4.4   Job table: (a) $t = 1291^+$; (b) $t = 1310^+$.

gathering routine each time the system changes its state. If we wish, however, to obtain job-related statistics—waiting time, response time—the information contained in the event list alone is no longer sufficient, and we need to keep track of the individual job's movement in the system. For this purpose we introduce a data structure called a *job table*. Conceptually the job table is a list of the jobs that are created during the simulation run. Associated with each job are the job's arrival time, job class, and service time. Like the event list, the size of the job table and its manipulation mechanism will depend on how the simulation program is written. As an extreme case, the job table may include all jobs that are to appear during the simulation run: It will inevitably introduce a significant waste of memory space. A more reasonable structure would be one in which job table entries are *created* and *destroyed*, as jobs *arrive* and *depart*, respectively.

Suppose that a job table is structured as in Fig. 4.4(a) in which the jobs are stored in the array JOB (. , .) according to the order of arrivals. Figure 4.4(a) shows that at time $t = 1291^+$ job 113 is still in service,* and there are 19 more time units to go. (We assume that job 113 arrived at $t = 1205$ and immediately started receiving service.) Since job 113 began receiving service, three additional jobs have arrived. Job 114 is the first among them, but belongs to class 2; thus jobs 115 and 116 have priority

---

* The expression "time 1291^+" means "just after time 1291."

Event type	Event time
Depart (Job 113)	1310
Arrival (Job 117)	1321

(a)

Event type	Event time
Arrival (Job 117)	1321
Depart (Job 115)	1322

(b)

Fig. 4.5   Event list: (a) $t = 1291^+$; (b) $t = 1310^+$.

over job 114. At time $t = 1205 + 105 = 1310$, job 113 will leave the system, and consequently the first row of the job table will be erased (Fig. 4.4b). Job 115 is now promoted to the top row, indicating that this is the job currently in service. The corresponding event lists may look like Figs. 4.5(a) and (b) at $t = 1291^+$ and $t = 1310^+$, respectively. Note that the next arrival (job 117) is already in the event list at $t = 1291^+$, although it is not listed in the job table yet. Conversely, those jobs that are in the waiting line do not appear in the event list (see Exercise 4.3.2).

Both the event list and the job table consist of elements that can be ranked according to a *total ordering*. In the case of the event list we can order the objects (that is, the events) according to their scheduled times. Similarly, the job table should be ranked in the order of scheduling priorities.

If we adopt data structures such as *ordered chains* or *linked lists*, then the manipulation of these arrays becomes in many cases substantially simpler and computationally efficient. This can be done by forming the linked table (or linked list) as shown conceptually on the left-hand side of Fig. 4.6(a). Here HEADER (or FIRST) is a link variable pointing to the first element in the list. Each element is chained to or points to its *successor*. The last element has a null pointer. A variable called TRAILER (or LAST) points to this last element. This linked structure is implemented by introducing a pointer field in the array JOB (,), as shown on the right-hand side of Fig. 4.6. The pointer field of an element (the last column in each row) has a value that contains the location or address of its successor. The address 0 is assumed to indicate that this element has no successor. We also assume that two memory locations are assigned to the two link variables HEADER and TRAILER. Figures 4.6(b) and (c) illustrate how the linked list changes as events occur at time $t = 1310$ (completion of job 113) and at $t = 1321$ (arrival of job 117). Dispatching a job for service is then done simply by selecting the job pointed to by the HEADER. When a new job arrives, a search is to be conducted along the chain until the right position for that job is located.

It goes without saying that this chaining technique is also applicable to the event list. Furthermore, the contents of the job table and the event list are closely related to each other. In fact, each time an event occurs, the corresponding system change should be reflected in the updating of

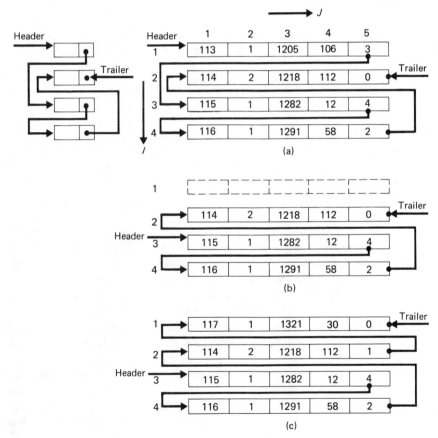

Fig. 4.6 Job table in linked list representation: (a) $t = 1291^+$; (b) $t = 1310^+$; (c) $t = 1321^+$.

both. Hence, the manipulation of the tables will be facilitated by introducing pointers between the job table and the event list for the jobs that have entries in both.

The data representations outlined above appear not only in simulation programs but also in a variety of computer programs—sorting routines, sparse matrix operations, compilers, operating systems, and data-base managers. The linked list representation discussed above and its variants are commonly called by the name of *list processing*. Programming languages such as PL/I, ALGOL68, and most of the simulation programming languages provide list-processing features. See Knuth (1968) for further reading on various data structures and their applications.

Exercises

4.3.1 Let $F_X(t)$ be the distribution function of interarrival time X. Suppose that m time units have elapsed since the most recent arrival. What is the probability that a job will arrive during the present time unit?

4.3.2 In the simulation model of a single-server queueing system discussed in Section 4.3.2, suppose that we modify the job table to include only jobs in the waiting line. Show that every job in the system appears either in the event list or in the job table.

4.3.3 Use a doubly linked list for the job table—that is, each element points to its predecessor as well as to its successor. Describe some circumstances under which such a list is useful.

4.4 TECHNIQUES FOR GENERATING RANDOM VARIABLES

By its nature, a Monte Carlo or self-driven simulator requires a mechanism for generating sequences of events that essentially govern the dynamic behavior of the system in question. In general, the random nature of events is characterized by the underlying probability distributions: If the system is a queueing system, the interarrival-time distribution $F_X(x)$ and service-time distribution $F_S(s)$ are sufficient to characterize the system behavior, provided that the sequences of interarrival times $\{X_i\}$ and service times $\{S_i\}$ are both independent and identically distributed. Then the simulator must be capable of producing sequences of variates* from such continuous probability distributions. Not all random variables required in a simulation experiment are continuous. For example, the number of messages that arrive in a unit-time interval is a discrete random variable, and so is the number of of bits contained in such a

---

* A particular outcome or sample value of a random variable is usually called a *variate*.

message. Generation of variates from any specified distribution is possible, once we know how to generate a sequence of independent variates drawn from the uniform distribution. This assertion will be demonstrated in Section 4.4.4. We will therefore first concentrate on the generation of the uniform variates.

4.4.1 The Generation of Random Numbers

Historically the generation of variates has been achieved in a variety of ways: manually, mechanically, or by means of some random physical process. If a digital computer is to be used for executing the simulation (which we assume throughout this chapter), it is convenient to have the computer itself generate the variates. Since a computer represents a real number with only finite accuracy, we normally generate *integers* Z_i between zero and some positive integer m. Then, the fraction

$$Y_i = Z_i/m \tag{4.1}$$

lies between zero and one. The most common method of generating such a sequence of *random numbers* Z_i is by means of a simple *recurrence relation* such as

$$Z_i = aZ_{i-1} + c \pmod m, \tag{4.2}$$

where a is a positive integer and c is a nonnegative integer. In order to properly understand Eq. (4.2) it is necessary to introduce the following definitions.

Definition 4.1 (Congruent modulo m).   Two integers a and b are said to be *congruent modulo m* if their difference is an integral multiple of m. The congruence relation is expressed as

$$a = b \pmod m \tag{4.3}$$

which reads a is congruent to b modulo m.

Definition 4.2 (Residue modulo m).   For a given a the smallest positive integer n such that $n = a \pmod m$ is said to be the residue modulo m of a.

For instance, $2 = 5 \pmod 3$, $1 = 13 \pmod 3$, etc. The recurrence relation (4.2) signifies that Z_i is the *residue modulo m* of $aZ_{i-1} + c$.

We call a the multiplier, c the increment, and m the modulus. The generation of a sequence of numbers according to a congruence relationship such as (4.2) is thus called the congruential method. Advantages of using such a simple recurrence formula are: (1) Statistical properties of the resulting sequence can be reasonably well understood, so that we can choose optimal values of a, m, c, and the initial value Z_0, which we often call a *seed*; (2) it requires little computational time and memory space; and (3) the sequence can be easily reproduced by just saving the seed Z_0. Similarly, the sequence generation can be interrupted and restarted by saving the last number.

The sequence $\{Z_i\}$ generated by (4.2) is completely determined once the four parameters are chosen; a, c, m, and Z_0. Therefore, it is not a random sequence in the sense that we defined it in Chapter 2. But for all practical purposes we may be content with accepting such sequences as random sequences, if they *appear* to be sufficiently random, that is, if no important statistical tests reveal a significant discrepancy from the behavior that a truly random sequence is supposed to demonstrate. Sequences generated in a deterministic way such as (4.2) are usually called *pseudo-random* or *quasi-random* sequences.

An arbitrary choice of the parameters a, c, m, and Z_0 does not generate an acceptable pseudo-random sequence. For example, let us choose arbitrarily $a = 13$, $c = 10$, and $m = 10$. Then $\{Z_i\}$ will be a sequence of integers ranging from 0 to 9. By selecting the seed $Z_0 = 2$, the sequence of Z's generated by (4.2) is 2, 6, 8, 4, 2, 6, 8, 4, ... This is obviously not a valid sequence of random numbers since only four of ten possible numbers $(0, 1, 2, \ldots, 9)$ ever appear. Since the sequence is cyclic with the period four, it is not satisfactory if more than four random numbers are required. Therefore, great discretion must be exercised in selecting the combinations of a, c, m, and Z_0. Number-theoretic analysis has revealed that *only* a few combinations yield satisfactory sequences.

The generation formula of the form (4.2) is called the *linear congruential method*. The special case $c = 0$ is most frequently used, and it is called the *multiplicative congruential method*. The case for $c \neq 0$ is called the *mixed congruential method*.

4.4.2 Multiplicative Congruential Generators

The multiplicative congruential method (often called the *power residue method*) computes a sequence $\{Z_i\}$, as defined above, according to the following simple relation:

$$Z_i = aZ_{i-1} \quad (\text{mod } m). \tag{4.4}$$

Certainly this method has the advantage of being slightly faster than the mixed congruential method in the generation process.

For this case, the following results have been derived based on *number-theoretic* arguments (see the appendix to Chapter 4).

Theorem 4.1 When we choose a modulus m such as

$$m = 1, 2, 4, p^e \quad \text{or} \quad 2p^e$$

where p is an odd *prime* and e is a positive integer, there exist elements a such that
$$a^{\phi(m)} = 1 \qquad (\text{mod } m).$$

Such an element is called a *primitive root* of m (see Definition 4A-5 in the appendix to Chapter 4). If we choose a primitive root as the multiplier and require the initial value Z_0 to be relatively prime to m, the random-number sequence $\{Z_i\}$ of formula (4.4) has a period of $m - 1$.

Lewis, Goodman, and Miller (1969) discuss a random-number generator that uses the full capacity of the 32-bit registers of IBM System/360 computers. Out of the 32 bits, only 31 bits are available for computation, since one bit is used as a *sign bit*. The largest prime is conveniently $m = 2^{31} - 1 = 2147483647$. It can be shown that $a = 7$ is a positive primitive root of $m = 2^{31} - 1$. Hence the random-number sequence has the *full cycle period* of $m - 1$; within one period all integers in the set $\{1, 2, \ldots, m - 1\}$ appear once. From Theorem 4A-4 we know that a power of 7, say 7^k, is also a primitive root, provided k is not a factor of $2^{31} - 2 \ (= 2 \times 3^2 \times 7 \times 11 \times 31 \times 151 \times 331)$. Lewis, Goodman, and Miller (1969) applied various statistical tests to evaluate the generator for various values of a. They show that the multiplier $a = 7^5 = 16,807$, which yields the particular generator

$$Z_{i+1} = 7^5 Z_i \qquad (\text{mod } 2^{31} - 1), \tag{4.5}$$

is one of the few values that provide random-number sequences with satisfactory statistical properties. A System/360 assembly language program implementing (4.5) is given in their article. The modular arithmetic in that program is accomplished by the divide instruction, with the desired random number Z_{i+1} equal to the remainder. The generator (4.5) is also adopted in Subroutine GGL, which is written in FORTRAN, of IBM Subroutine Library-Mathematics (IBM, 1974).

On most computers, the division operation is a much slower operation than others, such as shift and add. Thus, the modulo operation is the most time-consuming step. A technique called *division simulation*, however, makes the execution of (4.5) substantially faster. The division simulation algorithm is discussed by Payne, Rabung, and Bogyo (1969) and its application to the particular generator (4.5) is discussed by Gustavson and Liniger (1970) and Learmonth and Lewis (1973a). Let aZ_i be represented as

$$aZ_i = 2^{31} q_i + r_i, \tag{4.6}$$

where q_i is the quotient and r_i is the remainder, $0 \leq r_i < 2^{31}$. A simple algebraic manipulation of (4.6) shows that if there is no overflow in the addition of $q_i + r_i$, then

$$Z_{i+1} = aZ_i \quad (\mathrm{mod}\ 2^{31} - 1)$$

$$= q_i + r_i.$$

(4.7)

If there is overflow, $2^{31} - 1$ must be subtracted from $q_i + r_i$ to obtain the correct Z_{i+1}. Alternatively, this can be done by adding a constant of 1, and taking the modulo 2^{31}:

$$Z_{i+1} = q_i + r_i + 1 \quad (\mathrm{mod}\ 2^{31}),$$

(4.8)

where the congruence modulo 2^{31} can be done simply by retaining the low order 31 bits of $q_i + r_i + 1$. Note that in order to take advantage of the division simulation a program must be written in the assembler or machine language, since there is no easy way of explicitly dealing with q_i and r_i in a high-level language. Subroutines GGL1 and GGL2 (IBM, 1974) are written in IBM System/360 Basic Assembly language, using the division simulation algorithm; hence, they are more efficient than GGL. GGL1 uses a software test instruction to check, during each computation of a random number, whether or not an overflow in $r_i + q_i$ occurred. GGL2 uses hardware detection of overflow; hence it is faster than GGL1.

Learmonth and Lewis (1973a) describe a random-number generation package, LLRANDOM, which is also written in System/360 assembly language; it can be invoked in a FORTRAN IV program. The package, LLRANDOM, has an additional feature, namely a built-in *shuffling* mechanism. Essentially what it does is to take chunks of 128 numbers from the basic sequence and shuffle them according to some permutation rule in order to further randomize the sequence and obtain a better appearance of randomness. See also Knuth (1969) for various *shuffling* procedures.

As was observed in connection with the division simulation algorithm, the choice of modulus of the form

$$m = 2^b$$

(4.9)

has the advantage of computational efficiency, where b is the word length of the machine. Then, the congruence modulo m operation is accomplished by truncating and retaining only the low order of b bits. Furthermore, the division in (4.1) required for the conversion of Z_i to Y_i involves only shifting the binary point by b positions to the left, which is certainly a much faster operation than ordinary division. The same advantages will also be gained in decimal computers by choosing $m = 10^d$, where d is the corresponding word length. In fact, this case has been most frequently discussed in the past, and many random-number generator packages are based on this choice. Theorem 4.1 suggests, however, that we cannot have the full period of $m - 1$ in the resultant random sequence $\{Z_i\}$. Instead, we find the following property, again based on number-theoretic arguments.

Theorem 4.2 The sequence $\{Z_i\}$ generated by the multiplicative congruential method with the modulus (4.9) has the period $m/4$ provided that the multiplier a satisfies $a = 3$ or 5 (modulo 8) and the seed Z_0 is an odd integer. (See the discussions in the Appendix to Chapter 4.)

The discussions presented thus far have been concerned with (1) the simplicity of computation and (2) the maximum period of the sequence. Another feature that we must consider is (3) the serial independence of the sequence. A *necessary* (but not *sufficient*) condition for independence is *uncorrelatedness*. The correlation coefficient between adjacent sequence values $\rho(Z_i, Z_{i+1})$ is called the *(first-order)* *serial correlation coefficient*. From the results derived by Coveyou (1960) and Greenberger (1961) it can be shown that the serial correlation coefficient lies approximately between the values $a^{-1} \pm a/m$. Thus, $a = \sqrt{m}$ will minimize the upper bound of the correlation coefficient and we obtain $0 < \rho(Z_i, Z_{i+1}) < 2/\sqrt{m}$. We note, however, that some departure from $a = \sqrt{m}$ is not so critical.

As an example, consider $m = 2^{31} = 2147483648$. Then the choice of the multiplier $a = 2^{16} + 3 = 65539$ satisfies both criteria: maximization of the sequence period, and minimization of the serial correlation. The IBM Scientific Subroutine package RANDU (IBM, 1966) is a FORTRAN implementation of this particular generator that has been widely used. However, recent studies have revealed some undesirable property of the multiplicative congruential method with $m = 2^b$ and $a \cong \sqrt{m}$. Although the first-order serial correlation can be made sufficiently small, successive triples all lie on fifteen parallel planes in the unit cube. Because of this finding, RANDU has been replaced by GGL in the IBM Scientific Subroutine Library. The reader is directed to Fishman (1973a) and Learmonth and Lewis (1973b) for further discussions on the subject.

4.4.3 Mixed Congruential Generators

If we remove the restriction $c = 0$ in the recurrence equation (4.2), we obtain the mixed congruential generator as defined earlier. An algebraic manipulation shows that the ith value in the sequence is given by

$$Z_i = a^i Z_0 + \frac{a^i - 1}{a - 1} c \quad (\text{mod } m). \tag{4.10}$$

It has been shown by Hull and Dobell (1962) that a sequence of the full period m can be generated by properly choosing the set of parameters a, c, and Z_0. The rules are:

1. c is relatively prime to m,

2. $a = 1 \pmod q$ for any prime factor q of m, and

3. $a = 1 \pmod 4$ if 4 is a factor of m.

Knuth (1969) discusses the mixed congruential method in great depth, and suggests the following additional rules:

4. $a = 5 \pmod 8$ if m is a power of 2.

5. $\sqrt{m} < a < m - \sqrt{m}$, and preferably $a > m/100$. The digits in the binary representation of a should not have a simple, regular pattern.

6. The increment c should satisfy, in addition to (1), the condition that $c/m = 1/2 - \sqrt{3}/6$, lest the serial correlation be high.

Let us assume the 31-bit binary machine. Then the most convenient choice of the modulus is obviously $m = 2^{31}$. Take haphazardly some constant a that satisfies the rules listed above to be the multiplier. For example, $a = 314159269$ (the first 9 digits of π). A choice of the increment constant is, for instance, $c = 453806245$ (Exercise 4.4.3). Thus, the mixed congruential generator (Knuth, 1969; Fuller, 1975)

$$Z_{i+1} = 314159269Z_i + 453806245 \pmod{2^{31}} \qquad (4.11)$$

meets the above six rules. Note that the period of this pseudo-random sequence is $m = 2^{31}$ as compared with $m/4 = 2^{29}$ in the multiplicative method such as RANDU.

The choice of $m = 2^{31}$ is convenient not only for the implementation of the generator in assembly language, but also for programming in high-level languages. If the multiplication aZ_i creates an overflow, it may turn on the sign bit (the bit position 32) of the register, which makes the number appear as a negative integer. However, an addition* of $2^{31} = 2147483647 + 1$ will turn off the sign bit, resulting in the correct number $Z_{i+1} = aZ_i \pmod{2^{31}}$. The FORTRAN subroutine RANDU takes advantage of this operation. Care must be exercised, however, since different machines and compilers have different ways of turning off overflow.

Besides the multiplicative and mixed congruential methods discussed above, a number of other types of generators—the midsquare technique,

---

* Note that this addition must be done in two steps, since $2147483647 = 2^{31} - 1$ is the largest acceptable number in the 31-bit register.

the midproduct technique, the additive congruential method, feedback shift register generators—and various shuffling schemes have been proposed. Some of the methods are quite ad hoc and/or are known to produce rather poor pseudo-random sequences. As discussed in the last two sections, number theory can be successfully applied to some generators to select parameters wisely so that the maximum possible cycle length is obtained. The theory of mathematical statistics provides some additional guidelines to minimize serial correlation. These rules and guidelines are necessary conditions, but not sufficient conditions. A number of statistical tests of the randomness of pseudo-random sequences have been proposed and discussed in the literature. Widely known tests include the run test, the serial test, the chi-square goodness-of-fit test, the Kolmogorov-Smirnov test, and the spectral test. For more extensive treatments on this subject, the reader is referred to Knuth (1969), Fishman (1973a, 1973b), Learmonth and Lewis (1973b), and references therein. It appears, however, that there are some disagreements among researchers in the field concerning the relevance and interpretation of these statistical tests (see Kleijnen, 1975). It is fair to state that there is still no foolproof random-number generator.

4.4.4   Generation of Variates for Simulation

The random-number generation method discussed above generates integers $\{Z_i\}$ between 0 and $m - 1$ with a uniform frequency. Thus the fractions $\{Y_i\}$ of (4.1) are uniformly distributed between 0 and 1. How can we then generate a sequence of random observations from a given probability distribution? We will now discuss some of the more commonly used techniques.

The transform method

Let X be the random variable of our concern and $F(x)$ be the distribution function, that is,

$$F(x) = P[X \le x]. \tag{4.12}$$

Set $F(X) = Y$; then Y is defined over the range 0 and 1. Now we show that if Y is a random variable uniformly distributed between 0 and 1, the variable X defined by

$$X = F^{-1}(Y) \tag{4.13}$$

has the cumulative distribution $F(x)$ (see Fig. 4.7):

$$P[X \le x] = P[Y \le F(x)] = F(x). \tag{4.14}$$

The inverse mapping $F^{-1}(\ )$ can be done by writing the equation for this function, or by developing a table giving the values of X for a finite (but sufficiently dense) set of points of Y from 0 to 1.

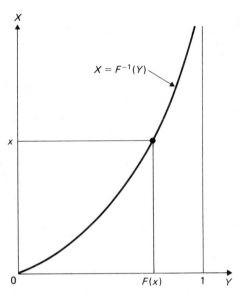

Fig. 4.7 Transformation of the uniform random variable into random variable X with the distribution $F(x)$.

Example 4.1 Consider random variable X with the *exponential* distribution

$$F(x) = 1 - e^{-\mu x}, \qquad x \geq 0. \tag{4.15}$$

Applying the procedure outlined above, set this function equal to a random decimal number Y

$$Y = 1 - e^{-\mu X} \tag{4.16}$$

so that

$$X = F^{-1}(Y) = -\{\ln(1 - Y)\}/\mu. \tag{4.17}$$

Since $1 - Y$ is itself a random decimal number between 0 and 1, we can use a simpler transformation

$$X = F^{-1}(1 - Y) = -(\ln Y)/\mu. \tag{4.18}$$

Thus, one can generate a sequence of random observations from an exponential distribution by applying the transformation (4.17) or (4.18) to a random decimal sequence.

Although this algorithm based on the logarithm transformation is easy to program, it is not the fastest method. Two other algorithms that do not use a natural logarithm subroutine are discussed by Knuth (1969): the random minimization method and the rectangle-wedge-tail method.

The rejection method

It is often possible to calculate the probability density function $f(x)$ but difficult to evaluate its integral $F(x)$ or the inverse $F^{-1}(x)$. A technique called the *rejection method* has been developed to deal with this situation. Let $f(x)$ be bounded by M and have a finite range (or support), say $a \leq x \leq b$, as shown in Fig. 4.8.

Let us generate pairs of random decimal numbers (R_1, R_2) between 0 and 1. Then

$$X_1 = a + (b - a)R_1 \tag{4.19}$$

is a random number in $[a, b]$. Whenever we encounter a pair (R_1, R_2) that satisfies the relationship

$$MR_2 \leq f(X_1), \tag{4.20}$$

we accept X_1 and reject otherwise. The probability density function of accepted X_1's will then be $f(x)$.

The number of trials before a successful pair is found is a random variable n with geometric distribution

$$P[n] = \rho(1 - \rho)^{n-1} \tag{4.21}$$

with

$$\rho = 1/M(b - a); \tag{4.22}$$

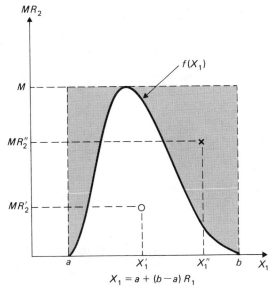

Fig. 4.8 The rejection method to generate a random variable with the probability density function $f(x)$. (The point "o" is to be accepted, whereas the point "x" is to be rejected.)

its mean value n is

$$E[n] = 1/\rho = M(b - a). \tag{4.23}$$

This implies that the method may not be efficient for probability density functions with large $M(b - a)$.

The composition method

Suppose that the distribution $F(x)$ is represented as the mixture of two distributions $F_1(x)$ and $F_2(x)$:

$$F(x) = pF_1(x) + (1 - p)F_2(x). \tag{4.24}$$

We can obtain a variate X from the distribution $F(x)$ by taking the following two steps: First, we generate a uniform variate U. Then if $U < p$, we set X equal to a variate with distribution $F_1(x)$; otherwise, we draw X from the other distribution $F_2(x)$. This composite procedure is directly applicable to the hyperexponential distribution (see Exercise 4.4.7).

In some cases the distribution $F(x)$ of random variable X is such that the variable is representable in terms of one or more independent random variables with simple distributions. A notable example is the Erlangian distribution defined by (3.30): If X is a random variable with k-stage Erlangian distribution of mean $1/\mu$, then X can be represented as the sum of k independent exponential random variables

$$X = X_1 + X_2 + \cdots + X_k, \tag{4.25}$$

each of which has mean $1/k\mu$. Hence the Erlangian variate can be derived by generating k exponential variates and summing them. A more efficient procedure is obtained (Exercise 4.4.8) by noting the following equivalency

$$X = -\frac{\ln\left(\prod_{i=1}^{k} Y_i\right)}{k\mu}, \tag{4.26}$$

where $Y_1, Y_2, \ldots, Y_k$ are k independent uniform variates between 0 and 1.

As k increases, the distribution of X of (4.25) will approach the normal or Gaussian distribution by virtue of the *central limit theorem* (see Section 2.7 for details). This property of *asymptotic normality* holds for any distributional forms of the component variables $\{X_i\}$ so long as their means and variances are finite. Let us define a random variable S by

$$S = Y_1 + Y_2 + \cdots + Y_n, \tag{4.27}$$

where $Y_1, Y_2, \ldots, Y_n$ are independent samples of the uniform variates between 0 and 1. Then for large n, the variable S is approximately normally distributed with mean $n/2$ and variance $n/12$. Then the variable X defined by

$$X = \frac{\left(S - \frac{n}{2}\right)\sigma}{\sqrt{n/12}} + \mu \tag{4.28}$$

approximates the normal variable with mean μ and variance σ^2. A convenient choice is $n = 12$, since it eliminates the square root term from the last expression. This value of n truncates the distribution at $\pm 6\sigma$ limits and is unable to generate values beyond 3σ. It will be worth mentioning here that most of the existing subroutine programs under the name "Gaussian Random Generator" are based on this method with a fairly small size of n; thus they are not appropriate when one is concerned with the tail of the distribution. In order to improve the accuracy of the approximation, the following procedure has been proposed and is known by the name of Teichroew's method (see Knuth, 1969, pp. 112–113; and Muller, 1959). Let us choose $n = 12$, $\mu = 0$, and $\sigma = \frac{1}{4}$, and denote the resulting variable by R:

$$R = (\tfrac{1}{4})(Y_1 + Y_2 + \cdots + Y_{12} - 6). \tag{4.29}$$

We set

$$X = [\{((a_9 R^2 + a_7)R^2 + a_5)R^2 + a_3\}R^2 + a_1]R, \tag{4.30}$$

where

$$a_1 = 3.949846138,$$
$$a_3 = 0.252408784,$$
$$a_5 = 0.076542912, \tag{4.31}$$
$$a_7 = 0.008355968,$$
$$a_9 = 0.029899776.$$

Then X is a fairly good approximation to a variate with the standard normal distribution.

There are other procedures for generating variates from the normal distribution: these include the polar method and the rectangle-wedge-tail method. The procedure of the polar method is summarized as follows (see Exercise 4.4.11): Let Y_1 and Y_2 be independent random numbers from the uniform distribution over $[0, 1)$. Then the variates

$$X_1 = (-2 \ln Y_1)^{1/2} \cos 2\pi Y_2 \tag{4.32}$$

and

$$X_2 = (-2 \ln Y_1)^{1/2} \sin 2\pi Y_2 \tag{4.33}$$

are independent and each represents a variate from the standard normal distribution. An improved version of the polar method that does not require the sine and cosine functions of (4.32) and (4.33) is obtained by Marsaglia, MacLaren, and Bray (1964). Knuth (1969) discusses this fast algorithm also.

In the rectangle-wedge-tail method, the probability density function is divided into a number of pieces: Some are rectangles, some are wedge-shaped, and the tail is the remainder of the function. Although this method is complicated in implementation and requires higher memory space than the other methods, it provides the fastest method for generating normal variates. See Knuth (1969) for a detailed discussion of this method. The reader is also directed to Ahrens and Dieter (1972), who give a survey of various generation methods of the normal and exponential variates.

Exercises

4.4.1 Using the multiplicative method, set $m = 2^5$, and $a = 3$. What is the period if the seed Z_0 is an odd number? Find the sequence when $Z_0 = 1$. Do the same for $Z_0 = 5$. What will happen if an even number is chosen as a seed?

4.4.2 Using the mixed congruential method, set $m = 2^5$, $a = 5$, and $c = 3$. What is the period of the resultant sequence? Generate the sequence with $Z_0 = 2$.

4.4.3 Examine whether the mixed congruential generator (4.11) satisfies rules 1–6 of Section 4.4.3.

4.4.4 Program the mixed congruential generator (4.11) in a language with which you are familiar.

4.4.5 Suppose that the first-order serial correlation coefficient in a sequence generated by the mixed congruential method is given by

$$\rho(Z_i, Z_{i+1}) = f(a, c, m).$$

Find the expression for the kth order serial correlation coefficient of the sequence.

4.4.6 Consider the following p.d.f.:

$$f_X(x) = \begin{cases} 2x, & 0 \le x \le 1 \\ 0, & \text{elsewhere.} \end{cases}$$

Use the rejection technique to generate random variates according to this distribution.

4.4.7 *Hyperexponential distribution.* Find a way to generate a sequence of variates that have the two-phase hyperexponential distribution:

$$F_X(x) = 1 - pe^{-\mu_1 X} - qe^{-\mu_2 X},$$

where $p + q = 1$.

4.4.8 Show that the relation (4.26) holds. Write a subroutine program for the Erlangian distribution.

4.4.9 Suppose that the random variable X is defined as

$$X = \min\{X_1, X_2\}$$

where X_1 and X_2 are independent variables with distributions $F_1(x)$ and $F_2(x)$.
a) What is the distribution of X?
b) Assume that $F_1(x)$ and $F_2(x)$ are exponential distributions of means $1/\mu_1$ and $1/\mu_2$, respectively. Find the distribution of X.

4.4.10 *Poisson distribution.* Suppose that we generate a sequence of uniform random variates $U_1, U_2, U_3, \ldots$. Let X be defined as an integer variable such that

$$\prod_{i=1}^{X+1} U_i < e^{-\lambda} \leq \prod_{i=1}^{X} U_i.$$

Then show that X has the Poisson distribution with mean λ. *Hint:* Consider a Poisson arrival process with rate λ and count the number of arrivals in the unit-time interval.

4.4.11 *The polar method for generating the Gaussian variate: Box and Muller* (1958). Derive formulas (4.32) and (4.33) by the following steps: Transform the pair (X_1, X_2) into the polar coordinates (R, Θ) according to

$$X_1 = R \cos \Theta \quad \text{and}$$
$$X_2 = R \sin \Theta,$$

where X_1 and X_2 are independent variables, both of which are from the Gaussian distribution of mean zero and variance one.

a) Show that the probability distribution function is given by

$$F_R(r) = 1 - \exp\left(-\frac{r^2}{2}\right)$$

and Θ is a uniform distribution over $[0, 2\pi)$.
b) Set $Y_1 = 1 - \exp(-R^2/2)$, $Y_2 = \Theta/2\pi$.

4.5 IMPLEMENTATION OF SIMULATORS

4.5.1 Selection of Simulation Languages

In this section we discuss how to select the best simulation language in which to program the model. Construction of a simulation program is often the most time-consuming phase in a simulation effort, and the use of a suitable simulation language is critical to the economic feasibility of the entire study.

The purpose of most simulation studies is to compare alternatives of, say, system configuration, system parameters, scheduling policies, etc. Therefore, the simulation program must be *flexible* enough to readily accommodate the alternatives that will be considered; a provision for *rapid modifications* should be built into the program. Most of the instructions in a simulation program are logical operations, whereas the actual arithmetic work required is relatively little and is of a very simple type. The essential feature required of a simulation program is that it be able to reproduce the *dynamic behavior* of a system as it operates in time. These considerations have provided part of the motivation for the development of *simulation programming languages* that has taken place since the 1960s. These languages are designed to optimize the features of programming unique to simulation. Thus, the languages (1) provide a convenient representation of elements that commonly appear in simulation models, (2) expedite configuration changes of the system model, (3) provide an internal timing and control mechanism required to execute a simulation run, and (4) facilitate collection of data and statistics on the aggregate behavior of the simulated system and production of reports in a proper format.

For all of these reasons, many simulation programs today are written in one of the existing simulation programming languages. The resulting significant savings in programming time usually compensate for a possible loss in computer running time. Some of the best known languages for discrete-event system simulation are GPSS, SIMSCRIPT, SIMULA, CSL, and SIMPL/1.

Despite all the convenience and possible advantages of simulation programming languages, it is often preferable or necessary to write a simulator in a general-purpose programming language such as ALGOL, FORTRAN, PL/1, or APL. This will be the case if your computing facility does not provide any simulation language package, or if none of your associates is familiar with simulation languages and you cannot afford to spend extra time learning such a language. Another factor that you should consider in making your decision is that the debugging facilities of simulation programming languages are generally not as good as those of general-purpose programming languages. Even without difficulties of the kind listed above, you may still wish to write a simulator in a general-purpose programming language. For example, you may want to write a simulator that runs more efficiently, or you may want to build into your simulator a special control scheme such as a variance reducing method and/or a special sampling technique.

4.5.2 Case Study 1: Simulation of a Cyclic Queueing System in FORTRAN

In this section we will demonstrate, through a rather simple case study, how to construct a simulator using a general-purpose programming

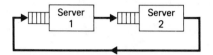

Fig. 4.9 A cyclic queueing system.

language such as FORTRAN. The same model will be discussed in later sections in which the simulators are written in GPSS and SIMPL/1.

Consider a two-stage cyclic queueing system such as the one shown in Fig. 4.9. there are two servers, connected in tandem and cyclic form. There exists a fixed number of jobs in this system and these jobs circle the two servers in the FCFS (first come, first served) manner. An analytical solution of the queue distribution at steady state is obtainable if the service-time distribution at either server 1 or server 2 is exponential. (See Sections 3.8.4 and 3.11.3.) Here we assume nonexponential service-time distributions at both servers.

The events that change the state of a queueing system are (1) an arrival of a job at a server, (2) a start of service, and (3) a completion of service. In the system under consideration, however, there are no arrivals from outside. Therefore, an arrival at one server is always the result of a departure from the other. A start of service at server 1 is caused by either the completion of the previous job at server 1 or the completion of a job at server 2. Therefore, there are only two independent events to be considered in the program, that is, "event 1" (completion of a job at server 1, and "event 2" (completion of a job at server 2).

The event list (or calendar) thus contains the scheduled times of only two future events:

SCHEDT(I): The scheduled time of the next event I, $I = 1, 2$.

The aggregate behavior of the system is characterized in terms of the queue size at a given time. This information is stored in the integer variables

QSIZE(I): The number of jobs at server I, $I = 1, 2$.

Clearly $QSIZE(1) + QSIZE(2) = NJOB$, where NJOB is the (fixed) number of jobs in the system. In addition to these variables we introduce the following:

CLOCK: The simulator clock to be set to the time of the imminent future event;

OLDCLK: The clock that stores the event time of the most recent event.

With this preparation we are ready to explain Fig. 4.10, the flow diagram of this simulation program. In the following discussion we use

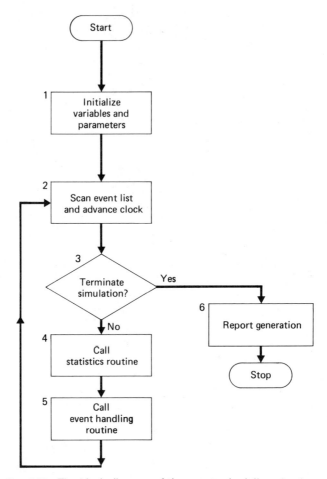

Fig. 4.10 The block diagram of the event-scheduling simulator.

FORTRAN statements for illustration. Needless to say, you could write an equivalent program in any other language.

The "main routine" shown in Fig. 4.10 is composed of six blocks; of course, there are other ways of decomposing the main routine into the component blocks and subroutine calls.

Main routine

Block 1: Initialization of the system variables and parameters

Here we make necessary declarations, read data cards, and set the initial conditions of the system. This block may consist of the following statements:

```
      REAL SCHEDT(2), TQTIME(2, 20), TOTJOB(2),
      CLOCK, OLDCLK
      INTEGER QSIZE(2), NJOB
      COMMON /A/ SCHEDT, TQTIME, TOTJOB, QSIZE
           (Read data NJOB, QSIZE(1))
      DO 120 I=1,2
  120 SCHEDT(1)=0.
      QSIZE(2)=NJOB-QSIZE(1)
      CLOCK=0.
```

In addition, we initialize the variables of STATIS, a statistic-gathering routine.

Block 2: Event-list scanning and clock updating

This is the core of the event-scheduling approach. In this sample problem, the scanning of the event list is so trivial that there is no need for sophisticated list processing techniques such as those discussed in Section 4.3.2.

```
  200 OLDCLK=CLOCK
      IF(SCHEDT(2).LT.SCHEDT(1)) GO TO 220
      I=1
  210 CLOCK=SCHEDT(1)
      GO TO 230
  220 I=2
      CLOCK=SCHEDT(2)
  230 CONTINUE
```

Block 3: Test for terminating simulation

Suppose we want to stop a simulation run at time $t = $ TMAX. This can be done by simply testing whether the scheduled time of the next event (which has just been stored in the variable CLOCK) exceeds TMAX or not. Thus, this block should be something like the following,

```
  300 IF(CLOCK.LT.TMAX) GO TO 310
      GO TO 600
  310 CONTINUE
```

where statement 600 corresponds to a subroutine call for report generation (see the discussion of block 6 below).

When to terminate a simulation run (that is, what value to choose for the parameter TMAX) is not a trivial question in many simulation problems. This is the subject to be discussed in Section 4.8. In practice, we often execute a simulator for a short period as a *pilot run*, and after the validity of the simulator is reasonably assured, then a number of *production runs* may be made. In this case, each run is terminated by a jump to block 6.

Block 4: Subroutine call for statistics collection

In the main routine, this block is a single statement, say,

```
400 CALL STATIS(I, CLOCK, OLDCLK)
```

where I (= event type), CLOCK, and OLDCLK are the set of arguments required for this subroutine. Additional parameters or variables may be necessary, depending on the type and amount of statistics we want to collect. An example of a statistics collection routine will be discussed in subroutine (2) given below.

Block 5: Subroutine call for event handling

In a general event-scheduling simulation model, we have different "event handlers" for different types of events. In the particular problem in question, the two events—event 1 and event 2—are of a similar nature, that is, the completion of service at one of the servers. Thus, it is sufficient to write only one event handler, which we denote as HANDLE. Therefore, block 5 is given by the statement

```
500 CALL HANDLE(I)
    GO TO 200
```

Block 6: Report generation

When a simulator run is terminated, a "report generation" routine will be called, which prints out summary statistics of the simulation run:

```
600 CALL REPT(CLOCK)
```

All the data required for the report generation should be found in STATIS—the statistics collection routine. Thus, in practice we may choose to have the report generation routine contained within the STATIS routine. In this case, block 3—the branching statement—should also be contained in the STATIS routine.

Subroutines

1. The event-handling subroutine (block 5)

Event I creates the following changes in the system: (1) It decreases by one the number of jobs in server I, and increases by one at the other server (server J), (2) it puts a new job (if any) in service at server I, (3) it puts server J into service, if that server was idle prior to event I, and (4) it updates the event list.

The subroutine HANDLE defined in the discussion on block 5

should thus be as follows:

```
      SUBROUTINE HANDLE(I)
            (declarations)
      J=3-I
      QSIZE(I)=QSIZE(I)-1
      QSIZE(J)=QSIZE(J)+1
      IF(QSIZE(I).EQ.0) GO TO 10
      SCHEDT(I)=CLOCK+ST(I,IZ)
   10 CONTINUE
      IF(QSIZE(J).GT.1) GO TO 20
      SCHEDT(J)=CLOCK+ST(J,IZ)
   20 CONTINUE
      RETURN
      END
```

Here ST(I, IZ) is a function that generates a variate drawn from the service-time distribution of server I. The sequence of values that the integer variable IZ takes on represents the pseudo-random integer sequence $\{Z_i\}$: Its initial value is Z_0, the seed of this sequence (see also the discussions on GGL below). Assume, for instance, that $F_1(x)$ is a two-stage hyperexponential distribution (with mean service times ST11 and ST12, and variates are drawn from the two exponential distributions with probabilities p and $1 - p$, respectively). Assume that $F_2(x)$ is the k-stage Erlangian distribution in which each stage is exponentially distributed with mean ST2. Then the service-time function ST(I, IZ) at server I will be defined as follows:

```
      FUNCTION ST(I,IZ)

      (declarations)

      IF(I.EQ.2) GO TO 20
      CALL GGL(IZ,X,1,IER)
      IF(X.GT.P) GO TO 15
      CALL GGL(IZ,Y,1,IER)
      ST=-ST11*ALOG(Y)
      GO TO 30
   15 CALL GGL(IZ,Y,1,IER)
      ST=-ST12*ALOG(Y)
      GO TO 30
   20 PROD=1
      DO 22 L=1,K
      CALL GGL(IZ,Y,1,IER)
   22 PROD=PROD*(Y)
      ST=-ST2*ALOG(PROD)
   30 RETURN
      END
```

Here the subroutine GGL is the random-number generator of IBM Scientific Library Mathematics. It generates for a given starting value a sequence of pseudo-random real numbers (independently and uniformly distributed between 0 and 1, excluding 0, 1), and supplies a starting value for the next call. It has the following format (IBM, 1974, p. 79):

```
CALL GGL(IX,X,N,IER)
```

where

> *IX:* GIVEN integer variable containing the starting value (seed) for the generator with $0 < IX < 2^{31} - 1$.
>
> RESULTANT pseudo-random integer (can be used as the starting value for the next call of GGL).
>
> *X:* RESULTANT real vector of dimension $N \geq 1$, containing the N pseudo-random real numbers.
>
> *N:* GIVEN number of pseudo-random real numbers to be generated.
>
> *IER:* RESULTANT error indicator (See the IBM manual for details.)

Thus, if $N = 1$, the FORTRAN statement

```
CALL GGL(IZ,Y,1,IER)
```

produces both the next pseudo-random integer in the sequence and the corresponding uniform variate between 0 and 1.

2. The statistics collection routine (block 4)

In this example, the main statistics of interest to us are the queue size distributions. The array TQTIME(I, L) is to be used to store the sum of intervals during which the number of jobs at server I is $L - 1$, $L \geq 1$. Variable TOTJOB(I) stores the cumulative number of event I (that is, the cumulative number of job service completions at server I). We write the routine as follows:

```
SUBROUTINE STATIS(I,CLOCK,OLDCLK)

    (declarations)

TOTJOB(I)=TOTJOB(I)+1
L=QSIZE(I)+1
TQTIME(I,L)=TQTIME(I,L)+(CLOCK-OLDCLK)
J=3-I
M=QSIZE(J)+1
TQTIME(J,M)=TQTIME(J,M)+(CLOCK-OLDCLK)
RETURN
END
```

As mentioned earlier, the statistics gathering routine will be substantially more involved if the response-time or waiting-time distribution is required. In that case, we must maintain the job table discussed in Section 4.3.2, which keeps track of the movements of the individual jobs.

3. The report generation subroutine (block 6)

Assume that we terminate the simulation run at the occurrence of the first event after time $t = $ TMAX, rather than exactly at $t = $ TMAX. This procedure introduces a slight bias into the resultant statistics, but simplifies the calculation of the average queue size, the queue distribution, etc. The array TQTIME(I, L) is now used to store the probability that the number of jobs at server I is $L - 1$, $L \geq 1$.

```
SUBROUTINE REPT(CLOCK)

(declarations)

(print CLOCK, the simulation termination time.)

      DO 20 I=1,2
      NJOBI=NJOB+1
      AVGQ=0.
      DO 10 L=2,NJOB1
   10 AVGQ=AVGQ+FLOAT(L-1)*TQTIME(I,L)
      AVGQ=AVGQ/CLOCK

         (print I and AVGQ)

      DO 20 L=1,NJOB1
      TQTIME(I,L)=TQTIME(I,L)/CLOCK
      L1=L-1

         (print L1 and TQTIME in table form)

   20 CONTINUE
      RETURN
      END
```

4.5.3   Simulation Programming Languages

Among several features of simulation programming languages discussed in Section 4.5.1, the core of a given simulation programming language consists of (1) the representation of the *static structure* of a given system, and (2) the representation of the *dynamic mechanism* of the system. A system can be viewed as a collection of *objects* that interact in a specified environment. An object is also called an *entity, transaction, facility,* or *process.* The data structure of a simulation model is a framework within which system states are defined, where system states can be viewed as possible configurations of these objects. The dynamic mechanism of the system acts on the data structure, changing data values and thereby causing state transitions.

State transitions are handled in different ways in different languages, depending on the representation of the objects. In some languages all objects are passive in the sense that actions happen to them, whereas in some others objects are active as well; that is, they can move around the system and initiate actions. In order to relate objects, such relational structures as sets, queues, lists, etc., are used (Section 4.3.2).

Informally, a simulation program can be decomposed into a three-level hierarchical structure. At the top level is a *simulation control program* (or *timing control routine*). Blocks of statements that handle specific system events or activities occupy the intermediate level. Miscellaneous routines such as random-number generators and report generators fill the bottom level. The blocks of statements are called *events, activities,* or *processes,* depending on the modeling approach (Fishman, 1973a, 1973b). The approach outlined in Sections 4.3.1 and 4.3.2 and adopted in the FORTRAN simulation program of Section 4.5.2 is called the *event-scheduling approach.* In this model the simulation control program scans the event list, identifies the next event, and executes the corresponding event block (the event-handling routine). SIMSCRIPT is an event-oriented language. The event-scheduling approach is generally efficient in terms of run times, and the event list or calendar is relatively easy to create when the scheduling statements are primarily time-oriented. The DELAY and WAIT commands, which interrupt the execution of a subprogram until a specified period of time has passed, are examples of time-oriented statements. Modeling based on the event-scheduling approach becomes complicated when scheduling involves condition-oriented statements such as WAIT UNTIL, which interrupts the execution of a subprogram until a stated set of conditions becomes satisfied.

In order to cope with difficulties such as condition-oriented scheduling, the *activity scanning approach* is often taken. In the single-server queueing system there is only one activity: serving a job. But in a simulation model of a computer system, relevant activities are, for example, (1) holding a job in main memory, (2) executing a job on the CPU, or (3) seeking the cylinder of a disk request. The objects are these activities, each having its own clock. The simulation control program scans the current conditions and clocks of the activities and determines which activities can be initiated or terminated.

In such simulation programming languages as SIMULA, GPSS, and SIMPL/1, the run-time efficiency of event scheduling and the modeling efficiency of activity scanning are combined. This modeling method is called the *process interaction approach.* The system behavior is described by a collection of processes (a process is defined here as a sequence of events that are associated with a system behavior). Each process may have several points at which it interacts with other processes. Then a single program is made to act as though it were several programs, independently controlled either by activity-type scans or event scheduling.

We do not intend to describe in detail existing simulation languages, but we do wish to give the readers a brief introduction to GPSS, one of the most widely used simulation languages, and to SIMPL/1, a relatively new language developed also by IBM.

SIMSCRIPT is one of the most available languages, perhaps second only to GPSS. SIMSCRIPT is a simulation language with its origin in FORTRAN. There are several versions of this language. The original SIMSCRIPT was developed by Markowitz, Karr, and Hauser (1963) at the Rand Corporation. SIMSCRIPT I.5 (Karr, Kleine, and Markowitz, 1965), SIMSCRIPT II (Kiviat, Villanueva, and Markowitz, 1969; Kiviat and Villanueva, 1969), and SIMSCRIPT II.5 (Consolidated Analysis Centers, Inc. 1971) are the successive improvements and extensions.

SIMULA (Dahl and Nygaard, 1966) is an ALGOL-based simulation language, and is used more widely in Europe than in the United States. There are a number of other simulation programming languages, but their availability and documentation are quite limited compared with GPSS and SIMSCRIPT. Interested readers are directed to an article by Teichroew and Lubin (1966), which gives a comparative discussion of various discrete-event simulation languages.

4.5.3   Simulation Languages for Computer System Simulation

The simulation languages described in the previous section can handle a large class of discrete-event system simulation. Simulation of computer system/subsystem models is merely one of many possible applications to which these general simulation languages are found useful. As was shown above, use of a simulation language such as GPSS alleviates the need for a great deal of time-consuming programming.

As the complexity of computer systems has grown, there has developed a need for an even higher level language tailored to simulation studies of computer system performance. IBM developed CSS (Computer System Simulator), a special language for simulating IBM's computer systems and subsystems. CSS is similar in concept to GPSS, because the basic idea evolved from GPSS programming experience for computer system modeling. CSS is *not* built on GPSS, but is coded in basic assembly language. Its structure is designed to alleviate the inefficiencies and difficulties found in GPSS models of computer systems. Seaman and Soucy (1969) describe the historical details and the earlier version of CSS. A later version CSS II (IBM, 1971d, 1971e) is available as an IBM program product.

The primitive elements of CSS are entities that describe actual computer system components such as processors, channels, control units, tapes, communication lines, and terminals. In the case of direct-access storage devices, CSS specifically models IBM 2302, 2311, 2314, and 3330 disk units and the 2321 data cell. The seek characteristics of these units are built into the CSS program. After the system configuration is described in terms of these *equipment entities*, both control programs and application programs must be specified. For this purpose, CSS provides an instruction set that consists of 41 instructions. Some of them are similar to macro instructions of operating systems (e.g., READ, WRITE, BRANCH, ALLOCATE). Other instructions are used for manipulation of the simulation model (e.g., test instruction, probabilistic branch, queueing instruction, arithmetic instruction). In addition, there are instructions for statistics collection and report generation (e.g., TABULATE, PRINT).

The programs represented by instruction sequences are classified into three categories: (1) application programs that model the user jobs, (2) control programs that model the operating system, controlling scheduling and resource allocation, and (3) environment programs that model the operations outside the system, such as terminal operators.

CSS models all IBM System/360 and System/370 configurations and can be modified to model new equipment or special-purpose systems. Since CSS is more direct in its representations, it usually runs faster than GPSS in most cases of computer system modeling.

4.6   SIMULATION IN GPSS

4.6.1   GPSS

GPSS (General Purpose System Simulator) is an interpretive simulation language developed at IBM. Its first version appeared in 1961; the second version, GPSS II, appeared in 1963 and was followed by GPSS III in 1965 and GPSS 360 in 1969. The current version, GPSS V (IBM, 1971a, 1971b, 1971c), is an extension of GPSS III and GPSS 360, and provides some new facilities and greater ease of use.

One of the special features of GPSS is that it describes directly the functional flow of the jobs (called *transactions*) through the system. The static structure of the system is described by entities such as *facilities* and *storages*. Facilities are entities that can be occupied by only one transaction at a time, while storages are entities that may be occupied by more than one transaction simultaneously. Therefore, in a typical computer system model, such resources as the CPU and disks are treated as facilities, whereas main memory is modeled as storage.

Transactions have numerical characteristics called *parameters*. Facilities and storages have numerical *attributes*. These parameters and attributes are collectively termed *standard numerical attributes*. The dynamic mechanism of the system is modeled in terms of *block commands*: Each block command represents an *operation* that acts on individual transactions or entities. The operation is accomplished by means of *field information* or a collection of *operands* that accompany each block statement.

Corresponding to each block command is a block-type subroutine. A GPSS simulation is the *interpretive* execution of these subroutines. In order to execute simulated events in the correct time sequence, GPSS maintains a clock that records the current simulation clock time. All clock times in the simulator are integer values. The GPSS clock is updated to indicate the time of occurrence of the most imminent event. Because time can take on only integer values in GPSS, it is the user's responsibility to select the GPSS time unit to obtain the desired precision.

4.6.2 Case Study 2: Simulation of the Cyclic Queueing System in GPSS

Our purpose here is to show how a GPSS program should be prepared. Just as for other computer languages, the easiest way to learn this language is to go through a sample program. We will discuss here the same queueing system as that discussed in Section 4.5.2. Figure 4.11 is a diagram of the functional segments of the cyclic queueing system. Conceptually, this diagram is much simpler than Fig. 4.10 because it is essentially the flow of transactions in the queueing system in question. We now discuss how to map this transaction flow diagram into GPSS statements.

We assume that there are eight jobs in this closed system, and that the service-time distribution at server 1 is a two-stage hyperexponential distribution

$$F_1(x) = 1 - pe^{-\mu_{11}t} - (1 - p)e^{-\mu_{12}t},$$

where $p = 0.9$, $\mu_{11} = \frac{1}{5}[\text{sec}^{-1}]$, and $\mu_{12} = \frac{1}{15}[\text{sec}^{-1}]$. The service-time distribution $F_2(t)$ at server 2 is the two-stage Erlangian distribution of

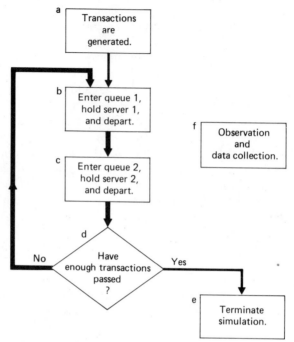

Fig. 4.11 Transaction flow diagram in the cyclic queueing system.

mean service time 5 [sec]. We choose the time unit to be $\frac{1}{100}$ [sec], and we will run the simulator until 500 transaction flows are observed at server 2. The reader should be able to modify the program when we employ the same stopping decision as that used in case study 1 (see Exercise 4.6.4).

A. Generation of transactions

The GENERATE block creates transactions for entry into the model. This block statement takes the form GENERATE A, B, C, D in which operands A and B specify that the intervals between transactions are uniformly distributed with range $[A - B, A + B]$. If $B = 0$, transaction arrivals are regular. The C operand specifies the delay until the first transaction is created by this block. The D operand is a count limiting the total number of transactions to be created by the GENERATE block; if omitted, the block continues to create transactions indefinitely. To generate other than uniform interarrival times, B may be a user-provided tabled function. In such a case, the interarrival time is the product of A and the value of function B.

The statement

$$\text{GENERATE} \quad ,,,8$$

creates eight transactions instantaneously, since in this case the operands
A, B, and C have a default value of zero. Additional operands E, F, G,
and H may be specified in the GENERATE block.

B. Servicing the transactions at server 1

Since server 1 is a single server, it is a facility in GPSS terminology.
SEIZE and RELEASE block commands are used to reserve and release
the facility, named SERV1:

```
           SEIZE      SERV1
             .
             .
             .
           RELEASE    SERV1
```

If another transaction is currently using the facility, entering transactions
must wait; that is, queueing is done at the SEIZE block. A transaction
may seize any number of facilities at one time.
    The interval (the service time) for which the facility is reserved is
specified by an ADVANCE block. If the distribution of the interval is
uniform with the mean A and the spread B, then we write

```
           ADVANCE    A,B
```

Thus, the A and B operands are similar to those of the GENERATE
block. To specify other than uniform service-time distributions, the
operand B is not a numeric number but is a *function*. In GPSS, a function
$y = f(x)$ is defined by a table that consists of a set of (x, y) values. A user
can specify the function using a *control statement* FUNCTION. One of the
most frequently used functions is $Y = -\ln(1 - x)$, which transforms a
uniform variate into an exponential variate. We define this function,
named EXPON, as follows:[*]

```
EXPON    FUNCTION    RN1,C24
0,0/.1,.105/.2,.223/.3,.356/.4,.510/.5,.693/.6,.916
.7,1.20/.75,1.39/.8,1.61/.84,1.83/.88,2.12/.9,2.30
.92,2.52/.94,2.81/.95,2.99/.96,3.22/.97,3.50
.98,3.91/.99,4.60/.995,5.30/.998,6.21/.999,6.90/.9997,8.11
```

The operand A of a FUNCTION defines the argument (independent
variable) of the function. Hence, in the EXPON function, the argument is
RN1, random-number stream 1: GPSS has eight pseudo-random number
generators, which are specified as RN1 through RN8. C24 in the B
operand shows that the function is a *continuous* valued function specified

---

[*] The EXPON function defined in the GPSS manual (IBM, 1971a) seems
inaccurate.

by 24 pairs of (x_i, y_i) values, $i = 1, 2, \ldots, 24$; $(0, 0)$, $(0.1, 0.105)$, ..., and $(0.9997, 8.11)$. Whenever the argument value lies between two successive points x_i and x_{i+1}, the GPSS program interpolates linearly to obtain the function value between the two associated points y_i and y_{i+1}.

Whenever the value of this function is used as an operand of a GPSS block statement, it is written as FN$EXPON: In GPSS, when a symbolically addressed function name, parameter, or attribute is used as an operand, a dollar sign ($) must be used as a symbol prefix. Thus, when FN$EXPON is encountered in execution, the output of random-number stream 1 is transformed according to the above function, yielding exponentially distributed random variates of mean 1.

The service-time distribution at server 1 is the hyperexponential distribution $F_1(x)$; such a server can be represented by two parallel exponential servers and a probabilistic split. The TRANSFER block statement is used for the probabilistic split:

```
TRANSFER .100, STG1, STG2
```

A transaction entering this block goes next to location STG1 with probability $1 - 0.100 = 0.900$, and to location STG2 with probability 0.100.

In order to gather queue statistics at a specified point in the model, we use QUEUE and DEPART blocks. The statement

```
QUEUE     A,B
```

adds B units to the contents of queue A. If the B operand is omitted (which is often the case), it is assumed to be 1. The program maintains the cumulative time integral of the queue size contributed by all transactions, that is, $\int_0^t Q(u)\, du$, defined by (3.58) (see Fig. 3.14). Of course, the integration in the above expression is reduced to the sum of queue size and time products, since $Q(t)$ is a staircase function. The average queue size over the simulation interval $[0, \tau]$ is obtained according to formula (3.54). The mean queueing time per transaction is computed by (3.53).

Similarly, the statement

```
DEPART    A,B
```

reduces the contents of queue A by B units. If the operand B is omitted, it is assumed to be 1.

By combining the GPSS block commands introduced above, we can represent the sequence of actions that take place at server 1 as follows:

```
CYCLE     QUEUE       QUE1
          SEIZE       SERVI
          TRANSFER    .100,STG1,STG2
STG1      ADVANCE     X$ST11,FN$EXPON
          TRANSFER    ,EXIT
STG2      ADVANCE     X$ST12,FN$EXPON
EXIT      DEPART      QUE1
          RELEASE     SERVI
```

The QUEUE block is named (CYCLE), since it is referenced by the TEST block to be discussed in part D. Note that the DEPART block comes after the ADVANCE block, since queue size, in our definition, includes a transaction in service as well as those in the waiting line (Exercise 4.6.1). The A operands of the ADVANCE blocks, X$ST11 and X$ST12, are the numerical values stored in the *save value* locations named ST11 and ST12, respectively. A dollar sign ($) is used since the save value location is symbolically addressed. These values are initialized using INITIAL statements:

```
INITIAL     X$ST11,500

INITIAL     X$ST12,1500
```

Since we chose the time unit of 10^{-2} [sec], the values 500 and 1500 represent 5 [sec] and 15 [sec], respectively.

C.   Servicing the transactions at server 2

The service-time distribution at server 2 is a two-stage Erlangian distribution. Recall that a k-stage Erlangian service time is equivalent to that of a job looping through a fictitious exponential server k times. Thus, the portion of programs related to activities at server 2 is as follows:

```
ST2       VARIABLE    X$KST2/X$ERLN
            .
            .
          ASSIGN      1,X$ERLN
          QUEUE       QUE2
          SEIZE       SERV2
STAGE     ADVANCE     V$ST2,FN$EXPON
          LOOP        1,STAGE
          DEPART      QUEUE2
COUNT     RELEASE     SERV2
            .
            .
          INITIAL     X$ERLN,2
          INITIAL     X$KST2,500
```

GPSS allows only a simple arithmetic statement to define a VARI-ABLE. Here, the VARIABLE, named ST2, represents the mean service time of the (fictitious) exponential server. It is set to the ratio of X$KST2 to X$ERLN, where X$KST2 is the value stored in the save value location KST2; X$ERLN is the number of Erlangian stages.

When a transaction is created in a GENERATE block, all parameters are initially zero. The statement

```
ASSIGN A,B
```

means that *parameter A* of a transaction is assigned the value *B*. Thus, when a transaction enters the block

```
ASSIGN 1,X$ERLN
```

the value of its parameter 1 (P1) is set to the value (2 in this case) stored in save value ERLN.

The statement LOOP allows a transaction to loop through a segment of the model a given number of times. The *A* operand specifies the parameter that is used as a counter. So in the present case, parameter P1 is chosen as the counter; its value is ASSIGNed equal to the number of Erlangian stages. Each time a transaction enters the LOOP block, the *A* operand parameter value is decreased by one. When the value of that particular parameter becomes 0, the transaction exits from the loop and enters the next block. If the parameter value is not 0, the transaction returns to the block specified by the *B* operand. In the present case, the LOOP statement is used to generate a *k*-stage Erlangian variate, where $k = 2$ in the example.

D.   Testing a simulation run length

The TEST block, like the IF statement in FORTRAN, checks the following relations between its operands:

L   Less than $(A < B)$

LE   Less than or equal to $(A \le B)$

E   Equal to $(A = B)$

G   Greater than $(A > B)$

GE   Greater than or equal to $(A \ge B)$

If the defined relation is *true*, the transaction proceeds to the next sequential block; if the relation if *false*, the transaction is transferred to the location of operand *C*. If the *C* operand is blank, the transaction is denied entry to the TEST block until the specified relations between the *A* and *B* operands become true. So block (d) of Fig. 4.11 can be represented by the statement:

```
TEST E     N$COUNT, X$SAMPL,CYCLE
```

Each time a transaction enters this TEST E block, the total number of transactions that have entered the RELEASE block (named COUNT) is compared with the save value SAMPL. If they are not equal, this block directs the transaction to the block named CYCLE of part **B**. When the *entry count* reaches SAMPL, the transaction is sent to the TERMINATE block. If we want to terminate when server 2 achieves, say, 500 service completions, we write

```
INITIAL    X$SAMPL,500
```

E. Termination of the simulation

We want to terminate the simulation run when the test of part D is passed, that is, when a transaction enters box (e) of Fig. 4.11. This can be achieved by using the TERMINATE block statement

```
TERMINATE 1
```

The A operand specifies the number of units by which the *run termination count* is decreased. The termination count is initially set by field A of a START control statement. The START statement indicates that all input data have been provided and the simulation may now proceed. When the termination count is decreased to zero or less, the simulation ends. Thus, if we have the START statement

```
START     1
```

the simulation run terminates when the first transaction enters the TER-MINATE block.

F. Statistics collection

GPSS provides built-in statistics-gathering capabilities. The output of a GPSS simulation includes statistics on the utilization of all facilities, storages, and queues in the system. However, the queue size *distributions* are not provided in the standard QUEUE statistics, and it is necessary to TABULATE them. The nature of the tabulation is determined by the TABLE definition statement. In order to collect the distributions of the numbers of transactions in server 1 and server 2, we write the TABLE definition statement

```
TAB1    TABLE     Q$QUE1,0,1,10
TAB2    TABLE     Q$QUE2,0,1,10
```

In the tabular representation, we group the observed results in *classes*, and record the *frequencies* of observations of these classes. The *A* operand specifies the numerical attribute to be tabulated, the *B* operand is the upper limit of the first class, the *C* operand is the size of the other contiguous classes, and the *D* operand specifies the total number of classes. Thus, TAB1 will contain the frequency counts of the value of QUE1 in the classes $(-\infty, 0]$, $(0, 1]$, $(1, 2], \ldots$, $(7, 8]$, and $(8, \infty)$. Since the queue size is always an integer, these class intervals are equivalent to the integers $0, 1, 2, \ldots, 8$ and $[9, \infty)$.

The tabulation is done by periodic sampling. We generate periodically a sequence of transactions (which are entirely separate from the transactions that go through the simulation model); when a transaction enters a TABULATE block, it updates the specified table. Such a procedure is done by the following set of GPSS statements:

```
GENERATE    100
TABULATE    TAB1
TABULATE    TAB2
TERMINATE   0
```

The GENERATE block generates a transaction at every 100 time units. Each time a transaction enters the first TABULATE block, the queue size of QUE1 is recorded in TAB1. Similarly, the next block TABU-LATEs the queue distribution of QUE2 in TAB2. The transactions that play the role of data collectors are absorbed by the TERMINATE block as they flow into this block.

We are now ready to combine the programs of the functional segments **A–F**, and complete the program. If a GPSS simulation run is desired, a SIMULATE statement must be included somewhere in the program. If no SIMULATE statement is provided, the job is terminated after the assembly phase. The operand *A* in the SIMULATE statement specifies the maximum run time in minutes. Therefore, if we write

```
SIMULATE    1
```

the model will run for no more than one minute. The SIMULATE statement may be placed anywhere in the model input.

In GPSS a detailed flow diagram is often used in which each of the GPSS macro statements (such as GENERATE, QUEUE, ENTER) is drawn in a unique *block symbol*. In this example, we dispense with such a detailed block diagram and present instead a complete GPSS simulation program for the cyclic queueing model (Fig. 4.12). The GPSS statements are converted by the GPSS assembly program into a numeric format acceptable for execution. The reader is directed to GPSS manuals for coding formats and run procedures.

```
        SIMULATE 1
EXPON FUNCTION RN1,C24
0,0/.1,.105/.2,.223/.3,.356/.4,.510/.5,.693/.6,.916
.7,1.20/.75,1.39/.8,1.61/.84,1.83/.88,2.12/.9,2.30
.92,2.52/.94,2.81/.95,2.99/.96,3.22/.97,3.50
.98,3.91/.99,4.60/.995,5.30/.998,6.21/.999,6.90/.9997,8.11
*
*        DEFINITIONS OF VARIABLE AND TABLES
*
  ST2      VARIABLE     X$KST2/X$ERLN
  TAB1     TABLE        Q$QUE1,0,1,10
  TAB2     TABLE        Q$QUE2,0,1,10
*
*        JOB GENERATION
*
         GENERATE     ,,,8
*
*        SERVICING JOBS AT SERVER 1
*
CYCLE    QUEUE        QUE1
         SEIZE        SERV1
         TRANSFER     .100,STG1,STG2
STG1     ADVANCE      X$ST11,FN$EXPON
         TRANSFER     ,EXIT
STG2     ADVANCE      X$ST12,FN$EXPON
EXIT     DEPART       QUE1
         RELEASE      SERV1
*
*        SERVICING JOBS AT SERVER 2
*
         ASSIGN       1,X$ERLN
         QUEUE        QUE2
         SEIZE        SERV2
STAGE    ADVANCE      V$ST2,FN$EXPON
         LOOP         1,STAGE
         DEPART       QUE2
COUNT    RELEASE      SERV2
*
*        TESTING SIMULATION RUN LENGTH
*
         TEST E       N$COUNT,X$SAMPL,CYCLE
*
*        TERMINATION OF SIMULATION
*
(cont.)
```

Fig. 4.12 A GPSS program of the cyclic queueing system.

```
        TERMINATE    1
*
*       STATISTICS COLLECTION
*
        GENERATE     100
        TABULATE     TAB1
        TABULATE     TAB2
        TERMINATE    0
*
*       INITIALIZATION
*
        INITIAL      X$SAMPL,500
        INITIAL      X$ERLN,2
        INITIAL      X$ST11,500
        INITIAL      X$ST12,1500
        INITIAL      X$KST2,500
*
*       SIMULATION PROCEEDS
*
        START        1
        END
```

Fig. 4.12 (*continued*)

The simulation run continues until the transaction of the 500th (= X$SAMPL) service completion at server 2 reduces the terminate count to zero. Upon termination, "facility statistics" and "queue statistics" are automatically presented as results of the built-in statistics collection routines of GPSS. If a simulation model included storages, "storage statistics" should follow facility statistics.

The user-specified statistic is based on the periodic sampling (as discussed in part F), whereas GPSS computes the queue statistics using the time-integration approach (as discussed in connection with the QUEUE block).

By means of the sample program, we have discussed most of the numerical attributes, GPSS block statements, and control statements that are frequently used in system modeling. However, there are some omissions. As described earlier, GPSS includes, in addition to the facility, another type of entity called storage, which can be viewed as a bank of facilities. The ENTER and LEAVE blocks are used to represent the use of storages.

The ENTER statement performs the same function as the SEIZE statement, except that the corresponding entity is a storage rather than a facility. The block statement ENTER A, B means that a transaction enters storage A and occupies B units of storage space. If the B field is left blank, it is assumed to be 1. For each storage device modeled in a simulation, a STORAGE definition statement is needed to specify the capacity of storage space, which cannot exceed $2^{31} - 1$. If the B operand specifies more units than the storage can accommodate presently, the transaction attempting to enter the ENTER block is refused entry and it must wait.

Note that a station with m parallel servers is equivalent to a storage of capacity m units (see Exercise 4.6.3). The simulation program should include a control statement

```
STORAGE A,m
```

and a block statement

```
ENTER   A,1
```

The statement LEAVE A, B removes B units from the contents of storage A, when a transaction enters this block.

Other important features not covered in the sample program include the QTABLE statement and *priority* and related blocks. The QTABLE statement is used to tabulate the distribution of *waiting time* that transactions spend in a queue. The A operand of a QTABLE statement refers to the name of the queue for which delay times are to be tabulated. In the sample program we have shown that transactions have parameters (up to eight parameters), which are given values by an AS-SIGN block. A transaction has another type of attribute, priority, which determines how it is processed by blocks. The priority value can be reset up or down by a PRIORITY block. The PREEMPT block controls the use of facilities in which preemptive priority scheduling is required; the priority value alone is used for nonpreemptive priority scheduling. Similarly, the INTERRUPT block represents a higher level use of the facility by a transaction. The facility remains interrupted until the transaction exits from the INTERRUPT block. In the case of the PREEMPT block, the conclusion of the interrupt is signaled by means of an explicit RETURN block. See GPSS manuals and books for further details and sample programs.

4.6.3   Timing Control and Data Structure in GPSS

The simulation control program or timing control routine in GPSS is called the *scanning routine.* The scanning operation performs the essential task of a simulation program, that is, *sequencing* and *executing* code blocks in the order in which they are actually supposed to take place in the simulated world. In GPSS, the scanning operation takes into consideration the combined features of the *scheduled event list* and the *conditional event list.* The scheduled event list contains those unconditional events whose occurrence epochs are determined directly from block statements (such as ADVANCE, GENERATE). The conditional event list is a collection of events incurred by such statements as ENTER and SEIZE: The actual time at which the transaction in question can acquire a storage or facility is conditioned on the departure of the transaction (if any) that is currently occupying that resource.

The GPSS scanning operation accordingly performs the ordering of simulated events in two steps, as illustrated in Fig. 4.13. Each time the system state changes, the GPSS scanning routine examines whether the new system condition (e.g., the result of a release of a resource) satisfies the requirements of any of the conditional events in the list. If so, the corresponding code block for such an event is executed. The execution of the event generally creates one or more future events, which will be then filed in the scheduled event list (together with the event time) or into the conditional event list (together with the set of conditions required). After all the conditional events are examined and appropriate actions taken, the scanning routine then scans the scheduled event table, identifies the most imminent event, advances the simulator clock to that event time, and executes the corresponding block statement. This will move the system into a new state; consequently, a new cycle of the scanning operation begins: The scanning routine examines the updated conditional event list and scheduled event list in the manner just described.

In order to minimize the scanning time, it is necessary to order entire events in the scheduled event list. This is accomplished, as discussed

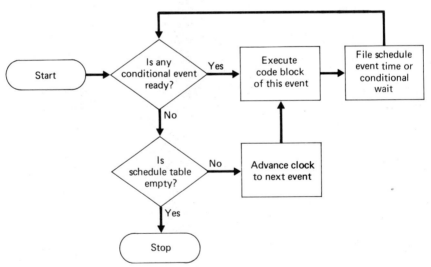

Fig. 4.13 GPSS timing control diagram.

earlier, by *chaining* events: Each event is chained to the following event as well as to the preceding event. When a new event is to be filed, the chain is revised by inserting the event into an appropriate place. The first and last entries on the ordered chain are appropriately identified. In GPSS, this chain is called the *future events chain*. It contains those transactions whose scheduled departure times (from the current activities) are known. Such transactions are placed in the chain in the order of the time at which they are scheduled to leave the chain.

The conditional event list is also organized in terms of a chain and is called the *current events chain*, which connects events according to their priority classes (within a priority class, transactions are sequenced as they joined the chain, that is, in FIFO order). Each transaction in the chain is in either *active* status or *delayed* (or *blocked*) status. If a transaction is in active status, then the GPSS scanning routine continuously moves the transaction into its next block. On the other hand, if the transaction is unable to proceed further because of the unavailability of some resource, it will be placed in the inactive status. Transactions in this status are skipped by the scan and are said to be in a *delay* chain; a delay chain is a push-down list of transactions that are waiting for the change in status of some resource. Associated with *each* resource (facility or storage) we assign several classes of chains—different chains corresponding to different conditions of that resource (e.g., "not-in-use" delay chain, "interrupted" delay chain, "unavailable" delay chain, etc.). When the system state changes, only those transactions that have been blocked by that *particular* condition at that *particular* resource are considered for advancement. This technique substantially reduces the scanning time.

Exercises

4.6.1 Discuss the difference between the following two cases in terms of statistics collected by the QUEUE blocks.

```
a)  QUEUE      QUE1
    SEIZE      SERV1
    DEPART     QUE1
    ADVANCE    10,FN$EXPON
    RELEASE    SERV1
        .
        .
        .

b)  QUEUE      QUE1
    SEIZE      SERV1
    ADVANCE    10,FN$EXPON
    DEPART     QUE1
    RELEASE    SERV1
        .
        .
        .
```

4.6.2 Write a GPSS simulation program of the $M/M/1$ queueing system (Section 3.8.2) with the parameter $\rho = \lambda/\mu = 0.8$. Obtain the response-time distribution, as well as the queue-length distribution.

4.6.3 Extend the program of Exercise 4.6.2 to an $M/M/n$ queueing system.

4.6.4 In the GPSS program discussed in this section, the simulation run is stopped after X$SAMPL ($=500$) of events are observed at server 2. Modify the stopping rule in such a way that it will stop at time $t = $ TMAX.

4.6.5 *Open queueing network.* Modify the GPSS program given in this section into a simulation program of the following open queueing network: Jobs arrive at server 1 according to the Poisson process with rate $\lambda = \frac{1}{8}$ [sec^{-1}]. They move cyclically between server 1 and server 2. Each time a transaction leaves server 2, it departs from the system with probability 0.2, and returns to server 1 with probability 0.8.

4.6.6 *Multiprogrammed computer system model.* If we consider server 1 and server 2 as the CPU and I/O processors, respectively, the model of Exercise 4.6.5 may be interpreted as a simple model of a multiprogrammed computer system. Extend the model by considering the storage constraint. Before an arriving job is allowed entry to the system, it must receive some amount of storage space according to the size of the job program. If the currently available storage is not sufficient to accommodate, the job is prevented from entering the multiprogramming system, and must wait in the queue associated with storage (the job scheduling queue). Assume that two thirds of the jobs require 10 units of storage, while the remaining ones require 40 units of storage. The total storage capacity is 80 units. Write a GPSS simulator to obtain the resource utilization, the average degree of multiprogramming, and the response-time distribution.

4.7 SIMULATION IN SIMPL/1

4.7.1 SIMPL/1

SIMPL/1 (Simulation Language based on PL/1) is a process-oriented language recently developed by IBM (IBM, 1972). A simulation model written in SIMPL/1 may contain PL/1 statements as well as SIMPL/1 statements, which we will describe below. The model is processed by the SIMPL/1 preprocessor, which translates it into a PL/1 code suitable for input to the PL/1 optimizing compiler. SIMPL/1 allows the user to write a discrete-event simulation model in terms of SIMPL/1 statements, which correspond to GPSS blocks discussed in the previous section. While retaining all the capabilities of PL/1, the language provides additional modeling and high-level list processing features.

A model of a given system contains a number of components, and in SIMPL/1 these components are represented in terms of *processes, entities, lists, procedures,* and *functions.*

Processes. A *process* is an element or object that possesses dynamic characteristics. For example, the server of a queueing system is a process. We define a process named SERVER by declaring

```
DCL SERVER PROCESS;
```

The *behavior* is a sequence of actions that occur over time. The behavior of the process SERVER is specified as follows:

```
SERVER:BEHAVIOR;
    IF VOID(QUEUE) THEN HOLD;        When queue empty, wait.
    FIRST_IN_Q=FIRST(QUEUE);         Get first job in queue.
    REMOVE FIRST FROM (QUEUE);       Release the job from
                                     queue.
    TAKE(ERLANG(1,M,K));             Draw service time from K-
                                     stage Erlang of mean MK.
    DESTROY FIRST_IN_Q;              The job leaves the model.
    END SERVER;
```

A group of statements such as those above is called a *behavior group*. When the last statement in the behavior group has been executed (that is, when the END statement has been reached), control returns automatically to the first statement of the group. A behavior group may appear anywhere within a SIMPL/1 model.

A process is introduced into the model through the START statement, such as in

```
START SERVER;
```
or
```
START SERVER SET (S);            Start server named S.
```

When the SET *option* is specified, it provides a name to the process just brought into the model. This is done by using an ordinary PL/1 pointer variable, which must be declared in advance:

```
DCL S POINTER;
```

Setting the pointer allows other processes to refer to this process; this mechanism enables us to represent interactions between different processes.

Entities. Not all elements or components of the system are processes. For instance, we view jobs as passive elements that are acted on by processes. In SIMPL/1, such elements are called *entities*. An entity, unlike a process, has no dynamic behavior of its own: Its principal function is to contain data and to be manipulated in lists. An entity is CREATEd rather than STARTed. We specify the arrival of jobs in the queueing system as follows:

```
DCL JOB ENTITY;
DCL ARRIVAL PROCESS;
    .
    .
START ARRIVAL;
    .
    .
ARRIVAL:BEHAVIOR;
  TAKE(NEGEXP(2,T));          Poisson arrival.
  CREATE JOB SET(J);          Create a job named J.
  INSERT J LAST IN (QUEUE);   Put job J last in queue.
  NOTIFY S;                   Tell server S about arrival.
END ARRIVAL;
```

In the above example, jobs are created through a process called ARRI-VAL. This process has the corresponding behavior group that specifies the sequences of actions of the process in SIMPL/1 statements.

Lists. One of the most useful features of SIMPL/1 is that processes and entities can be arranged into *sets* or *lists*. The lists themselves must be declared; thus:

```
DCL QUEUE LIST;
```

The lists can be examined at any time, and processes and entities can be inserted or removed at will. Examples are some of the statements that appeared above:

```
IF VOID(QUEUE) THEN HOLD;
REMOVE FIRST FROM (QUEUE);
INSERT J LAST IN (QUEUE);
```

Quite often we wish to gather statistics of the data items in the list. This can be achieved by adding the STATS option when the list is declared:

```
DCL QUEUE LIST STATS;
```

Procedures. If a program contains entity-type declarations and list-handling statements but no process-type declarations or process-handling statements, it can be written as a SIMPL/1 procedure. A procedure statement is defined as in a PL/1 external procedure. Control passes to the procedure by a CALL statement or a function reference.

Functions. SIMPL/1 provides a variety of functions useful for both simulation and list processing. The function library may be divided into list-handling functions, process-handling functions, statistical functions, and histogram functions. We give a brief explanation of some of these functions in the case study below.

4.7.2 Case Study 3: Simulation of the Cyclic Queueing Model in SIMPL/1

In this section we discuss a sample program written in SIMPL/1. The system to be modeled is the two-stage cyclic queueing system discussed in Sections 4.5.2 and 4.6.2.

The main program

First we present the skeleton of the SIMPL/1 program by deferring discussions on the behavior groups, procedures, and declarations. The main program is as follows:

```
CYCLIC: MODEL OPTIONS (MAIN);
    (DECLARATIONS)
            .
            .
            .
    DO J=1 TO NJOB;
        CREATE JOB SET(J);
        INSERT J IN (QUEUE1);
    END;
    START SERVER1 SET(S1) AFTER TIME(0);
    START SERVER2 SET(S2) AFTER TIME(0);
    TAKE(RUN_TIME);
    CALL INTEG_Q;
    CALL STATISTICS;
    TERMINATE;
    (BEHAVIOR GROUPS)
    (PROCEDURES)
END CYCLIC;
```

The MODEL statement assigns the name CYCLIC to the main routine. We first create NJOB (= 8 in the example) jobs and place all of them in a list called QUEUE1. An INSERT statement inserts an element (entity or process) in a SIMPL/1 list. For example, the statement

```
INSERT J LAST IN (QUEUE);
```

puts the entity (or process) referenced by J at the bottom of QUEUE LIST. Another option

```
INSERT J FIRST IN (QUEUE);
```

puts it at the top. If we omit the position option and simply say

```
INSERT J IN (QUEUE);
```

then LAST is assumed.

Immediately after the job creation, the two processes SERVER1 and SERVER2 are introduced into the model. If the SET option is present, it establishes a pointer by which the process may be referenced. The TIME option (AFTER TIME(0) in the above example) indicates when the new process is to be first activated, that is, when control is to be passed to its behavior group.

After starting up the processes that will carry out the simulation, the model can TAKE a time interval equal to the designed simulation run time through the specification

```
TAKE(RUN_TIME);
```

The variable RUN_TIME should be declared and assigned a value as in the ordinary PL/1 statements. Procedures INTEG_Q and STATISTICS are for statistics-gathering purposes, and will be described below.

A TERMINATE statement removes a process or all processes of a certain type from the model. For instance, the statement

```
TERMINATE P;
```

removes P from the model. If the reference to a process is omitted, that is,

```
TERMINATE;
```

then the CURRENT process, which is the main routine in this case, terminates itself. With the TERMINATE statement, a set of standard statistics is printed out.

Behavior groups

The behavior of the process SERVER1 is specified as follows:

```
SERVER1: BEHAVIOR;
    IF VOID(QUEUE1) THEN HOLD;
    FIRST_IN_Q1=FIRST(QUEUE1);
    TAKE(SERV_TIME(1));
    REMOVE FIRST FROM (QUEUE1);
    INSERT FIRST_IN_Q1 IN (QUEUE 2);
    CALL INTEG_Q;
    NOTIFY S2;
END SERVER1;
```

The VOID function determines whether the list QUEUE1 is empty or not. If the queue is empty, the HOLD statement prevents further activation of the process. The FIRST function finds the first element in the list QUEUE1 and assigns it to a variable called FIRST_IN_Q1.

SERV_TIME(1) represents the amount of service time and is defined below as a procedure. The TAKE statement causes the process to suspend execution of the next statement until this amount of simulation time has elapsed. The REMOVE statement is the converse of the INSERT statement. The REMOVE statement followed by the INSERT statement transports the job ($=$ FIRST_IN_Q1) from QUEUE1 to QUEUE2. Then the process invokes procedure INTEG_Q, which maintains the time integration of the queue size process at QUEUE1 (see the discussion of procedures below). The NOTIFY statement reports the job completion to the process S2 (server 2), which has been held until NOTIFIED.

The behavior group of the process SERVER2 is essentially the same as that of SERVER1:

```
SERVER2: BEHAVIOR;
    IF VOID(QUEUE2) THEN HOLD;
    FIRST_IN_Q2=FIRST(QUEUE2);
    TAKE(SERV_TIME(2));
    REMOVE FIRST FROM (QUEUE2);
    INSERT FIRST_IN_Q2 IN (QUEUE1);
    CALL INTEG_Q;
    NOTIFY S1;
END SERVER2;
```

Procedures

We define below the three procedures: INTEG_Q, STATISTICS, and SERV_TIME.

INTEG_Q: This procedure is invoked every time the system state changes. The procedure updates the variable SUMTQ ($=$ sum of time-queue product) defined for server 1:

$$\text{SUMTQ}(t) = \int_0^t q_1(u)\,du,$$

where $q_1(t)$ is the number of jobs at server 1.

```
INTEG_Q: PROC;
    SUMTQ=SUMTQ+(CLOCK-OLDCLK)*OLDQUE;
    OLDCLK=CLOCK;
    OLDQUE=ITEMS(QUEUE1);
END INTEG_Q;
```

CLOCK is one of the system variables used by SIMPL/1 during execution of a model. It represents the absolute simulated time in the model. It is increased by the timing routine to represent the passage of time. The variables SUMTQ and OLDCLK (= old clock) are initially set to zero, whereas the initial value of variable OLDQUE (= old queue size) is determined by the initial condition of QUEUE1. The ITEMS function determines the number of items in the list QUEUE1 and assigns the number to the variable OLDQUE.

STATISTICS: Upon termination of a simulation run at time $t =$ RUN_TIME, this procedure is called to compute the average queue size at server 1 (see the main program on p. 275):

```
STATISTICS: PROC;
    DCL AVG_Q FLOAT BIN;
    AVG_Q=SUMTQ/RUN_TIME;
    PUT DATA (AVG_Q);
END STATISTICS;
```

The result AVG_Q is printed out by the PUT statement.

SERV_TIME: This procedure computes random variates from the hyperexponential distribution (for server 1) or the Erlangian distribution (for server 2).

```
SERV_TIME: PROC(TYPE);
    DCL TYPE FIXED BIN;
    DCL ST FLOAT BIN;
    IF TYPE=1 THEN
        IF RANDF(1))0.1 THEN
            DO;
                ST=NEGEXP(2,5);
                RETURN(ST);
            END;

        ELSE
            DO;
                ST=NEGEXP(2,15);
                RETURN(ST);
            END;

    ELSE
        DO;
            ST=ERLANG(2,2.5,2);
            RETURN(ST);
        END;
END SERV_TIME:
```

The RANDF function generates a uniformly distributed real random number in the interval. The argument should be a binary fixed half-word integer in the interval $[1, 20]$, specifying the random-number stream. Thus, RANDF(1) is a sample value from random-number stream 1. This function returns a binary floating single-precision random number. The multiplicative congruential generator of the type discussed in Section 4.4.2 is used (see Eqs. 4.1 and 4.5):

$$Z_{i+1} = aZ_i \quad (\text{modulo } m),$$

where $a = 7^5 = 16{,}807$ and $m = 2^{31} - 1$.

The NEGEXP function chooses a variate from the exponential distribution of the specified mean. Its format is

$$\text{NEGEXP } (j, m)$$

where the argument j is a binary fixed half-word integer in the interval $[1, 20]$, specifying the random-number stream to be used. The mean m of the distribution is a binary float single-precision number. The value is calculated from the formula

$$X = - m \ln Y$$

and is returned as a binary float single-precision number. The ERLANG function returns an ERLANG variate of the specified stage and mean. Its format is

$$\text{ERLANG } (j, m, k),$$

where j specifies the random-number stream, k is the number of stages of the Erlangian distribution, and m is the mean of the fictitious exponential distributions. It is generated according to the formula (Eq. 4.26)

$$X = - m \ln \left\{ \prod_{i=1}^{k} Y_i \right\}$$

and is represented as a binary float single-precision number. Note that the mean of this variate is km, not m.

Histogram and model output statistics

A histogram of some observed data can be created in a SIMPL/1 model by declaring it an array with the HISTOGRAM attribute. For instance,

```
DCL H1(8) HISTOGRAM(1.0,0);
```

defines a histogram with the name H1 having eight frequency classes. The first frequency class starts at 0 and the width of each class is 1.0. The ENTER statement records an observation into a histogram. Its general format is

```
ENTER OBSERVED(X) IN (H);
```

The value of X is examined, and the entry of the appropriate frequency class of histogram H is incremented by 1. In order to specify when the action of ENTER is to be taken, we use the UPON statement. In our example, we wish to see that each time a job enters server 1, the number of jobs at that server is observed and recorded in the histogram H1:

```
UPON INSERT (QUEUE1) ENTER OBSERVED (ITEMS(QUEUE1)-1) IN (H1);
```

The PLOT statement prints a histogram graphically on SYSPRINT. For instance, we state

```
PLOT H1;
```

or

```
PLOT H1 CLEAR;
```

The use of the CLEAR option sets all frequency classes to zero after the plot.

By putting together the main program, the behavior groups, and the procedures discussed above and adding necessary declaration statements, we obtain the complete source program shown in Fig. 4.14.*

4.7.3   The SIMPL/1 Timing Routine

Passage of time in the real world is simulated in a SIMPL/1 model by incrementing the variable CLOCK. The simulation control program called the timing routine in SIMPL/1 controls the sequence in which processes are activated. It does this by maintaining a number of lists: (1) the active list, (2) the ready list, (3) the hold list, and (4) the schedule list. The timing routine of SIMPL/1 is in its concept similar to that of GPSS, but there are some important differences, which we discuss below.

The active list.   Normally this list contains only one process, the CURRENT PROCESS. However, if this process begins execution of another process (e.g., by a START statement), the new process enters the active list at the top, "pushing down" the old process. When the new CURRENT process leaves the active list, the original process is "pushed up" again, resuming the status of the CURRENT process. The execution of the CURRENT process will yield changes in the system state and perhaps in the contents of the schedule list or hold list, depending on the type of statements executed. It may also result in a notification of held processes.

---

* This sample program was prepared with the assistance of T. L. Moeller.

```
1    CYCLIC: MODEL OPTIONS(MAIN);
2       DCL SERVER1 PROCESS;
3       DCL SERVER2 PROCESS;
4       DCL (QUEUE1,QUEUE2) LIST STATS;
5       DCL JOB ENTITY;
6       DCL (S1,S2,J) POINTER;
7       DCL (FIRST_IN_Q1,FIRST_IN_Q2) POINTER;
8       DCL ERLANG ENTRY(FIXED BIN,BIN FLOAT,FIXED BIN(31,0))
              RETURNS(BIN FLOAT);
9       DCL RANDF ENTRY(FIXED BIN) RETURNS(BIN FLOAT);
10      DCL NEGEXP ENTRY(FIXED BIN,BIN FLOAT) RETURNS(BIN FLOAT);
11      DCL FIRST ENTRY RETURNS(PTR);
12      DCL VOID ENTRY RETURNS(BIT(1));
13      DCL ITEMS RETURNS(FIXED BIN(15,0));
14      DCL SUMTQ FLOAT BIN INIT(0);
15      DCL OLDCLK FLOAT BIN INIT(0);
16      DCL OLDQUE FLOAT BIN;
17      DCL H1(8) HISTOGRAM (1.0,0);
18      DCL RUN_TIME FIXED BINARY;
19      DCL NJOB FIXED BINARY;
20      GET DATA (RUN_TIME,NJOB);
21      DO J=1 TO NJOB;
22         CREATE JOB SET(J);
23         INSERT J IN (QUEUE1);
24      END;
25      OLDQUE=ITEMS(QUEUE1);
26      START SERVER1 SET(S1) AFTER TIME(0);
27      START SERVER2 SET(S2) AFTER TIME(0);
28      UPON INSERT (QUEUE1) ENTER OBSERVED (ITEMS(QUEUE1)-1) IN (H1);
29      TAKE(RUN_TIME);
30      CALL INTEG_Q;
31      CALL STATISTICS;
32      PLOT H1;
33      TERMINATE;
34   SERVER1: BEHAVIOR;
35      IF VOID(QUEUE1) THEN HOLD;
36      FIRST_IN_Q1=FIRST(QUEUE1);
37      TAKE(SERV_TIME(1));
38      REMOVE FIRST FROM (QUEUE1);
39      INSERT FIRST_IN_Q1 IN (QUEUE2);
40      CALL INTEG_Q;
41      NOTIFY S2;
42   END SERVER1;
```

(cont.)

Fig. 4.14 SIMPL/1 program for the cyclic queueing system simulation.

```
43    SERVER2: BEHAVIOR;
44        IF VOID(QUEUE2) THEN HOLD;
45        FIRST_IN_Q2=FIRST(QUEUE2);
46        TAKE(SERV_TIME(2));
47        REMOVE FIRST FROM (QUEUE2);
48        INSERT FIRST_IN_Q2 IN (QUEUE1);
49        CALL INTEG_Q;
50        NOTIFY S1;
51    END SERVER2;
52    INTEG_Q: PROC;
53        SUMTQ=SUMTQ+(CLOCK-OLDCLK)*OLDQUE;
54        OLDCLK=CLOCK
55        OLDQUE=ITEMS(QUEUE1);
56    END INTEG_Q;
57    STATISTICS: PROC;
58        DCL AVG_Q FLOAT BIN;
59        AVG_Q=SUMTQ/RUN_TIME;
60        PUT DATA (AVG_Q);
61    END STATISTICS;
62    SERV_TIME: PROC(TYPE);
63        DCL TYPE FIXED BIN;
64        DCL ST FLOAT BIN;
65        IF TYPE=1 THEN
66            IF RANDF(1))0.1 THEN
67                DO;
68                    ST=NEGEXP(2,5);
69                    RETURN(ST);
70                END;
71            ELSE
                   DO;
72                    ST=NEGEXP(2,15);
73                    RETURN(ST);
74                END;
75        ELSE
                   DO;
76                    ST=ERLANG(2,2.5,2);
77                    RETURN(ST);
78                END;
79    END SERV_TIME;
80    END CYCLIC;
```

Fig. 4.14 (continued)

The ready list. This list contains processes that are ready for activation at this point of simulated time. When the active list becomes empty, the timing routine moves the first process on the ready list to the active list, thus making the process the new CURRENT process. Processes enter the ready list to be activated.

The hold list.   This list contains all the processes interrupted by a HOLD statement. If such a process receives its required notifications, the process will be reactivated at that point of simulation time.

The schedule list.   This list contains those processes that are to be activated at some scheduled future time. For instance, a process that is started at time CLOCK = 0

`START PROC 1 AFTER(5);`

will be placed in the schedule list with a time value of 5. The schedule list is chained in ascending order of time values.

When both the active and the ready lists are empty, the timing routine sets the value of CLOCK to the time at which the process at the top of the schedule list is due to be activated. The imminent process(es) will then be moved to the ready list.

In comparison with the GPSS scanning routine, SIMPL/1 processes in either the active or the ready list correspond to GPSS transactions in the CURRENT EVENTS CHAIN; SIMPL/1 processes in the hold list are similar to GPSS transactions contained in the various DELAY CHAINs; and the schedule list of SIMPL/1 is more or less equivalent to the FUTURE EVENTS CHAIN of GPSS.

Note that in SIMPL/1, entities do not play active roles in the time control mechanism, whereas in GPSS the transactions form various ordered chains upon which the scanning operation is performed. Another major difference between GPSS and SIMPL/1 lies in the fact that conditional events or processes in the hold list of SIMPL/1 become activated as a direct consequence of *process-handling statements* such as NOTIFY, UPON START, etc. In GPSS, on the other hand, it is the major responsibility of the scanning routine to determine which conditional events are due for execution.

Exercises

4.7.1 Write a SIMPL/1 program of the *M/M/*1 queueing system.

4.7.2 In the sample program, the lists QUEUE1 and QUEUE2 include jobs in service at SERVER1 and SERVER2, respectively. Modify the program so that the list includes only those in the waiting lines.

4.7.3 In the sample program, the histogram H1 collects the queue distribution seen by jobs arriving at server 1. Modify the program in the following manner.

   a) Collect the time average distribution of the queue size at server 1.

b) Define a separate process that generates "observers" at regular intervals. Upon arrival of each observer, the queue length is observed and stored in the histogram table.

4.7.4 Refer again to the sample program discussed in Section 4.7.2. Extend the simulation program so that the *response-time* distributions at both servers are obtained.

4.8 ANALYZING A SIMULATION RUN

4.8.1 Starting Conditions, Transients, and Equilibrium

In many cases, the objective of a simulation study is to investigate the behavior of a simulated system in its steady-state operation condition. We must then give special consideration to *starting conditions* and *transient periods,* since the behavior of the simulation model will not represent the typical behavior of the simulated system until the model reaches a steady-state condition. Therefore, the data observed during this transient period should be discarded. Consequently, we must start the simulation model in a state that is as representative of steady-state conditions as possible in order to minimize the length of the unwanted transients.

To determine whether the model has reached its steady-state condition is generally not a simple matter, because a steady state of a stochastic system or its model is defined in terms of the *probability distribution* of the system state, and not a particular value of the state. That is to say, the notion of the transient in a stochastic system is different, for instance, from that of a deterministic system (such as an electrical circuit), where the transient behavior is completely characterized by its impulse response function. It should be recognized that the equilibrium is a limiting condition that may be approached but never attained exactly. There is no single point in simulation time beyond which the system is in equilibrium, but we can choose some reasonable point beyond which we are willing to neglect the error that is made by considering the system to be in equilibrium. From now on we speak of a transient period in this sense. The transient period is, in general, dependent on the starting condition. For example, in the case of a queueing system, we often start the simulation model with an empty queue. This is probably not too bad with a single-server queue in which this condition is simply equivalent to starting the simulation at the beginning of a busy period. In more complex systems such as queueing networks, these starting conditions often represent quite atypical system states.

Starting the simulator in a more typical state accelerates the approach to a steady-state condition, but we still have to estimate the transient period and exclude the data collected in that period in order not to bias the results to preconceived conclusions. Ideally we wish to select

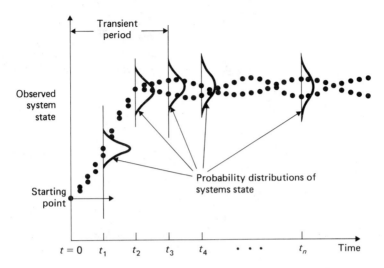

Fig. 4.15　The observed distribution of the system state at various ages.

starting conditions probabilistically, according to the equilibrium-state probability distribution. But had we such information, we would have no reason to execute a simulation. Therefore, in practice, the search for good starting conditions should be based on some prior knowledge of the system or on results of pilot runs or earlier studies.

The choice of reasonable starting conditions can diminish the transient period but cannot eliminate it completely. In order to estimate the transient duration, we make a number of preliminary pilot runs from the *same starting point* and compare the observed distribution of the state of the system at various ages. Figure 4.15 shows typical results of such preliminary runs. Needless to say, the initial values (often called "seeds") of the pseudo-random generator should be different in different runs or replications; otherwise we would observe exactly the same system output.

4.8.2　Choice of Sample Sizes*

The choice of the sample size is clearly among the most important factors in a simulation experiment. Unfortunately, it is often the case that the simulation analyst selects these sample sizes somewhat arbitrarily and then hopes that the estimates thereby obtained are sufficiently precise. Such a procedure is clearly inappropriate. The correct procedure is to conduct a statistical analysis to determine the required sample sizes that will satisfy the required precision.

---

* The reader may wish to study Sections 5.3, 5.5, and 5.6 before proceeding to study the present section.

Suppose that we wish to estimate μ, the mean of Y, which is a chosen measure of a system's performance. Assume that the observations of this measure, Y_1, Y_2, $\ldots$, Y_N, are *statistically independent* with *normal distribution* with the unknown mean μ. A *confidence interval* for the sample mean

$$\bar{Y} = \frac{\sum_{i=1}^{N} Y_i}{N} \tag{4.34}$$

can be obtained by the procedure to be discussed in Section 5.6.2. That is, the variable

$$Z = \frac{(\bar{Y} - \mu)}{s_Y/\sqrt{N}} \tag{4.35}$$

has a t distribution with $(N - 1)$ degrees of freedom, where s_Y^2 is the sample variance defined by

$$s_Y^2 = \frac{\sum_{i=1}^{N}(Y_i - \bar{Y})^2}{N - 1}. \tag{4.36}$$

Therefore

$$-t_{\alpha/2;\,N-1} \le \frac{\sqrt{N}(\bar{Y} - \mu)}{s_Y} \le t_{\alpha/2;\,N-1} \Bigg] = 1 - \alpha, \tag{4.37}$$

where $t_{\alpha/2;\,N-1}$ is the upper $100 \times \alpha/2$ percentage point of the t-distribution with $(N-1)$ degrees of freedom (see Sections 5.5.2 and 5.6.2). Inverting this inequality leads to

$$P\Bigg[\bar{Y} - \frac{t_{\alpha/2;\,N-1} s_Y}{\sqrt{N}} \le \mu \le \bar{Y} + \frac{t_{\alpha/2;\,N-1} s_Y}{\sqrt{N}} \Bigg] = 1 - \alpha \tag{4.38}$$

so that the random variables

$$\bar{Y} - \frac{t_{\alpha/2;\,N-1} s_Y}{\sqrt{N}} \tag{4.39}$$

and

$$\bar{Y} + \frac{t_{\alpha/2;\,N-1} s_Y}{\sqrt{N}} \tag{4.40}$$

are the lower and upper confidence limits, respectively. This confidence interval can be made as small as desired by making the sample size sufficiently large. As N increases, the t-distribution approaches the normal distribution. For practical purposes, when N is greater than 30 or so, we can replace $t_{\alpha/2;\,N-1}$ in the above formula by $z_{\alpha/2}$, the upper $100 \times \alpha/2$ percentage point of the standard normal distribution (Section 5.6.2), so that

$$P\left[\bar{Y} - \frac{z_{\alpha/2}s_Y}{\sqrt{N}} \le \mu \le \bar{Y} + \frac{z_{\alpha/2}s_Y}{\sqrt{N}}\right] = 1 - \alpha. \qquad (4.41)$$

Thus, for a given confidence interval, the required sample size can be estimated by approximating the standard deviation by s_Y obtained from pilot runs or early observations.

In most simulations, however, the assumption of statistical independence and normality will not apply to the observed data. If the Y_i's are not normally distributed, some transformation $g(\ )$ may be made on them, so that the resultant data $g(Y_i)$'s are approximately normally distributed. Such a transformation as $g(y) = \log y$, or $g(y) = y^{1/2}$ may reduce the effect of the long tail of the distribution often encountered in system simulation. In most situations, however, we need not perform such a transformation. By virtue of the central limit theorem, the distribution of the sample mean $\bar{Y}$ (often called the *sampling distribution*) is asymptotically (that is, for sufficiently large N) normal regardless of the distribution of Y_i's, provided that their mean and variance are finite. Then the confidence interval formula given above is still valid if N is sufficiently large.

If the data of simulation output is correlated, the above confidence formula can no longer be used, and we must introduce some model that explicitly recognizes the *correlation properties* among observations. Let Y_i be the ith observation collected in an experiment. We assume that the sequence of observations $\{Y_i;\ i = 1, 2, \ldots\}$ defines a covariance (or wide-sense) stationary random process; that is to say, the process $\{Y_i\}$ has an index invariant mean

$$\mu = E[Y_i] \qquad (4.42)$$

and an autocovariance function

$$R_j = E[(Y_i - \mu)(Y_{i+j} - \mu)] < \infty, \qquad (4.43)$$

which is a function of only the difference between indexes i and $i + j$. Suppose that we are given N observations $\{Y_i;\ i = 1, 2, \ldots, N\}$. The existence of correlation does not affect estimation of the population mean μ: The best estimate of μ is still the sample mean

$$\bar{Y} = \frac{\sum_{i=1}^{N} Y_i}{N}. \qquad (4.44)$$

It can be shown that the variance of the estimate is (Exercise 4.8.2)

$$\text{Var}\,[\bar{Y}] = \frac{\sum_{j=-N+1}^{N-1}\left(1 - \frac{|j|}{N}\right)R_j}{N}$$

$$= \frac{\sigma^2\left\{1 + 2\sum_{j=1}^{N-1}\left(1 - \frac{j}{N}\right)\rho_j\right\}}{N}, \tag{4.45}$$

where σ^2 is the (unknown) variance of Y_i's, that is, $\sigma^2 = R_0$; and ρ_j is the autocorrelation function (or autocorrelation sequence), that is, $\rho_j = R_j/R_0$ (see (5.50)). Letting N approach infinity we have

$$\lim_{N\to\infty} N\,\text{Var}\,[\bar{Y}] = \sum_{j=-\infty}^{\infty} R_j = \sigma^2\xi \tag{4.46}$$

where

$$\xi = \sum_{j=-\infty}^{\infty} \rho_j = 1 + 2\sum_{j=1}^{\infty} \rho_j \tag{4.47}$$

summarizes the effect of the correlation property on the variance of the sample mean: If $\{Y_i\}$ is an uncorrelated sequence, $\xi = 1$. In many cases, we will find that $\xi > 1$—for example, the case where $\{Y_i\}$ is the waiting time of the ith job. Although possible in theory, we rarely have the situation in which $1 > \xi \geq 0$.

It is instructive to note that the quantity ξ is related to the *spectrum* of the stochastic sequence $\{Y_j\}$ by

$$\xi = \frac{2\pi P(0)}{\sigma^2} = \frac{P(0)}{\frac{1}{2\pi}\int_{-\pi}^{\pi} P(\lambda)\,d\lambda} \tag{4.48}$$

where the spectrum $P(\lambda)(-\pi \leq \lambda \leq \pi)$ is defined by (5.56).

From (4.46) we see that for sufficiently large N

$$\text{Var}\,[\bar{Y}] = \frac{\sigma^2\xi}{N} = \frac{\sigma^2}{N/\xi}. \tag{4.49}$$

Thus, we may interpret that N/ξ represents the *effective* size of the independent samples when the size of the correlated samples is N. On the basis of the central limit theorem, we can show again that the sample mean $\bar{Y}$ is asymptotically normally distributed:

$$P\left[-z_{\alpha/2} \leq \frac{\bar{Y} - \mu}{\sqrt{\sigma^2\xi/N}} \leq z_{\alpha/2}\right] = 1 - \alpha. \tag{4.50}$$

Thus, the confidence interval for μ is given by

$$\bar{Y} \pm z_{\alpha/2} \sigma \sqrt{\frac{\xi}{N}}. \tag{4.51}$$

In general, the quantity $\sigma^2 \xi$ defined by Eq. (4.46) is unknown. One way of solving the problem is, of course, to estimate the autocovariance function R_k or the spectrum $P(\lambda)$. Such time-series analysis or spectral analysis is not very appealing since a substantial computation effort is required. Furthermore, such a procedure provides us with more information than necessary: All that we need is an effective way of estimating the quantity $\sigma^2 \xi$. To this end, we usually adopt one of the following three methods in establishing confidence intervals.

The independent-replication method

One method is to *replicate* the simulation experiment. We run the experiment many times using different (and presumably independent) streams of random numbers for different runs. Suppose that we replicate the experiment m times, and each replication generates n steady-state observations, $Y_i^{(j)}$; $1 \le i \le n$, $1 \le j \le m$. Thus, we have the total $N = mn$ usable observations. We denote the sample mean of the jth replication by $\bar{Y}^{(j)}$:

$$\bar{Y}^{(j)} = \frac{\sum_{i=1}^n Y_i^{(j)}}{n}, \qquad j = 1, 2, \ldots, m. \tag{4.52}$$

Then, the set $\{\bar{Y}^{(j)}; 1 \le j \le m\}$ forms m independent and identically distributed random variables. The best estimates of the mean μ and variance σ_Y^2 of the variables $\bar{Y}^{(j)}$'s are given by the *overall sample mean*

$$\bar{Y} = \frac{1}{m} \sum_{j=1}^m \bar{Y}^{(j)} = \frac{1}{mn} \sum_{j=1}^m \sum_{i=1}^n Y_i^{(j)} \tag{4.53}$$

and the *sample variance*

$$s_Y^2 = \frac{1}{m-1} \sum_{j=1}^m (\bar{Y}^{(j)} - \bar{Y})^2, \tag{4.54}$$

respectively. When n is sufficiently large, the variables $\bar{Y}^{(j)}$'s are approximately normally distributed. Then, the distribution of the variable

$$\bar{Y} - \frac{\mu}{\sqrt{s_Y^2/m}}$$

can be approximated by the t-distribution with $(m-1)$ degrees of freedom. Thus, the confidence interval for μ is given by

$$\bar{Y} \pm \frac{t_{\alpha/2;\, m-1} s_Y}{\sqrt{m}}. \tag{4.55}$$

Furthermore, if m is large,

$$P\left[-z_{\alpha/2} \leq \frac{\bar{Y} - \mu}{\sqrt{s_Y^2/m}} \leq z_{\alpha/2}\right] = 1 - \alpha. \tag{4.56}$$

Hence we can replace the critical value $t_{\alpha/2;\, m-1}$ by $z_{\alpha/2}$ in (4.55).

By comparing (4.50) and (4.56), we see that the replication method gives us the following estimate of $\sigma^2\xi$:

$$\sigma^2\xi \approx ns_Y^2. \tag{4.57}$$

If the estimated confidence interval (4.55) is not as tight as we wish to see, then we must run the simulator for a longer period. Suppose we want the confidence interval to be $\bar{Y} \pm \delta$. Then the required sample size $\hat{N}$ is estimated from (4.50) and (4.57) as

$$\hat{N} \approx \left(\frac{z_{\alpha/2}}{\delta}\right)^2 \sigma^2\xi \approx \left(\frac{z_{\alpha/2}s_Y}{\delta}\right)^2 n. \tag{4.58}$$

Thus, the required sample size for each of the m replications is given by

$$\hat{n} = \left(\frac{z_{\alpha/2}s_Y}{\delta}\right)^2 \frac{n}{m}. \tag{4.59}$$

Therefore, we should run each replication for an additional $\hat{n} - n$ observations so that we have the total $\hat{N} = m\hat{n}$ usable data. Alternatively, we maintain n as the size of each replication and make additional $(\hat{m} - m)$ replications of size n, where

$$\hat{m} = \left(\frac{z_{\alpha/2}s_Y}{\delta}\right)^2. \tag{4.60}$$

Again we will have the total $\hat{N} = \hat{m}n$ of observations.

The main disadvantage of the independent-replication method is that each replication run requires an initial stabilization period before approaching its steady-state condition, so that much of the simulation time may be unproductive.

The single-run method

The second method, and probably the one more commonly used, is to make the runs consecutively, using the final condition of one run as the steady-state starting condition for the next run. In other words, we make one long continuous simulation run, which is then divided into contiguous segments (or batches), each of which has length n. The sample mean $\bar{Y}^{(j)}$ of the jth segment is then treated as an individual observation. In the *single-run* method, the unproductive portion of simulation time is just

one initial stabilization period. Therefore, this method seems advantage-
ous over the independent-replication method in terms of simulation run
time. The price we pay for this apparent benefit is that the set of sample
means $\{\bar{Y}^{(j)}; \; j = 1, 2, \ldots, m\}$ is not, strictly speaking, statistically
independent. For most practical purposes, however, the correlation between these observations may be neglected if each of the batches is
sufficiently long. Estimation of the confidence interval for the single-run
method can be done by following the same procedure as that used for the
replication method: We just replace the jth replication by the jth batch.
The single run method is sometimes referred to as the method of batch
means.

Example 4.2 (Confidence interval calculation in a queueing system
simulation). Consider an $M/G/1$ queueing system with the arrival rate
$\lambda = 1$[job/sec], and a two-stage hyperexponential service distribution
with $\pi_1 = 0.744$, $\mu_1 = 1.009$, and $\mu_2 = 20.18$. Then the server utilization is computed as

$$\rho = \lambda E[S] = \lambda\left(\frac{\pi_1}{\mu_1} + \frac{1 - \pi_1}{\mu_2}\right) \cong 0.75.$$

A simulation program was written and the following experiment
conducted.*

1. The system was initially empty.
2. The initial 500-second portion of output data was discarded.
3. A single run of $T = 40000$ seconds was made, and was divided
   into $m = 20$ segments of equal length $\tau = T/m = 2000$ sec.

The observed process is a queue length $Q(t)$ as a function of simulated
time t. The sample mean of this quantity in the jth segment is given by

$$\bar{Q}^{(j)} = \frac{\displaystyle\int_{(j-1)\tau}^{j\tau} Q(t)\, dt}{\tau}, \qquad j = 1, 2, \ldots, m, \qquad (4.61)$$

which is the continuous-time analog of the expression (4.52) (see also
Exercise 4.8.3). The overall mean of the queue size process is then

$$\bar{Q} = \frac{\sum_{j=1}^{m} \bar{Q}^{(j)}}{m} = \frac{\displaystyle\int_{0}^{T} Q(t)\, dt}{T}. \qquad (4.62)$$

---

* This simulation experiment was done by Phillip S. Yu of Stanford University.

TABLE 4.1   MEAN QUEUE SIZES $\bar{Q}^{(j)}$ FOR $j = 1, 2, \ldots, 20$

Batch j	Mean queue size	Batch j	Mean queue size
1	3.0067	11	3.8689
2	2.8691	12	3.2124
3	3.2807	13	4.0369
4	3.5868	14	3.5707
5	3.9536	15	4.1673
6	3.8611	16	4.3745
7	3.9517	17	2.8854
8	4.1430	18	3.1784
9	3.6877	19	4.3381
10	3.0358	20	4.7597

The realizations of the sample means of the 20 batches observed in this experiment are tabulated in Table 4.1. By ranking these 20 results in order of magnitude, we obtain the cumulative frequency curve (see Eq. (5.15)), as shown in Fig. 4.16. (A more appropriate graphical representation is the fractile diagram discussed in Section 5.4.1.) From this plotted curve, it is reasonable to judge that the random variates $\bar{Q}^{(j)}$'s are approximately normally distributed. Thus, the t-distribution of $m - 1 = 19$ degrees of freedom (d.f.) is our model for the variable

$$\frac{(\bar{Q} - \mu)}{\sqrt{s_Q^2 / m}},$$

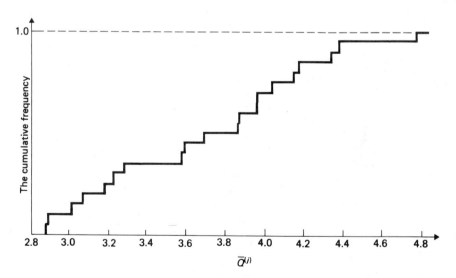

Fig. 4.16   The cumulative frequency curve of the twenty batch means.

where μ is the population mean $\mu = E[Q(t)]$. The sample mean and variance based on the $m(=20)$ data are

$$\bar{Q} = 3.6884$$

and

$$s_Q^2 = \frac{1}{m-1} \sum_{j=1}^{m} (\bar{Q}^{(j)} - \bar{Q})^2 = 0.302425.$$

The critical value that leaves 2.5 percent of the probability in the upper tail is

$$t_{0.025; 19} = 2.093.$$

Hence, the 95-percent $(=1-\alpha)$ confidence interval is calculated as

$$\bar{Q} \pm t_{0.025; 19} \sqrt{\frac{s_Q^2}{20}} = 3.6884 \pm 0.2573.$$

From the result of the $M/G/1$ queue (see Eq. (3.330)), the true mean μ is 3.6752, which is included in the 95-percent confidence interval obtained above.

In the example above, the choice of 500 seconds for the initial transient period was made not on the basis of several pilot runs, but on the basis of a simple formula due to the *diffusion approximation.* In a single-server queueing system (a $G/G/1$ queue), the transient time (see Kobayashi, 1974b) is approximately given by

$$T_0 = \tau_0 \frac{E[S](C_s^2 + C_a^2 \rho)}{(1-\rho)^2}, \tag{4.63}$$

where $E[S]$ = the mean service time; $\tau_0 \cong 5$; $\rho (= \lambda E[S])$ = the server utilization; C_s^2 = the squared coefficient of variation of service time; and C_a^2 = the squared coefficient of variation of interarrival time. In the example above, these parameters are computed as

$$E[S] = 0.75, \quad \rho = 0.75, \quad C_s^2 = 1.6, \quad \text{and} \quad C_a^2 = 1,$$

which yields

$$T_0 \cong 140 \text{ seconds.}$$

Hence, the choice of $T_0 = 500$ is judged to be sufficiently long to avoid a possible bias in observed data due to initial conditions.

The important properties of formula (4.63) are that:

1. The transient time becomes longer as the server utilization increases in the proportion $1/(1-\rho)^2$.

2. The larger the coefficients of variation of service time and interarrival time, the longer the transient period.

A formula similar to (4.63) holds for the cyclic queueing system studied in Section 4.5.2:

$$T_0 = \frac{\tau_0 E[S_1](C_1^2 + rC_2^2)}{(1 - r)^2},$$

(4.64)

where $\tau_0 \cong 5$; $E[S_i]$ = the mean service time at server i, $i = 1$, 2; C_i^2 = the squared coefficient of variation of service time at server i, $i = 1$, 2; and $r = E[S_1]/E[S_2]$. Note that if the two servers are balanced (i.e., $r = 1$), the transient period tends to be long.

The regenerative method

The regenerative method has been investigated recently by Crane and Iglehart (1974a, 1974b, 1975), Fishman (1973b), and Iglehart (1975, 1976a, 1976b). This method eliminates the problem of determining the transient period, which was necessary in both the replication method and the single-run method to provide valid confidence intervals. A probabilistic (or stochastic) system is said to be *regenerative* if there exists a particular system state, called a *regenerative state*, such that whenever the system returns to that state the history of past states of the system has no influence on the future of the system.

A sequence of épochs at which the system returns to such a regenerative state are called *regeneration* (or *renewal*) *points*, and the time between the kth and $(k + 1)$th regeneration points is called the *kth cycle*. Thus, for a *regenerative* process $\{X(t); t \geq 0\}$, the continuation of the process beyond a regeneration point, say t_1, is a probabilistic replica of the whole process commencing at epoch 0, independent of $\{X(t); 0 \leq t \leq t_1\}$ (Feller, 1966, p. 365). The definition is also applicable to regenerative processes in discrete time.

If the time between two successive regeneration points is finite, then observations made in this cycle are statistically independent of the observations made in other cycles. In addition, the proper collection of measurements made during such cycles are identically distributed.

We denote a given regenerative process by $\{X(t): t \geq 0\}$, or simply by $X(t)$. Let X be a random variable that represents $X(t)$ in the equilibrium condition; that is,

$$\lim_{t \to \infty} P[X(t) \leq x] = P[X \leq x]$$

(4.65)

for every x in $(-\infty, \infty)$. The value we want to estimate with our simulation is the expected value of some function f of X

$$r = E[f(X)].\qquad(4.66)$$

Let each cycle generate a pair (Y_i, α_i), where Y_i is the integral of $f(X(t))$ over the ith cycle, and α_i is the length of the ith cycle. Then the random variable pairs (Y_1, α_1), (Y_2, α_2), $\ldots$, (Y_i, α_i), $\ldots$ are i.i.d. and

$$r = \lim_{t \to \infty} \frac{\displaystyle\int_0^t f(X(u))\, du}{t} = \frac{E[Y_i]}{E[\alpha_i]}.\qquad(4.67)$$

This relation is a direct result of the *strong law of large numbers* (see, for example, Ross, 1970, p. 52).

For example, consider a $G/G/1$ queueing system. We can define the regeneration points as those instants when the system starts busy periods (that is, when a job arrives at the empty server). Note that if the system is $M/G/1$ or $M/M/1$, there are other obvious choices for the regenerative state (Exercise 4.8.5).

Suppose that the simulator runs for n cycles and $\bar{Y}$ and $\bar{\alpha}$ are the sample means of $\{Y_i\}$ and $\{\alpha_i\}$, respectively; s_Y^2 and s_α^2, the *sample variances*; and $s_{Y\alpha}$, the *sample covariance* between $\{Y_i\}$ and $\{\alpha_i\}$. Then Eq. (4.67) suggests an estimator of r to be the ratio of the two sample means:

$$\hat{r} = \frac{\bar{Y}}{\bar{\alpha}},\qquad(4.68)$$

which is called the *ratio estimator*. An approximate expression for the $100 \times (1 - \alpha)$ percent confidence interval can be derived (Crane and Iglehart, 1975) using the asymptotic normality of the variable $Y_i - r\alpha_i$:

$$\hat{r} - \frac{z_{\alpha/2}\hat{s}}{\bar{\alpha}\sqrt{n}} \le r \le \hat{r} + \frac{z_{\alpha/2}\hat{s}}{\bar{\alpha}\sqrt{n}},\qquad(4.69)$$

where $z_{\alpha/2}$ is the $100 \times \alpha/2$ percent point of the standard normal distribution as defined before, and $\hat{s}^2$ is an estimate of the variance of $Y_i - r\alpha_i$:

$$\hat{s}^2 = s_Y^2 - 2\hat{r}s_{Y\alpha} + \hat{r}^2 s_\alpha^2.\qquad(4.70)$$

The ratio estimator (4.68) converges to the population mean r of (4.67) as n approaches infinity. For finite sample size n, however, it is a *biased* estimator. Fishman (1973a, p. 303) and Iglehart (1975) discuss other estimators for r and compare them in terms of bias and variance.

One major difficulty of the regenerative method lies in identifying a proper regenerative state. The regenerative state should be such that regeneration points are sufficiently dense in the passage of simulation time because the formula (4.69) for the confidence interval is based on the asymptotic normality of the joint variable $(\bar{Y}, \bar{\alpha})$. Further discussions and applications of the regenerative method are found in Law (1975), Sauer (1975), Lavenberg and Slutz (1975), Sargent (1976), Fishman (1977), and Iglehart (1978). Iglehart and Shedler (1978a, 1978b) discuss a method of estimating passage times in a network of queues.

Exercises

4.8.1 Discuss what factors determine the transient period of a single-server system. Do the same for the cyclic queueing system and the machine servicing model.

4.8.2 Derive Eq. (4.45).

4.8.3 Consider a time-continuous process $\{Y(t);\ 0 \le t \le T\}$ with (unknown) mean μ and covariance function $R_Y(\tau)$, where τ is the *time lag*.

   a) What is the best estimate of μ that you can obtain?

   b) Find the expression for the variance of that estimate.

4.8.4 Suppose that the observed data is a time-continuous process $Y(t)$. Discuss how the replication method can be applied to such a case.

4.8.5 Identify possible regenerative states for an $M/G/1$ queueing system. Do the same for an $M/M/1$ queueing system. What about a general network of queues with exponential servers?

4.8.6 Show that Eq. (4.67) holds even if α_i is some measure of the ith cycle other than the cycle length (for example, the number of entities that have arrived and departed during the ith cycle). Discuss how to estimate the average response time in a $G/G/1$ system using the regenerative simulation method.

4.8.7 Apply the three different methods discussed in this section to the cyclic queueing system simulator constructed in Section 4.5.2. Compare their confidence intervals for various cases of simulation run length.

4.8.3 Comparison of Alternatives

When the purpose of a simulation exercise is to compare *alternatives*, we can improve the efficiency of the data-gathering procedure by focusing on the *relative results* rather than the *absolute results*. In conventional physical experiments, we often attempt to sharpen the contrast between alternatives by using the most homogeneous experimental units or media that we can obtain. Such a procedure is called a *block design* in the experimental design (see Chapter 5). In a simulation experiment, the corresponding experimental unit or medium is a sequence of *exogenous events*, which supposedly describe the activities of the outside world to the model. For example, this exogenous-event sequence can be job arrivals and departures in a queueing system, and this is a function of pseudo-random number sequences; or it can be drawn from actual operations as in trace-driven simulations. In either case, we can reproduce and reuse the same sequence of events for different runs of the model, and this ability of attaining perfect homogeneity of experimental media makes simulated experiments quite different from physical experiments.

In order to support this approach with a more quantitative argument, let us consider the following example. Suppose we wish to compare the performance of two different versions of the system under study. Let Y be the selected measure of performance, and let the population mean and variance of Y under version j be μ_j and σ_j^2, respectively ($j = 1, 2$). Given observation data $\{Y_{j,i}: j = 1, 2; i = 1, 2, \ldots N\}$, a natural thing to do is to compare the sample means

$$\bar{Y}_1 = \frac{\sum_{i=1}^N Y_{1,i}}{N} \tag{4.71}$$

and

$$\bar{Y}_2 = \frac{\sum_{i=1}^N Y_{2,i}}{N}. \tag{4.72}$$

Their difference satisfies the following properties:

$$E[\bar{Y}_1 - \bar{Y}_2] = \mu_1 - \mu_2 \tag{4.73}$$

and

$$\mathrm{Var}\,[\bar{Y}_1 - \bar{Y}_2] = \mathrm{Var}\,[\bar{Y}_1] + \mathrm{Var}\,[\bar{Y}_2] - 2\,\mathrm{Cov}\,[\bar{Y}_1, \bar{Y}_2]$$

$$= \frac{\sigma_1^2 + \sigma_2^2}{N} - 2\,\mathrm{Cov}\,[\bar{Y}_1, \bar{Y}_2]. \tag{4.74}$$

If two separate and independent pseudo-random sequences are used in versions 1 and 2, then the covariance term of the last equation is zero. If a common random sequence is used, then there may exist a certain degree of *positive correlation* between the random variates $\bar{Y}_1$ and $\bar{Y}_2$. If that is the case, the variance of $\bar{Y}_1 - \bar{Y}_2$ will be reduced accordingly, and this reduction is often substantial. The use of a common pseudo-random sequence to test all alternatives is thus the most important single procedural option in simulation. Furthermore, in practice, this procedure will be easier and more economical than generating different pseudo-random sequences or traced data for different runs. The idea developed in this section will be used, with some modification, in a variance-reduction technique called the control-variate method, which will be discussed in Section 4.9.3.

4.9 EFFICIENT STATISTICAL SIMULATION

4.9.1 Monte Carlo Techniques

In a simulation experiment, samples of many thousands of observations are often required to estimate some performance measure with sufficient confidence. In view of the cost of computer run time, it is clearly important that one should attempt to reduce the volume of sampling. Unfortunately, it has been a wide practice to apply simulation techniques uncritically with little thought to the efficiency of simulation runs.

Various methods for improving the efficiency of statistical simulation are often called Monte Carlo techniques (in a narrower sense than the same term that is sometimes used in referring to probabilistic simulation techniques in general), and the literature on this subject is extensive. Hammersley and Handscomb (1964) give a full account of Monte Carlo methods. In this chapter we will discuss these techniques in the context of stochastic simulation systems.

A statistical simulation may be regarded as a way of estimating the *expected values* of random variables in question. This way of looking at a simulation experiment is useful in relating the design of simulation experiments to a procedure of estimating the means of the underlying distributions by a *sampling* process. Define a random vector $\mathbf{R}$ to represent a stream of random numbers of length m, where m is the total number of random variates to be generated during a simulation run and is assumed to be finite and fixed:

$$\mathbf{R} = (R_1, R_2, \ldots, R_m). \tag{4.75}$$

Since the elements R_i's are statistically independent and uniformly distributed between 0 and 1, the joint probability density function of $\mathbf{R}$ is given by

$$f_{\mathbf{R}}(\mathbf{r}) = \begin{cases} 1; & 0 \le r_i \le 1 \quad \text{for all} \quad i = 1, 2, \ldots, m \\ 0; & \text{elsewhere.} \end{cases} \tag{4.76}$$

We view the *response variable* Y as a random variable implicitly defined by the simulation procedure. In other words, the simulator maps a given value $\mathbf{r}$ of the random vector $\mathbf{R}$ into value y of the random variable Y (Fig. 4.17).

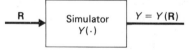

Fig. 4.17 A simulator viewed as a mapping from random vector $\mathbf{R}$ to random variable Y.

The variable Y can be vector-valued, but we will restrict our attention here to a scalar-valued function. For example, Y may be the mean waiting time of jobs in a queueing system. Then the purpose of the simulation is merely to estimate the expected value of Y:

$$E[Y] = \int_0^1 \cdots \int_0^1 Y(\mathbf{r}) f_{\mathbf{R}}(\mathbf{r}) \, d\mathbf{r}. \qquad (4.77)$$

The basic idea behind various Monte Carlo techniques is that the efficiency of statistical simulation can be substantially enhanced by proper exploitation of any available knowledge of the situation. Even though the functional form $Y(\mathbf{R})$ is seldom known explicitly (otherwise, we would probably not have recourse to simulation), we often know approximately how the response variable Y depends on the generated random variable sequence $\mathbf{R}$. For example, in a simple queueing system, the waiting times increase as the relative number of large service times and/or short interarrival times increases. That is, if many jobs arrive and their service demands tend to be high, then we can expect a large value for the average waiting time. This qualitative knowledge can be profitably used in designing efficient methods to estimate the response variable.

4.9.2 The Antithetic-Variate Method

As discussed above, a simulation is a statistical method of estimating the expected value of a random variable $Y = Y(\mathbf{R})$. Suppose that another random variable $X = X(\mathbf{R})$ is made available to us and that X has the same (unknown) expectation as Y and possesses a high degree of negative correlation with Y. Then

$$\alpha Y(\mathbf{R}) + (1 - \alpha)X(\mathbf{R}) \qquad (4.78)$$

has the same mean as Y, but its variance can be made significantly smaller than $\text{Var}[Y]$ by a suitable choice of α.

The key in applying this method to any simulation is to find a suitable auxiliary variable X. A very simple *system-independent* method for obtaining X is to let

$$X(\mathbf{R}) = Y(\mathbf{R}^*), \qquad (4.79)$$

where the vector $\mathbf{R}^* = \mathbf{1} - \mathbf{R}$; that is, $R_i^* = 1 - R_i$ for all $i = 1, 2, \ldots,$ m. Clearly, $\mathbf{R}^*$ has the same probability density function as $\mathbf{R}$; thus, the expectation of X is the same as that of Y. The optimal value of α in this case is $\alpha = \frac{1}{2}$. A simulation is performed by using a random-number sequence $\mathbf{R}$ to compute values of Y, and only then are the values of the auxiliary variable X calculated by re-running the simulation, using its antithetic partner $\mathbf{R}^*$. These two steps are completely independent except that in performing the random sampling in calculating Y, provisions must be made for obtaining data that will be needed later in calculating X's. If the above procedure creates negative correlation between the two responses X and Y, then their mean $(X + Y)/2$ will have a smaller variance than that of Y (or X). This variance-reducing technique is called the *antithetic-variate method*.

Page (1965) describes the use of this technique in queueing problems. Suppose that the simulation of estimating the mean waiting time in a single-server model is conducted by forming interarrival time variate* T_i and service time variate S_i from the random-number vector $\mathbf{R}$:

$$T_i = F_T^{-1}(R_{2i-1}) \tag{4.80}$$

and

$$S_i = F_S^{-1}(R_{2i}), \tag{4.81}$$

where $F_T(\bullet)$ and $F_S(\bullet)$ are the distribution functions of T and S, respectively. The functional relationship between the waiting-time variate Y and the random-number vector $\mathbf{R}$ is difficult to characterize even in this rather simple case. But we can explain why the antithetic-variate method can possibly reduce the variance of the estimate of mean waiting time. In this queueing model, a period of rapid arrivals of jobs needing much service (that is, a sequence of small T's and large S's) will cause a queue to develop. Conversely, a sequence of large T's and small S's will cause a queue existing at the start of the sequence to diminish. Therefore, if we estimate the mean waiting time from busy and slack periods combined, it is likely to have a much smaller error than if we estimate from a single period. The antithetic-variate approach, in this case, is to obtain busy periods (in a simulation run of producing X) corresponding to the slack ones (in a run of producing Y), and vice versa.

The antithetic variable defined by $X = Y(\mathbf{1} - \mathbf{R})$ is, in principle, applicable to any simulation system and for any response variable Y, although its effectiveness is critically dependent on the system structure and the variables to be estimated. In fact, in a more complex simulation there is no simple way to show whether the assumption of negative correlation between X and Y holds at all.

The following method, on the other hand, is applicable only to a queueing system or its equivalent. We define an antithetic variable $X(\mathbf{R})$ by interchanging pairs of random numbers associated with interarrival

---

* In earlier sections, we denoted interarrival time by X, but here we use T, since X denote the auxiliary variable in this section.

time T_i and service time S_i for each i. That is, corresponding to (4.80) and (4.81), we now compute a sequence of pairs (T'_i, S'_i) by

$$T'_i = F_T^{-1}(R_{2i}) \tag{4.82}$$

and

$$S'_i = F_S^{-1}(R_{2i-1}) \tag{4.83}$$

and the sequence yields the antithetic variate $X(\mathbf{R})$.

Even in the simple example given above, the correlation between $Y(\mathbf{R})$ and its auxiliary variable $X(\mathbf{R})$ is difficult to assess by analysis since consecutive waiting times are not statistically independent. Page (1965) reports that the techniques described above can result in reducing the number of observations by a factor of two in most cases. Of course, the efficiency depends on the arrival and service time distributions and also on the model structure. It should be noted, however, that the use of the antithetic-variate method requires an addition or amendment of only a few statements in a simulation program; yet it is likely to reduce the computing time substantially. Mitchell (1973) also discusses the antithetic variate method in $G/G/1$ queueing simulation.

Gaver (1969) also discusses an application of the antithetic-variate method to a single-server problem in which he is concerned with the transient behavior in the oversaturated case. The numerical results are compared with those of other variance-reduction techniques. Shedler and Yang (1971) discuss an application of antithetic variables to simulation of a cyclic queue model of paging in a virtual storage system.

4.9.3   The Control-Variate Method

The *control-variate* method is another Monte Carlo technique for reducing the variation of sample observations, thereby increasing the precision of the estimate. Consider a random variable Z defined by

$$Z(\mathbf{R}; \beta) = Y(\mathbf{R}) - \beta\{X(\mathbf{R}) - E[X(\mathbf{R})]\}, \tag{4.84}$$

where $X(\mathbf{R})$, called the auxiliary variable, is a random variable whose expectation $E[X(\mathbf{R})]$ is known. Clearly, Z is an unbiased estimate of $E[Y]$ for any β and its variance is given by

$$\text{Var}[Z] = \text{Var}[Y] + \beta^2 \text{Var}[X] - 2\beta \text{Cov}[X, Y]. \tag{4.85}$$

The coefficient β is selected to minimize the variance $\text{Var}[Z]$, which leads to

$$\beta_0 = \text{Cov}[X, Y]/\text{Var}[X] \tag{4.86}$$

and the minimized variance is therefore given by

$$\text{Var}[Z] = \text{Var}[Y](1 - \rho_{XY}^2) \leq \text{Var}[Y], \tag{4.87}$$

where ρ_{XY} is the correlation coefficient between X and Y. In practice, the covariance between X and Y will not be known; hence it must be estimated from data. For a given N independent observations (or replications) $X^{(j)}$ and $Y^{(j)}$ ($1 \le j \le N$), an estimated optimum β_0 will be of the form

$$\hat{\beta}_0 = \frac{\sum_{j=1}^{N}(Y^{(j)} - \bar{Y})(X^{(j)} - E[X])}{N \, \text{Var}[X]} \tag{4.88}$$

or

$$\hat{\beta}_0 = \frac{\sum_{j=1}^{N}(Y^{(j)} - \bar{Y})(X^{(j)} - E[X])}{\sum_{j=1}^{N}(X^{(j)} - E[X])^2}, \tag{4.89}$$

depending on whether the population variance $\text{Var}[X]$ is known or not.

The above theory is used in a stochastic simulation as follows. We wish to estimate the expected value of the response Y, where Y is related to the random vector $\mathbf{R}$ in unknown functional form $Y(\mathbf{R})$. For a chosen control variable $X(\mathbf{R})$, we then observe simulated outputs $Y^{(j)}$ and $X^{(j)}$ for random-number stream $\mathbf{R}$. We approximate $E[Z]$ by $\bar{Z}$:

$$\bar{Z} = \frac{1}{N} \sum_{j=1}^{N} (Y^{(j)} - \beta_0 X^{(j)}) + \beta_0 E[X]. \tag{4.90}$$

Recall that we assumed that we can calculate the expectation of X. Suppose we simplify the original simulation model to the extent that we can find an analytic solution for it. (For example, the simplified version may assume the exponential distribution for all the service or interarrival times.) Then we choose the auxiliary variable X as the response variable in the simplified model, in the same way that the variable Y is defined in the original model. We then run the original simulator and a simulator of the simplified version, using the same random-number stream. In this case, the optimal coefficient β_0 is often close to unity. We may then wish to skip the step for computing β_0 and reduce (4.90) to

$$\bar{Z} = \frac{1}{N} \sum_{j=1}^{N} (Y^{(j)} - X^{(j)}) + E[X]. \tag{4.91}$$

Sometimes this estimation method is called the *straight control-variate method*, whereas the estimate of Eq. (4.90) is called the *regression-adjusted control-variate method*.

When the control variable X is an input variable actually used in the simulation (such as the service time or interarrival time), X is often called a *concomitant variate*. The concomitant-variate method has an advantage in that $X^{(j)}$ can be collected for practically no additional programming or run-time cost.

The idea developed above can be readily extended to a set of *multiple control variates* $X_1, X_2, \ldots, X_k$. Now we define random variable Z, rather than (4.84), by

$$Z(\mathbf{R}) = Y(\mathbf{R}) - \sum_{i=1}^{k} \beta_i \{X_i(\mathbf{R}) - E[X_i]\}. \tag{4.92}$$

We denote by $\mathbf{Q}$ the covariance matrix of $\mathbf{X} = [X_1, X_2, \ldots, X_k]$ and by $\mathbf{c}$ the cross-covariance vector between $\mathbf{X}$ and Y:

$$Q_{ij} = \text{Cov}[X_i, X_j], \qquad i, j = 1, 2, \ldots, k \tag{4.93}$$

and

$$c_i = \text{Cov}[X_i, Y], \qquad i = 1, 2, \ldots, k. \tag{4.94}$$

Then the optimal choice for $\boldsymbol{\beta} = [\beta_1, \beta_2, \ldots, \beta_k]$ is

$$\boldsymbol{\beta}_0 = \mathbf{c}\mathbf{Q}^{-1} \tag{4.95}$$

which leads to

$$\text{Var}[Z] = \text{Var}[Y] - \mathbf{c}\mathbf{Q}^{-1}\mathbf{c}' = \text{Var}[Y](1 - R_{Y\mathbf{X}}^2) \le \text{Var}[Y], \tag{4.96}$$

where $R_{Y\mathbf{X}}$ is the multiple correlation coefficient between Y and $\mathbf{X}$. The square of the correlation coefficient is often called the *coefficient of determination* (see Section 5.9.4) and it is the portion of the total variation in Y explained by the variations in $\mathbf{X}$. Thus $R_{Y\mathbf{X}}^2$ measures the significance of the control variates $\mathbf{X}$. The covariance matrix $\mathbf{Q}$ and the cross-covariance vector $\mathbf{c}$ are generally not known; thus we substitute them by their sample estimates.

The idea behind the control-variate variance-reduction method is quite similar to that of *regression analysis* (especially *analysis of covariance*), which is discussed in Section 5.9. The variation of the response variable Y can be minimized by taking advantage of the information furnished by the predictor variables $\mathbf{X}$. In the analysis of covariance, the term "concomitant variates" also refers to a set of variates whose variation we wish to eliminate. We should note, however, the following difference between the regression-analysis and the control-variate methods: In the regression analysis we usually wish to investigate the power of a set of predictive variables X in explaining the variation of the response variable Y, and thus we tend to include any variable that will improve our prediction, whereas in the simulation with the control-variate method, we explicitly evaluate the additional reduction in the variance against the additional computation involved. Remember we can always achieve any desired reduction in the variance of the estimates by sufficiently long simulation runs.

Gaver (1969) applies the control-variate method to estimating the mean waiting time in a single-server queueing system. Beja (1969) discusses a similar case in which he estimates the *mean* waiting time in a queueing system with priorities. He reports the multiple control-variate method (three control variates) cuts the variance to about eight percent (that is, by a factor of 12.5) of the initial value under a favorable circumstance. Of course, the above gain in variance reduction should be offset to some degree by the extra computer time needed for the calculation of the values of the control variates and their optimal coefficients.

Gaver and Shedler (1971) discuss the use of the control-variate method in their simulation model of a demand paging computer system with explicit consideration of system overhead. The response variables are the CPU utilization and the DTU (data transfer unit) utilization. The control variates are the corresponding response variables in a simplified version of a cyclic queueing system simulator. Recall that the server utilization of a cyclic queueing model can be computed if one of the service distribution functions is exponential (see Chapter 3). They report that the variance of the CPU utilization estimate is reduced, based on the straight control-variate method, by a factor ranging from 8 to 12, depending on the value of utilization.

Lavenberg, Moeller, and Welch (1977) report that *work variates* are efficient concomitant variates in the simulation of closed queueing network models. The work variate W_j is defined as the total amount of work completed by server j, divided by the total count of service completions observed within the network during a simulation run. Thus the variation in W_j reflects variations in both the sample mean service time and the job arrival rate of that server. It is interesting to note that the work variates are essentially empirical estimates of the workload parameters $\bar{W}_j$ defined by (3.223). Recall that the queue size distribution and related quantities (that is, utilization, mean queue size, mean response, etc.) of a queueing network with exponential servers depend on the workloads only through the parameters $\bar{W}_j$'s.

For more discussions on these and different variance-reduction techniques, the reader is referred to Kleijnen (1975), Gaver and Thompson (1973), Fishman (1973a), Tocher (1963), and references therein.

Exercises

4.9.1 Refer to the two-state cyclic queueing simulation discussed in Sections 4.5–4.7. Apply the antithetic method using the antithetic pair **R** and **R***.

4.9.2 In the simulation problem of the cyclic queueing model, apply the control-variate method. The auxiliary variable X should be defined over a simplified version of the model, where at least one of the servers is exponential.

4.10 VALIDATION AND TESTING OF THE SIMULATION MODEL

Once the model is constructed and verified, we wish to test the validity or credibility of that simulation model. In order to draw inference about the real system from results obtained from the simulation, the model must be a reasonably valid representation of the real system. The process of validation sounds straightforward enough in principle. But, in practice, conclusive validation tests are difficult to arrange. In some cases, there is no existing counterpart for any of the simulated alternatives. Such a situation occurs when an entirely new system is to be designed and simulation experiments are adopted to make a choice among design alternatives. If the real system under consideration or a similar system is available, we would obtain some assurance of validity by demonstrating that for one or two alternative versions of the simulated system and a set of conditions, the simulator produces results that are not inconsistent with the known performance of the real system. If the model fails to pass, then it is exceedingly suspect. On the other hand, we cannot make any strong statement about the credibility of the model even if the model passes the test under certain variations and sets of conditions: There is always the *uncertainty* associated with drawing a general conclusion from a limited number of tests. How to deal with such inherent uncertainty is within the realm of *statistical design* and the *analysis of experiments*, which is the theme of Chapter 5.

The level of details required in the validation of a simulator should depend on how that simulator is to be used in decision making. In other words, we must return to the principal objective of the simulation study and choose some performance measure that indicates whether the observation data generated by the simulator agree sufficiently with those of the real system. If the performance measure thus obtained is some mean value (e.g., CPU utilization, the average response time), then the notion of *significance level* and *confidence interval* should be applied to quantify the statistical significance of the difference between measured and simulated effects. The *analysis-of-variance* technique can be used to test the hypothesis that the mean of a series of data generated by the simulator is equal to the mean of the corresponding observed data of the real system. This technique will be discussed in Section 5.7 at length.

In some cases the performance criterion is not just the mean value of observations, but also its frequency distribution. Various graphical presentation methods to be discussed in Section 5.4 are useful for this purpose. Several statistical techniques exist for testing the "goodness of fit" of the distribution: notably, the chi-square (χ^2) test and the Kolmogorov–Smirnov test. For these statistical tests, we refer the reader to Kendall and Stuart (1961, Chapter 30), and Cox and Lewis (1968). Knuth (1969), Fishman (1973a), and Mihram (1972) also discuss these tests in connection with the statistical validation of random-number generators.

APPENDIX TO CHAPTER 4

Much of the discussion presented in Section 4.4 is based on number theory. For those readers unfamiliar with the subject, a set of basic definitions and theorems relevant to the congruential methods are given in this appendix. For a more complete treatment of the subject, the reader is directed to books on number theory—see, for example, Ore (1948), Uspensky and Heaslet (1939), and LeVeque (1962).

Definition 4A-1 (Euler's phi function). For a given positive integer m, let $\phi(m)$ be the number of values among $1, 2, \ldots, m - 1$ that are relatively prime to m. The function $\phi(\bullet)$ is called *Euler's phi-function*. It is clear that $\phi(1) = 1$, $\phi(2) = 1$, $\phi(3) = 2$, $\phi(4) = 2$, etc.

Theorem 4A-1 (Euler). (1) When m is a prime, $\phi(m) = m - 1$. (2) When m is factored into primes, that is, when

$$m = \prod_i p_i^{e_i}$$

then

$$\phi(m) = \prod_i (p_i - 1)p_i^{e_i-1}.$$

Definition 4A-2 (Power residue). The residues of the successive powers of an integer a modulo m are called power residues. If we denote the ith power residue by n_i, it must satisfy the congruence relation

$$n_i = a^i \quad (\text{modulo } m), \qquad i = 1, 2, 3, \ldots.$$

Example 4A-1 When $a = 5$ and $m = 31$, the power residues are $n_1 = 5$, $n_2 = 25$, and $n_3 = 1$. Therefore, beyond $i = 3$, the same pattern will repeat itself: $n_4 = 5$, $n_5 = 25$, $n_6 = 1$, etc. When $a = 3$ and $m = 31$, then we will find that $n_1 = 3$, $n_2 = 9$, $n_3 = 27$, $n_4 = 19$, $n_5 = 26$,

$n_6 = 16, \ldots, n_{28} = 7, n_{29} = 29$, and $n_{30} = 1$. Thus the sequence $\{n_i\}$ has the period $\phi(31) = 30$. Another way of looking at the above example is as follows. In the first case, the set $\{a, a^2, a^3 (= 1)\}$ forms a *cyclic group of order 3* generated by the element $a = 5$; for the second case, the element $a = 3$ generates a cyclic group of order 30. Here the multiplication in these groups is, of course, "multiplication modulo m." Therefore, we have the following.

Definition 4A-3 (Order of a).   Let a and m be relatively prime, and let λ be the least positive exponent such that $a^\lambda = 1 \pmod{m}$. Then λ is called the *order of a* modulo m.

Clearly the order λ is equal to the total number of *distinct power residues*, and is thus the period of the sequence $\{n_i\}$, $i = 1, 2, \ldots$. Any value of a that gives the maximum possible order (mod m) is referred to by the following special name.

Definition 4A-4 (Primitive element modulo m).   Let $\lambda(m)$ be the maximum possible order modulo m. An element a that is relatively prime to m is called a *primitive element modulo m*, if

$$a^{\lambda(m)} = 1 \pmod{m}.$$

There exists some relationship between the maximum possible order $\lambda(m)$ and Euler's phi-function $\phi(m)$. First, we state the following.

Theorem 4A-2 (Euler).   When m and a are relatively prime, the relation holds:

$$a^{\phi(m)} = 1 \pmod{m}.$$

From this theorem and the definition of $\lambda(m)$, it follows that $\lambda(m) \leq \phi(m)$ and $\lambda(m)$ is a *divisor* of $\phi(m)$.

Definition 4A-5 (Primitive root of m).   An element a that has $\phi(m)$ as its order modulo m is called a *primitive root* of m.

Theorem 4A-3   Primitive roots exist when $m = 1, 2, 4, p^e$, and $2p^e$ for odd prime p (see Knuth, 1969, pp. 19–20).

Thus, for those values of m that are stated in Theorem 4A-3, the set $C = \{1, 2, \ldots, m - 1\}$ forms a cyclic group of order $\phi(m) = \lambda(m)$. A primitive root a of m generates this group, that is, $C = \{a, a^2, \ldots, a^{\phi(m)}\}$. It is known that there are $\phi(\phi(m))$ such generators of C; in other words, there are $\phi(\phi(m))$ primitive roots of m. Then we state the following theorems without proof.

Theorem 4A-4   If a is a primitive root of m, then a^k is also a primitive root of m, if and only if k and $\phi(m)$ are relatively prime.

Multiplicative congruential method with $m = 2^e$

Historically, the most popular choice of the modulus m has been

$$m = 2^e,$$

where e is the word length of a computer. For this choice of m, the mod m operation and division by m (as required in Eq. (4.1)) are simplified. But as Theorem 4A-3 suggests, there exist no *primitive roots* for values of m. Hence the order of a primitive element modulo m, $\lambda(m)$, is strictly less than $\phi(m) = 2^{e-1} = m/2$.

Since an element a to be considered here should be relatively prime to $m = 2^e$, it must be an odd integer. Then either $a - 1$ or $a + 1$ (not both) is a multiple of 4. Thus we can write $a \mp 1 = (2r + 1)2^f$ with some unique integers r and $f > 1$. It follows that $\pm a = 1 \pmod{2^f}$ and $\pm a \neq 1 \pmod{2^{f+1}}$. We can then show (Knuth, 1969) that for $e > f$

$$a^{2^{e-f}} = (\pm a)^{2^{e-f}} = 1 \pmod{2^e}$$

but

$$(\pm a)^{2^{e-f-1}} \neq 1 \pmod{2^e}.$$

Therefore, the order of $a \pmod{2^e}$ divides 2^{e-f}, but not 2^{e-f-1}. The maximum period of power residues is, therefore, $2^{e-2} = m/4$. This is achieved when $f = 2$ (hence, $e \geq 3$), which in turn determines the element a:

$$a \mp 1 = 4(2r + 1)$$

or, equivalently,

$$a = 5 \quad \text{or} \quad 3 \pmod 8.$$

This result then leads to Theorem 4.2 of Section 4.4.

REFERENCES

Ahrens, J. H., and U. Dieter (1972). "Computer Methods for Sampling from the Exponential and Normal Distributions." *Communications of the Association for Computing Machinery* **15:** 873–882.

Beja, A. (1969), "Multiple Control Variates in Monte Carlo Simulation with Applications to Queueing Systems with Priorities." In B. Avi-Itzhak (ed.), *Developments in Operations Research*, Vol. I. New York: Gordon and Breach.

Consolidated Analysis Centers, Inc. (1971). *SIMSCRIPT II.5 Reference Handbook*, Santa Monica, California.

Coveyou, R. R. (1960). "Serial Correlation in the Generation of Pseudo-Random Numbers." *Journal of the Association for Computing Machinery* **7:** 72–74.

Cox, D. R., and P. A. W. Lewis (1968). *The Statistical Analysis of Series of Events.* London: Methuen.

Crane, M. A., and D. L. Iglehart (1974a). "Simulating Stable Stochastic Systems, I: General Multiserver Queues." *Journal of the Association for Computing Machinery* **21** (No. 1): 103–113.

Crane, M. A., and D. L. Iglehart (1974b). "Simulating Stable Stochastic Systems, II: Markov Chains." *Journal of the Association for Computing Machinery* **21** (No. 1): 114–123.

Crane, M. A., and D. L. Iglehart (1975a). "Simulating Stable Stochastic Systems, III: Regenerative Processes and Discrete-Event Simulations." *Operations Research* **23** (No. 1): 33–45.

Crane, M. A., and D. L. Iglehart (1975b). "Simulating Stable Stochastic Systems, IV: Approximation Techniques." *Management Science* **21:** 1215–1224.

Crane, M. A., and A. J. LeMoine (1977). "An Introduction to the Regenerative Method for Simulation Analysis." *Lecture Notes in Control and Information Science* Vol. 4. Berlin: Springer-Verlag.

Dahl, O., and K. Nygaard (1966). "SIMULA—an ALGOL-Based Simulation Language." *Communications of the Association for Computing Machinery* **9** (No. 9): 671–678.

Emshoff, J. R., and R. L. Sisson (1970). *Design and Use of Computer Simulation Models.* New York: Macmillan.

Feller, W. (1966). *An Introduction to Probability Theory and Its Applications,* Vol. 2. New York: John Wiley.

Fishman, G. S. (1967). "Problems in the Statistical Analysis and the Length of Sample Records." *Communications of the Association for Computing Machinery* **10** (No. 2): 94–99.

Fishman, G. S. (1973a). *Concepts and Methods in Discrete Event Digital Simulation.* New York: John Wiley.

Fishman, G. S. (1973b). "Statistical Analysis for Queueing Simulations." *Management Science* **20** (No. 3): 363–369.

Fishman, G. S. (1977). "Achieving Specific Accuracy in Simulation Output Analysis." *Communications of the Association for Computing Machinery* **20** (No. 5): 310–315.

Fuller, S. H. (1975). "Performance Evaluation." In H. S. Stone (ed.), *Introduction to Computer Architecture,* pp. 474–545. Chicago: Science Research Associates.

Gaver, D. P. (1969). "Statistical Methods for Improving Simulation Efficiency." *Proceedings of the Third Conference on the Applications of Simulation* (December): 38–46.

Gaver, D. P., and G. S. Shedler, (1971). "Control Variable Methods in the Simulation of a Model of a Multiprogrammed Computer System." *Naval Research Logistics Quarterly* **18:** 435–450.

Gaver, D. P., and G. L. Thompson (1973). *Programming and Probability Models in Operations Research.* Monterey, Calif.: Brooks/Cole Publishing Company.

Greenberger, M. (1961). "Notes on a New Pseudo-Random Number Generator." *Journal of the Association for Computing Machinery* **8:** 163–167.

Gustavson, F. G., and W. Liniger (1970). "A Fast Random Number Generator with Good Statistical Properties." *Computing* **6:** 221–226. Berlin: Springer-Verlag.

Hammersley, J. M., and D. C. Handscomb (1964). *Monte Carlo Methods.* London: Methuen.

Hillier, F. S., and G. J. Lieberman (1968). *Introduction to Operations Research.* San Francisco: Holden-Day.

Hull, T. E., and A. R. Dobell (1962). "Random Number Generators." *SIAM Review* **4** (No. 3): 230–254.

Iglehart, D. L. (1975). "Simulating Stable Stochastic Systems, V: Comparison of Ratio Estimator." *Naval Research Logistics Quarterly* **22** (No. 3).

Iglehart, D. L. (1976). "Simulating Stable Stochastic Systems, VI: Quantile Estimation." *Journal of the Association for Computing Machinery* **23** (No. 2): 347–360.

Iglehart, D. L. (1977). "Simulating Stable Stochastic Systems, VII: Selecting Best System." *TIMS Studies in Management Sciences* **7:** 37–49.

Iglehart, D. L. (1978). "The Regenerative Method for Simulation Analysis." In K. M. Chandy and R. T. Yeh (eds.), *Current Trends in Programming Methodology, Vol. III: Software Modeling,* pp. 52–71. Englewood Cliffs, N.J.: Prentice-Hall.

Iglehart, D. L., and G. S. Shedler (1978a). "Regenerative Simulation of Response Times in Networks of Queues." *Journal of the Association for Computing Machinery* **25** (3).

Iglehart, D. L., and G. S. Shedler (1978b). "Simulation of Response Times in Finite Capacity Open Networks of Queues." *Operations Research* **26.** (Also IBM Research Report RJ 1886, San Jose, California, 1976.)

IBM (1966). "Subroutine RANDU." In *IBM Application Program, System/360 Scientific Subroutine Package, Version III,* GH20-0205-4, p. 77. IBM Corporation, Data Processing Division, White Plains, New York.

IBM (1971a). *General Purpose Simulation System V: User's Manual,* SH20-0851-1, 2nd ed. IBM Corporation, Data Processing Division, White Plains, New York.

IBM (1971b). *General Purpose Simulation System V: Introductory User's Manual,* SH20-0866-1, 2nd ed. IBM Corporation, Data Processing Division, White Plains, New York.

IBM (1971c). *General Purpose Simulation System V: OS (GPSS V-OS) Operations Manual,* SH20-0867-3, 3rd ed. IBM Corporation, Data Processing Division, White Plains, New York.

IBM (1971d). *Computer System Simulator II (CSS II): General Information,*

GH20-0874-1, 2nd ed. IBM Corporation, Data Processing Division, White Plains, New York.

IBM (1971e). *Computer System Simulator II (CSS/II): Program Description and Operations Manual*, SH20-0875-1, 2nd ed. IBM Corporation, Data Processing Division, White Plains, New York.

IBM (1972). *SIMPL/1 (Simulation Language Based on PL/1): Program Reference Manual*, SH19-5060-0. IBM Corporation, Data Processing Division, White Plains, New York.

IBM (1974). "Subroutine GGL." In *IBM Subroutine Library—Mathematics, User's Guide*, SH12-5300-1, pp. 79–82. IBM Corporation, Data Processing Division, White Plains, New York.

Karr, H. W., H. Kleine, and H. Markowitz (1965). *SIMSCRIPT I.5*, Consolidated Analysis Centers, Inc., CACI65-INT-1, Santa Monica, Calif.

Kendall, M. G., and A. Stuart (1961). *The Advanced Theory of Statistics, Vol. II: Inference and Relationship*. London: Charles Griffin.

Kiviat, P. J., and R. Villanueva (1969). *The SIMSCRIPT II Programming Language Reference Manual*. Englewood Cliffs, N.J.: Prentice-Hall.

Kiviat, P. J., R. Villanueva, and H. Markowitz (1969). *The SIMSCRIPT II Programming Language*. Englewood Cliffs, N.J.: Prentice-Hall.

Kleijnen, J. P. C. (1975). *Statistical Techniques in Simulation*, Parts I and II. New York: Marcel Dekker.

Knuth, D. E. (1968). *The Art of Computer Programming, Vol. 1: Fundamental Algorithms*, Ch. 2. Reading, Mass.: Addison-Wesley.

Knuth, D. E. (1969). *The Art of Computer Programming, Vol. 2: Seminumerical Algorithms*. Reading, Mass.: Addison-Wesley.

Kobayashi, H. (1974a). "Application of the Diffusion Approximation to Queueing Network I: Equilibrium Queue Distributions." *Journal of the Association for Computing Machinery* **21** (No. 2): 316–328.

Kobayashi, H. (1974b). "Application of the Diffusion Approximation to Queueing Networks II: Nonequilibrium Distributions and Applications to Computer Modeling." *Journal of the Association for Computing Machinery* **21** (No. 2): 459–469.

Lavenberg, S. S., and D. R. Slutz (1975). "Regenerative Simulation of Queueing Model of an Automated Tape Library." *IBM Journal of Research and Development* **19** (No. 5): 463–475.

Lavenberg, S. S., T. L. Moeller, and P. D. Welch (1977). "Control Variables Applied to the Simulation of Queueing Models of Computer Systems." In K. M. Chandy and M. Reiser (eds.), *Proceedings of the International Symposium on Computer Performance Modelling, Measurement and Evaluation*. Amsterdam: North-Holland.

Law, A. M. (1975). "Efficient Estimators for Simulated Queueing Systems." *Management Science* **22:** 30–41.

Learmonth, G. P., and P. A. W. Lewis (1973a). "Naval Postgraduate School Random Generator Package LLRANDOM." Naval Postgraduate School, Monterey, Calif.

Learmonth, G. P., and P. A. W. Lewis (1973b). "Statistical Tests of Some Widely Used and Recently Proposed Uniform Random Number Generators." *Proceedings of Computer Science and Statistics: Seventh Annual Symposium on the Interface*, pp. 163–171. Ames: Iowa State University.

LeVeque, W. J. (1962). *Elementary Theory of Numbers.* Reading, Mass.: Addison-Wesley.

Lewis, P. A. W., A. S. Goodman, and J. M. Miller (1969). "A Pseudo-Random Number Generator for the System/360." *IBM System Journal* **8** (No. 2): 136–146.

MacDougal, M. H. (1970). "Computer System Simulation: An Introduction." *Computing Surveys* **2** (No. 3): 191–209.

MacLaren, M. D., and G. Marsaglia (1965). "Uniform Random Number Generators." *Journal of the Association for Computing Machinery* **12** (No. 1): 83–89.

MacLaren, M. D., G. Marsaglia, and T. A. Bray (1964). "A Fast Procedure for Generating Exponential Random Variables." *Communications of the Association for Computing Machinery* **7** (No. 5): 298–300.

Markowitz, H. M., H. W. Karr, and B. Hauser (1963). *SIMSCRIPT: A Simulation Programming Language.* Englewood Cliffs, N.J.: Prentice-Hall.

Marsaglia, G., and T. A. Bray (1964). "A Convenient Method for Generating Normal Variables." *SIAM Review* **6** (3): 260–264.

Marsaglia, C., M. D. MacLaren, and T. A. Bray (1964). "A Fast Procedure for Generating Normal Random Variables." *Communications of the Association for Computing Machinery* **7:** 4–10.

Mihram, G. A. (1972). *Simulation: Statistical Foundations and Methodology.* New York: Academic Press.

Mitchell, B. (1973). "Variance Reduction by Antithetic Variates in GI/G/1 Queueing Simulations." *Operations Research* **21** (4): 988–997.

Moeller, T., and H. Kobayashi (1974). "Use of the Diffusion Approximation to Estimate Run Length in Simulation Experiments." *Proceedings of COMPSTAT Symposium*, pp. 363–372. Vienna (October).

Muller, M. V. (1959). "A Comparison of Methods for Generating Normal Deviates on a Computer." *Journal of the Association for Computing Machinery* **6:** 376–383.

Naylor, T. H. (ed.) (1969). *The Design of Computer Simulation Experiments.* Durham, N.C.: Duke University Press.

Naylor, T. H., J. L. Balintfy, D. S. Burdick, and K. Chu (1967). *Computer Simulation Techniques.* New York: John Wiley.

Noetzel, A. S., and L. A. Herring (1976). "Experience with Trace-Driven Modeling." *Proceedings of the Symposium on the Simulation of Computer Systems,* pp. 111–118. National Bureau of Standards, Boulder, Colorado (August).

Ore, O. (1948). *Number Theory and Its History.* New York: McGraw-Hill.

Page, E. S. (1965). "On Monte Carlo Methods in Congestion Problems, II: Simulation of Queueing Systems." *Operations Research* **13:** 300–305.

Payne, W. H., J. R. Rabung, and T. P. Bogyo (1969). "Coding the Lehmer Pseudo-Random Number Generator." *Communications of the Association for Computing Machinery* **12** (No. 2): 85–86.

Ross, S. M. (1970). *Applied Probability Models with Optimization Applications.* San Francisco: Holden-Day.

Sargent, R. G. (1976). "Statistical Analysis of Simulation Output Data." *Proceedings of Symposium on Simulation of Computer Systems,* pp. 39–50. National Bureau of Standards, Boulder, Colorado (August).

Sauer, C. H. (1975). "Simulation Analysis of Generalized Queueing Networks." *Proceedings of 1975 Summer Computer Simulation Conference,* pp. 75–81. San Francisco (July).

Sauer, C. H., and L. Woo (1977). "Hybrid Simulation of a Distributed Network." IBM Research Report RC 6341, IBM T. J. Watson Research Center, Yorktown Heights, N.Y.

Schatzoff, M., and C. C. Tillman (1975). *Design of Experiments in Simulator Validation* **19** (No. 3): 252–262.

Seaman, P. H., and R. C. Soucy (1969). "Simulating Operating Systems." *IBM Systems Journal* **8** (No. 4): 264–279.

Shannon, R. E. (1975). "Simulation: A Survey with Research Suggestions." *American Institute of Industrial Engineers (AIIE) Transactions* **7** (No. 3): 289–301.

Shedler, G. S., and S. S. Yang (1971). "Simulation of a Model of Paging System Performance." *IBM System Journal* **10:** 113–128.

Sherman, S. W. (1976). "Trace-Driven Modeling: An Update." *Proceedings of Symposium on Simulation of Computer Systems,* pp. 87–91. National Bureau of Standards, Boulder, Colorado (August).

Sherman, S. W., F. Baskett, and J. C. Browne (1972). "Trace-Driven Modeling and Analysis of CPU Scheduling in a Multiprogramming System." *Communications of the Association for Computing Machinery* **15:** 1063–69.

Sherman, S. W. and J. C. Browne (1973). "Trace-Driven Modeling: Review and Overview." *Proceedings of Symposium on Simulation of Computer Systems,* pp. 200–207. National Bureau of Standards, Gaithersburg, Maryland (June).

Smith, C. S. (1971). "Multiplicative Pseudo-Random Number Generators with Prime Modulus." *Journal of the Association for Computing Machinery* **18** (No. 4).

Teichroew, D., and J. F. Lubin (1966). "Computer Simulation: Discussion of the Technique and Comparison of Languages." *Communications of the Association for Computing Machinery* **9:** 723–741.

Tocher, K. D. (1963). *The Art of Simulation.* London: The English Universities Press.

Uspensky, J. V., and M. A. Heaslet (1939). *Elementary Number Theory.* New York: McGraw-Hill.

5
Data
Analysis

Although some need still exists for the improvement and economization of measurement techniques, it is more important and more difficult to decide which parameters of a system should be measured than it is to determine how the measurements are to be made. More often than not, we observe poor practice in both the planning of the measurement activities and the interpretation of the collected data. The main purpose of this chapter is to explain those statistical techniques with which computer scientists and system analysts engaged in system performance evaluation should be familiar. We do not intend to make this chapter a comprehensive treatment of all aspects of statistical methodologies that might be useful to performance analyses and model constructions. Our purpose is, rather, to provide fundamental knowledge on statistical techniques that should help the reader to determine the main features of important relationships among significant system variables hidden or implied in masses of data.

5.1 MEASUREMENT, ANALYSIS, AND MODEL CONSTRUCTION

In Chapters 3 and 4, we studied analytic modeling techniques and simulation methods pertaining to system performance analysis. These techniques play important roles in system design and implementation, particularly in their early stages. However, the multiple interactions among various hardware and software components of contemporary computing systems are generally so complex that many performance issues cannot be fully anticipated at design time. Obviously, a prediction model fails to capture those implications that are incurred by performance factors not included in the model construction. When the design is complete and the implementation is under way, we are able to use an additional methodology to complement the analytic and simulation efforts: We can *measure* and *evaluate* the actual system in operation. Although each component of a computing system can be unambiguously specified by the system designers and its function can be logically *debugged*, there is usually plenty of room for performance improvement. This is simply because the complexity of today's computer systems has outpaced our capability to infer the overall system behavior from system component performance figures, such as CPU instruction processing rate, storage access time, and channel data rates.

Measurement and evaluation are important not only in the implementation and integration stages, but also in the installation and operational stages. Since each installation has its own work-load environment and performance objective, the ultimate choice of system configuration and scheduling and resource allocation strategies can only be meaningfully addressed through continuous measurement and evaluation. In fact, the importance of measurement and evaluation has been so keenly recognized that most contemporary computer systems are equipped with *built-in* measurement facilities, so that measurement takes place throughout the life of a system.

In operational systems, daily measurements are made at the very least for the purpose of job accounting. Accounting measurements are primarily concerned with an individual user's resource consumptions such as CPU time, storage space, the number of lines of print, etc. In addition, some measurements are usually available on the overall utilization of system components. The summary statistics provided by such measurements are certainly not sufficient to characterize the dynamic behavior of the system in operation, yet they can reveal some information pertaining to system performance. Thus, accounting measurement facilities are used for both accounting and work-load characterization. IBM 360/370 operating systems, for example, provide a software monitoring program called the System Management Facility (SMF), which collects data to be used for these purposes.

Another motivation for obtaining measurement data is to estimate *input parameters* required for analytic and simulation models. Even after the system is operational and stable measurement data become available, predictive models still play important roles in the performance improvement and capacity planning. Suppose that a computer center manager wishes to improve the service capability of his or her installation and has a number of options from which to choose: to replace the CPU with a more powerful one; to expand main-memory capacity; to increase the number of access paths to auxiliary storage devices; or to change some resource allocation algorithms. Examining these options by actually re-configuring the system is certainly infeasible. Perhaps the manager will resort to analytic or simulation models for performance comparisons and make some sensible decision. Inputs to these models (for example, distribution functions of various service demands or event sequences to be fed into a trace-driven simulator) should be abstracted from measurement data taken from the installation in question.

Another important role of measurement and evaluation, although frequently neglected, is the validation of a performance-prediction model. An ultimate guarantee of the predictability of any model is achieved only through calibrating and validating the predicted performance against the measured figures of the actual system. Any major discrepancy between the two should be carefully examined, since it should lead to implementation errors in the actual system or to a refinement of the prediction model.

5.2 MEASUREMENT TOOLS

5.2.1 Hardware Monitors

Measurement techniques can be grouped into two classes: hardware instrumentation techniques (using hardware monitors) and programmed measurement techniques (using software monitors). A *hardware monitor* typically consists of (1) a set of electronic probes or sensors, (2) a logic plugboard, (3) a set of counters, and (4) a display or recording unit. The probes monitor electronically the state of chosen terminal points, usually resources such as the CPU, channels, and peripheral devices. The signal detected at the CPU probe may indicate, for instance, whether the CPU is in the busy state or idling at any instant. The monitored signals, which are typically on/off binary signals, are processed in a logic circuitry to transform or select raw signals into a set of interpretable signals. For example, an AND operation of signals from a channel and CPU will reveal information relevant to the evaluation of "channel-CPU overlap." The counters are used for summary statistics: to count the number of specific events or the time duration of a system activity. The duration of some activity can be measured by means of internally generated clock pulses: The monitored state is used as a gate signal to control the entry of clock pulses to the counter, so that the total number of clock ticks accumulated indicates the duration of that system state. Utilization of an individual resource is typically measured in this manner. The output of summary data may take various forms: The counter contents may be periodically displayed in real time on a graphic console, or they may be written out onto magnetic tapes for later processing.

For transformations and selections of probed signals, basic Boolean logic operations such as AND, OR, and NOT are typically used. Additional operations conventionally used in the hardware monitor include the latch (flip/flop) function and comparators.

In some recently developed monitors, a minicomputer is included as the controller and processor of the hardware monitor. This allows the hardware monitor to have additional capabilities, such as the generation of histograms rather than merely averages. The use of a minicomputer permits the monitor outputs to be connected to a range of peripherals, including disks and display scopes. If necessary, after sampling some real-time processing can be performed by the minicomputer before the collected data is stored or displayed on output devices. The minicomputer may also facilitate on-line modification of measurements and experiments, so that the analyst can effectively conduct the measurement and evaluation.

5.2.2 Software Monitors

As outlined above, the hardware monitor can collect information concerning resource usage and various system activities without disturbing the system. Its major limitation, however, is the lack of capability of sensing software-related events. For a performance evaluation, it is often important to have the capacity to observe sequences of state changes that the system and individual programs go through. Such information is especially useful when we wish to study the effect of various operating system components (e.g., the CPU dispatcher or the memory allocation policy) on system performance. Such detailed information can be attained through a *software monitor.* There are generally two types of software monitors: the event-tracing monitor and the sampling monitor.

An event-tracing monitor is a collection of system routines that are brought into execution upon occurrence of interruptions of the CPU and other major events such as scheduling, dispatching, and lockout. The monitor records a sequence of significant events. By granting the monitor an access to the system's clock or internal timer, the time of occurrence can be recorded together with the individual event records, and such data is often called "time-stamped data." This data can reveal information concerning how individual programs are making progress in the system. The software monitor can also collect system status information by scanning various system tables and queues related to these events. Thus, a software monitor can measure such things as the queue length at a device, the frequency of access to devices and data sets, or the seek time and rotational delay to meet a request on a direct-access storage device. Information concerning memory usage is collected much more easily using the software technique rather than the hardware monitor. The types of data listed above are of great value in finding out where the individual programs spend their time and in identifying possible performance bottlenecks of the system.

In addition to the collection of performance statistics, an interrupt-driven software monitor is also capable of generating *event traces* to supply input data for a trace-driven simulator such as the one discussed in Chapter 4. Many operating systems include an event-tracing facility as a debugging aid. IBM's OS/360 and VS/370 provide a software monitor called GTF (Generalized Trace Facility). It records the sequence of interruptions of a System 360/370. In the *internal trace mode*, GTF records interrupt-associated events into a memory-resident table. When the table becomes full, GTF simply overwrites the old data; thus the table size determines the number of most recent events that the system can memorize. If a system failure or user program failure occurs, the information in the table can be used to diagnose the error in the system or user programs. In the *external trace mode*, GTF transfers the traced data to tape or direct-access storage when the internal table is filled. In order to avoid the loss of trace information due to overwriting, the table size must be made sufficiently large and/or the types of events for recording must be limited. For example, an installation can choose specific SVC (super-visor call) interruptions during a trace session.

The versatility and richness of the information captured by the software monitor described above cannot be obtained without sacrifice. Unlike the hardware monitor, data collection and recording via the software monitor does place a burden on the system. Each time the measurement routine intercepts a major event and collects information, it certainly consumes CPU time, occupies some main memory for buffering data, and uses a channel and device to transfer and store data. Therefore, measurement via a software monitor has a danger of degrading the system performance during the monitoring process. If the monitor puts appreciable loads on some of the system resources (the CPU in particu-lar), it not only annoys the system users, but also introduces biases or distortions in measurement data: The collected data no longer reflects the system and user behavior that would have occurred without the measure-ment activity.

Such difficulty may be, in some cases, overcome through the use of the *sampling technique*. The software monitor invokes the monitoring routine at regular intervals by permitting the processor to be interrupted by the internal timer. At these instants, the monitor program inspects the contents of those memory-resident tables that contain information of system resource usage, programs, data-set reference activity, etc. In other words, the sampling monitor takes "snapshots" of the system status at periodic intervals. The sampling rate is determined within the trade-off between the desirable time resolution and the tolerable system degradation. For instance, when a sampling monitor is used to determine data-set reference activity, the sampling rate can be relatively slow. On the other hand, if the monitor is used to estimate software module activity by a single job, which may last for a relatively short period, a much higher sampling rate will be required. In general, the sampling rate should be based on (1) the rate of state changes (or the span of correlation in time), (2) the desired accuracy in estimating the parameters of distributions, and (3) the cost of measurement. The statistical analysis to be discussed in later sections can be used in dealing with such problems.

A disadvantage of the sampling monitor is that not all major events can be captured. For example, using the sampling monitor, it would be very difficult to estimate such quantities as the input/output interrupt rates and SVC interruption rate. It is possible to invoke a software monitor on the basis of event occurrence or the sample timer, since the interruption caused by the interval time is an external interruption. Thus, in software monitors, the interrupt-interception technique and sampling technique coexist, and measurement analysts can switch at will from one mode of operation to another.

Many software monitors provide data reduction routines and print out summary statistics such as utilization, queue distribution, and various types of histograms in predetermined formats. In many cases, these built-in statistics gathering facilities are not sufficient for the needs of performance analysts. In the following sections we will discuss how to process and interpret measurement data. Needless to say, the design and analysis of simulation experiments have a great deal in common with those of measurement and evaluation of real systems.

5.3 BASIC STATISTICAL CONCEPTS

In Chapter 2 we studied the theory of probability, aiming at a mathematical description of random events. The notion of "probabilities" was originally derived from that of "relative frequencies," but modern probability theory is founded on the axioms of probability. Set theory furnishes the machinery for handling such concepts as sample spaces, sample points, and events.

The *theory of statistics* involves interpreting a set of finite observations as a *sample point* drawn at random from a sample space. The study of statistics has the following three objectives: (1) to make the *best estimate* of important parameters of the population; (2) to assess the *uncertainty* of the estimate; and (3) to reduce a bulk of data to understandable forms.

In much the same way that an examination of the properties of probability distribution function forms the basic theory of probability, the foundation of statistical analysis is to examine the empirical distributions and certain descriptive measures associated with them.

5.3.1 Sample Mean and Sample Variance

Suppose that $\{X_i; 1 \leq i \leq n\}$ is a sample of size n (that is, n independent observations) from a population whose distribution has the population mean μ and variance σ^2. The *sample mean* $\bar{X}$ is defined as the arithmetic mean:

$$\bar{X} = \frac{1}{n} \sum_{i=1}^{n} X_i. \tag{5.1}$$

Taking the expectation or mean of both sides, we have

$$E[\bar{X}] = \frac{1}{n} \sum_{i=1}^{n} E[X_i]. \tag{5.2}$$

But since $X_1, X_2, \ldots, X_n$ are independent and identically distributed (i.i.d.) random variables, we have

$$E[X_1] = E[X_2] = \cdots = E[X_n] = \mu. \tag{5.3}$$

Substituting these values into (5.2), we have

$$E[\bar{X}] = \mu. \tag{5.4}$$

Without attempting a discussion of statistical estimation theory here, we remark that (5.4) asserts that $\bar{X}$ is an *unbiased estimate* of μ. An unbiased estimate is one that is, on the average, right on target.

Now let us consider the variance of $\bar{X}$. We have

$$\mathrm{Var}\,[\bar{X}] = E[\bar{X} - E[\bar{X}]]^2, \tag{5.5}$$

where the term $\bar{X} - E[\bar{X}] = \bar{X} - \mu$ can be rewritten as

$$\bar{X} - E[\bar{X}] = \frac{1}{n} \sum_{i=1}^{n} (X_i - \mu). \tag{5.6}$$

Therefore, by substituting (5.6) into (5.5), we find

$$\mathrm{Var}\,[\bar{X}] = \frac{1}{n^2} \sum_{i=1}^{n} E[(X_i - \mu)^2] + \frac{1}{n^2} \sum_{\substack{i=1 \\ (i \neq j)}}^{n} \sum_{j=1}^{n} E[(X_i - \mu)(X_j - \mu)]. \tag{5.7}$$

Since the random variables $\{X_i - \mu ; 1 \le i \le n\}$ are statistically independent with zero mean and variance σ^2, we finally have

$$\text{Var}\,[\bar{X}] = \frac{\sigma^2}{n}. \tag{5.8}$$

Thus, the variance of the sample mean is inversely proportional to the sample size.

The deviations of the individual observations from the sample mean provide information about the dispersion of X_i's about $\bar{X}$. We define the *sample variance* s_X^2, or simply s^2, by

$$s^2 = \frac{1}{n-1} \sum_{i=1}^{n} (X_i - \bar{X})^2. \tag{5.9}$$

We can write this as

$$s^2 = \frac{1}{n-1} \sum_{i=1}^{n} \left[(X_i - \mu) - \frac{1}{n} \sum_{j=1}^{n} (X_j - \mu) \right]^2$$

$$= \frac{1}{n} \sum_{i=1}^{n} (X_i - \mu)^2 - \frac{1}{n(n-1)} \sum_{\substack{i=1 \\ (i \ne j)}}^{n} \sum_{j=1}^{n} (X_i - \mu)(X_j - \mu). \tag{5.10}$$

Taking the expectations, we have

$$E[s^2] = \sigma^2. \tag{5.11}$$

The reason for using $n - 1$ rather than n as the divisor in (5.9) is to make $E[s^2]$ equal to σ^2, that is, to make s^2 an unbiased estimate of σ^2. The positive square root of the variance, s, is called the *standard deviation*.

5.3.2   Relative Frequency and Histograms

Observations are generally listed in the order in which they are obtained. This comprises our *primary data*, and we often *rank* the primary data according to the magnitude. When the observed data takes on discrete values* (e.g., the number of jobs in a queue), we can just count the number of occurrences for the individual values. Suppose that a sample of size n is given and k $(\le n)$ distinct values exist. Let $n(j)$ be the number of

---

* Strictly speaking, any observed data is discrete, since either the number representation or the resolution of measurement devices limits the number of significant digits. For practical purposes, however, we will still distinguish continuous variables and discrete variables, depending on whether the possible values the variable may take are sufficiently dense or not.

times that the jth value is observed, $1 \le j \le k$. Then the fraction

$$f(j) = \frac{n(j)}{n}, \qquad 1 \le j \le k \tag{5.12}$$

is, as defined in Eq. (2.1), the *relative frequency* of the jth value.

When the underlying random variable X is a continuous variable, we often adopt the method of "grouping" or "classifying" the data: The range of observations is divided into k intervals, called *class intervals*, at points $x_0, x_1, x_2, \ldots, x_k$. Let us designate the interval $(x_{j-1}, x_j]$ as the jth class, $1 \le j \le k$. Note that the lengths of the class intervals $\Delta x_j = x_j - x_{j-1}$ need not be equal. Let $n(j)$ denote the number of observations in the jth class interval, that is, the number of observations satisfying

$$x_{j-1} < X \le x_j. \tag{5.13}$$

Then the relative frequency of the jth class takes the same form as (5.12). The grouped distribution may be represented graphically as the following "step function" in an (x, h)-coordinate system:

$$h(x) = \frac{f(j)}{\Delta x_j} = \frac{n(j)}{n\Delta x_j}, \quad \text{for} \quad x_{j-1} < x \le x_j. \tag{5.14}$$

Note that the frequency divided by the class length is used as the ordinate. In this manner, the relative frequency of the jth class is represented by a rectangular area of size $f(j)$. Such a diagram is called a *histogram* and can be regarded as an estimate of the probability density function of the population. If the class lengths Δx_j are all the same, the shape of the histogram remains unchanged even if we use the relative frequency of the classes $\{f(j)\}$, or the frequency counts of the classes $\{n(j)\}$, as the ordinate. Such diagrams are also called histograms. In Fig. 5.1 we show a histogram that is obtained from measurement data of the CPU service time of an interactive system (Anderson and Sargent, 1972): The class lengths are constant with $\Delta x_j = \frac{1}{60}[\sec]$, and the sample size is approximately 120,000. We show the ordinate in both $f(j)$, the relative frequency of the class, and h_j, the value of $h(x)$ in the jth class.

Choice of the class intervals in the histogram representation is by no means trivial. Certainly we should choose them in such a way that the characteristic features of the distribution are emphasized and chance variations are obscured. If the class lengths are too small, chance variations dominate because each interval includes only a small number of observations. The variance of the histogram's height is approximately inversely proportional to the class length Δx_j (Exercise 5.3.2). On the other hand, if the class lengths are too large, a great deal of information concerning the characteristics of the distribution will be lost. A more

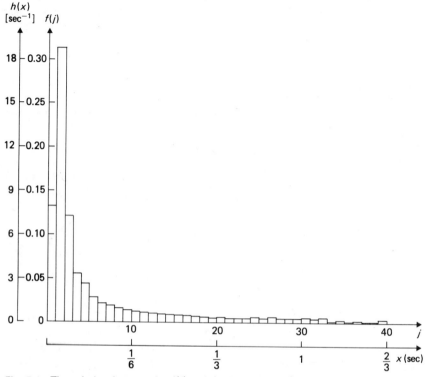

Fig. 5.1 The relative frequencies $f(j)$ and the histogram $h(x)$ of the computer service time demand (Anderson and Sargent, 1972).

systematic study on the choice of the class lengths is related to the problem of *fitting distribution forms* to data. It involves such advanced notions as the χ^2-test and *maximum likelihood estimation* (see, for example, Kendall and Stuart, 1961; Daniel and Wood, 1971; Fishman, 1973).

The empirical distribution analog of the cumulative distribution function is the *cumulative relative frequency distribution*. Let $X_1, X_2, \ldots, X_n$ denote n observations in the order observed, and let $X_{(1)}, X_{(2)}, \ldots, X_{(n)}$ denote the same n observations (ungrouped) ranked in order of magnitude. The frequency $H(x)$ of observations that are smaller than or equal to x, called the *cumulative relative frequency*, is

$$
H(x) = \begin{cases}
0, & \text{for } x < X_{(1)} \\[2mm]
\dfrac{i}{n}, & \text{for } X_{(i)} \le x < X_{(i+1)}, \quad i = 1, 2, \ldots, n-1 \\[2mm]
1, & \text{for } x \ge X_{(n)}.
\end{cases}
\tag{5.15}
$$

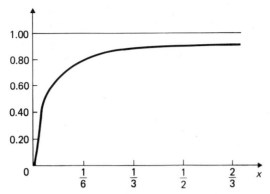

Fig. 5.2 The cumulative relative frequency distribution of the computer service time demand (Anderson and Sargent, 1972).

The graphical plot of $H(x)$ is a nondecreasing step curve, which increases from 0 to 1 in "jumps" of $1/n$ at points $x = X_{(1)}, X_{(2)}, \ldots, X_{(n)}$. If several observations take on the same value, the jump is a multiple of $1/n$. Figure 5.2 is obtained from the same measurement data as that used in Fig. 5.1. Since the sample size is quite large in this case, the plotted curve looks essentially continuous.

When *grouped data* are presented as a cumulative relative frequency distribution, it is usually called the *cumulative histogram*. The cumulative histogram is far less sensitive to variations in class lengths than the histogram (Exercise 5.3.3). It is because the accumulation is essentially equivalent to integration along the x-axis, which *filters out* the chance variations contained in the histogram. The cumulative relative frequency distribution or the cumulative histogram is, therefore, quite helpful in portraying the gross features of data.

Exercises

5.3.1 Prove the following recursive formulas for the sample mean and variance:

$$\bar{X}_i = \bar{X}_{i-1} + \frac{(X_i - \bar{X}_{i-1})}{i}, \quad i \geq 1$$

and

$$s_i^2 = \left(\frac{i-2}{i-1}\right) s_{i-1}^2 + \frac{(X_i - \bar{X}_{i-1})^2}{i}, \quad i > 1$$

with the initial values

$$\bar{X}_0 = 0, \quad \text{and} \quad s_0^2 = s_1^2 = 0.$$

Then the last values of the sequence—that is, $\bar{X}_n$ and s_n—are the desired quantities:

$$\bar{X} = \bar{X}_n \quad \text{and} \quad s^2 = s_n^2.$$

5.3.2 Let the underlying (unknown) probability density function and cumulative distribution function of a random variable be $f(x)$ and $F(x)$, respectively. Show that the height h_j of the histogram for the jth class based on a sample of size n has the mean

$$E[h_j] = \frac{F(x_j) - F(x_{j-1})}{\Delta x_j} \cong f(x_j)$$

and variance

$$\text{Var}\,[h_j] = \frac{[F(x_j) - F(x_{j-1})][1 - F(x_j) + F(x_{j-1})]}{n \Delta x_j^2}$$

$$\cong \frac{f(x_j)}{n \Delta x_j}.$$

5.3.3 Suppose that the underlying comulative distribution function of a random variable X is given by $F_X(x)$. What is the mean and variance of H_j, the height of the cumulative histogram in the jth interval? Explain why the shape of the cumulative histogram is rather insensitive to the choice of class lengths $\{\Delta x_j\}$.

5.4   GRAPHICAL REPRESENTATIONS

Reducing primary data to the sample mean, sample variance, and histogram can reveal a great amount of information concerning the nature of the population distribution. But sometimes important features of the underlying distribution are obscured or hidden by the data reduction procedures. In this section we will discuss some graphical methods that have been found to be quite valuable in exploratory analyses of measurement data. They are (1) the fractile diagram, (2) the log survivor function curve, (3) the concentration curve, (4) the dot diagram and correlation coefficient, and (5) the correlogram and periodogram.

5.4.1   The Fractile Diagram

As we stated in Section 2.7, some random variables occurring in physical situations have the normal (or Gaussian) distribution, or at least can be treated approximately as normal random variables. As we shall see in subsequent sections, most statistical analysis techniques are based on the assumption of normality of measured variables. Thus, when we collect measurement data and obtain some empirical distribution, the first thing we might do is to examine whether the underlying distribution is normal. A *fractile diagram* (Hald, 1952) is useful for this purpose.

For a given (cumulative) distribution function $F(x)$

$$P = F(x) \tag{5.16}$$

provides the dependence of the cumulative distribution on the variable x.

The inverse function

$$x_P = F^{-1}(P) \tag{5.17}$$

gives the value of the variable x that corresponds to the given cumulative probability P. The value x_P is called the P-fractile. Some authors use the terms *percentile* or *quantile* to mean fractile.

The distribution function of the standard normal distribution defined in (2.217) is often denoted by $\Phi(\bullet)$:

$$\Phi(u) = \frac{1}{\sqrt{2\pi}} \int_{-\infty}^{u} \exp\left(-\frac{t^2}{2}\right) dt. \tag{5.18}$$

Then the fractiles, u_P, of the standard normal distribution are derived as

$$u_P = \Phi^{-1}(P). \tag{5.19}$$

Suppose that for a given cumulative relative frequency $H(x)$ we wish to test whether this empirical distribution resembles a normal distribution, that is, to test whether

$$H(x) \cong \Phi\left(\frac{x - \mu}{\sigma}\right) \tag{5.20}$$

holds for some parameters μ and σ. Testing this relation is equivalent to testing the relation

$$u_{H(x)} \cong \frac{x - \mu}{\sigma}. \tag{5.21}$$

According to the definition $H(x)$, the function $u_{H(x)}$ is a step function that may be written as

$$u_{H(x)} = \begin{cases} -\infty, & \text{for} \quad x < X_{(1)} \\ u_{i/n}, & \text{for} \quad X_{(i)} \le x < X_{(i+1)}, \quad i = 1, 2, \ldots, n-1 \\ \infty & \text{for} \quad x \ge X_{(n)}. \end{cases} \tag{5.22}$$

Therefore, the step function

$$u = u_{H(x)} \tag{5.23}$$

provides an estimate of the straight line

$$u = \frac{x - \mu}{\sigma} \tag{5.24}$$

in the same way that the cumulative frequency distribution $y = H(x)$ forms an estimate of the cumulative distribution function $y = F(x)$. The graphical plot of the function (5.23) in an (x, u)-coordinate system is called the *fractile diagram*.

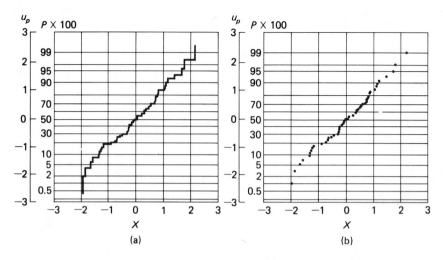

Fig. 5.3 The fractile diagram of normal variates: (a) step curve; (b) dot diagram.

Instead of plotting (x, u_P) on ordinary graph paper, we may plot (x, P) directly on a special graph paper called *probability paper*. On the ordinate axis of a probability paper, the corresponding values of $P = \Phi(u)$ are marked, rather than the u values. Probability paper is used in the same manner as other special graph papers, such as logarithmic paper. Figure 5.3(a) shows a probability paper with step curve $u = u_{H(x)}$ based on $n = 50$ sample points drawn from a normal distribution with mean 0 and variance 1. Instead of the step curve, we often plot n points $(X_{(i)}, (i - \frac{1}{2})/n)$ which are situated at the midpoints of the vertical parts of the step curve. The advantages are that it is easier to plot n points than to draw a step curve, and that possible systematic deviations from a straight line are more easily detected from this dot diagram. The result of this procedure is shown in Fig. 5.3(b).

If the theoretical distribution is normal, the points of the fractile diagrams vary randomly about a straight line. The variance of the fractile u_H corresponding to the cumulative relative frequency H is given approximately by (Exercise 5.4.1)

$$\text{Var}[u_H] \cong \frac{\Phi(u_P)\Phi(-u_P)}{n[\phi(u_P)]^2}, \tag{5.25}$$

where $\phi(u) = \Phi'(u)$: the density function of the standard normal variable. Thus, the variance is inversely proportional to the number of observations. The quantity $n\,\text{Var}[u_H]$ depends only on u_P, and has a minimum at $u_P = 0$ (that is, $P = 0.50$).

In a small sample, say $n < 20$, the permissible random variation of points in the fractile diagram is so large that it is generally difficult to examine whether systematic deviations from a straight line exist.

5.4.2 The Log Survivor Function Curve

Given the distribution function $F(x)$ of a random variable X, its complement

$$F^c(x) = 1 - F(x) = P[X > x] \tag{5.26}$$

is called the *complementary distribution function* (Chapter 2), *reliability function*, or *survivor function*. The last two terms originated from the theory of reliability in which the random variable X represents the interval between failures. The natural logarithm of Eq. (5.26) is known as the *log survivor function* (Cox and Lewis, 1968):

$$\ln F^c(x) = \ln\{P[X > x]\}. \tag{5.27}$$

The log survivor function will show the details of the tail end of the distribution more effectively than the distribution itself. If, for instance, $F(x)$ is an exponential distribution with mean $1/\alpha$, then its log survivor function is a straight line: $\ln e^{-\alpha x} = -\alpha x$. If $F(x)$ is a two-stage hyperexponential distribution

$$F(x) = \pi_1(1 - e^{-\alpha_1 x}) + \pi_2(1 - e^{-\alpha_2 x}), \qquad \alpha_1 > \alpha_2 \tag{5.28}$$

then its log survivor function has two asymptotic straight lines, since

$$\ln F^c(x) = \ln\left[\pi_1 e^{-\alpha_1 x} + \pi_2 e^{-\alpha_2 x}\right]$$
$$\cong \begin{cases} -\alpha_1 x + \ln \pi_1 & \text{for small } x \\ -\alpha_2 x + \ln \pi_2 & \text{for large } x. \end{cases} \tag{5.29}$$

The *sample* (or *empirical*) *log survivor function* is similarly defined as

$$\ln[1 - H(x)], \tag{5.30}$$

where $H(x)$ represents the cumulative relative frequency (ungrouped data) or the cumulative histogram (grouped data). In the ungrouped case we find from (5.15) that

$$\ln\left(1 - \frac{i}{n}\right), \qquad 1 \le i \le n \tag{5.31}$$

should be plotted against x_i, where the subscript i represents the rank. In order to avoid difficulties at $i = n$, we may sometimes modify (5.31) into

$$\ln\left[1 - \frac{i}{n+1}\right], \qquad 1 \le i \le n. \tag{5.32}$$

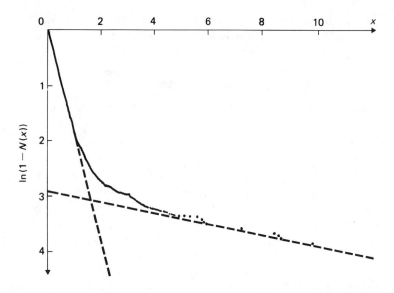

Fig. 5.4 The log survivor function of the two-phase hyperexponential distribution with $\pi_1 = 0.0526$, $\alpha_1 = 0.1$, and $\alpha_2 = 2.0$.

As an example, we plot in Fig. 5.4 the log survivor function using a sample of size 1000 drawn from the hyperexponential distribution with parameters

$$\pi_1 = 0.0526, \quad \alpha_1 = 0.1, \quad \text{and} \quad \alpha_2 = 2.0.$$

Out of the 1000 samples taken, 18 sample points that exceed $x = 10$ are outside the scale of the figure; hence they are not shown. The two asymptotes of (5.29) can be easily recognized from this log survivor function.

Characteristically, the log survivor function of the mixed exponential distribution (5.28) is convex with a linear tail as shown in Fig. 5.4. Observations of (or departures from) such characteristic shapes are used to postulate a functional form for a distribution. See Lewis and Shedler (1973), who discuss use of empirical log-survivor function in the page fault data in a computer system operating under the LRU (least recently used) replacement algorithm. See also Gaver, Lavenberg, and Price (1976) and Lewis and Shedler (1976).

Other curves that can be derived from the histogram or distribution function are the *completion rate curve* (Exercise 5.4.4) and the *mean residual life curve* (Exercise 5.4.5).

5.4.3 The Concentration Curve

Consider a random variable X with the distribution function $F(x)$ and the corresponding density function $f(x)$. Define the function $Q(x)$ by

$$Q(x) = \frac{\int_0^x uf(u)\, du}{\int_0^\infty uf(u)\, du}. \qquad (5.33)$$

A plot of $Q(x)$ versus $F(x)$ is called the *concentration curve* or the *curve of concentration* (Kendall and Stuart, 1958) and illustrates the percentage contribution to the *mean value* from the $100 \times F(x)$ percentiles of the job population. The area between the concentration curve and the line $Q = F$ is called the *area of concentration*. The denominator of $Q(x)$ is the mean value $E[X]$. Using the formula

$$\int_a^b uf(u)\, du = -[u(1 - F(u))]_a^b + \int_a^b \{1 - F(u)\}\, du \qquad (5.34)$$

we have an alternative expression for $Q(x)$:

$$Q(x) = \frac{-x[1 - F(x)] + \int_0^x [1 - F(u)]\, du}{\int_0^\infty [1 - F(u)]\, du}. \qquad (5.35)$$

Thus, once the cumulative relative frequency distribution $H(x)$, an estimate of $F(x)$, is obtained, the empirical value of $Q(x)$ is easily computable from the last equation. Figure 5.5 is the concentration curve derived from the cumulative distribution shown in Fig. 5.2. It shows, for example, that the upper 10 percentiles of the job population contribute approximately 95 percent of the total work load. Also shown in this diagram are the concentration curves for the uniform and exponential distributions (Exercise 5.4.4).

Another example of the concentration curve is as follows. Suppose that we measure the frequencies of access to N different data records in a computer file. We rank the records in decreasing order of the access frequencies; hence f_j represents the relative frequency of the jth most frequently used data record, $1 \le j \le N$. Then a set of points

$$Q(j) = \frac{-j(1 - F_j) + \sum_{i=1}^{j} (1 - F_{i-1})}{\sum_{i=1}^{N} (1 - F_{i-1})} = \frac{jF_j - \sum_{k=1}^{j-1} F_k}{N - \sum_{k=1}^{N-1} F_k}, \qquad (5.36)$$

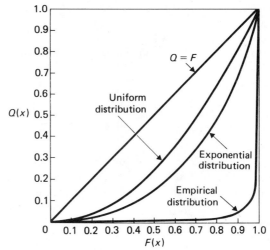

Fig. 5.5 The concentration curves of computer service demands (Anderson, 1972).

versus

$$F_j = \sum_{i=1}^{j} f_i \qquad (5.37)$$

will produce the concentration "dot" curve.

5.4.4 The Dot Diagram and the Correlation Coefficient

In the preceding sections we were concerned with various graphical presentation techniques to extract some significant features contained in the empirical distribution of a sample of *one* random variable. These techniques are especially valuable in determining actual parametric distribution models of inputs to analytic or simulation models. So we may deem these techniques to be primarily useful to *input analyses* in modeling efforts.

In analyzing a simulation model or an operational system, we usually measure a number of variables, and we wish to find possible statistical associations among them. Thus, the search for *correlations* between two or more quantities is one of the most important functions in the *output analyses* of the measurement and evaluation process. A typical method of graphically examining correlations between two variables X and Y based on n observations of the pair $\{(X_i, Y_i); 1 \le i \le n\}$ is to plot the points (X_i, Y_i) one by one as coordinates. Such a diagram is called a *dot* or *scatter diagram*. The density of dots in a given region is proportional to the relative frequency of the pairs (X, Y) in the region. An example is shown in Fig. 5.6, which is based on the measurement data of an IBM APL/360 system. Here the variable X_i represents the number of disk accesses in the ith interval period (where each interval is 10 minutes) and Y_i is the average length of CPU bursts (or periods of continuous CPU requirement) during the same period. This figure clearly indicates that the variables Y and X are *negatively correlated* (in the sense defined below). An increase in X results, on the average, in a decrease in Y.

    The most frequently used measure of statistical association between a pair of variables is the *correlation coefficient*. For a given pair of random variables X and Y, the covariance of X and Y, written $\mathrm{Cov}\,[X, Y]$ or σ_{XY}, is defined as*

$$\sigma_{XY} = E[(X - \mu_X)(Y - \mu_Y)] = E[XY] - \mu_X\mu_Y. \qquad (5.38)$$

If X and Y are statistically independent, it follows (see Exercise 2.5.5) that

$$\sigma_{XY} = 0. \qquad (5.39)$$

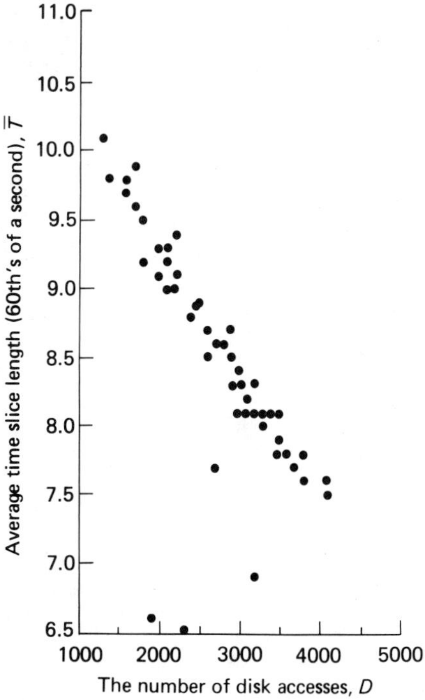

Fig. 5.6 An example of the dot diagram (Anderson and Sargent, 1972).

---

* In some literature, σ_{XY}^2 is used rather than σ_{XY}. We drop the square term, since the covariance can be negative.

The converse is not true: The condition $\sigma_{XY} = 0$ does not imply that X and Y are independent (Exercise 5.4.7). The *correlation coefficient* ρ_{XY} between X and Y is defined as

$$\rho_{XY} = \frac{\sigma_{XY}}{\sigma_X \sigma_Y}, \tag{5.40}$$

which may be simply written as ρ when no ambiguity arises as to which random variables are involved. The correlation coefficient always satisfies the condition (Exercise 5.4.8)

$$-1 \le \rho_{XY} \le 1. \tag{5.41}$$

We say that X and Y are *properly linearly dependent* if there exist nonzero constants a and b such that $aX - bY$ is a constant c, that is,

$$P[aX - bY = c] = 1. \tag{5.42}$$

Therefore,

$$\text{Var}[aX - bY - c] = 0, \tag{5.43}$$

from which we have (Exercise 5.4.9)

$$\rho_{XY} = +1 \quad \text{or} \quad -1 \tag{5.44}$$

depending on whether ab is positive or negative. Conversely, if $\rho = \pm 1$, then it implies (Example 5.4.8) that

$$P\left[\mp \frac{(X - \mu_X)}{\sigma_X} + \frac{Y - \mu_Y}{\sigma_Y} = 0\right] = 1. \tag{5.45}$$

The *sample covariance* of the two variables based on observations $\{(X_i, Y_i); 1 \le i \le n\}$ is defined as

$$S_{XY} = \frac{1}{n-1} \sum_{i=1}^{n} (X_i - \bar{X})(Y_i - \bar{Y})$$

$$= \frac{1}{n-1} \sum_{i=1}^{n} X_i Y_i - \frac{n}{n-1} \bar{X}\bar{Y}, \tag{5.46}$$

where $\bar{X}$ and $\bar{Y}$ are the sample means. The *sample correlation coefficient* is defined accordingly:

$$r_{XY} = \frac{s_{XY}}{s_X s_Y}, \tag{5.47}$$

where s_X^2 and s_Y^2 are the sample variances of $\{X_i\}$ and $\{Y_i\}$, respectively.

5.4.5 The Correlogram and the Periodogram

Thus far we have assumed that the sample $\{X_j; 1 \leq j \leq N\}$ is N independent observations. In practice, however, we often must deal with the cases
in which the serial number i of X_i is some time index, that is, the order in
which the random variables appear in time. For instance, $\{X_j\}$ may
represent the CPU utilization measured at a regular timed interval
$t = j\Delta$, or $\{X_j\}$ may be the sequence of waiting times of requests at a disk
queue, or it may be the output of a random-number generator. In any of
these cases, we should be interested in determining the extent of correlation that may exist in the sequence of data.

   As defined in Section 2.9, a *time series* or *discrete-time random
process* $\{X_i; -\infty < i < \infty\}$ is said to be *wide-sense stationary*, if

$$E[X_j] = \mu \quad \text{for all} \quad j \tag{5.48}$$

and

$$E[(X_j - \mu)(X_{j+k} - \mu)] = R_k \quad \text{for all} \quad j \quad \text{and} \quad k. \tag{5.49}$$

That is, the mean is constant throughout the sequence, and the covariance
between any pair X_j and X_{j+k} is a function of their distance k in the time
indexes. The function $\{R_k\}$ is called the autocovariance function of $\{X_j\}$.

   For a given *wide-sense stationary* time series $\{X_i\}$ we define the
autocorrelation sequence $\{\rho_k\}$ by

$$\rho_k = \frac{R_k}{R_0} = \frac{R_k}{\sigma^2}, \quad -\infty < k < \infty. \tag{5.50}$$

We sometimes call ρ_k the *serial correlation coefficient* of *lag k* (or *order k*).
Clearly,

$$-1 \leq \rho_k \leq 1, \quad \text{and} \quad \rho_0 = 1. \tag{5.51}$$

   For an observed sequence $\{X_j; 1 \leq j \leq N\}$, an estimator of the
autocovariance function R_k is given by

$$\hat{R}_k = \frac{1}{N-k} \sum_{j=1}^{N-k} (X_j - \bar{X})(X_{j+k} - \bar{X}), \tag{5.52}$$

where

$$\bar{X} = \frac{1}{N} \sum_{j=1}^{N} X_j. \tag{5.53}$$

We can show that $\hat{R}_k$ is an asymptotically unbiased estimator of R_k:

$$\lim_{N \to \infty} E[\hat{R}_k] = R_k. \tag{5.54}$$

An estimator for the serial correlation function ρ_k on the basis of a finite sample is called the *correlogram* and is usually given by

$$\hat{\rho}_k = \frac{\hat{R}_k}{\hat{R}_0}. \tag{5.55}$$

It can be shown that $\hat{\rho}_k$ is an asymptotically unbiased estimator of ρ_k.

Although the estimated correlation function reveals much information about a time-dependent sequence, the distribution theory for the sample correlation function $\hat{\rho}_k$ is not well developed, except for its asymptotic property and for normal random variates. It is therefore difficult to apply any of the formal hypothesis tests available in statistical theory. The theory of *spectral analysis*, on the other hand, is well developed (see, for example, Kendall and Stuart, 1966; Cox and Lewis, 1968); we shall study some of the key concepts in the remaining part of this section. We define the *Fourier transform* of the autocovariance function R_k by

$$P(\lambda) = \frac{1}{2\pi} \sum_{k=-\infty}^{\infty} R_k e^{-ik\lambda}$$

$$= \frac{1}{2\pi} \left[R_0 + 2 \sum_{k=1}^{\infty} R_k \cos(k\lambda) \right], \quad -\pi \le \lambda \le \pi \tag{5.56}$$

where $i = \sqrt{-1}$. The inverse relationship is given by

$$R_k = \int_{-\pi}^{\pi} P(\lambda) e^{ik\lambda} \, d\lambda$$

$$= \int_{-\pi}^{\pi} P(\lambda) \cos k\lambda \, d\lambda. \tag{5.57}$$

The transform pair (5.56) and (5.57) is known as the *Wiener-Khinchine* theorem. By setting $k = 0$ in the last equation, we find

$$\sigma^2 = \int_{-\pi}^{\pi} P(\lambda) \, d\lambda. \tag{5.58}$$

In other words, the variance σ^2 is made up of infinitesimal contributions $P(\lambda) \, d\lambda$ in small bands around each *frequency* λ. Thus, the function $P(\lambda)$ is called the (*power*) *spectrum*. Its normalized version

$$\frac{P(\lambda)}{\sigma^2} = \frac{1}{2\pi} \sum_{k=-\infty}^{\infty} \rho_k e^{-ik\lambda} \tag{5.59}$$

is called the (*power*) *spectral density function*.

For the observed sequence $\{X_j;\ 1 \le j \le N\}$ let us consider the Fourier transform

$$C(\lambda) = \frac{1}{\sqrt{N}} \sum_{j=1}^{N} (X_j - \bar{X})e^{ij\lambda}, \qquad -\pi < \lambda < \pi \qquad (5.60)$$

where $i = \sqrt{-1}$. We restrict our attention to values of λ of the form $\lambda = 2\pi m/N$, $m = 1, 2, \ldots, [N/2]$ (where $[z]$ is the largest integer not exceeding z). Although other values of λ may be considered, no additional information is obtained thereby, since $C(\lambda)$ can be interpolated with weighting functions of the form $\sin[\lambda - (2\pi m/N)]/[\lambda - (2\pi m/N)]$. So we write

$$C_m = C\!\left(\frac{2\pi m}{N}\right) = \frac{1}{\sqrt{N}} \sum_{j=1}^{N} (X_j - \bar{X})e^{2\pi ijm/N}$$

$$= \begin{cases} \dfrac{1}{\sqrt{N}} \displaystyle\sum_{j=1}^{N} X_j e^{2\pi ijm/N}, & m = 1, 2, \ldots, N-1 \\[4mm] 0, & m = 0, N. \end{cases} \qquad (5.61)$$

The relation (5.61) is the so-called *discrete Fourier transform* of $\{X_j - \bar{X}\}$, and its inverse transform is

$$X_j - \bar{X} = \frac{1}{\sqrt{N}} \sum_{m=1}^{N-1} C_m e^{-2\pi ijm/N}. \qquad (5.62)$$

The transformed sequence C_m is complex-valued. We define the *periodogram* by

$$I_m = |C_m|^2 = \frac{1}{N}\left| \sum_{j=1}^{N} X_j e^{2\pi ijm/N} \right|^2, \qquad m = 1, 2, \ldots, N-1. \qquad (5.63)$$

If we rearrange the double sum involved in (5.63) we can show that

$$I_m = \sum_{k=-N+1}^{N-1} \left(1 - \frac{|k|}{N}\right) \hat{R}_k e^{2\pi ikm/N}. \qquad (5.64)$$

If we take the expectation of both sides

$$E[I_m] = \sigma^2 \sum_{k=-N+1}^{N-1} \left(1 - \frac{|k|}{N}\right) \rho_k \cos\left(\frac{2\pi km}{N}\right) \qquad (5.65)$$

under weak conditions, this tends to

$$E[I_m] \to \sigma^2 \sum_{k=-\infty}^{\infty} \rho_k \cos\left(\frac{2\pi km}{N}\right) = 2\pi P\!\left(\frac{2\pi m}{N}\right) \qquad (5.66)$$

as $N \to \infty$.

We can write the term C_m of (5.61) as

$$C_m = A_m + iB_m, \qquad m = 1, 2, \ldots, N - 1, \qquad (5.67)$$

where

$$A_m = \frac{1}{\sqrt{N}} \sum_{j=1}^{N} X_j \cos\left(\frac{2\pi jm}{N}\right) \qquad (5.68)$$

and

$$B_m = \frac{1}{\sqrt{N}} \sum_{j=1}^{N} X_j \sin\left(\frac{2\pi jm}{N}\right). \qquad (5.69)$$

It is not difficult to show that A_m and B_m have zero mean and variance $\sigma^2/2$. Furthermore, they are uncorrelated because of the orthogonality between $\sin(2\pi jm/N)$ and $\cos(2\pi jm/N)$. Also, by virtue of the central limit theorem, they are asymptotically (that is, as $N \to \infty$) normally distributed; consequently they are asymptotically independent. The individual components $\{I_m\}$ for different values of m are asymptotically independent. (Note that if the X_j's are independently normally distributed, so are $\{A_m\}$ and $\{B_m\}$ for any *finite* sample size N.) Therefore, for a given index m, the variable

$$I_m = A_m^2 + B_m^2 \qquad (5.70)$$

has asymptotically (or exactly, for normal X_j's) a distribution proportional to the chi-square distribution with two degrees of freedom, which is equivalent to an *exponential distribution* (Section 5.5). Thus, the coefficient of variation of the variable I_m remains 1, no matter how large the sample size N becomes. This property, together with the asymptotic independence of I_m and $I_{m'}$ $(m \neq m')$, implies that the periodogram fluctuations appear highly erratic when plotted against m. Therefore, the periodogram is seldom used to estimate the spectrum. Instead, the correlogram is first computed; then the Fourier transform of the correlogram is taken, as suggested by the Wiener-Khinchine theorem. In order to obtain a "smoother" estimate of the spectrum, the correlogram may be multiplied by a "weight function" (or window function) before the transformation is taken. See Hannan (1969) for further details on this subject.

The periodogram $\{I_m\}$ is a convenient statistic to use in testing for independence of the sequence $\{X_j\}$. If the variables $\{X_j\}$ are independent, then the variables $\{I_m; 1 \leq m \leq [N/2]\}$ are i.i.d. with an exponential distribution. Hence, if we form a point process with interarrival times $\{I_m\}$, then it is a Poisson process! A convenient way of testing for the uniformity of this associated Poisson process is done graphically through

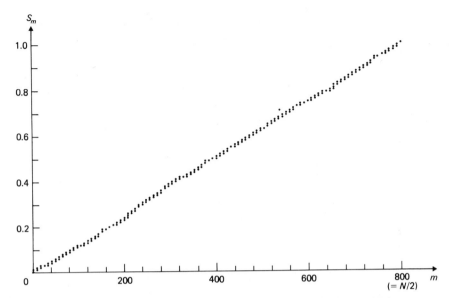

Fig. 5.7 An example of the cumulative periodogram (Yue, 1971).

the *normalized cumulative periodogram.* Let

$$S_m = \frac{\sum_{j=1}^{m} I_j}{\sum_{j=1}^{M} I_j}, \qquad m = 1, 2, \ldots, M \, (= [N/2]). \tag{5.71}$$

Figure 5.7 plots the cumulative periodogram for the CPU times $\{X_j\}$, which are measured for $N = 1600$ consecutive jobs in a teleprocessing information retrieval system (Yue, 1971). From this graph, it may be reasonable to judge that the CPU times of the system in question are i.i.d. random variables. For the same data, it was found that the CPU distribution is approximated by the gamma distribution with the coefficient of variation $\beta^{-1/2} \cong 2.4$.

More formal procedures of testing for uniformity are usually done by the Kolmogorov-Smirnov test and the chi-squared test (see, for example, Kendall and Stuart, 1961).

Exercises

5.4.1 Derive the expression (5.25). *Hint:* $\mathrm{Var}\,[u_H] \cong \mathrm{Var}\,[H]\,(du/dP)^2$.

5.4.2 Plot the sample log survivor function by generating 1000 values of a random variable X that has the two-stage Erlangian distribution of mean 1. Do the same for the four-stage Erlangian distribution.

5.4.3 Find the expression for the log survivor function and the completion rate function, when the service time is
  a) constant a;
  b) uniformally distributed between $[a, b]$.

5.4.4 a) Let X be a continuous random variable with a uniform distribution $F(x)$. Show that the concentration curve is given by

$$Q = F^2, \quad 0 \le F \le 1.$$

  b) Let X be an exponentially distributed random variable. Show that its concentration curve is

$$Q = F + (1 - F)\ln(1 - F), \quad 0 \le F \le 1.$$

5.4.5 *The completion rate curve.* If $F(x)$ represents the distribution function of a service time variable, we define the function

$$z(x) = \frac{f(x)}{F^c(x)} = \frac{f(x)}{1 - F(x)}$$

which is called the *completion rate function* (or the *failure rate* or *hazard function*).
  a) Find the completion rate function when $F(x)$ is an exponential distribution with mean $1/\alpha$.
  b) Find the relation between the log survivor function and the completion rate function.
  c) Show that $z(x)$ of the hyperexponential distribution is monotone decreasing.
  d) Show that if $z(x)$ is monotone increasing, then the coefficient of variation is less than one.

5.4.6 *The mean residual life curve.* Let X be a service time variable with the distribution $F_X(\bullet)$. Given that X is greater than x, we call the difference

$$R = X - x$$

the *residual life* conditioned on that $X > x$.
  a) Show that the mean *residual life function* is given by

$$R(x) = E[R \mid X > x] = \frac{\displaystyle\int_x^\infty [1 - F_X(u)]\, du}{1 - F_X(x)}.$$

  What is $R(0)$?
  b) Show that $R(x)$ is a monotone-decreasing function if and only if the completion rate function $z(x)$ is monotone increasing.
  c) For the hyperexponential distribution (5.28), show that

$$\lim_{x \to \infty} R(x) = \frac{1}{\alpha_2}.$$

d) Show that for the gamma distribution

$$f(x) = \frac{e^{-\alpha x}}{\Gamma(\beta)} \alpha(\alpha x)^{\beta-1}, \qquad x > 0$$

$R(x)$ is a monotone-increasing (decreasing) function if $\beta < 1$ ($\beta > 1$). Find $R(0)$ and $\lim_{x \to \infty} R(x)$.

5.4.7 Suppose that random variables X and Y are functionally related according to

$$Y = \cos X.$$

Let the probability density function of X be given by

$$f_X(x) = \begin{cases} \dfrac{1}{2\pi}, & -\pi < x < \pi \\[2mm] 0, & \text{elsewhere.} \end{cases}$$

Find $\text{Cov}[X, Y]$.

5.4.8 Given two random variables X and Y, define a new random variable

$$Z = \left[t\left(\frac{X - \mu_X}{\sigma_X}\right) + \frac{Y - \mu_Y}{\sigma_Y} \right]^2$$

where t is a real constant.

     a) Compute $E[Z]$.
     b) Show that $-1 \le \rho_{XY} \le 1$, where ρ_{XY} is the correlation coefficient between X and Y.

5.4.9 Show that if $\rho = \pm 1$, then (5.45) holds.

5.4.10 Show that the sample covariance s_{XY} is an unbiased estimate of σ_{XY}.

5.4.11 Generalize the recursive computation formula of Exercise 5.3.1 to the sample covariance.

5.5   DISTRIBUTIONS DERIVED FROM THE NORMAL DISTRIBUTION

In Section 2.7 we defined the normal (or Gaussian) distribution and discussed its properties. The normal distribution plays a central role in the mathematical theory of statistics for at least two reasons. First, the normal distribution often describes a variety of physical quantities observed in the real world. In Chapter 3, we discussed that the queue size in a finite population queueing system is approximately normally distributed when the population size is moderate or large. The response-time distribution in that model is also given in terms of a distribution closely related to the normal distribution. Some empirical studies indicate that the distribution of working set size (Denning, 1968) of a program behavior in a virtual-storage system environment is well approximated by a normal distribution. These instances cited here may be perhaps exceptions: The underlying probability distributions of quantities of direct interest in a computer system are seldom normal. However, statistical estimation of these distributions or distribution parameters involves an extensive use of the normal distribution or related distributions.

The second reason for the frequent use of the normal distribution is its mathematical tractability. For instance, sums of independent normal random variables are themselves normally distributed. Such reproductivity of the distribution is enjoyed only by a limited class of distributions (that is, binomial, gamma, Poisson). Many important results in the theory of statistics are founded on the assumption of normal distribution. Of course, whenever we adopt such a distribution assumption, we must be aware of the discrepancy between the reality and its model. Great care must be exercised in interpreting the results that the model produces.

5.5.1   The Chi-Square Distribution

Let us assume that $X_1, X_2, \ldots, X_n$ are independent observations from a population distributed according to $N(\mu, \sigma^2)$. An estimate of σ^2 is provided by the sample variance

$$s^2 = \frac{1}{n-1} \sum_{i=1}^{n} (X_i - \bar{X})^2. \tag{5.72}$$

If the population mean μ is known, which is very seldom the case, the estimate s^2 should be replaced by

$$s^{*2} = \frac{1}{n} \sum_{i=1}^{n} (X_i - \mu)^2. \tag{5.73}$$

The n variables $X_1 - \mu, X_2 - \mu, \ldots, X_n - \mu$ in the above expression are i.i.d. with the common distribution $N(0, \sigma^2)$. By normalizing these variables by σ, we find

$$s^{*2} = \frac{\sigma^2}{n} \sum_{i=1}^{n} U_i^2 \tag{5.74}$$

where

$$U_i = \frac{X_i - \mu}{\sigma}, \qquad 1 \leq i \leq n \tag{5.75}$$

are i.i.d. random variables with the *standard normal distribution* $N(0, 1)$. Denoting the sum of n independent standard normal variables squared by χ_n^2

$$\chi_n^2 = \sum_{i=1}^{n} U_i^2, \tag{5.76}$$

s^{*^2} may be written as

$$s^{*^2} = \frac{\sigma^2}{n} \chi_n^2. \tag{5.77}$$

The distribution of the χ_n^2-value defined above is called the *chi-square* (χ^2) *distribution with n degrees of freedom (d.f.)*.

If we write s^2 in a manner similar to s^{*^2}, we have

$$s^2 = \frac{\sigma^2}{n-1} \chi^2 \tag{5.78}$$

where

$$\chi^2 = \sum_{i=1}^{n} \left(\frac{X_i - \bar{X}}{\sigma}\right)^2. \tag{5.79}$$

The n variables $\{(X_i - \bar{X})/\sigma; \ 1 \le i \le n\}$ included in the last expression satisfy the relation

$$\sum_{i=1}^{n} \frac{X_i - \bar{X}}{\sigma} = 0 \tag{5.80}$$

and therefore they are *linearly dependent*. We can show, however, that χ^2 may be transformed to a sum of $n - 1$ independent standard normal variables (Exercise 5.5.1). Thus, χ^2 may be written as χ_{n-1}^2, that is,

$$s^2 = \frac{\sigma^2}{n-1} \chi_{n-1}^2. \tag{5.81}$$

The distribution function of χ_n^2 depends solely on n, the degrees of freedom. The probability that χ_n^2 lies in the interval $(v, v + dv)$ is found (Exercise 5.5.2):

$$f_{\chi_n^2}(v) \, dv = \frac{v^{(n/2)-1} e^{-v/2}}{2^{n/2} \Gamma\left(\frac{n}{2}\right)} \, dv, \qquad 0 \le v < \infty \tag{5.82}$$

where $\Gamma(z)$ denotes the gamma function:

$$\Gamma(z) = \int_0^\infty t^{z-1} e^{-t} \, dt. \tag{5.83}$$

For the argument $z = n/2$, where n is a positive integer, we find

$$\Gamma(1) = 1, \qquad \Gamma\left(\frac{1}{2}\right) = \sqrt{\pi} \tag{5.84}$$

and for $n > 2$

$$\Gamma\left(\frac{n}{2}\right) = \begin{cases} \left(\dfrac{n}{2} - 1\right)!, & \text{for } n \text{ even} \\[2em] \left(\dfrac{n}{2} - 1\right)\left(\dfrac{n}{2} - 2\right)\cdots\dfrac{3}{2}\cdot\dfrac{1}{2}\sqrt{\pi}, & \text{for } n \text{ odd.} \end{cases}$$ (5.85)

For $n = 1$, we have

$$f_{\chi_1^2}(\nu) = \frac{\nu^{-1/2}e^{-\nu/2}}{\sqrt{2\pi}}, \qquad \nu > 0.$$ (5.86)

The probability density function curve is monotonically decreasing, the abscissa axis forming the asymptote, as shown in Fig. 5.8. For $n = 2$, we have the following density function:

$$f_{\chi_2^2}(\nu) = \frac{e^{-\nu/2}}{2}, \qquad \nu \geq 0$$ (5.87)

which is the exponential distribution with mean $E[\chi_2^2] = 2$. For $n = 3$, we have

$$f_{\chi_3^2}(\nu) = \frac{\nu^{1/2}e^{-\nu/2}}{\sqrt{2\pi}}, \qquad \nu \geq 0.$$ (5.88)

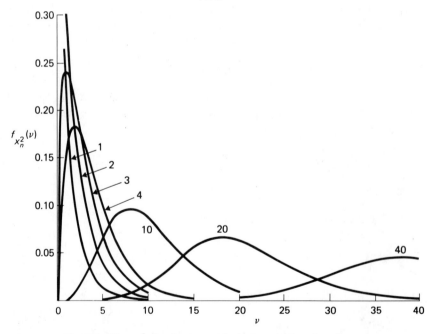

Fig. 5.8   The χ^2 distribution with degrees of freedom (n_1, n_2).

The probability density function curve originates at the point $(0, 0)$ and increases until $\nu = 1$, beyond which it decreases monotonically. For the value $n > 3$, the distribution curve takes a course similar to that for $n = 3$. Figure 5.8 gives the probability density function curves for several values of n. The expectation of χ_n^2 is equal to the number of d.f.:

$$E[\chi_n^2] = n, \tag{5.89}$$

which is immediate from the definition of the χ^2 variable. The *mode*, the abscissa of the maximum of the curve, is equal to $n - 2$, and the variance is

$$\text{Var}[\chi_n^2] = 2n. \tag{5.90}$$

The χ^2 distribution is related to a number of the probability distribution functions we studied in Chapter 3: the gamma distribution, the Erlangian distribution, and the Poisson distribution. In order to demonstrate this, we make the change of variable

$$Y_n = \frac{\chi_n^2}{2} \tag{5.91}$$

in the probability density function of the χ_n^2 distribution. We then obtain

$$f_{Y_n}(y) = \frac{y^{(n/2)-1} e^{-y}}{\Gamma\left(\dfrac{n}{2}\right)} \tag{5.92}$$

which is a special case of the gamma distribution (3.25) in which the parameters α and β are

$$\alpha = 1, \qquad \beta = \frac{n}{2}. \tag{5.93}$$

If we consider only the case in which n is an even integer, that is,

$$n = 2k, \tag{5.94}$$

then Eq. (5.92) is reduced to

$$f_{Y_{2k}}(y) = \frac{y^{k-1} e^{-y}}{(k-1)!} \tag{5.95}$$

which is the k-stage Erlangian distribution with mean k. The above result is easily understood if we recognize that the sum of the squares of two independent standard normal variables is distributed exponentially with mean two (see Eq. (5.87) and Exercise 5.5.4). Hence, Y of (5.91) is equivalent to the sum of k independent exponential variables, each of which has mean unity.

From the set of results shown above, we find the following relation between the chi-square distribution and the Poisson distribution:

$$P[\chi_{2k}^2 > 2\lambda] = \int_\lambda^\infty \frac{y^{k-1}e^{-y}}{(k-1)!}\, dy$$

$$= \int_\lambda^\infty P(k-1; y)\, dy = Q(k-1; \lambda) \qquad (5.96)$$

where the function $\{P(k;\lambda); k = 0, 1, 2, \ldots\}$ is the Poisson distribution with mean λ and $\{Q(k;\lambda); k = 0, 1, 2, \ldots\}$ is its cumulative distribution (see Section 3.9.2).

5.5.2 The Student's t-Distribution

From the reproductive property of the normal distribution, we can show that the sample mean $\bar{X}$ of n independent observations $\{X_1, X_2, \ldots, X_n\}$ from the population $N(\mu, \sigma^2)$ is normally distributed according to $N(\mu, \sigma^2/n)$. Thus, the variable U defined by

$$U = \frac{(\bar{X} - \mu)\sqrt{n}}{\sigma} \qquad (5.97)$$

is a standard normal variable. If σ is known and μ is to be estimated from the sample mean, then we can use tables of the standard normal distribution to test whether U is significantly different from zero. (See Section 5.6.2 on the significant test and confidence statement.) In practice, however, we do not know the population variance σ^2, hence we must replace σ^2 by its estimate s^2, the sample variance defined in Eq. (5.9). Thus, we introduce a new statistic:

$$t_{n-1} = \frac{(\bar{X} - \mu)\sqrt{n}}{s}. \qquad (5.98)$$

By using the relation between s^2 and χ_{n-1}^2 given by (5.81), we can write

$$t_{n-1} = \frac{(\bar{X} - \mu)\sqrt{n}/\sigma}{s/\sigma} = \frac{U}{\sqrt{\chi_{n-1}^2/(n-1)}}. \qquad (5.99)$$

Thus, the distribution of t_{n-1} depends only on $n - 1$, the d.f. for s^2. The distribution of the variable t_{n-1} is called the Student's t-distribution (or simply the t-distribution) with $(n - 1)$ degrees of freedom. We can obtain (Exercise 5.5.5) the probability density function of the t-distribution for k

degrees of freedom as

$$f_{t_k}(t) = \frac{\Gamma\left(\dfrac{k+1}{2}\right)}{\Gamma\left(\dfrac{k}{2}\right)\sqrt{\pi k}} \left(1 + \frac{t^2}{k}\right)^{-(k+1)/2}, \qquad -\infty < t < \infty. \qquad (5.100)$$

For $k = 1$, the distribution reduces to

$$f_{t_1}(t) = \frac{1}{\pi(1 + t^2)} \qquad (5.101)$$

which is Cauchy's distribution (discussed in Section 2.7). For $k = 2$, we have

$$f_{t_2}(t) = (2 + t^2)^{-3/2} \qquad (5.102)$$

which has zero mean but infinite variance. As one may expect, the t-distribution is more dispersed than the normal distribution is, since the use of s rather than σ introduces additional uncertainty. Moreover, while there is one standard normal distribution, there is a whole family of t-distributions. With small sample size, this distribution is considerably more spread out than the normal distribution, but as sample size increases, the t-distribution approaches the normal distribution. Figure 5.9 shows the distribution curves for various values of k.

Since the t-distribution is symmetric around $t = 0$, all odd moments of the distribution (5.100) that exist are zero. As for the even moments

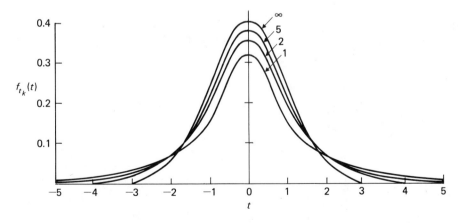

Fig. 5.9 The student's t-distribution with k degrees of freedom ($k = 1, 2, 5, \infty$).

that exist, we have from (5.99)

$$E[t_k^{2r}] = E[(\chi_1^2)^r]E\left[\left(\frac{\chi_k^2}{k}\right)^{-r}\right]$$ (5.103)

since U^2 is equivalent to the χ_1^2 variable. Hence, using the result of Exercise 5.5.6, we find

$$E[t_k^{2r}] = \frac{k^r\Gamma\left(\frac{1}{2} + r\right)\Gamma\left(\frac{k}{2} - r\right)}{\Gamma\left(\frac{1}{2}\right)\Gamma\left(\frac{k}{2}\right)},$$ (5.104)

which shows that the 2rth moment exists if and only if $-1 < 2r < k$. The *mean* and *variance* of the t_k-distribution can, therefore, be defined for $k > 1$ and $k > 2$, respectively, and have values

$$E[t_k] = 0, \qquad \text{Var}\,[t_k] = \frac{k}{k - 2}.$$ (5.105)

Applications of the t-distribution will be given in later sections.

5.5.3 The F-Distribution

Suppose that random variables V_1 and V_2 are statistically independent, having the chi-square distributions with n_1 and n_2 degrees of freedom, respectively. We define the variable F_{n_1,n_2}, or simply F, by

$$F = \frac{V_1/n_1}{V_2/n_2}.$$ (5.106)

Then we can show that the probability that F falls in the interval $(x, x + dx)$ is given by

$$f_F(x)\,dx = \frac{\Gamma\left(\frac{n_1 + n_2}{2}\right)\left(\frac{n_1}{n_2}\right)^{n_1/2}}{\Gamma\left(\frac{n_1}{2}\right)\Gamma\left(\frac{n_2}{2}\right)}\,x^{(n_1/2)-1}\left(1 + \frac{n_1 x}{n_2}\right)^{-(n_1+n_2)/2}\,dx, \quad x > 0$$ (5.107)

which is called the *F-distribution* (F stands for Fisher[*]) with n_1, n_2 degrees of freedom. The F-distribution is often referred to as the

---

[*] However, the random variable originally proposed by Fisher was z defined by $z = \frac{1}{2}\ln F$.

variance-ratio distribution or the *Snedecor distribution*. The above distribution can be derived in a manner similar to the derivation of the *t*-distribution (Exercise 5.5.7): Start with the joint probability density function of V_1 and V_2; then obtain the joint probability density function of F and V_2, and take the marginal distribution of F.

The *r*th moment of the *F*-distribution is given by (Exercise 5.5.6)

$$E[F^r] = \frac{\left(\dfrac{n_2}{n_1}\right)^r \Gamma\left(\dfrac{n_1}{2} + r\right)\Gamma\left(\dfrac{n_2}{2} - r\right)}{\Gamma\left(\dfrac{n_1}{2}\right)\Gamma\left(\dfrac{n_2}{2}\right)} \tag{5.108}$$

which exists only for $-n_1 < 2r < n_2$. Thus, the mean and variance of F are given by

$$E[F] = \frac{n_2}{n_2 - 2} \quad \text{for} \quad n_2 > 2 \tag{5.109}$$

and

$$\text{Var}[F] = \frac{2n_2^2(n_1 + n_2 - 2)}{n_1(n_2 - 2)^2(n_2 - 4)} \quad \text{for} \quad n_2 > 4. \tag{5.110}$$

The *mode*, the value for which F is maximum, is given by

$$\text{mode } F = \frac{n_2(n_1 - 2)}{n_1(n_2 + 1)}. \tag{5.111}$$

Figure 5.10 shows the *F*-curves for several pairs of (n_1, n_2).

Suppose that we have two normal populations $N(\mu_i, \sigma_i^2)$, $i = 1, 2$. Assume that we have independent observations of sample size n_i, with s_i^2 as their sample variances. In the previous section we have seen that s_i^2/σ_i^2 is χ^2-distributed with $(n_i - 1)$ degrees of freedom, $i = 1, 2$. Then the ratio of the sample variances is

$$\frac{s_1^2}{s_2^2} = \frac{\sigma_1^2}{\sigma_2^2} F_{n_1-1, n_2-1}. \tag{5.112}$$

Therefore, the *F*-distribution is used to test the equality of two sample variances. It will be extensively discussed in the analysis of variance (Section 5.7).

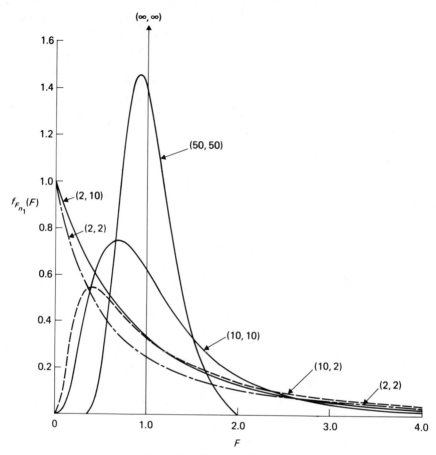

Fig. 5.10 The F-distribution.

Exercises

5.5.1 Show that χ^2 of (5.79) is a sum of $(n - 1)$ independent standard normal variables.

5.5.2 *Derivation of the χ^2-distribution.* The region of the $\mathbf{U} = (U_1, U_2, \ldots, U_n)$ space such that

$$\chi < \sqrt{U_1^2 + U_2^2 + \cdots + U_n^2} < \chi + d\chi, \qquad \chi > 0$$

is a hypershell with inner radius χ and outer radius $\chi + d\chi$. The volume dV of such a shell is proportional to its thickness $d\chi$ and to the $(n - 1)$ power of its radius χ:

$$dV = A\chi^{n-1}\, d\chi$$

where the constant A will be determined below.

a) Show that the probability density function of χ_n is given by

$$f_{\chi_n}(\chi) \, d\chi = \frac{A}{(2\pi)^{n/2}} \chi^{n-1} e^{-\chi^2/2} \, d\chi, \qquad \chi > 0.$$

b) Show that the probability density function of χ_n^2 is given by

$$f_{\chi_n^2}(v) \, dv = \frac{A}{2(2\pi)^{n/2}\sqrt{v}} v^{(n-1)/2} e^{-v/2} \, dv, \qquad v > 0.$$

c) Show that the constant A is given by

$$A = \frac{2(2\pi)^{n/2}}{\Gamma\!\left(\dfrac{n}{2}\right) 2^{n/2}}.$$

5.5.3 *Moments and characteristic functions of the gamma and χ^2-distributions.*

a) Consider the gamma distribution

$$f_X(x) = \frac{x^{\beta-1} e^{-x}}{\Gamma(\beta)}.$$

Show that the mth moment is

$$E[X^m] = \frac{\Gamma(\beta + m)}{\Gamma(\beta)}, \qquad m = 1, 2, \ldots,$$

and that its characteristic function is

$$\phi_X(\Theta) = (1 - i\Theta)^{-\beta}.$$

b) Show that the χ_n^2 has the mth moment

$$E[(\chi_n^2)^m] = \frac{2^m \Gamma\!\left(\dfrac{n}{2} + m\right)}{\Gamma\!\left(\dfrac{n}{2}\right)}, \qquad m = 1, 2, 3, \ldots,$$

and its characteristic equation

$$\phi_{\chi_n^2}(\Theta) = (1 - 2i\Theta)^{-n/2}.$$

5.5.4 Show (without having recourse to (5.87)) that if X_1 and X_2 are independent standard normal variables, their squared sum

$$Y = X_1^2 + X_2^2$$

is exponentially distributed with mean 2.

5.5.5 *Derivation of the t-distribution.*

a) Show that the joint probability density function of U and χ_{n-1}^2 is given by

$$f_{U, \chi_{n-1}^2}(u, v) \, du \, dv = \frac{1}{2\sqrt{2\pi}\Gamma\!\left(\dfrac{n-1}{2}\right)} \left(\frac{v}{2}\right)^{(n-3)/2} e^{-(u^2+v)/2}.$$

b) By applying the transformation (5.99) and noting the Jacobian of this transformation is $\sqrt{\nu/n - 1}$, show that the joint probability density function of t_{n-1} and χ^2_{n-1} is

$$f_{t_{n-1}\chi^2_{n-1}}(t, \nu) \, dt \, d\nu = \frac{1}{2\sqrt{\pi(n-1)}\,\Gamma\left(\dfrac{n-1}{2}\right)} \left(\frac{\nu}{2}\right)^{(n-2)/2} e^{-(\nu/2)[1+t^2/(n-1)]} \, dt \, d\nu.$$

c) Taking the marginal distribution of t, show that the distribution of t_{n-1} is

$$f_{t_{n-1}}(t) = \frac{\Gamma\left(\dfrac{n}{2}\right)}{\sqrt{\pi(n-1)}\,\Gamma\left(\dfrac{n-1}{2}\right)} \left(1 + \frac{t^2}{n-1}\right)^{-n/2}.$$

5.5.6 Show that the rth moment of the F-distribution is given by Eq. (5.108). *Hint:* Use the result of Exercise 5.5.3 on the χ^2-distribution.

5.5.7 Show that when the degree of freedom in the numerator of F is one, the F- and t-distributions have a simple relation.

5.6 EXPERIMENTS AND STATISTICAL INFERENCE

5.6.1 Controlled Variables and Uncontrolled Variables

Before mathematics can be used to answer questions about a given physical situation, it is necessary to describe the situation in mathematical terms. The mathematical description contains certain assumptions or approximations whose purpose is to keep unimportant details from obscuring the problem. This description, if it is properly done, can become a mathematical model. We are now interested in setting up a mathematical model to describe inference problems about the aggregate or population on the basis of a sample of results actually observed.

Our model for experimental measurement involves the assumption that we can obtain a random sample from the population, and it is this assumption that most often causes troubles. When the population in which we are interested and the population from which we can sample are not identical, any statements we make about the former population are only as good as our assumption that the two populations are equivalent with respect to the characteristics that we measure in the latter.

We will begin with a basic quantitative experiment measuring a single quantity. We will use the equation

$$Y = \mu + \varepsilon(\mathbf{U}) \tag{5.113}$$

as the basis for a mathematical model for inference. Here Y represents an observation, μ is the "true" value of the quantity being measured, and $\mathbf{U}$ is the set of *uncontrolled* variables that cause the discrepancy $\varepsilon(\mathbf{U})$ between μ and Y. The quantity $\varepsilon(\mathbf{U})$ represents the effect of uncontrolled factors or "noise" inherent in the measurement. The conceptual quantity μ belongs to the population, while Y and $\mathbf{U}$ vary from one observation to another. Let us consider a very simple example, in which we wish to measure the utilization factor μ of the CPU of a given computer system. If an experiment is performed several times in quick succession, the contributors to $\mathbf{U}$ that change slowly compared with the intervals between measurements—such as the number of active processes (or tasks) in the system—will remain fairly constant. Our results will then look much more consistent than would be the case if the experiment were repeated at longer intervals. Clearly, the trouble here is that we are sampling from a small, homogeneous population and trying to make inferences to a much larger population whose variability we have not observed.

The difficulty mentioned above arose because we did not clearly state what and how we were to measure. We see that there are several courses of action open to us:

1. We may take further readings on randomly chosen times during a day or several days, getting a better estimate of the average value of CPU utilization μ.

2. We may control presumably significant parameters of system work load (such as the number of active processes) at some value that is of interest to us.

3. We may measure the number of active processes each time we run the experiment, and try to determine quantitatively the relationship between μ and the number of processes.

Which approach we should take depends on our objectives. Courses 2 and 3 are, of course, not open to us until we recognize the number of processes as a major cause of variability in μ.

The notion of controlled versus uncontrolled variables introduced above motivates us to distinguish between two approaches in experiments on computer systems or simulators. The first is one in which we use the same and fixed work load during many experimental runs; the second approach is one in which measurement is taken during periods of actual system operation with real and uncontrollable work loads. The first case includes benchmark tests of real systems (see Chapter 1) and experiments on trace-driven (or deterministic) simulators (see Chapter 4). It has the advantage of providing a completely controlled environment with reproducible results. The shortcoming of the benchmark tests or simulation is that conclusions inferred from such experiments are often critically dependent on the specific work load chosen, and it is difficult to extrapolate the results to other work loads. The advantage of the second approach is, of course, that we are sampling from a large population of work loads encountered at a particular installation. However, the results we collect are subject to larger variations because of the uncontrollable work load. The statistical theory of design of experiments, to be discussed in Section 5.8, provides techniques to eliminate or substantially reduce the effects of such uncontrolled variations. The variance-reducing techniques discussed in Section 4.9 are examples of such techniques available to self-driven (or probabilistic) simulation.

Let $\mathbf{X}$ represent *a set of controlled* (or at least measured) *variables*. An observation Y depends not only on $\mathbf{X}$, but also on a set of uncontrolled factors, which we again represent by $\mathbf{U}$. Now we have the following mathematical model:

$$Y = f(\mathbf{X}) + \varepsilon(\mathbf{X}, \mathbf{U}). \qquad (5.114)$$

Here $f(\mathbf{X})$ represents the dependence on $\mathbf{X}$ of μ, the true value of the quantity that we wish to measure, and $\varepsilon(\mathbf{X}, \mathbf{U})$ represents the experimental error or the effect of uncontrolled factors $\mathbf{U}$.

In fitting the present model to a problem, we often have a choice as to whether we should include a certain factor in $\mathbf{X}$ or leave it in $\mathbf{U}$. Whenever we leave a factor in $\mathbf{U}$, we are hoping that its effect will average out. Situations described by our model can be classified into two categories depending on whether $\mathbf{X}$ is a *qualitative* or *quantitative* variable. For example, in the experiment to study the CPU utilization, one component of $\mathbf{X}$ may represent a CPU dispatching algorithm, which is a qualitative variable. Or it could be the variable representing the average number of processes in the system, a quantitative variable. If $\mathbf{X}$ represents several variables, there may be some of each type.

When all the components of $\mathbf{X}$ are qualitative, the experiment becomes one of comparing the populations of Y's at the various levels of $\mathbf{X}$. The *analysis of variance method*, to be discussed in Section 5.7, is a standard statistical tool used to handle such comparisons. The effect of $\mathbf{U}$ on Y is often nearly independent of the levels of $\mathbf{X}$. In such a case our model becomes

$$Y = f(\mathbf{X}) + \varepsilon(\mathbf{U}). \qquad (5.115)$$

If all the components of $\mathbf{X}$ are quantitative, the remarks we made concerning qualitative variables still apply, but there are additional features that can now be introduced. Since the values of $\mathbf{X}$ at which observations can be made are ordered numbers, it now makes sense, for example, to try to infer from the experimental results what might take place at values of $\mathbf{X}$ between or beyond those actually used. In order to do this we must have some knowledge about the function $f(\mathbf{X})$ but this cannot be provided by experimental data. This knowledge comes from a structural model or from empirical evidence accumulated by large numbers of experiments. For example, if X is the page fault rate of a virtual memory computing system and if Y represents the percentage of time that the CPU is in the supervisor state, it is often true that

$$f(X) = \alpha + \beta X; \qquad (5.116)$$

that is, $f(X)$ is linear (at least approximately in some range of values of X). When this is the case, the entire problem may be reduced to that of estimating the parameters α and β. This problem will be treated further in the section on *regression*.

5.6.2 Degrees of Uncertainty: Significance Level and Confidence Intervals

Any inference about the population is subject to some uncertainty, unless the observed sample consists of the entire population. The degree of uncertainty can be described quantitatively by various statistical techniques. The use of significance tests and confidence intervals are among the important techniques for measuring degrees of uncertainty in making inferences about population characteristics from sample data.

Test of significance

A *significance test* can be regarded as a special case of *hypothesis testing*, which will be discussed in Section 5.7. It consists of determining whether or not a result obtained from sampled data could reasonably have been expected if a *hypothesis* about the population were assumed to be true. Some variation in properties of samples is expected due to random variations in the selection of sample observations. But if there is a *significant* deviation of an observed value from its expected value, then we are led to *reject* the hypothesis. To test any hypothesis on the basis of a random sample of observations, we must divide the sample space (that is, all possible sets of observations), $\mathbf{S}$, into two regions. If the observed sample point $\mathbf{Y} = [Y_1, Y_2, \ldots, Y_n]$ falls into one of these regions, say $\mathbf{R}$, we shall *reject* the hypothesis; if $\mathbf{Y}$ falls into the complementary region, $\mathbf{S} - \mathbf{R}$, we shall *accept* the hypothesis. $\mathbf{R}$ is called the *critical region* of the test, and $\mathbf{S} - \mathbf{R}$ is called the *acceptance region*.

If we know the probability distribution of the observation, $F_0(\mathbf{Y})$, under the hypothesis H_0 being tested, we can determine $\mathbf{R}$ in such a way that, given H_0, the probability of rejecting H_0 (that is, the probability that **Y** falls in **R**) is equal to a preassigned value α:

$$P[\mathbf{Y} \in \mathbf{R} \mid H_0] = \alpha. \qquad (5.117)$$

The value α is called the *signficance level* (or the *size*) of the test. The probability α can be arbitrarily fixed, but statistics literature often uses 0.05 and 0.01 in illustrative examples and these figures have gained much popularity as an arbitrary level to use. There is no inherent virtue in the number 0.05 or 0.01, but it is convenient to use when there is no particular basis for decision.

Perhaps it is appropriate to clarify the use of rather preemptory terms "reject" and "accept," which are conventional in statistical decision theory. These terms are not intended to imply that any hypothesis is ever finally accepted or rejected. If you cannot overcome your philosophical dislike of these admittedly inappropriate expressions, you will perhaps agree to regard them as code words, "reject" standing for "decide that the observations are unfavorable to," and "accept" for the opposite (Kendall and Stuart, 1961).

Confidence Intervals

We begin with an example concerning the mean μ of a *normal* distribution with known variance. Suppose a sample contains n observations Y_1, $Y_2, \ldots, Y_n$ and its sample mean is $\bar{Y}$. Then it is reasonable to assume that the sample mean $\bar{Y}$ is an approximation to μ, the mean of the population. But, of course, $\bar{Y}$ has some discrepancy or variation from μ, so that we should try to estimate some interval around $\bar{Y}$ such that we can predict with some *confidence* that μ falls within that interval.

We normalize the random variable $\bar{Y}$ by the transformation

$$Z = \frac{(\bar{Y} - \mu)\sqrt{n}}{\sigma}, \qquad (5.118)$$

where σ is the population variance and is assumed to be known. Thus, Z has the standard normal distribution $\phi(z)$ of Fig. 5.11, which was defined earlier in Section 2.7. This distributional form clearly does not depend on knowledge of μ; rather, the transformed variable Z involves the unknown μ. Then by letting $z_{\alpha/2}$ denote the upper $\alpha/2 \times 100$ percentile of the standard normal distribution, as shown in Fig. 5.11, we have

$$P\left[-z_{\alpha/2} \leq \frac{(\bar{Y} - \mu)\sqrt{n}}{\sigma} \leq z_{\alpha/2}\right] = 1 - \alpha. \qquad (5.119)$$

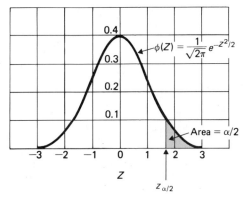

Fig. 5.11 The standard normal distribution $\phi(z)$ and its upper $100 \times \alpha/2$ percentile value $z_{\alpha/2}$.

It is not difficult to see that the inequality about Z in (5.119) can be transformed into an inequality about μ as follows:

$$P\left[\bar{Y} - z_{\alpha/2}\frac{\sigma}{\sqrt{n}} \le \mu \le \bar{Y} + z_{\alpha/2}\frac{\sigma}{\sqrt{n}}\right] = 1 - \alpha. \qquad (5.120)$$

The random interval $\bar{Y} \pm z_{\alpha/2}\sigma/\sqrt{n}$ is called a *confidence interval* and $1 - \alpha$ is the *confidence coefficient* or the *confidence level*. Very often the conventional value 0.95 is used as a confidence coefficient, for which $z_{0.025} = 1.96$. The frequency interpretation of the probability statement (5.120) is as follows: If the procedure of taking random and independent observations and constructing the associated random interval, $\bar{Y} \pm z_{\alpha/2}\sigma/\sqrt{n}$ (see Fig. 5.12), is repeated many times, approximately $(1 - \alpha) \times 100$ percent of these random intervals will contain μ. Note that the random interval in any particular case may or may not contain the value μ.

The result just obtained was based on the assumption that the population standard deviation σ was known. The experimenter is rarely so fortunate as to have such precise prior knowledge. Hence, in searching for a confidence interval of μ, it is necessary to estimate σ^2 by the sample variance s^2. If we proceed analogously with the case for known σ^2, we obtain a random variable

$$t = \frac{(\bar{Y} - \mu)\sqrt{n}}{s}. \qquad (5.121)$$

The distribution of the variable t is the Student's t-distribution with $(n - 1)$ degrees of freedom, as defined in Section 5.5.2.

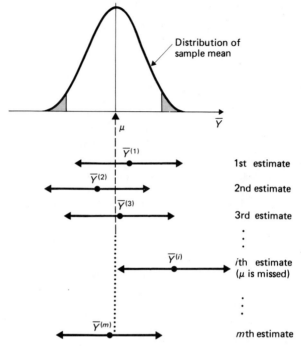

Fig. 5.12 The unknown population mean of a normal random variable and a set of m confidence intervals, each of which is based on n independent observations.

Proceeding again as in the case in which σ^2 was known, we can assert that

$$P\left[-t_{\alpha/2;n-1} \le \frac{(\bar{Y} - \mu)\sqrt{n}}{s} \le t_{\alpha/2;n-1}\right] = 1 - \alpha \qquad (5.122)$$

which is equivalent to

$$P\left[\bar{Y} - t_{\alpha/2;n-1}\frac{s}{\sqrt{n}} \le \mu \le \bar{Y} + t_{\alpha/2;n-1}\frac{s}{\sqrt{n}}\right] = 1 - \alpha. \qquad (5.123)$$

Thus, $\bar{Y} \pm t_{\alpha/2;n-1}(s/\sqrt{n})$ is a confidence interval with confidence coefficient $1 - \alpha$.

Exercises

5.6.1 *Estimating the CPU utilization factor.* Consider the problem of estimating the utilization factor μ of the CPU. We define a simple random variable Y by

$$Y = \begin{cases} 0; & \text{if CPU is idle} \\ 1; & \text{if CPU is busy.} \end{cases}$$

Assume that the time separation between successive observation instants is sufficiently large that the sample values can be regarded as statistically independent. Show that the $(1 - \alpha)$ confidence interval for the proportion, for large n, is given by

$$\bar{Y} \pm z_{\alpha/2} \sqrt{\frac{\bar{Y}(1 - \bar{Y})}{n}},$$

where $\bar{Y}$ is the sample mean given by

$$\bar{Y} = \frac{1}{n} \sum_{i=1}^{n} Y_i.$$

Hint: Use the asymptotic normality of the binomial distribution.

5.6.2 *Estimating the mean of exponential distribution.* Suppose that the CPU processing time of jobs in a certain computer system is known to be exponentially distributed with unknown mean τ. Each job is allocated a *quantum* of q seconds of CPU service. If a job is finished within the quantum, it is called a *trivial* job. Suppose that a total of N jobs are observed in a given period, out of which n jobs are trivial and the rest, $(N - n)$ jobs, are nontrivial. Show that the $(1 - \alpha)$ confidence interval for estimating τ is, for sufficiently large N, given by $[\tau^-, \tau^+]$, where

$$\tau^+ = -\frac{q}{\ln(1 - \theta^-)},$$

$$\tau^- = -\frac{q}{\ln(1 - \theta^+)},$$

and where

$$\theta^+ = \frac{n}{N} + z_{\alpha/2} \frac{\sqrt{n\left(1 - \dfrac{n}{N}\right)}}{N},$$

$$\theta^- = \frac{n}{N} - z_{\alpha/2} \frac{\sqrt{n\left(1 - \dfrac{n}{N}\right)}}{N}.$$

5.7 THE ANALYSIS OF VARIANCE

It is often useful to resolve the sample variance of a given variable into separate components of variance, that is to say, into a sum of several distinct *sums of squares*, each corresponding to a source of variation. This process is sometimes called the *analysis of variance.*

As an example, suppose that there are m different scheduling algorithms available to a given computer system. The first question we might ask is, "Does the scheduling algorithm in fact have a significant effect on the system's performance?" In order to answer this question, we compare the algorithms by choosing the CPU problem state factor (that is, the proportion of time that the CPU is doing useful work) as the measure of performance. We set up an experiment in which the system work load is set to a normal level and the CPU problem state factor can be directly measured for a specified interval. The mathematical model we set up to answer this question is similar to (5.115):

$$Y = f(X) + \varepsilon(\mathbf{U}), \tag{5.124}$$

where X is the *controlled variable* that represents the chosen scheduling algorithm and Y is an observed CPU problem state value for the specified X. Although we claim that the experiment should be conducted under a similar load condition, generally we cannot control the system work load completely, and there might possibly be other inexplicable factors; the set of these uncontrolled variables is represented by $\mathbf{U}$. Note that the variable X is a qualitative variable and let us denote by μ_i the population mean of the CPU problem state factor under scheduling algorithm i:

$$\mu_i = f(i), \qquad i = 1, 2, \ldots, m. \tag{5.125}$$

A random sample of n measurement periods is then obtained for each algorithm. Table 5.1 shows an example of a data table when $m = 3$ and $n = 5$. The table entry Y_{it} represents the CPU problem state factor of the tth period under algorithm i. The plausible first step one may take is to compute the sample average $\bar{Y}_{i.}$ of Y_{it}, $i = 1, 2, \ldots, m$:

$$\bar{Y}_{i.} = \frac{\sum_{t=1}^{n} Y_{it}}{n}, \qquad i = 1, 2, \ldots, m \tag{5.126}$$

which are also listed in Table 5.1. Now our original question can be paraphrased as follows: Are the sample means $\bar{Y}_{i.}$ in Table 5.1 different

TABLE 5.1 An example of data table Y_{it}; The CPU problem state factor of the tth measurement period under Algorithm i

Period Algorithm	$t = 1$	$t = 2$	$t = 3$	$t = 4$	$t = 5$	$\bar{Y}_{i.}$
$i = 1$	54.6	45.7	56.7	37.7	48.3	48.6
$i = 2$	53.4	57.5	54.3	52.3	64.5	56.4
$i = 3$	56.7	44.7	50.6	56.5	49.5	51.6

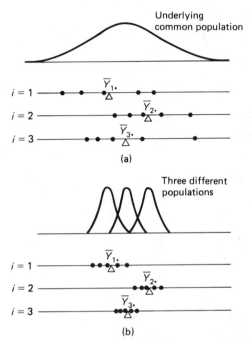

Fig. 5.13 (a) A case in which the null hypothesis is acceptable; (b) a case in which H_0 is not acceptable.

for different i because of differences in the underlying population means μ_i? Or can these differences be reasonably attributed to chance fluctuations alone?

In order to answer this, we proceed by using the formal statistical procedures called *hypothesis testing* and the corresponding analysis of variance. The hypothesis of "no difference" in the population mean is usually called the *null hypothesis* and is represented as

$$H_0: \quad \mu_1 = \mu_2 = \cdots = \mu_m = \mu, \qquad (5.127)$$

where μ is some unknown but common mean value of μ_i's. Figure 5.13(a) illustrates the situation we envision under the null hypothesis; that is, all samples could be drawn from the same population and the differences in sample means may be explained by *chance*.

Figure 5.13(b), on the other hand, shows the case in which the H_0 is not acceptable: The (same) differences in sample means can hardly be explained by chance alone, because the variance in sample means $\bar{Y}_i$. seems large in relation to the chance fluctuation within each row. In order to proceed more formally, consider the total sum of squares of the error defined by

$$Q = \sum_{i=1}^{m} \sum_{t=1}^{n} (Y_{it} - f(i))^2$$

$$= \sum_{i=1}^{m} \sum_{t=1}^{n} (Y_{it} - \mu_i)^2. \qquad (5.128)$$

The minimum value of Q *subject to the null hypothesis* H_0 is attained by choosing the following estimate of the common population mean

$$\mu^* = \bar{Y}.. = \frac{1}{m} \sum_{i=1}^{m} \bar{Y}_{i.}, \qquad (5.129)$$

where $\bar{Y}_{i.}$ is the sample mean of Y_{it} in the ith class as defined in (5.126) and $\bar{Y}..$ is the overall mean. Therefore, the minimum value of Q is given by

$$Q_T = \min_{\mu} \sum_{i=1}^{m} \sum_{t=1}^{n} (Y_{it} - \mu)^2$$

$$= \sum_{i=1}^{m} \sum_{t=1}^{n} (Y_{it} - \bar{Y}..)^2 = \sum_{i=1}^{m} \sum_{t=1}^{n} Y_{it}^2 - mn\bar{Y}...^2. \qquad (5.130)$$

This is the *total sum of squares* of deviations from the overall mean $\bar{Y}...$

The minimum value of Q *without the restriction* of the null hypothesis H_0 is achieved when we choose $\bar{Y}_{i.}$ as an estimate of the population mean μ_i:

$$Q_w = \sum_{i=1}^{m} \min_{\mu_i} \sum_{t=1}^{n} (Y_{it} - \mu_i)^2$$

$$= \sum_{i=1}^{m} \sum_{t=1}^{n} (Y_{it} - \bar{Y}_{i.})^2 = \sum_{i=1}^{m} \left(\sum_{t=1}^{n} Y_{it}^2 - n\bar{Y}_{i.}^2 \right). \qquad (5.131)$$

The quantity Q_w is a measure of the variation *within class treatment* of X (the scheduling algorithm in this example), and is usually called the *sum of squares within treatment*. Our numerical example shows that $Q_w = 429$ and $Q_T = 583.8$, hence $Q_w < Q_T$. In fact, it generally holds that $Q_w \leq Q_T$: Q_T is the minimum value under the constraint H_0, whereas Q_w is the minimum value without the constraint; hence, Q_w can be smaller than Q_T. It will then be reasonable to attribute the difference $Q_T - Q_w$ to the (possible) differences in the population means. In fact, we can show the following relation by a simple algebraic manipulation:

$$Q_b = Q_T - Q_w = n \left(\sum_{i=1}^{m} \bar{Y}_{i.}^2 - m\bar{Y}..^2 \right)$$

$$= n \sum_{i=1}^{m} (\bar{Y}_{i.} - \bar{Y}..)^2 \qquad (5.132)$$

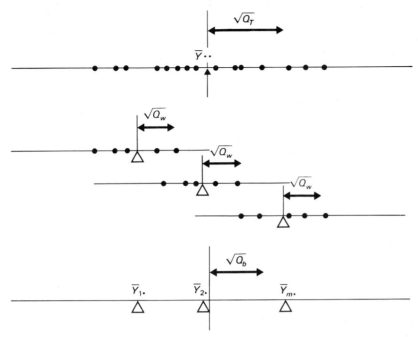

Fig. 5.14 The relationship among the total sum of squares Q_T, the sum of squares within treatment Q_w, and the sum of squares between treatments Q_b.

which is clearly a measure of dispersion *between* the m different sample means $\bar{Y}_i$.'s. Therefore, Q_b is called the *sum of squares between treatments.*

Any sum of squares has associated with it a number called its *degrees of freedom* (d.f.). This number indicates how many independent pieces of information are needed to compile the sum of squares. The total sum of squares Q_T has the degrees of freedom $mn - 1$, since all mn terms $Y_{11} - \bar{Y}.., \ldots, Y_{it} - \bar{Y}.., \ldots, Y_{mn} - \bar{Y}..$ sum to zero by definition of the total mean Y. The sum of squares Q_w has $mn - m = m(n - 1)$ degrees of freedom, since $Y_{i1} - \bar{Y}_{i.}, \ldots, Y_{it} - \bar{Y}_{i.}, \ldots, Y_{in} - \bar{Y}_{i.}$ sum to zero, for $i = 1, 2, \ldots, m$. The sum of squares Q_b has $(m - 1)$ degrees of freedom, since it contains m random variables $\bar{Y}_{i.} - \bar{Y}..$ which again add up to zero. Note that the degrees of freedom for the two components Q_b and Q_w of Q_T add to the corresponding total figure. Figure 5.14 summarizes these relationships.

Note that Q_w can be rewritten from its definition as

$$Q_w = \sum_{i=1}^{m} (n - 1)s_i^2, \tag{5.133}$$

where s_i^2 is the sample variance within the ith treatment and is an unbiased estimate of $\sigma^2 = E[\varepsilon^2(\mathbf{U})]$, the variance of observations due to the uncontrolled factor $\mathbf{U}$:

$$E[s_i^2] = \sigma^2, \qquad i = 1, 2, \ldots, m. \tag{5.134}$$

Therefore, the expectation of Q_w is

$$E[Q_w] = m(n-1)\sigma^2 \tag{5.135}$$

so that the *mean squared deviations within treatments*, $Q_w/m(n-1)$, is an unbiased estimate of σ^2. Similarly, we can show (Exercise 5.7.2) that the *mean squared deviation between treatments*, $Q_b/(m-1)$, is an unbiased estimate of

$$\sigma^2 + \frac{n}{m-1} \sum_{i=1}^{m} (\mu_i - \mu^*)^2, \tag{5.136}$$

where

$$\mu^* = \frac{1}{m} \sum_{i=1}^{m} \mu_i. \tag{5.137}$$

Now if the H_0 is true, that is, if $\mu_1 = \mu_2 = \cdots = \mu_m = \mu^*$, then the sum of squares appearing in (5.136) will be zero, and $Q_w/m(n-1)$ and $Q_b/(m-1)$ should have comparable values since they both estimate σ^2. Therefore, the original question can now be stated: "Is $Q_b/(m-1)$ large relative to $Q_w/m(n-1)$?" So we examine the ratio

$$F = \frac{Q_b/(m-1)}{Q_w/m(n-1)} \tag{5.138}$$

called the *variance ratio* or *F-ratio*. The distribution of this statistic is the F-distribution discussed earlier in Section 5.5.3. If H_0 is true, the F-ratio will have, on the average, a value near 1. On the other hand, if H_0 is not true, F will be larger than 1. The formal test of H_0 exploits the distribution of the test statistic F. When H_0 of (5.127) is true in the example of Table 5.1, the exact distribution of F should look like Fig. 5.15. The critical $F_{0.05}$ value, cutting off five percent of the upper tail of the distribution, is also shown. For the data in Table 5.1, an evaluation of (5.138) yields $F = 77.4/35.75 = 2.165$. Since this is below the critical $F_{0.05}$ value of 3.89, the hypothesis H_0 cannot be rejected; in other words, the observed differences in the means are not significant enough and can be reasonably explained by chance fluctuations. This formal test confirms our earlier intuitive conclusion.

The computation procedure discussed in this section can be summarized in the form presented in Table 5.2. This analysis of variance

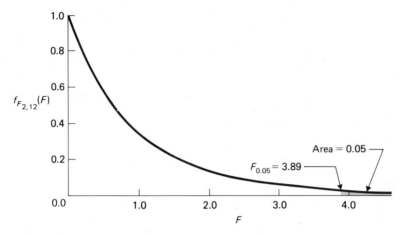

Fig. 5.15 The distribution of the F-statistic for the degrees of freedom $2 \, (=m-1)$ and $12 \, (=m(n-1))$.

table, often called the ANOVA table, has been almost universally accepted as the particular form for reporting computation results. The numerical example that we discussed in this section (Table 5.1) can therefore be reported in Table 5.3.

The F-distribution in Fig. 5.15 is only one of many, as was shown in Fig. 5.10; there are different distributions depending on the degrees of freedom $m - 1$ and $m(n - 1)$ in the numerator and the denominator, respectively. The more degrees of freedom in calculating both numerator and denominator, the closer these two estimates of variance will be to their target σ^2; thus, the more closely their ratio will concentrate around 1. This is illustrated in Fig. 5.10. Critical points for the F-distributions are tabulated in most mathematical handbooks and statistics textbooks.

TABLE 5.2   THE ANALYSIS OF VARIANCE (ANOVA) TABLE.

Source of variation	Degrees of freedom	Sum of squares	Mean squared deviation	Test statistic
Between classes	$m - 1$	$Q_b = n\left(\sum\limits_{i=1}^{m} \bar{Y}_{i\cdot}^2 - m\bar{Y}_{\cdot\cdot}^2 \right)$	$s_b^2 = Q_b/(m - 1)$	
Within classes	$m(n - 1)$	$Q_w = Q_T - Q_b$	$s_w^2 = Q_w/m(n - 1)$	$F = s_b^2/s_w^2$
Total	$mn - 1$	$Q_T = \sum\limits_{i=1}^{m} \sum\limits_{t=1}^{n} Y_{it}^2 - mn\bar{Y}_{\cdot\cdot}^2$		

TABLE 5.3   THE ANOVA TABLE THAT CORRESPONDS TO THE DATA OF TABLE 5.1.

Source of variation	Degrees of freedom	Sum of squares	Mean squared deviation	Test statistic
Between algorithms	2	$Q_b = 154.8$	$s_b^2 = 77.4$	
Within algorithms	12	$Q_w = Q_T - Q_b = 429$	$s_w^2 = 35.75$	$F = 2.17$
Total	14	$Q_T = 583.8$		

Exercises

5.7.1 Suppose that the entries of Table 5.1 are replaced by the table given below.

Algorithm \ Period	$t = 1$	$t = 2$	$t = 3$	$t = 4$	$t = 5$
$i = 1$	48.4	49.7	48.7	48.5	47.7
$i = 2$	56.1	56.3	56.9	57.6	55.1
$i = 3$	52.1	51.1	51.6	52.1	55.1

Conduct the analysis of variance. Will you reject the hypothesis (5.127) at the significance level of five percent?

5.7.2 Prove Eq. (5.136). *Hint:* Show

$$E[(\bar{Y}_{i.} - \bar{Y}_{..} - \eta_i)^2] = E[(\bar{Y}_{i.} - \bar{Y}_{..})^2] - \eta_i^2$$

where

$$\eta_i = \mu_i - \mu^* = E[\bar{Y}_{i.} - \bar{Y}_{..}].$$

5.7.3 *Analysis of variance with samples of unequal sizes.* Generalize the analysis of variance method to samples with unequal sizes. Let the size of the samples in the ith class (or treatment) be denoted by n_i, and let

$$\sum_{i=1}^{m} n_i = N.$$

The hypothesis we test is H_0 of (5.127).

    a) Find the expression for Q_T, Q_w, and Q_b.
    b) How should we generalize the F-ratio of (5.138)?
    c) Write down the analysis of variance table.

5.7.4 Two page replacement algorithms—algorithms A and B—were implemented on a virtual machine system.* In order to eliminate the effects of work-load variations, the algorithm was switched between A and B every five

---

* A more comprehensive treatment of this experimental data is given in Y. Bard and M. Schatzoff (1978).

minutes (see Bard (1973) for details of this experimental procedure). A summary of the resulting data is presented below.

RESULTS OF PAGING EXPERIMENT

Day	Response time		Problem state time		Page Read Rate	
	A	*B*	*A*	*B*	*A*	*B*
1	7.0	8.4	45.6	42.6	29.0	29.7
2	7.6	8.5	49.7	43.6	30.0	32.6
3	7.7	10.4	39.5	37.5	26.9	32.1
4	12.1	16.6	42.8	39.3	33.1	36.1
Average	8.6	11.0	44.0	40.7	19.7	32.6

Conduct the analyses of variance, and discuss the significance of the performance difference between the two algorithms.

5.8 DESIGN OF EXPERIMENTS

5.8.1 Principles of Randomization

Thus far we have lumped all of the causes of error into one category called the uncontrolled variables $\mathbf{U}$; the corresponding error term $\varepsilon(\mathbf{U})$ represents any deviation from the quantity we wish to measure. In order to describe some of the problems that arise in practice, it is helpful to classify the causes of error according to the physical circumstances that generate them. In computer system performance evaluation, we can think of at least the following three categories: (1) variation due to system changes, (2) uncontrolled conditions on system work load, and (3) measurement errors.

The first of the above list is clear. Any experiment that involves system changes during the measurement period will introduce variations that are often difficult to assess. Such changes may include hardware changes (e.g., the capacity of main storage, the number of channels, etc.) and/or software changes (e.g., choice of resource allocations policies, scheduling parameters, etc.). The second of the list—uncontrolled conditions—are those factors that may effect the outcome of the experiment, but are not controlled by the experimentor as are the factors represented by the variable $\mathbf{X}$. Measurements and evaluations carried out with live work loads are such instances, whereas evaluations with fixed benchmark work loads may be regarded as controlled experiments. The third category—measurement errors—refers to measurements made on **X** as well as those made on the response variable *Y*.

In almost any sampling situation we rarely obtain *uncorrelated* (or *random*) *errors*. For example, several measurements of a system taken in a short interval will usually resemble one another more closely than will measurements taken randomly in time: In other words, errors have a natural tendency to be correlated. It is usually easier to collect samples all at one time than to spread the measurement efforts out over a longer period of time. It is clear, however, that such sampling tends to provide a poor basis for inference except for the particular time at which sampling was done. Furthermore, the apparent consistency among the observations tends to lead us into a false feeling of confidence in the answer. The difficulty is that the subpopulation chosen for sampling tends to be more homogeneous than the entire population, so the expected *random errors* are actually an unseen *systematic error* or *bias*. We can regard systematic error or bias as being the result of sampling from the wrong population, that is, from some population different from the one to which inferences are to be made. Often, in assessing various system configurations or scheduling algorithms, an unrecognized causal factor may change during the course of the sequence of experiments in such a way as to favor a particular treatment (e.g., a particular scheduling algorithm); this treatment will then appear to be highly effective, when it is really the unrecognized factor that is producing the apparently good results.

A device called *randomization* is used to circumvent this difficulty. The *principle of randomization* originally propounded by R. A. Fisher (1935) is as follows.

1. Randomize the allotment of treatments to experimental units so that every treatment will have an equal chance of being assigned to each experimental unit.

2. Randomize the sequence in which treatments are applied so that we can keep the effect of uncontrolled variables that vary slowly with time from being confused with the effect of the controlled variable.

3. Randomize places at which experiments take place. (This procedure may not usually apply to the measurement and evaluation of computer systems, since it is rare that we conduct measurements of more than one system in parallel.)

The arrangement specified above is called a *completely randomized design*. Randomization is a mechanism which tends to put systematic errors (unknown to the experimenter) into the random errors. The advantage of replacing systematic error by random error is that with repeated observations random errors can be measured—for example, by computing the observed variance. In other words, randomization provides a basis for probabilistic measures of uncertainty such as confidence intervals or significance levels.

5.8.2 Restricted Randomization and One-Factor Experimental Design

We have seen how randomization can help us to avoid the appearance of bias even in the presence of unrecognized or uncontrolled variables, but this means only that our experimentation is valid on the average. In order to achieve high *precision*, we generally need to take many observations. As we have seen above, complete randomization is effective in helping us to remove bias, even if we know nothing about the nature of uncontrolled variables. In many practical cases, however, some knowledge of the patterns in uncontrolled conditions is available, which makes certain systematic arrangements very attractive. With some prior knowledge of unattended causal factors, it is then possible to make more precise comparisons of different treatments by grouping the experimental units into *blocks* of units, so that units within a block resemble each other with respect to the uncontrolled variables more than units in different blocks do. This layout is called a *randomized block design*. An application example of the *blocking* technique to compute performance evaluation is discussed in a paper by Bard (1973). His objective is to compare the performance of two different page replacement algorithms under live load conditions. The system is instrumented so that the page replacement algorithm is switched automatically back and forth every five minutes. Thus, each ten-minute interval forms a block, which includes two experimental units. Work-load variations between blocks can then be eliminated from the comparison of the two algorithms. Randomization was not used in Bard's experiment since he felt that there was no possibility of systematic or biased behavior in work loads over successive ten-minute intervals.

In general, the manner in which the experimental units are arranged into blocks, the method of assigning various treatments (or combinations of treatments) to the units within blocks, and a plan for analysis and interpretation of the results together constitute the theory of *statistical design of experiments*. The effects of the variations between blocks in block experiments will be eliminated by applying the analysis of variance as a computational device. Consider, for example, a time-sharing system that uses round-robin scheduling. We want to examine whether the value of time slice q affects the average response time Y. We will measure Y

for m different values of the quantum size, q_i, $i = 1, 2, \ldots, m$. However, we expect that the work load slowly changes during the time of the day and this uncontrolled causal factor may vary in such a way as to dominate the effect of the quantum size. One obvious method used to avoid such an effect is the completely randomized design, in which different time quantum sizes are assigned randomly to different observation intervals. Let Y_{it} stand for the average response of the tth experimental unit under the ith treatment (that is, quantum size q_i), where $i = 1, 2, \ldots, m$ and $t = 1, 2, \ldots, n$ (in this case, an experimental unit represents one observation interval and we assume that each treatment is given n experimental units). Thus, the total sum of squares of deviation from the mean value $\bar{Y}..$ is

$$\sum_{i=1}^{m} \sum_{t=1}^{n} (Y_{it} - \bar{Y}..)^2 = \sum_{i=1}^{m} \sum_{t=1}^{n} (Y_{it} - \bar{Y}_{i.})^2 + n \sum_{i=1}^{m} (\bar{Y}_{i.} - \bar{Y}..)^2$$

or

$$Q_T = Q_w + Q_b \tag{5.140}$$

where Q_T, Q_w, and Q_b stand for the total sum of squares, the sum of squares within-treatments, and the sum of squares between-treatments, respectively, as defined in (5.130)–(5.132). Then the "variance ratio" is given, as we saw in Section 5.7, by

$$F = \frac{Q_b/(m-1)}{Q_w/m(n-1)}. \tag{5.141}$$

If the "time of the day" effect is changing slowly compared with the length of an observation interval, then the following *restricted randomization* will be effective. Number the observation intervals consecutively along the time of day, $1, 2, \ldots, m, \ldots$. Count these off in blocks of size m $(1, 2, \ldots, m)$, $(m + 1, m + 2, \ldots, 2m)$, $(2m + 1, 1m + 2, \ldots, 3m), \ldots$. Now within each block assign m different time quanta (or treatments) at random to the m observation intervalus (or experimental units). This arrangement is an example of a *randomized block design*. The analysis of variance can be performed by assuming that the block and treatment effects are additive; the total sum of the squares of deviation from the mean value is then

$$\sum_{i=1}^{m} \sum_{t=1}^{n} (Y_{it} - \bar{Y}..)^2 = n \sum_{i=1}^{m} (\bar{Y}_{i.} - \bar{Y}..)^2 + m \sum_{t=1}^{n} (\bar{Y}_{.t} - \bar{Y}..)^2$$

$$+ \sum_{i=1}^{m} \sum_{t=1}^{n} \{Y_{it} - \bar{Y}_{.t} - (\bar{Y}_{i.} - \bar{Y}..)\}^2$$

$$\tag{5.142}$$

or

$$Q_T = Q_b + Q_B + Q_E, \qquad (5.143)$$

where Q_B and Q_E stand for sums of squares for *blocks* and for *errors*, respectively. What was called Q_w is now divided into two parts:

$$Q_w = Q_B + Q_E. \qquad (5.144)$$

Now the effect of the variations between blocks is evaluated, and we wish to eliminate it from our test. The variance ratio we use for testing whether or not the time quantum (i.e., different treatments) affects the response time (i.e., the observable) is now given by

$$F = \frac{Q_b/(m-1)}{Q_E/(m-1)(n-1)}. \qquad (5.145)$$

5.8.3   Factorial Experiments

We often wish to test various types of treatments, each with several different choices. For example, one might wish to compare two different paging algorithms (say, $X_1 = \text{LRU}$, $X_2 = \text{FIFO}$), and two different page sizes (say, $Z_1 = 1k$ words, $Z_2 = 4k$ words), giving a total of four treatment combinations $(X_1Z_1, X_2Z_1, X_1Z_2, X_2Z_2)$; this is called a 2×2, or 2^2 *factorial experiment.* Each variable that is to be controlled in a designed experiment is called a *factor.* Each value that a factor can take is called a *level* of that factor. For instance, in an experiment of comparing the two page replacement algorithms, the algorithm is a factor and its two choices (LRU and FIFO) are its levels. A factorial experiment with two factors, one at m levels and the other at m' levels, is called an $(m \times m')$-factorial experiment, and contains $m \times m'$ different treatments. The theory of the design of experiments is concerned with principles for setting up experiments so as to estimate the *effects* of the different treatments on the response variable(s) of interest as efficiently as possible.

A general model for a factorial experiment with two factors X and Z is given by

$$Y = f(X, Z) + \varepsilon(X, Z, \mathbf{U}), \qquad (5.146)$$

where $\mathbf{U}$ again represents a set of uncontrolled variables. Using the factorial model, the effect of any treatment combination is considered to be the sum of three effects: the two *main effects* (the X-effect and the Z-effect) and the *interaction effect* of X and Z. A main effect is one that corresponds to variation of a single factor. The interaction effect is one that corresponds to simultaneous variation of the two factors; it measures whether the effect of various X-levels is the same for each level of Z or conversely, the Z-effect on each level of X. The model generalizes in an obvious fashion to an experiment with p (>2) factors. An important principle inherent in factorial experiments is that we should vary factors simultaneously rather than one factor at a time. This is because only simultaneous variation permits us to estimate the interactions. Needless to say, each of the main effects can also be estimated from the observations of a factorial experiment.

Let us consider an $(m \times m')$-factorial experiment with n observations in each treatment $Y_{ij1}, Y_{ij2}, \ldots, Y_{ijn}$, $1 \leq i \leq m$, $1 \leq j \leq m'$, which are distributed according to $E[Y_{ijt}] = \mu_{ij}$ and $\mathrm{Var}[Y_{ijt}] = \sigma^2$. Let us derive the following parameters from μ_{ij}:

$$\mu_{i\cdot} = \frac{1}{m'} \sum_{j=1}^{m'} \mu_{ij}, \tag{5.147}$$

$$\mu_{\cdot j} = \frac{1}{m} \sum_{i=1}^{m} \mu_{ij}, \tag{5.148}$$

and

$$\mu = \frac{1}{m} \sum_{i=1}^{m} \mu_{i\cdot} = \frac{1}{m'} \sum_{j=1}^{m'} \mu_{\cdot j} = \frac{1}{mm'} \sum_{i=1}^{m} \sum_{j=1}^{m'} \mu_{ij}. \tag{5.149}$$

Then we may write the following identity

$$\mu_{ij} = \mu + (\mu_{i\cdot} - \mu) + (\mu_{\cdot j} - \mu) + (\mu_{ij} - \mu_{i\cdot} - \mu_{\cdot j} + \mu). \tag{5.150}$$

Letting $\alpha_i = \mu_{i\cdot} - \mu$, $\beta_j = \mu_{\cdot j} - \mu$, and $\gamma_{ij} = \mu_{ij} - \mu_{i\cdot} - \mu_{\cdot j} + \mu$, it may be shown that

$$\sum_{i=1}^{m} \alpha_i = \sum_{j=1}^{m'} \beta_j = \sum_{i=1}^{m} \gamma_{ij} = 0. \tag{5.151}$$

If we assume that the error term ε is independent of X and Z, our model becomes

$$Y_{ijt} = \mu_{ij} + \varepsilon_{ijt}(\mathbf{U}) \tag{5.152}$$

$$\mu_{ij} = \mu + \alpha_i + \beta_j + \gamma_{ij}, \tag{5.153}$$

where the parameters are referred to as follows: μ = the overall mean; α_i = the main effect of factor X at level i; β_j = the main effect of factor Z at level j; and γ_{ij} = the interaction effect of factor X at level i and factor Z at level j. This model is often called the *fixed-effects* analysis of variance model, which is essentially a special case of the linear regression model to be discussed in Section 5.9.

The main hypotheses we wish to test are

$$H_0: \alpha_i = \beta_j = \gamma_{ij} = 0 \quad \text{for} \quad i = 1, 2, \ldots, m; j = 1, 2, \ldots, m' \tag{5.154}$$

and

$$H_1: \gamma_{ij} = 0 \quad \text{for} \quad i = 1, 2, \ldots, m; j = 1, 2, \ldots, m'. \tag{5.155}$$

If H_0 is true, then there is no difference between the means of the various treatments (or level combinations). The hypothesis H_1 says that effects due to factors X and Z are additive. If H_1 is rejected, the conclusion is that these factors are not additive or that factors X and Z interact, and the difference between X-levels cannot be specified without reference to a particular Z-level and vice versa.

Following the same procedure that we adopted in Section 5.7, we first compute the minimum value of the sum of squares of error

$$Q = \sum_{i=1}^{m} \sum_{j=1}^{m'} \sum_{t=1}^{n} (Y_{ijt} - \mu_{ij})^2 \tag{5.156}$$

subject to the conditions of the various hypotheses. Let us consider first the minimization of Q under H_0. By differentiating

$$Q = \sum_{i=1}^{m} \sum_{j=1}^{m'} \sum_{t=1}^{n} (Y_{ijt} - \mu)^2 \tag{5.157}$$

with respect to μ and setting it to zero, we obtain the solution

$$\mu^* = \frac{1}{mm'n} \sum_{i=1}^{m} \sum_{j=1}^{m'} \sum_{t=1}^{n} Y_{ijt} = \bar{Y}_{....} \tag{5.158}$$

Therefore, the minimum value of Q under the constraint of H_0 is given as

$$Q_T = \min_{H_0} Q = \sum_{i=1}^{m} \sum_{j=1}^{m'} \sum_{t=1}^{n} (Y_{ijt} - \mu^*)^2$$

$$= \sum_{i=1}^{m} \sum_{j=1}^{m'} \sum_{t=1}^{n} Y_{ijt}^2 - mm'n\bar{Y}_{....}^2. \tag{5.159}$$

which represents the total sum of the squares of deviation from the overall mean $\bar{Y}_{....}$.

Similarly, we compute the minimum value of Q under the hypothesis H_1:

$$Q_1 = \min_{H_1} Q = \min_{\alpha_i \beta_j} \left\{ \sum_{i=1}^{m} \sum_{j=1}^{m'} \sum_{t=1}^{n} (Y_{ijt} - \alpha_i - \beta_j)^2 \right\}$$

$$= Q_T - m'n \left(\sum_{i=1}^{m} \bar{Y}_{i..}^2 - m\bar{Y}_{...}^2 \right) - mn \left(\sum_{j=1}^{m'} \bar{Y}_{.j.}^2 - m'\bar{Y}_{...}^2 \right), \tag{5.160}$$

where

$$\bar{Y}_{i..} = \frac{1}{m'n} \sum_{j=1}^{m'} \sum_{t=1}^{n} Y_{ijt} \qquad (5.161)$$

and

$$\bar{Y}_{.j.} = \frac{1}{mn} \sum_{i=1}^{m} \sum_{t=1}^{n} Y_{ijt.} \qquad (5.162)$$

The second and third terms of (5.160) represent the sum of the squares of dispersion between X-factor levels and Z-factor levels, respectively:

$$Q_{bX} = m'n \sum_{i=1}^{m} (\bar{Y}_{i..} - \bar{Y}_{...})^2 = m'n \left(\sum_{i=1}^{m} \bar{Y}_{i..}^2 - m\bar{Y}_{...}^2 \right), \quad (5.163)$$

and

$$Q_{bZ} = mn \sum_{j=1}^{m'} (\bar{Y}_{.j.} - \bar{Y}_{...})^2 = mn \left(\sum_{j=1}^{m'} \bar{Y}_{.j.}^2 - m'\bar{Y}_{...}^2 \right). \quad (5.164)$$

Hence, we can write (5.160) as

$$Q_T = Q_1 + Q_{bX} + Q_{bZ}. \qquad (5.165)$$

The minimum value of Q without any restriction is similarly calculated and given by

$$\begin{aligned}
Q_w &= \min_{\mu_{ij}} \left\{ \sum_{i=1}^{m} \sum_{j=1}^{m'} \sum_{t=1}^{n} (Y_{ijt} - \mu_{ij})^2 \right\} \\
&= \sum_{i=1}^{m} \sum_{j=1}^{m'} \left(\sum_{t=1}^{n} Y_{ijt}^2 - n\bar{Y}_{ij.}^2 \right) \\
&= Q_T - n \left(\sum_{i=1}^{m} \sum_{j=1}^{m'} \bar{Y}_{ij.}^2 - mm'\bar{Y}_{...}^2 \right), \qquad (5.166)
\end{aligned}$$

where

$$\bar{Y}_{ij.} = \frac{1}{n} \sum_{t=1}^{n} Y_{ijt.} \qquad (5.167)$$

The second term in the expression for Q_w is the dispersion of the mean of mm' cells, which we call Q_b, the sum of the squares between mm' cells:

$$Q_b = n \sum_{i=1}^{m} \sum_{j=1}^{m'} (\bar{Y}_{ij.} - \bar{Y}_{...})^2 = n \left(\sum_{i=1}^{m} \sum_{j=1}^{m'} \bar{Y}_{ij.}^2 - mm'\bar{Y}_{ij...}^2 \right); \qquad (5.168)$$

hence

$$Q_T = Q_w + Q_b. \qquad (5.169)$$

The dispersion between cells Q_b can be further decomposed into Q_{bX}, Q_{bZ}, and Q_{XZ}, which represent the sum of the squares between X-factor levels, Z-factor levels, and the *interaction* between X and Z, respectively:

$$Q_b = Q_{bX} + Q_{bZ} + Q_{XZ}, \tag{5.170}$$

where the interaction term is obtained from (5.163), (5.164), and (5.168), as

$$Q_{XZ} = Q_b - Q_{bX} - Q_{bZ}$$

$$= n \left\{ \sum_{i=1}^{m} \sum_{j=1}^{m'} (\bar{Y}_{ij \cdot} - \bar{Y}_{\cdots})^2 - m' \sum_{i=1}^{m} (\bar{Y}_{i \cdots} - \bar{Y}_{\cdots})^2 - m \sum_{j=1}^{m'} (\bar{Y}_{\cdot j \cdot} - \bar{Y}_{\cdots})^2 \right\}$$

$$= n \left\{ \sum_{i=1}^{m} \sum_{j=1}^{m'} \bar{Y}_{ij \cdot}^2 - m' \sum_{i=1}^{m} \bar{Y}_{i \cdots}^2 - m \sum_{j=1}^{m'} \bar{Y}_{\cdot j \cdot}^2 + mm' \bar{Y}_{\cdots}^2 \right\}. \tag{5.171}$$

The scheme of computation is summarized in Table 5.4, where the mean square term of each row is the sum of the squares divided by its degree of freedom. A variety of hypotheses can be tested:

1. The ratio $F = s_b^2/s_w^2$ is the test statistic for testing the hypothesis H_0: Under H_0 of (5.154), the random variable F will be distributed according to the F-distribution with degrees of freedom $(mm' - 1)$ and $(n - 1)mm'$. Therefore, H_0 will be rejected if F exceeds the critical value $F_{\alpha; mm'-1, (n-1)mm'}$.

2. The ratio $F = s_{XZ}^2/s_w^2$ is used to test the significance of the interaction effect between factors X and Z; that is, under H_1 of (5.155) the random variable F will be distributed according to the F-distribution with degrees of freedom $(m - 1)(m' - 1)$ and $(n - 1)mm'$.

3. The variance ratio $F = s_{bX}^2/s_w^2$ is used to test whether differences exist between classes of X-factors when averaged over all Z-classes used in the experiment (although there may be differences between X-classes for a particular level of Z-factor). In other words, the hypothesis to be tested is

$$H_2: \mu_{1 \cdot} = \mu_{2 \cdot} = \cdots = \mu_{m \cdot}. \tag{5.172}$$

Similarly, the variance ratio $F = s_{bY}^2/s_w^2$ is used to test

$$H_3: \mu_{\cdot 1} = \mu_{\cdot 2} = \cdots = \mu_{\cdot m'}. \tag{5.173}$$

A few examples of factorial experiments used to compute performance studies have been reported in recent years. Tsao, Comeau, and Margolin (1972) apply a factorial experiment and the corresponding analysis of variance to their study of the system performance in a paging

TABLE 5.4 THE ANOVA TABLE FOR AN $m \times m'$ FACTORIAL EXPERIMENT.

Source of variation	Degrees of freedom	Sum of squares	Mean squared deviation	Test statistics
Between X-factor levels	$m-1$	$Q_{bX} = m'n\left(\sum_{i=1}^{m} \bar{Y}_{i\cdot\cdot}^2 - m\bar{Y}_{\cdots}^2\right)$	$s_{bX}^2 = \dfrac{Q_{bX}}{m-1}$	$F = \dfrac{s_{bX}^2}{s_w^2}$ (for testing H_2)
Between Z-factor levels	$m'-1$	$Q_{bZ} = mn\left(\sum_{j=1}^{m'} \bar{Y}_{\cdot j\cdot}^2 - m'\bar{Y}_{\cdots}^2\right)$	$s_{bZ}^2 = \dfrac{Q_{bZ}}{m'-1}$	$F = \dfrac{s_{bZ}^2}{s_w^2}$ (for testing H_3)
Interaction between X and Z	$(m-1)(m'-1)$	$Q_{XZ} = Q_b - Q_{bX} - Q_{bZ}$	$s_{XZ}^2 = \dfrac{Q_{XZ}}{(m-1)(m'-1)}$	$F = \dfrac{s_{XZ}^2}{s_w^2}$ (for testing H_1)
Between mm' cells (subtotal)	$mm'-1$	$Q_b = n\left(\sum_{i=1}^{m}\sum_{j=1}^{m'} \bar{Y}_{ij\cdot}^2 - mm'\bar{Y}_{\cdots}^2\right)$	$s_b^2 = \dfrac{Q_b}{mm'-1}$	$F = \dfrac{s_b^2}{s_w^2}$ (for testing H_0)
Within cells	$mm'(n-1)$	$Q_w = Q_T - Q_b$	$s_w^2 = \dfrac{Q_w}{mm'(n-1)}$	
Total	$mm'n-1$	$Q_T = \sum_{i=1}^{m}\sum_{j=1}^{m'}\sum_{l=1}^{n} Y_{ijl}^2 - mm'n\bar{Y}_{\cdots}^2$		

environment. Schatzoff and Tillman (1975) discuss factorial experiments as a means of statistical calibration and validation of a trace-driven simulator.

As the number of factors for inclusion increases, the total number of different treatments grows quite rapidly: It is given by the product of the factor levels. In order to economize on the cost of experiments, an experimental design technique called *fractional factorial design* may be used, which eliminates some portion of the factor-level combinations. This is done at the expense of discarding information on higher-order interactions. Such an arrangement is justifiable in many cases when the main effects and low-order interactions are sufficient to characterize the performance problems in question. The aforementioned article by Schatzoff and Tillman discusses the use of the $\frac{1}{2}$-fraction of a 2^5 factorial design.

5.9   REGRESSION ANALYSIS AND EMPIRICAL MODELS

5.9.1   The Method of Least Squares and Regression Curves

The advantages of the experimental design and corresponding analysis of variance, as discussed in the previous section, are found mainly in those cases in which the objective of the experiment is to measure certain effects associated with *qualitative variables* and to measure their various interactions. Often we wish to obtain more than this: We may want to obtain a description of the function $f(X)$ over the range of some *quantitative variable(s)*. We now discuss situations involving such analysis.

Suppose there are m observations Y_i, where

$$Y_i = f(X_i; \ \alpha, \beta, \gamma, \ldots) + \varepsilon_i, \qquad i = 1, 2, \ldots, m \qquad (5.174)$$

and X_i represents the value of a quantitative variable X at which Y_i is observed. Note that the last equation is a generalization of (5.124) in which X was a qualitative variable. Here the variable X may be again a *controlled variable* fixed at each of several levels, whereas Y represents an *observed random variable*. The following argument can be extended, however, to the problem of considering the *joint variation* of two measurements, X_i and Y_i, neither of which is controlled–by the experimenter. The parameters α, β, γ, ... represent unknown constants, and the functional form $f(X; \alpha, \beta, \gamma, \ldots)$ is assumed known except for these parameters. Our prior knowledge of the structured model describes $f(X)$ except for certain parameters that are to be estimated from the data. When the theory is insufficient to provide this information, we may resort to the empirical expedient of using some arbitrarily selected function that seems to have about the right shape; this procedure may be useful for *interpolation*, but it cannot be safely used for *extrapolation*.

The estimation of the parameters α, β, γ, ... is usually done by the *method of least squares.* We let

$$Q = \sum_{i=1}^{m} \{Y_i - f(X_i;\ \alpha, \beta, \gamma, \ldots)\}^2 \tag{5.175}$$

represent, as a function of α, β, γ, ..., the sum of the squares of deviation of the observed points from the resulting curve. The reader will see that (5.175) is an extension of (5.128). The least-square estimates of α, β, γ, ... are those that minimize Q. Estimating an equation is equivalent to fitting a curve through a *scatter diagram* plotting Y_i versus X_i. This is called the *regression* of Y on X. More formally, the regression of Y on X is defined as the *conditional expectation* of Y given X, that is, the mean of the distribution of all Y's that may be observed for the given X. In this usage we shall speak of Y as a *dependent* or *response variable* and X as an *independent* or *predictor variable.* Suppose that $f(X;\ \alpha, \beta, \gamma, \ldots)$ is a linear in α, β, γ, ... : The function, for example, takes the form $f(X) = \alpha + \beta X + \gamma X^2$, $f(X) = \alpha + \beta X + \gamma \log X$, etc. Assume that X is measured without error, that the error ε in measuring Y has zero mean and constant variance σ^2, and that the errors in measuring Y are not correlated with one another. Then it can be shown (by what is known as the Gauss-Markov theorem) that the estimates of α, β, γ, ... provided by the method of least squares are *unbiased* and also have the least variance of any linear unbiased estimates.

In view of the analysis of variance discussed in the preceding sections, the total sum of the squares of deviation from the mean value is expressed as

$$Q_T = \sum_{i=1}^{m} (Y_i - \bar{Y})^2 = \sum_{i=1}^{m} (Y_i - \hat{Y}_i)^2 + \sum_{i=1}^{m} (\hat{Y}_i - \bar{Y})^2$$

$$= Q_{aR} + Q_{bR}, \tag{5.176}$$

where $\hat{Y}_i$ is the *predicted value*, that is, the value on the regression curve corresponding to X_i:

$$\hat{Y}_i = f(X_i;\ \alpha, \beta, \gamma, \ldots). \tag{5.177}$$

The term Q_{aR} represents variation *about the regression curve*, and Q_{bR} is the sum of the squares of deviation *between the values on the regression curve*, that is, the variation of Y explained by regression.

Example 5.1 (Linear regression).   Consider, for instance, the following simple regression equation

$$f(X) = \alpha + \beta X. \tag{5.178}$$

Then the sum of the squares of deviation is given by

$$Q = \sum_{i=1}^{m} (Y_i - \alpha - \beta X_i)^2 \tag{5.179}$$

and we obtain the least-square estimates of *regression coefficients* as

$$\hat{\beta} = \frac{\sum_{i=1}^{m} (X_i - \bar{X}) Y_i}{\sum_{i=1}^{m} (X_i - \bar{X})^2} \tag{5.180}$$

and

$$\hat{\alpha} = \bar{Y} - \hat{\beta} \bar{X}, \tag{5.181}$$

where

$$\bar{X} = \frac{1}{m} \sum_{i=1}^{m} X_i \tag{5.182}$$

and

$$\bar{Y} = \frac{1}{m} \sum_{i=1}^{m} Y_i. \tag{5.183}$$

Therefore, we obtain the following regression equation:

$$f(X) = \bar{Y} + \hat{\beta}(X - \bar{X}). \tag{5.184}$$

It can be shown (Exercise 5.9.1) that the estimators $\hat{\alpha}$ and $\hat{\beta}$ have the following properties:

$$E[\hat{\alpha}] = \alpha, \tag{5.185}$$

$$\text{Var}[\hat{\alpha}] = \frac{\sigma^2}{n} \frac{\sum_{i=1}^{m} X_i^2}{\sum_{i=1}^{m} (X_i - \bar{X})^2}, \tag{5.186}$$

$$E[\hat{\beta}] = \beta, \tag{5.187}$$

and

$$\text{Var}[\hat{\beta}] = \frac{\sigma^2}{\sum_{i=1}^{m} (X_i - \bar{X})^2}, \tag{5.188}$$

where the expectation is taken with respect to the Y for given X's; σ^2 is the variance of the error ε. The expression for the slope $\hat{\beta}$ can be transformed as follows:

$$\hat{\beta} = \frac{\sum_{i=1}^{m} (X_i - \bar{X})(Y_i - \bar{Y})}{\sum_{i=1}^{m} (X_i - \bar{X})^2} = \frac{r_{YX} s_Y}{s_X}, \tag{5.189}$$

where s_Y^2 and s_X^2 are sample variances of the data Y_i and X_i, respectively, and r_{YX} is the sample correlation coefficient between Y and X:

$$r_{YX} = \frac{1}{m-1} \sum_{i=1}^{m} \frac{(X_i - \bar{X})}{s_X} \cdot \frac{(Y_i - \bar{Y})}{s_Y}$$

$$= \frac{\sum_{i=1}^{m} (X_i - \bar{X})(Y_i - \bar{Y})}{\sqrt{\sum_{i=1}^{m} (X_i - \bar{X})^2 \cdot \sum_{i=1}^{m} (Y_i - \bar{Y})^2}}. \tag{5.190}$$

This close relationship between $\hat{\beta}$ and r_{YX} plays an important role in the following discussion.

From (5.184), we have

$$\hat{Y}_i - \bar{Y} = \hat{\beta}(X_i - \bar{X}). \tag{5.191}$$

Therefore, we can write Q_{bR} as

$$Q_{bR} = \hat{\beta}^2 \sum_{i=1}^{m} (X_i - \bar{X})^2 = r_{YX}^2 \sum_{i=1}^{m} (Y_i - \bar{Y})^2, \tag{5.192}$$

which leads to the following expression for r_{YX}^2:

$$r_{YX}^2 = \frac{Q_{bR}}{Q_T}$$

$$= \frac{\text{Variance of } Y \text{ explained by regression}}{\text{Total variation of } Y}. \tag{5.193}$$

This equation provides a clear intuitive interpretation of r_{YX}^2. The square of the correlation coefficient, r_{YX}^2, is therefore often called the *coefficient of determination*. It is the proportion of the total variation of Y explained by fitting the linear regression (see Fig. 5.16).

From the relation established by (5.176) and (5.193), the following null hypothesis test on β may be constructed: The question is whether the ratio of the explained variance Q_{bR} to the unexplained variance Q_{aR} is sufficiently large to reflect the hypothesis that Y is unrelated to X. Specifically, a test of the hypothesis

$$H_0: \beta = 0 \tag{5.194}$$

involves forming the ratio

$$F = \frac{Q_{bR}}{Q_{aR}/(m-2)} = \frac{\hat{\beta}^2 \sum_{i=1}^{m} (X_i - \bar{X})^2}{s_{aR}^2}, \tag{5.195}$$

which has an F-distribution with degrees of freedom 1 and $m-2$. The mean squared dispersion s_{aR}^2 defined in the last expression is an estimate of σ^2. Note that the same test can be performed by the t-statistic with

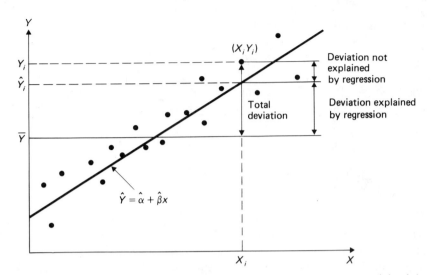

Fig. 5.16 Variation explained by regression versus variation not explained by regression.

$(m - 2)$ degrees of freedom:

$$t = \frac{\hat{\beta}}{\sqrt{s_{aR}^2 / \sum_{i=1}^{m}(X_i - \bar{X})^2}}. \tag{5.196}$$

In fact, the F- and t-distributions are related by $F = t^2$ when the degree of freedom in the numerator of F is one (Exercises 5.5.7 and 5.9.5).

5.9.2   Test for the Form of Regression Curve

As we mentioned earlier, we often discuss the fitting of an approximate regression curve in cases in which regressions are not exactly linear. To test the hypothesis regarding the form of the regression curve, we use the analysis of variance technique. Let

$$Y_{it} = f(X_i; \ \alpha, \beta, \gamma, \ldots) + \varepsilon_{it}, \qquad t = 1, 2, \ldots, n_i \tag{5.197}$$

be observed variables when the variable X takes on the ith level X_i, $i = 1, 2, \ldots, m$. With *multiple observations* for given X_i's, we now partition $Y_{it} - \bar{Y}_{..}$ into a sum of three deviations:

$$Y_{it} - \bar{Y}_{..} = (Y_{it} - \bar{Y}_{i.}) + (\bar{Y}_{i.} - \hat{Y}_i) + (\hat{Y}_i - \bar{Y}_{..}), \tag{5.198}$$

where $\hat{Y}_i$ is given by (5.177); in other words, the value of the regression $f(X)$ curve at $X = X_i$. $\bar{Y}_{i.}$ is the sample mean of class i:

$$\bar{Y}_{i.} = \frac{\sum_{t=1}^{n_i} Y_{it}}{n_i}, \qquad i = 1, 2, \ldots, m \tag{5.199}$$

and $\bar{Y}_{..}$ is the overall mean of Y_{it} given by

$$\bar{Y}_{..} = \frac{\sum_{t=1}^{n_i} \sum_{t=1}^{n_i} Y_{it}}{\sum_{i=1}^{m} n_i} = \frac{1}{N} \sum_{i=1}^{m} n_i \bar{Y}_{i\cdot}, \qquad (5.200)$$

where $N = \sum_{i=1}^{m} n_i$ is the total number of observations. Squaring and summing (5.198) leads to the following results:

$$
\begin{aligned}
Q_T &= \sum_{i=1}^{m} \sum_{t=1}^{n_i} (Y_{it} - \bar{Y}_{..})^2 \\
&= \sum_{i=1}^{m} \sum_{t=1}^{n_i} (Y_{it} - \bar{Y}_{i\cdot})^2 + \sum_{i=1}^{m} n_i(\bar{Y}_{i\cdot} - \hat{Y}_i)^2 + \sum_{i=1}^{m} n_i(\hat{Y}_i - \bar{Y}_{..})^2 \\
&= Q_w + Q_{aR} + Q_{bR}, \qquad (5.201)
\end{aligned}
$$

where Q_w is the variation within classes, Q_{aR} represents the variation about the regression curve, and Q_{bR} is the variation of Y that can be explained by the regression curve. Alternative expressions for Q_T, Q_w, and $Q_{aR} + Q_{bR} = Q_R$ are given as follows:

$$Q_T = \sum_{i=1}^{m} \sum_{t=1}^{n_i} Y_{it}^2 - N\bar{Y}_{..}^2; \qquad (5.202)$$

$$Q_w = \sum_{i=1}^{m} \left(\sum_{t=1}^{n_i} Y_{it}^2 - n_i \bar{Y}_{i\cdot}^2 \right); \qquad (5.203)$$

and

$$Q_R = Q_{aR} + Q_{bR} = \sum_{i=1}^{m} n_i(\bar{Y}_{i\cdot} - \bar{Y}_{..})^2 = \sum_{i=1}^{m} n_i \bar{Y}_{i\cdot}^2 - N\bar{Y}_{..}^2. \qquad (5.204)$$

Thus, we obtain the analysis of variance table, as given in Table 5.5.

The hypothesis regarding the form of the regression curve is tested by

$$F = \frac{s_{aR}^2}{s_w^2} = \frac{Q_{aR}/(m - 2)}{Q_w/(N - m)}, \qquad (5.205)$$

which has an F-distribution with degrees of freedom $m - 2$ and $N - m$, if the hypothesis is true and the observation errors are normally distributed.

Example 5.2 (Test for the straight line regression).   If the regression is a straight line, as we discussed in the previous section, the sum of the squared dispersions between the values on the regression line is given by

$$
\begin{aligned}
Q_{bR} &= \hat{\beta}^2 \sum_{i=1}^{m} n_i(X_i - \bar{X})^2 \\
&= \hat{\beta}^2 \left[\sum_{i=1}^{m} n_i X_i^2 - \frac{1}{N} \left(\sum_{i=1}^{m} X_i \right)^2 \right], \qquad (5.206)
\end{aligned}
$$

TABLE 5.5 THE ANOVA TABLE OF REGRESSION ANALYSIS.

Source of variation	Degrees of freedom	Sum of squares	Mean squared deviation	Test statistic
Between values on regression curve	1	$Q_{bR} = \sum_{i=1}^{m} n_i(\hat{Y}_i - \bar{Y}_{..})^2$	$s_{bR}^2 = Q_{bR}$	$F = \dfrac{s_{bR}^2}{s^2}$ (for testing $\beta = 0$)
About regression curve	$m - 2$	$Q_{aR} = Q_R - Q_{bR}$	$s_{aR}^2 = \dfrac{Q_{aR}}{m - 2}$	$F = \dfrac{s_{aR}^2}{s_w^2}$ (for testing linearity)
Subtotal	$m - 1$	$Q_R = \sum_{i=1}^{m} n_i \bar{Y}_{i.}^2 - N\bar{Y}_{..}^2$		
Within classes	$N - m$	$Q_w = Q_T - Q_R$	$s_w^2 = \dfrac{Q_w}{N - m}$	
Total	$N - 1$	$Q_T = \sum_{i=1}^{m}\sum_{t=1}^{n_i} Y_{it}^2 - N\bar{Y}_{..}^2$		

where

$$N = \sum_{i=1}^{m} n_i, \qquad \hat{Y}_i = f(X_i;\ \hat{\alpha}, \hat{\beta}, \hat{\gamma}, \ldots), \qquad \bar{Y}_{i.} = \frac{\sum_{t=1}^{n_i} Y_{it}}{n_i},$$

$$\bar{Y}_{..} = \frac{1}{N}\sum_{i=1}^{m}\sum_{t=1}^{n_i} Y_{it} = \frac{1}{N}\sum_{i=1}^{m} n_i \bar{Y}_{i.},$$

and

$$s^2 = \frac{Q_T - Q_{bR}}{N - 2} = \frac{1}{N - 2}\{(N - m)s_w^2 + (m - 2)s_{aR}^2\}.$$

where the expression of the regression coefficient $\hat{\beta}$ is obtained by a straightforward generalization of (5.189):

$$\hat{\beta} = \frac{\sum_{i=1}^{m} n_i (X_i - \bar{X}) \bar{Y}_{i.}}{\sum_{i=1}^{m} n_i (X_i - \bar{X})^2}$$

$$= \frac{\sum_{i=1}^{m} n_i (X_i - \bar{X})(\bar{Y}_{i.} - \bar{Y}_{..})}{\sum_{i=1}^{m} n_i (X_i - \bar{X})^2}. \qquad (5.207)$$

If the variance ratio F of (5.205) is significantly large, the hypothesis of linearity must be rejected. If F is not significant, then the hypothesis $\beta = 0$ can be tested by the test statistic

$$F = \frac{s_{bR}^2}{s^2}, \qquad (5.208)$$

where s^2 is the sample estimate of variation *not explained by regression*:

$$s^2 = \frac{\sum_{i=1}^{m} \sum_{t=1}^{n_i} (Y_{it} - \hat{Y}_i)^2}{\sum_{i=1}^{m} n_i - 2} = \frac{Q_w + Q_{aR}}{N - 2}, \qquad (5.209)$$

which is often referred to as the *residual variance*. The divisor $(N - 2)$ is used rather than $N - 1$, since in the calculation of s^2 two estimators $\hat{\alpha}$ and $\hat{\beta}$ are required; thus two degrees of freedom are lost for s^2.

5.9.3 Confidence Intervals of Linear Regression

Let us continue the linear regression discussed in the previous sections. For a given, perhaps new, value of X, say X_0, what is the interval that will predict the *mean value* of Y_0? The appropriate estimator of $E[Y_0]$ is clearly $\hat{Y}_0$, the value on our estimated regression line above X_0:

$$\hat{Y}_0 = \hat{\alpha} + \hat{\beta} X_0 = \bar{Y}_{..} + \hat{\beta}(X_0 - \bar{X}). \qquad (5.210)$$

But as a *point estimator*, this will almost certainly involve some error because of errors made in the estimates of $\hat{\alpha}$ and $\hat{\beta}$. It is not difficult to show that

$$\text{Cov}[\bar{Y}_{..}, \hat{\beta}] = 0; \qquad (5.211)$$

that is, $\bar{Y}_{..}$ and $\hat{\beta}$ are *uncorrelated* random variables. We can show that the variance of the predicted mean $\hat{Y}_0$ at a specific value X_0 is (Exercise 5.9.2):

$$\text{Var}[\hat{Y}_0] = \sigma^2 \left[\frac{1}{N} + \frac{(X_0 - \bar{X})^2}{\sum_{i=1}^{m} n_i (X_i - \bar{X})^2} \right], \qquad (5.212)$$

where σ^2 is the variance of observation errors ε_{it} of (5.197). Now, if we add the strong assumption that observation errors are normally distributed, it follows that $\bar{Y}_{..}$ and $\hat{\beta}$ are also normal. As a consequence, $\hat{Y}_0$

will be normal too. But even without assuming the normality of Y_{it}, the distributions of $\hat{\beta}$ and $\bar{Y}..$ will usually approach normality, as the sample size increases. It follows, therefore, that $\hat{Y}_0$ is also asymptotically normally distributed. Hence, the confidence interval for the mean value $E[Y_0]$ for the level of $(1 - \alpha)$ is

$$\hat{Y}_0 \pm z_{\alpha/2}\sigma \sqrt{\frac{1}{N} + \frac{(X_0 - \bar{X})^2}{\sum_{i=1}^{m} n_i(x_i - \bar{X})^2}}, \qquad i = 1, 2, \ldots, m$$

(5.213)

or in the usual case in which an unknown σ must be replaced with s:

$$\hat{Y}_0 \pm t_{\alpha/2;N-2}s \sqrt{\frac{1}{N} + \frac{(X_0 - \bar{X})^2}{\sum_{i=1}^{m} n_i(X_i - \bar{X})^2}}.$$

(5.214)

Here

$$s^2 = \frac{\sum_{i=1}^{m} \sum_{t=1}^{n_i} (Y_{it} - \hat{Y}_i)^2}{N - 2},$$

(5.215)

as was defined in (5.209). The t-distribution has $(N - 2)$ degrees of freedom.

Now, for a given X_0, what is the confidence interval of the predicted value of an *individual observation*? Once again, the best estimate is $\hat{Y}_0$, the point on the estimated regression line above X_0. But in this case, it is necessary to estimate the variance of the difference between the ordinate on the computed regression line $\hat{Y}_0$ and the corresponding true ordinate Y_0:

$$E[(Y_0 - \hat{Y}_0)^2] = \mathrm{Var}\,[Y_0] + \mathrm{Var}\,[\hat{Y}_0]$$

$$= \sigma^2 \left[1 + \frac{1}{N} + \frac{(X_0 - \bar{X})^2}{\sum_{i=1}^{m} n_i(X_i - \bar{X})^2}\right].$$

(5.216)

In other words, to our previous variance (5.212) is now added the inherent variance σ^2 of an individual Y observation. The prediction interval for Y_0 is, therefore, given in the following form:

$$\hat{Y}_0 \pm t_{\alpha/2;N-2}s \sqrt{1 + \frac{1}{N} + \frac{(X_0 - \bar{X})^2}{\sum_{i=1}^{m} n_i(X_i - \bar{X})^2}}.$$

(5.217)

The relationship between prediction and confidence intervals is shown in Fig. 5.17. Note how both bands expand as X_0 moves further away from its central value $\bar{X}$; this reflects the fact that $(X_0 - \bar{X})^2$ appears in both variances.

We emphasize that, in formulas (5.213) and (5.217), X_0 may be any value of X. If X_0 lies among the values $X_1, X_2, \ldots, X_m$, the process is

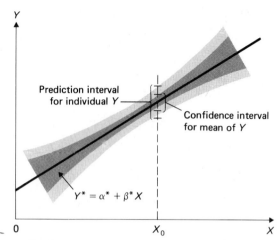

Fig. 5.17   Confidence interval of Y versus the predictor variable X.

called *interpolation*. If X_0 is out beyond the observed X's, then the process is called *extrapolation*. In both cases, there is no sharp division between safe interpolation and dangerous extrapolation. Rather, there is the continually increasing danger of misinterpretation as X_0 gets further and further away from its central value.

Exercises

5.9.1 Verify the properties (5.185)–(5.188) of the regression coefficient estimates.

5.9.2 Derive the expression (5.212). *Hint:* From (5.210) we have

$$\text{Var}\,[\hat{Y}_0] = \text{Var}\,[\bar{Y}..] + (X_0 - \bar{X})^2\,\text{Var}\,[\hat{\beta}].$$

5.9.3 *Sample correlation ratio.* Refer to the problem of analyzing the linearity of regression. Define the *sample correlation ratio* of Y on X by

$$e^2_{Y|X} = \frac{\sum_{i=1}^{m} n_i(\bar{Y}_{i\cdot} - \bar{Y}..)^2}{\sum_{i=1}^{m}\sum_{t=1}^{n_i}(Y_{it} - \bar{Y}..)^2}$$

$$= \frac{Q_R}{Q_T} = \frac{Q_{aR} + Q_{bR}}{Q_T}.$$

a) Show that

$$e^2_{Y|X} = 1 - \frac{Q_w}{Q_T}.$$

Also show that $e^2_{Y|X} = 1$ if and only if observed variables Y_{it}'s show no variation within classes of X_i; in other words, every observation lies on the *regression curve*, so that Y and X are strictly functionally related; $e^2_{Y|X}$ approaches zero when there is no reduction in error due to the use of knowledge about X.

b) Show that

$$r^2 \leq e^2_{Y|X}$$

with the equality holding only when the regression of Y on X is exactly linear.

c) Explain the relationship between X and Y for the following cases: (1) $r^2 = 0$; (2) $r^2 = e^2_{Y|X} = 1$; (3) $r^2 \leq e^2_{Y|X} = 1$; (4) $r^2 = e^2_{Y|X} < 1$; and (5) $r^2 < e^2_{Y|X} < 1$.

d) Show that the statistic $e^2_{Y|X} - r^2$ will provide a test of linearity of regression of Y on X, by proving that

$$\frac{(e^2_{Y|X} - r^2)/(m - 2)}{(1 - e^2_{Y|X})/(N - m)}$$

is equivalent to the F-value defined by (5.205).

5.9.4   Multiple Regression Analysis

Multiple regression is the extension of simple regression to take account of the effect of more than one independent X variable on the dependent variable Y. It is obviously an appropriate technique when we want to investigate the effect on Y of several variables simultaneously. Yet, even if we are interested in the effect of only one variable on Y, it is usually wise to include the other variables influencing Y in a multiple regression analysis for two reasons:

1. To reduce residual variance, i.e., stochastic error, which represents the variability of Y due to many omitted variables, each with an individually small effect. Statistical tests and confidence intervals are strengthened.

2. To eliminate a bias that might result if we were to ignore an uncontrolled variable that substantially affects Y.

Suppose that the response variable, Y, is now to be regressed on p independent variables (or factors) and assume that there are $n(\geq p)$ observations:

$$Y_t = \beta_0 + \beta_1 X_{1t} + \beta_2 X_{2t} + \cdots + \beta_p X_{pt} + \varepsilon_t, \qquad t = 1, 2, \ldots, n \tag{5.218}$$

where X_{jt} is the value of the jth variable at which Y_t is observed; $\beta_0, \beta_1, \ldots, \beta_p$ represent unknown regression coefficients, and the ε_t's are error variables (not necessarily normally distributed) with

$$E[\varepsilon_t] = 0 \tag{5.219}$$

and

$$E[\varepsilon_t \varepsilon_s] = \begin{cases} \sigma^2; & t = s \\ 0; & t \neq s. \end{cases} \qquad (5.220)$$

We now use matrix notation and rewrite the *regression plane* of (5.218) as

$$\mathbf{Y} = \mathbf{X}'\boldsymbol{\beta} + \boldsymbol{\varepsilon} \qquad (5.221)$$

where $\mathbf{Y}$ and $\boldsymbol{\varepsilon}$ are m-dimensional column vectors whose tth elements are Y_t and ε_t, respectively; $\boldsymbol{\beta}$ is a $(p + 1)$-dimensional column vector whose entries are $\beta_0, \beta_1, \ldots, \beta_p$:

$$\mathbf{Y} = \begin{bmatrix} Y_1 \\ Y_2 \\ \cdot \\ \cdot \\ \cdot \\ Y_t \\ \cdot \\ \cdot \\ \cdot \\ Y_n \end{bmatrix}, \quad \boldsymbol{\varepsilon} = \begin{bmatrix} \varepsilon_1 \\ \varepsilon_2 \\ \cdot \\ \cdot \\ \cdot \\ \varepsilon_t \\ \cdot \\ \cdot \\ \cdot \\ \varepsilon_n \end{bmatrix}, \quad \boldsymbol{\beta} = \begin{bmatrix} \beta_0 \\ \beta_1 \\ \beta_2 \\ \cdot \\ \cdot \\ \cdot \\ \beta_i \\ \cdot \\ \cdot \\ \cdot \\ \beta_p \end{bmatrix} \qquad (5.222)$$

and $\mathbf{X}'$ is an $n \times (p + 1)$ matrix and is the *transpose* of the following matrix $\mathbf{X}$:

$$\mathbf{X} = \begin{bmatrix} 1 & 1 & \cdots & 1 & \cdots & 1 \\ X_{11} & X_{12} & \cdots & X_{1t} & \cdots & X_{1n} \\ X_{21} & X_{22} & \cdots & X_{2t} & \cdots & X_{2n} \\ \cdot & \cdot & & & & \\ \cdot & \cdot & & & & \\ X_{j1} & X_{j2} & \cdots & X_{jt} & \cdots & X_{jn} \\ \cdot & & & & & \\ \cdot & & & & & \\ X_{p1} & X_{p2} & \cdots & X_{pt} & \cdots & X_{pn} \end{bmatrix} \qquad (5.223)$$

The matrix $\mathbf{X}$ is called the *design matrix* when it is determined prior to the experiment, since each row of $\mathbf{X}$ represents a combination of "factors" at which a certain response Y is observed.

The least-square method requires that we minimize the scalar sum of squares

$$Q = (\mathbf{Y} - \mathbf{X}'\boldsymbol{\beta})'(\mathbf{Y} - \mathbf{X}'\boldsymbol{\beta}) \qquad (5.224)$$

for variation in the regression coefficient vector $\boldsymbol{\beta}$. Differentiating Q with respect to $\boldsymbol{\beta}$ and setting it to zero, we obtain the following expression, which is often called the *normal equation*:

$$(\mathbf{XX'})\boldsymbol{\beta} = \mathbf{XY} \tag{5.225}$$

which gives for our least-square estimators the vector

$$\hat{\boldsymbol{\beta}} = (\mathbf{XX'})^{-1}\mathbf{XY}, \tag{5.226}$$

where we assume that $\mathbf{XX'}$, a $(p + 1) \times (p + 1)$ matrix, is nonsingular and therefore can be inverted. It is not difficult to show (Exercise 5.9.4) that $\hat{\boldsymbol{\beta}}$ is an unbiased estimator of $\boldsymbol{\beta}$ and its *covariance matrix* is given by

$$V(\hat{\boldsymbol{\beta}}) = E[(\hat{\boldsymbol{\beta}} - E[\hat{\boldsymbol{\beta}}])(\hat{\boldsymbol{\beta}} - E[\hat{\boldsymbol{\beta}}])'] = \sigma^2(\mathbf{XX'})^{-1}, \tag{5.227}$$

which is a generalization of (5.186) and (5.188). By inserting the solution (5.226) into (5.224) we obtain the variation about the regression plane that is equivalent to the minimized Q of (5.224):

$$Q_{aR} = \sum_{t=1}^{n} (Y_t - \hat{Y}_t)^2 = (\mathbf{Y} - \mathbf{X'}\hat{\boldsymbol{\beta}})'(\mathbf{Y} - \mathbf{X'}\hat{\boldsymbol{\beta}})$$

$$= (\mathbf{Y} - \mathbf{X'}\hat{\boldsymbol{\beta}})'\mathbf{Y} \tag{5.228}$$

where we use the property that the vector $\hat{\mathbf{Y}} = \mathbf{X'}\hat{\boldsymbol{\beta}}$ is *orthogonal* to the residual vector, $\mathbf{Y} - \mathbf{X'}\hat{\boldsymbol{\beta}}$. Note that

$$s_{aR}^2 = \frac{Q_{aR}}{n - p - 1} \tag{5.229}$$

is an unbiased estimator of σ^2, where $(n - p - 1)$ is the number of observations minus the number of parameters estimated.

The important relation discussed in the previous section

$$Q_T = Q_{aR} + Q_{bR} \tag{5.230}$$

also holds for the multiple regression model (not necessarily a linear model). The sum of the squares Q_{bR} may be obtained as

$$Q_{bR} = \sum_{t=1}^{n} (\hat{Y}_t - \bar{Y})^2$$

$$= \hat{\boldsymbol{\beta}}'\mathbf{XY} - n\bar{Y}^2. \tag{5.231}$$

The total squared sum of variance around the mean $\bar{Y}$ is

$$Q_T = \sum_{t=1}^{n} (Y_i - \bar{Y})^2 = \mathbf{Y'Y} - n\bar{Y}^2. \tag{5.232}$$

Hence, we obtain the analysis of variance of Table 5.6.

TABLE 5.6 THE ANOVA TABLE OF MULTIPLE REGRESSION ANALYSIS.

Source of variation	Degrees of freedom	Sums of squares	Mean squared deviation	Test statistic
Between points on regression plane	p	$Q_{bR} = \hat{\boldsymbol{\beta}}'\mathbf{XY} - n\bar{Y}^2$	$s_{bR}^2 = \dfrac{Q_{bR}}{p}$	$T = \dfrac{s_{bR}^2}{s_{aR}^2}$
Around regression plane	$n - p - 1$	$Q_{aR} = Q_T - Q_{bR}$	$s_{aR}^2 = \dfrac{Q_{aR}}{n - p - 1}$	
Total	$n - 1$	$Q_T = \mathbf{Y}'\mathbf{Y} - n\bar{Y}^2$		

In some cases we are not at all confident initially that any of the X_j's are related to Y. In this event, a significance test of the null hypothesis H: $\beta_1 = \beta_2 = \cdots = \beta_p = 0$ should be based on the statistic $F = s_{bR}^2/s_{aR}^2$. This statistic has an F-distribution with degrees of freedom p and $(n - p - 1)$.

An estimator $\hat{\beta}_j$ (the jth component of $\hat{\boldsymbol{\beta}}$) is a linear function of the observables $\{Y_i\}$, and is, therefore, normally distributed with mean β_j. The variance is, from (5.227), given by

$$\text{Var}\,[\hat{\beta}_j] = \sigma^2[(\mathbf{XX}')^{-1}]_{j,j}. \tag{5.233}$$

Recall that the estimator of σ^2 is given by s_{aR}^2 of (5.229). It follows that the statistic

$$t = \frac{\hat{\beta}_j - \beta_j}{\sqrt{s_{aR}^2[(\mathbf{X}'\mathbf{X})^{-1}]_{j,j}}} \tag{5.234}$$

has a Student's t-distribution with $(n - p - 1)$ degrees of freedom. This enables us to set confidence intervals for β_j or to test hypotheses concerning its value (Exercise 5.9.5).

Multiple and partial correlation

We define the *multiple correlation coefficient* R_{YX} between Y and the regressor variables as the ordinary correlation between the fitted $\hat{Y}$

$$\hat{Y} = \beta_0 + \hat{\beta}_1 X_1 + \hat{\beta}_2 X_2 + \cdots + \hat{\beta}_p X_p \tag{5.235}$$

and the observed Y, that is,

$$R_{YX} = r_{Y\hat{Y}}. \tag{5.236}$$

This quantity measures the significance of all the regressors $X_1, X_2, \ldots,$ X_p. Analogous to (5.193), we can express the square of the multiple correlation coefficient, which is often called the *coefficient of determination*, as

$$R^2_{YX} = \frac{Q_{bR}}{Q_T}$$

$$= \frac{\text{Variation of } Y \text{ explained by regression}}{\text{Total variation of } Y}. \qquad (5.237)$$

Note that this is identical to r^2_{YX} if there is only one regressor. Thus, as we add additional explanatory variables to our model, by observing how fast R^2_{YX} increases we can see in (5.237) how helpful the additional variables are in improving the explanation of Y. Our conclusion is the same as in simple correlation; the major value of calculating R^2_{YX} is to clarify how successfully the regression explains the variation in Y.

In general, if the response variable Y is correlated with a regressor variable X_j, this may be merely incidental to the fact that both are correlated with another variable or set of variables $X_1, X_2, \ldots, X_{j-1},$ $X_{j+1}, \ldots, X_p$. This consideration leads us to examine the correlation between variables X_j and Y when other regressors are kept constant. This is called the *partial correlation* and can be considered as the correlation between residuals

$$\varepsilon = Y - (\beta_0 + \beta_1 X_1 + \cdots + \beta_{j-1}X_{j-1} + \beta_{j+1}X_{j+1} + \cdots + \beta_p X_p) \tag{5.238}$$

and

$$\varepsilon' = X_j - (\beta'_0 + \beta'_1 X_1 + \cdots + \beta'_{j-1}X_{j-1} + \beta'_{j+1}X_{j+1} + \cdots + \beta'_p X_p) \tag{5.239}$$

after subtracting the corresponding regressions on $X_1, \ldots, X_{j-1}, X_{j+1},$ $\ldots, X_p$ from Y and X_j. It may be shown that this partial correlation coefficient is given by

$$r_{YX_j \cdot X_1 \cdots X_p} = \frac{-\rho_{0j}}{\sqrt{\rho_{00}\rho_{jj}}}, \tag{5.240}$$

where ρ_{ij} is the $(i - j)$ component of the inverse of the $(p + 1) \times (p + 1)$ matrix of correlation coefficients for the variables $X_0 (= Y), X_1, X_2, \ldots,$ X_p.

The partial correlations measure the significance of regressors one by one, whereas the multiple correlation coefficient measures the significance of all the regressors at once. We now show the relationship between correlation and the partial correlations. Letting R_{YX} be the multiple correlation between Y and the regressor variables $\mathbf{X}$ as before, we can show (see Kendall and Stuart, 1961) that

$$1 - R_{Y\mathbf{X}}^2 = (1 - r_{YX_1}^2)(1 - r_{YX_2 \cdot X_1}^2)(1 - r_{YX_3 \cdot X_1 X_2}^2)$$
$$\cdots (1 - r_{YX_p \cdot X_1 X_2 \cdots X_{p-1}}^2), \tag{5.241}$$

where $r_{YX_j \cdot X_1 X_2 \cdots X_{j-1}}^2$ is the partial correlation between Y and X_j with X_1, $X_2, \ldots, X_{j-1}$ fixed, $j = 1, 2, \ldots, p$. It is clear from the above expression that

$$1 - R_{Y\mathbf{X}}^2 \leq 1 - r_{YX_j \cdot X_1 X_2 \cdots X_{j-1}}^2. \tag{5.242}$$

It follows that if $R_{Y\mathbf{X}} = 0$, all the corresponding partial correlations are also zero so that Y is completely uncorrelated with all the other variables. On the other hand, if $R_{Y\mathbf{X}} = 1$, at least one partial correlation must also be 1 to make the right-hand side of (5.241) equal to zero. In this case

$$\sum_{t=1}^{n} (Y_t - \bar{Y})^2 - \sum_{t=1}^{n} (\hat{Y}_t - \bar{Y})^2 = \sum_{t=1}^{n} (Y_t - \hat{Y}_t)^2 = 0 \tag{5.243}$$

so that all points Y_t lie on the regression line, and Y is a strict linear function of $X_1, X_2, \ldots, X_p$. Thus, $R_{Y\mathbf{X}}$ is a measure of the linear dependence of Y on $\mathbf{X}$.

Selection of regressors in multiple regression

So far we have assumed that the complete set of predictors or independent variables $X_1, X_2, \ldots, X_p$ was given on which a linear regression equation for a chosen response or dependent variable Y was established. In the general model-construction process, however, selection of the regressors $X_1, X_2, \ldots, X_p$ is clearly not a trivial matter. Two opposed criteria are usually involved in this selection procedure:

1. We want to include as many X's as possible to account for all possible causal factors and obtain the most reliable predictor.

2. Because of the cost and system overhead involved in the measurement and reduction of raw data, we should like to include as few X's as possible. This will be the case particularly if the selected variables are subsequently used for performance tuning of a given computer system.

Therefore, we need to compromise between these two conflicting demands, but there is no unique statistical procedure for doing this. Several procedures have been proposed to select the "best regression equation," given a response variable (i.e., performance measure), a set of candidate predictor variables, and a series of observations on all of them. They are (1) all possible regressions, (2) backward elimination, (3) forward selection, (4) stepwise regression, and (5) stagewise regression.

Draper and Smith (1967) discuss the details and relative merits of these different methods.

In the *stepwise regression* method, one variable is added to the regression equation at each step. The variable added is the one that makes the greatest reduction in the sum of the squares of the errors. Equivalently, it is the variable that has the highest partial correlation with the dependent variable partialed on the variables which have already been added; and, equivalently, it is the variable which, if it were added, would have the highest F-value. An important property of the stepwise procedure is that it reexamines the significance of the variables incorporated into the model in previous stages. This provision is explained as follows. The effect of an X variable (say, X_j) in determining a response may be large when the regression equation includes only X_j. However, when the same variable is entered into the equation after other variables, it may affect the response very little, due to the fact that X_j is highly correlated with variables already in the regression equation. The stepwise regression uses a particular type of F-test, called a *partial F-test*. The insignificant variable is removed from the regression equation before adding an additional variable. This process is continued until no more variables will be admitted to the equation and no more are rejected. It is to be noted that the stepwise procedure starts by entering into the regression the X variable most highly correlated with the response, since partial correlation partialed on the null set is exactly the simple correlation.

Exercises

5.9.4 a) Verify the expression (5.227) for the covariance matrix of $\hat{\boldsymbol{\beta}}$.

   b) Show that the earlier results (5.186) and (5.188) proven in Exercise 5.9.1 can be derived as special cases of the result of part (a).

5.9.5 Derive (5.234). Show that for the case

$$Y_t = \beta_0 + \beta_1 X_t + \varepsilon_t$$

the expression reduces to (5.196).

5.9.5 A Case Study: Evaluating System Changes by the Analysis of Variance and Regression Models

This section illustrates how the analysis of variance and regression analysis can be used to evaluate computer system changes. The material presented below is from an article by Friedman and Waldbaum (1975). Their study was motivated by a proposed change in the APL time-sharing system at IBM's Thomas J. Watson Research Center. The APL system was run on a System/360 Model 91 under OS/MVT, and users' programs and data occupy blocks of storage called *work spaces*. Work spaces that are not being used are stored in libraries on disk; work spaces currently in use are *swapped* between main memory and disk. The proposed modifications to the system involved two system parameters: WSSIZE and IN-CORE. The parameter WSSIZE (=work-space size) specifies the maximum size of each work space in the system. Main storage and the area on disk used for swapping are formatted into fixed-size areas that are large enough to store the maximum-size work spaces. The other parameter, INCORE, specifies the number of work spaces that may be in main memory simultaneously. Thus, the value of INCORE is the highest level of multiprogramming possible in the APL system. The proposed experimental change was from

$$(INCORE, WSSIZE) = (3, 5)$$

to

$$(INCORE, WSSIZE) = (2, 7)$$

where the value of WSSIZE is in terms of the number of tracks on an IBM 2314 disk: Each track, when formatted for APL, can contain a maximum of 7248 bytes of data. Thus, storage areas that are five and seven tracks long can store work spaces as large as 36,000 bytes and 48K bytes (K = 1024), respectively. The above experimental change was proposed because a number of APL users required larger work spaces and a straightforward enlarging of APL work spaces (i.e., a change to (3, 7)) would reduce the amount of main memory available for OS batch users.

There arose a concern, however, about a possible serious performance degradation of the APL system that might be incurred by the implementation of such system change. The following factors were considered detrimental to the performance with the two 48K-byte work spaces:

1. Reducing the level of multiprogramming would increase the amount of swapping.
2. More time would be required for reading and writing the larger work spaces.

In order to evaluate quantitatively the possible performance degradation, the above authors performed a regression analysis based on measured data collected during a test period of 35 days, during which the following three different configurations were run:

1st day–18th day:	(INCORE, WSSIZE) = (3, 5),
19th day-27th day:	(INCORE, WSSIZE) = (2, 5),
28th day–35th day:	(INCORE, WSSIZE) = (2, 7).

The performance variable that is modeled is the system reaction time, that is, the time from detection of a user's carriage return until the user's work space is dispatched (i.e., receives its first time slice). As we discussed in Chapter 1, system reaction time indicates the effectiveness of the scheduler in dispatching service to a newly arrived input.

As response variables, Friedman and Waldbaum selected three points on the statistical distribution of the system reaction time:

Y = The 50th percentile for the system reaction time; that is, the system reaction time (in seconds) achieved or bettered by 50 percent of the inputs.

Y' = The 90th percentile for the system reaction time (in seconds).

Y'' = The 95th percentile for the system reaction time (in seconds).

The last three columns of Table 5.7 list these response variables observed over a period of 35 days.

Performance comparison ignoring work loads

First we formulate the problem as a simple analysis of variance. We regard the three configurations (3, 5), (2, 5), and (2, 7) as three *treatments* of the experiment: We call them treatments 1, 2, and 3, respectively. Let $\{Y_{it}; i = 1, 2, 3, t = 1, 2, \ldots, n_i\}$ denote the 50th percentile for the system reaction time on the tth day under the ith treatment; the size of the samples in the ith treatment is denoted by n_i:

$$n_1 = 18, \quad n_2 = 9, \quad n_3 = 8$$

and

$$N = n_1 + n_2 + n_3 = 35.$$

Then the observation variable from the treatment i can be written as

$$Y_{it} = \mu_i + \varepsilon_{it}(\mathbf{U}), \qquad t = 1, 2, \ldots, n_i, \qquad (5.244)$$

where the μ_i's are unknown means $i = 1, 2, 3$. The error term $\varepsilon_{it}(\mathbf{U})$ is assumed to be independent from sample to sample and have zero mean and a common variance σ^2.

TABLE 5.7 DATA USED FOR MODEL BUILDING

Day	Treatment		Predictive variables (work-load variables)						Response variables (reaction times)		
	X_1	X_2	X_3	X_4	X_5	X_6	X_7	X_8	Y [sec]	Y' [sec]	Y'' [sec]
1	1	0	1350	1.5	6.1	21.5	128	21	0.22	0.55	0.94
2	1	0	1541	1.9	18.4	15.5	134	22	0.31	0.92	1.61
3	1	0	1214	1.3	9.7	15.9	110	20	0.30	0.70	1.03
4	1	0	1218	1.5	21.1	28.5	104	19	0.29	0.72	0.97
5	1	0	1423	1.9	16.7	27.7	127	18	0.24	0.72	1.40
6	1	0	1803	1.6	11.3	18.1	130	21	0.26	0.66	1.04
7	1	0	1918	1.5	18.4	7.4	111	18	0.27	0.60	0.87
8	1	0	2006	1.5	15.7	13.8	173	23	0.26	0.64	1.02
9	1	0	1567	1.0	3.3	15.3	116	20	0.26	0.59	0.92
10	1	0	1373	1.4	6.7	13.7	136	21	0.26	0.64	1.12
11	1	0	1092	1.2	31.7	15.1	95	20	0.34	1.06	1.57
12	1	0	1015	0.9	28.2	15.0	102	16	0.32	1.24	1.88
13	1	0	1670	1.2	8.4	6.3	100	22	0.22	0.56	0.78
14	1	0	1148	1.5	21.2	20.9	96	18	0.26	0.75	1.35
15	1	0	1416	1.4	12.1	40.9	110	19	0.25	0.65	1.24
16	1	0	1341	1.8	8.4	18.3	109	19	0.24	0.61	1.17
17	1	0	1279	1.4	24.5	45.2	104	15	0.27	0.72	1.29
18	1	0	1665	1.6	10.9	17.1	135	21	0.26	0.59	0.91
19	0	0	1378	1.5	5.9	18.5	120	18	0.29	0.72	1.24
20	0	0	1469	1.3	18.2	22.6	107	19	0.31	0.84	1.26
21	0	0	1365	1.4	16.9	21.0	120	24	0.32	0.93	1.70
22	0	0	1542	1.7	18.9	20.9	137	18	0.29	0.71	1.17
23	0	0	1057	0.7	7.0	15.2	85	18	0.27	0.60	0.98
24	0	0	1394	1.5	19.2	7.5	108	22	0.26	0.62	1.20
25	0	0	1245	1.3	2.2	8.8	118	18	0.25	0.57	0.94
26	0	0	1195	1.2	6.2	13.6	120	18	0.27	0.65	1.21
27	0	0	1748	1.7	4.2	17.0	132	22	0.24	0.55	0.85
28	0	1	1197	1.2	7.5	14.9	131	19	0.39	1.43	2.57
29	0	1	2029	1.4	7.0	16.7	123	19	0.36	0.87	1.27
30	0	1	2394	1.8	10.3	19.4	150	26	0.42	1.08	1.78
31	0	1	2018	2.1	12.1	20.0	146	22	0.37	1.07	1.84
32	0	1	1606	2.1	9.6	17.8	126	21	0.31	0.76	1.21
33	0	1	1103	1.3	12.5	10.5	82	17	0.29	0.61	0.99
34	0	1	1729	1.2	3.7	9.9	96	16	0.28	0.69	1.08
35	0	1	2117	1.9	16.6	49.3	160	17	0.41	1.42	2.17

(Reprinted by permission from Friedman and Waldbaum, "Evaluating System Changes Under Uncontrolled Workload: A Case Study," *IBM Systems Journal.* © 1975 by International Business Machines Corporation.)

where

$$X_1 = \begin{cases} 0 & \text{when INCORE} = 2 \\ 1 & \text{when INCORE} = 3 \end{cases} \qquad X_2 = \begin{cases} 0 & \text{when WSSIZE} = 5 \\ 1 & \text{when WSSIZE} = 7 \end{cases}$$

Y = 50 percentile reaction time,

Y' = 90 percentile reaction time,

and

Y'' = 95 percentile reaction time.

We now ask: "How much do these treatments differ from each other?" Thus, the hypotheses we wish to test are the following three:

$$H_1:\quad \mu_2 = \mu_3 = \mu, \tag{5.245}$$

$$H_2:\quad \mu_1 = \mu_2 = \mu, \tag{5.246}$$

and

$$H_3:\quad \mu_1 = \mu_3 = \mu. \tag{5.247}$$

In order to test hypothesis H_1 (which says there is no difference between the performance under the configurations $(2, 5)$ and $(2, 7)$), we denote by Q_T the minimized total sum of squares under the constraint of H_1:

$$
\begin{aligned}
Q_T &= \min_{\mu_1} \sum_{t=1}^{n_1} (Y_{1t} - \mu_1)^2 + \min_{\mu} \sum_{i=2}^{3} \sum_{t=1}^{n_i} (Y_{it} - \mu)^2 \\
&= \left(\sum_{t=1}^{n_1} Y_{1t}^2 \right) - n_1 \bar{Y}_1^2. + \left(\sum_{i=2}^{3} \sum_{t=1}^{n_i} Y_{it}^2 \right) - \frac{(n_2 \bar{Y}_2. + n_3 \bar{Y}_3.)^2}{n_2 + n_3},
\end{aligned}
\tag{5.248}
$$

which has the degree of freedom $N - 2 = 33$. The variation within treatment, which we denote as Q_w, has the degree of freedom $N - 3 = 32$, and is given by

$$
\begin{aligned}
Q_w &= \sum_{i=1}^{3} \min_{\mu_i} \sum_{t=1}^{n_i} (Y_{it} - \mu_i)^2 \\
&= \sum_{i=1}^{3} (n_i - 1)s_i^2,
\end{aligned}
\tag{5.249}
$$

where $\bar{Y}_i.$ and s_i^2 in Eqs. (5.248) and (5.249) are the sample mean and variance of the ith treatment:

$$\bar{Y}_1. = 0.26833, \quad \bar{Y}_2. = 0.27777, \quad \bar{Y}_3. = 0.35373, \tag{5.250}$$

and

$$s_1^2 = 0.032585, \quad s_2^2 = 0.026822, \quad s_3^2 = 0.054232. \tag{5.251}$$

Therefore, we immediately have

$$Q_w = 0.0444. \tag{5.252}$$

The sum of the squares between the treatments is given, from (5.132) of Section 5.7, as

$$Q_b = Q_T - Q_w. \tag{5.253}$$

Since Q_w can be alternatively written as

$$Q_w = \sum_{i=1}^{3} \left(\sum_{t=1}^{n_i} Y_{it}^2 - n_i \bar{Y}_{i.}^2 \right), \tag{5.254}$$

we can obtain the numerical value of Q_b from (5.248) and (5.254):

$$Q_b = \sum_{i=2}^{3} n_i \bar{Y}_{i.}^2 - \frac{(n_2 \bar{Y}_{2.} + n_3 \bar{Y}_{3.})^2}{n_2 + n_3}$$

$$= \frac{n_2 n_3}{n_2 + n_3} (\bar{Y}_{3.} - \bar{Y}_{2.})^2, \tag{5.255}$$

which has $33 - 32 = 1$ degrees of freedom. Then the statistic to test hypothesis H_1 is given by the F-value

$$F = \frac{Q_b}{Q_w/32} = 17.6 \tag{5.256}$$

or, equivalently, the t-statistic with 32 degrees of freedom:

$$t = \sqrt{F} = \frac{\bar{Y}_{3.} - \bar{Y}_{2.}}{\sqrt{\dfrac{Q_w}{32}\left(\dfrac{1}{n_2} + \dfrac{1}{n_3}\right)}} = 4.20. \tag{5.257}$$

The 95- and 99-percent critical values of the t-statistic are $t_{0.025;32} = 2.038$ and $t_{0.005;32} = 2.740$, respectively. Hence, we conclude that the difference between treatment 2—the $(2, 5)$ configuration—and treatment 3—the $(2, 7)$ configuration—is deemed significant.

Similarly, the test statistic for hypothesis H_2 is calculated (see Exercise 5.9.6) as $t = 0.62$, which, unlike (5.257), is even smaller than the 50-percent critical value $t_{0.5;32} = 0.683$. Hence, we judge that there is no significant statistical difference between treatment 1—the $(3, 5)$ configuration—and treatment 3—the $(2, 5)$ configuration. The t-statistic for hypothesis H_3 is $t = 5.4$, which is substantially high. There is a real difference in the 50th percentile system reaction time between the pre-experimental configuration and the configuration after change.

Performance comparison considering work loads

The difference in the system reaction time we have shown above can be attributed to the system configuration only, if the system work loads are statistically similar over the entire 35-day period. If the work loads are appreciably different, it is desirable to compare the system performance after eliminating the work-load differences. The work-load variables available for the analysis are limited to those measured routinely by the APL system. The following six work-load variables, which we denote by X_3 through X_8, were selected for possible inclusion in the model for performance comparison:

X_3 = The number of conversational inputs per hour

X_4 = The percentage of CPU time consumed by all small CPU requests (that is, requests using two seconds or less of CPU time)

X_5 = The percentage of CPU time consumed by all large CPU requests (that is, requests using more than two seconds of CPU time)

X_6 = The number of large CPU requests per hour

X_7 = The number of commands per hour requiring two work spaces in main storage simultaneously

X_8 = The number of log-ons per hour

These six numerical variables are tabulated in columns 3 through 8 of Table 5.7. In addition to these, we introduce two categorical (dummy) variables, X_1 and X_2, as follows:

$$X_1 = \begin{cases} 0, & \text{if INCORE} = 2 \\ 1, & \text{if INCORE} = 3 \end{cases} \tag{5.258}$$

and

$$X_2 = \begin{cases} 0, & \text{if WSSIZE} = 5 \\ 1, & \text{if WSSIZE} = 7.} \end{cases} \tag{5.259}$$

We now attempt to fit data into the following simple linear model:

$$Y_t = \beta_0 + \beta_1 X_{1t} + \cdots + \beta_8 X_{8t} + \varepsilon_t, \qquad t = 1, 2, \ldots, N\ (= 35) \tag{5.260}$$

or in matrix notation

$$\mathbf{Y} = \mathbf{X'\beta} + \boldsymbol{\varepsilon}, \tag{5.261}$$

where $\mathbf{X}$ is the design matrix (5.223) in which $p = 8$ and $n = 35$. Then by solving the normal equation (5.226), we obtain the regression coefficients as follows:

$$\hat{\beta}_0 = 1.2802 \times 10^{-1},$$
$$\hat{\beta}_1 = -2.2159 \times 10^{-2},$$
$$\hat{\beta}_2 = 8.5586 \times 10^{-2},$$
$$\hat{\beta}_3 = -1.0305 \times 10^{-5},$$
$$\hat{\beta}_4 = -5.2215 \times 10^{-2}, \qquad (5.262)$$
$$\hat{\beta}_5 = 3.3267 \times 10^{-3},$$
$$\hat{\beta}_6 = 7.8640 \times 10^{-4},$$
$$\hat{\beta}_7 = 8.4086 \times 10^{-4},$$
$$\hat{\beta}_8 = 4.4911 \times 10^{-3}.$$

The sum of the squares of deviation about the regression plane is calculated as

$$Q_{aR} = 0.019268, \qquad (5.263)$$

which is also called the *residual sum of squares*. Similarly, the sum of the squares of deviation between the values on the regression plane (that is, the variation of Y explained by regression) is

$$Q_{bR} = 0.067429. \qquad (5.264)$$

Thus, the coefficient of determination (or multiple correlation coefficient squared) is

$$R^2 = 0.7778. \qquad (5.265)$$

From the definition of the on-off variables X_1 and X_2, we see that β_0 is the average of the Y's for configuration $(2, 5)$; $\beta_0 + \beta_1$ is the average of the Y's under $(3, 5)$; $\beta_0 + \beta_2$ is the average of the Y's under $(2, 7)$. Therefore, the hypotheses of (5.245)–(5.247) can be represented in terms of β_i:

$$H_1: \beta_1 - \beta_2 = 0, \qquad (5.266)$$
$$H_2: \beta_1 = 0 \qquad (5.267)$$

and

$$H_3: \beta_2 = 0. \qquad (5.268)$$

Recall that for a given design matrix $\mathbf{X}$, the estimated regression coefficient $\hat{\boldsymbol{\beta}}$ is an unbiased estimate of $\boldsymbol{\beta}$ with the covariance matrix (5.227), where σ^2 is the (unknown) variance of the residual error ϵ. The best estimate of σ^2 that we can provide is s_{aR}^2 of (5.229):

$$s_{aR}^2 = \frac{Q_{aR}}{35 - 8 - 1} = 0.000741, \qquad (5.269)$$

TABLE 5.8 RESULTS OF FITTING THE LINEAR
REGRESSION MODEL

	Y	Y'	Y''
$\hat{\beta}_0$	0.128	0.134	0.117
$\hat{\beta}_1$	−0.022	−0.030	−0.083
$\hat{\beta}_2$	0.086	0.400	0.640
$t(\hat{\beta}_1)$	1.9	0.5	0.7
$t(\hat{\beta}_2)$	5.6	4.9	4.3
R^2	0.78	0.71	0.66

(Reprinted by permission from Friedman and Waldbaum, "Evaluating System Changes Under Uncontrolled Workload: A Case Study," *IBM Systems Journal.*
© 1975 by International Business Machines Corporation.)

which is called the *residual mean square*. Assuming the normality of the
residual error (which we will examine later), the statistic for testing the
hypothesis $\beta_i = 0$ is given by the t-statistic of (5.234) with 26 d.f.

Table 5.8 summarizes the results of the analysis with the t-statistics
for the significance of coefficients β_i's. The large value of $t(\hat{\beta}_2)$ for all
three variables Y, Y', and Y'' substantiate our earlier observation that,
with the work-load level being taken into consideration, there is, in fact, a
real difference between configurations $(2, 7)$ and $(3, 5)$; the small values of
$t(\hat{\beta}_1)$ confirm that there exists no significant difference between the $(2, 5)$
and $(3, 5)$ conditions.

Examining the "goodness-of-fit" of the model

To examine whether the obtained linear regression—an empirical
model—fits the data, we plot the *residuals*, that is, the differences between fitted value, $\hat{Y}$, and observed value, Y. Such a graphical representation sometimes reveals whether there is some dependency of the
magnitude of the residual on the magnitude of the equation value. First of
all, in order for our model to be valid, the residual should show roughly
equal scatter for all values of Y; otherwise, the variance of the error term
ε cannot be considered independent of Y as assumed in the model
formulation. Quite often, some transformation, such as log Y, will eliminate nonuniform scatter of the residuals. (See Anderson and Sargent
(1972) and Tsao, Comeau, and Margolin (1972) for applications of the
logarithmic transformation to computer measurement data.)

Figure 5.18 shows the residual versus fitted Y based on the 35
observation data. We can say that there is no evidence of systematic

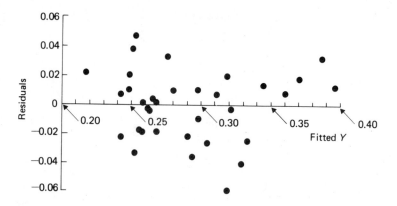

Fig. 5.18 Residuals versus fitted Y (courtesy of G. Waldbaum).

departure from nonconstancy. We do not find any outliers either. An *outlier* is a wild point or untypical value (that is, a point of extraordinarily large residual), introduced perhaps by some measurement or recording error. If outliers are, in fact, due to bad data points, then we should discard them; to retain them may invalidate the judgment we make. But when we detect outliers, we must take care before we decide that they are "bad" values: If the large residual occurs at an extreme Y value, the point may imply curvature in the true relation or a nonconstancy of variance with the value of Y. A close examination of outliers often leads to the discovery of important variables that are not previously considered.

Another important assumption used in the model construction is that the distribution of the uncontrolled error $\varepsilon(\mathbf{U})$ is a normal or Gaussian distribution. Recall that the test statistics—F-values, t-values—are based on the normality assumption. In order to check the near-normality of the error structure, we plot the fractile diagram—the cumulative distribution diagram with normal grid (see Section 5.4.1)—of the residual terms. Figure 5.19 shows the fractile diagram based on the set of residual terms in the linear regression model obtained above. The plot is found to be nearly straight, so we may judge that the error terms are normally distributed. Needless to say, the cumulative distribution based on a finite number of samples always contains random fluctuation from the theoretical curve—a straight line on probability paper. Thus, we need to acquire some feeling for an acceptable departure from normality. Daniel and Wood (1971) show a number of computer plots of a fractile diagram for various sample sizes ranging from 8 to 384. The amount of fluctuation tends to be large at ends of the fitted straight line (see Eq. (5.25) and Exercise 5.4.1).

We find from Table 5.8 that 78 percent of the variation in system reaction time Y (the 50th percentile point) can be explained by the model (that is, $R^2 = 0.78$). The square root of the variance estimated from the unexplained variation is 0.027 second. A reasonable question to raise then is: "Can we improve the model by fitting into a more complicated functional form (say, inclusion of X_i^2, X_iX_j, etc.) than the simple linear form?" This question could be most appropriately handled if we have independent replications of observations with the variables X_i's under control: We compute variance within Y's obtained for a given set of X_i's. If this variance is not smaller than the variance of the residual error, then it is of no use to attempt to obtain a better fit. Unfortunately, this estimation procedure is not applicable here, since the X's were not controlled in the experiment; we do not have replicated observations with the X's being fixed. In order to cope with a situation like this, we apply

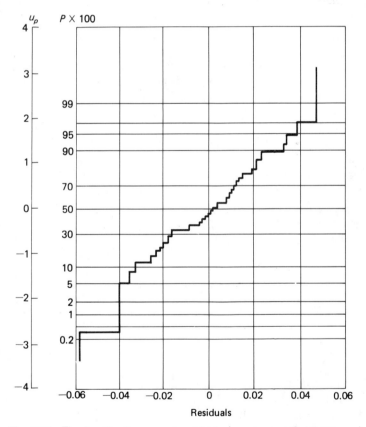

Fig. 5.19 The fractile diagram of residuals (courtesy of G. Waldbaum).

the concept of the *near replicates*: We look for pairs of observations that are taken far apart in time but under "nearly the same" X condition. The variation in the dependent variable for these pairs of observations is used to define another estimate of error variance, which is then compared with the residual mean square s_{aR}^2. This procedure is implemented in the computer program by Wood (1972) that was used by Friedman and Waldbaum. The estimate of error variation obtained from near-replication proved consistent with the residual error variance.

This leaves us with a model that has a significant amount of reaction time variation that can be explained neither by the system conditions nor by the measured work-load variables. Of course, part of the unexplained variation $Q_T - Q_{aR}$ is due to the fact that the variables in the model are specified at the macro level (that is, they are daily averages). It is also possible that there are other unmeasured variables that might account for the unexplained variation in reaction time.

Exercises

5.9.6 Refer to the case study problem. Verify that the test statistics used to test hypotheses H_2 and H_3 are the t-values given on p. 398.

5.9.7 Refer again to the case study. Consider the hypothesis

$$H_0: \mu_1 = \mu_2 = \mu_3 = \mu.$$

What is the F-value to test H_0? Do you accept or reject H_0 at the significance level of five percent? What about at the one-percent significance level?

5.9.8 Test hypotheses H_1, H_2, H_3, and H_0 with respect to the response variables Y' and Y''.

5.9.9 Ignoring the work loads $X_3, \ldots, X_8$, write the normal equation for the regression coefficients β_0, β_1, and β_2.

    a) Show that

$$\hat{\beta}_0 = \bar{Y}_{2.}, \quad \hat{\beta}_1 = \bar{Y}_{1.} - \bar{Y}_{2.}, \quad \hat{\beta}_2 = \bar{Y}_{3.} - \bar{Y}_{2.}.$$

    b) Show that the test statistics obtained by the analysis of variance—that is, (5.257), etc.—are equivalent to the statistics for testing the regression coefficients.

5.9.6   The Analysis of Covariance

In the case study of the previous section, the variables of main interest were the categorical variables X_1 and X_2; $X_3, \ldots, X_8$ were introduced in order to minimize chance fluctuations due to work-load changes. In other words, our objective was to test for *pure* effects of the treatments (i.e., X_1

and X_2 values) with greater accuracy by taking advantage of the information furnished by the work-load variables. The *analysis of covariance* is another technique used to accomplish this same objective. Variates whose variation we wish to eliminate are called *concomitant variates*. Recall that the term concomitant variate was introduced in Section 4.9 in the discussion of the variance reduction method via control variates. The reader will find a close relationship between the analysis of covariance and the control variate method. In the problem of Section 5.9.5, the six work-load variables are concomitant variables.

Let us assume that there are k concomitant variables $Z_1, Z_2, \ldots, Z_k$. Assuming the regression of dependent variable Y on concomitant variables to be linear, the observational equations containing the parameters $\boldsymbol{\beta}' = [\beta_1, \beta_2, \ldots, \beta_p]$ and the regression coefficients $\boldsymbol{\gamma}' = [\gamma_1, \gamma_2, \ldots, \gamma_k]$ can be written as

$$Y_t = \beta_0 + \beta_1 X_{1t} + \cdots + \beta_p X_{pt} + \gamma_1 Z_{1t}$$
$$+ \cdots + \gamma_j Z_{jt} + \cdots + \gamma_k Z_{kt} + \varepsilon_t, \quad t = 1, 2, \ldots, n \quad (5.270)$$

or in matrix notation

$$\mathbf{Y} = \mathbf{X}'\boldsymbol{\beta} + \mathbf{Z}'\boldsymbol{\gamma} + \boldsymbol{\varepsilon}, \quad\quad\quad (5.271)$$

where $\mathbf{X}$ is the design matrix of size $(p + 1) \times n$; $\mathbf{Z}$ is a $k \times n$ matrix with its jth row as $\mathbf{Z}'_j$ representing the n observations $\{Z_{jt}; t = 1, 2, \ldots, n\}$ on the jth concomitant variable. Referring again to the case study problem of the previous section, we see that the design matrix of that experiment is given from Table 5.7 by

$$
\mathbf{X} = \begin{bmatrix} \overbrace{\begin{matrix}1 & 1 & \cdots & 1\end{matrix}}^{18} & \overbrace{\begin{matrix}1 & 1 & \cdots & 1\end{matrix}}^{9} & \overbrace{\begin{matrix}1 & 1 & \cdots & 1\end{matrix}}^{8} \\ 1 & 1 & \cdots & 1 & 0 & 0 & \cdots & 0 & 0 & 0 & \cdots & 0 \\ 0 & 0 & \cdots & 0 & 0 & 0 & \cdots & 0 & 1 & 1 & \cdots & 1 \end{bmatrix}. \quad (5.272)
$$

It is worthwhile to make a few remarks here: The setup (5.271) is mathematically equivalent to the multiple linear regression model with the unknown parameter vector $[\boldsymbol{\beta}'\boldsymbol{\gamma}']$, the design matrix $[\mathbf{X}, \mathbf{Z}]$, and the observation vector $\mathbf{Y}$. Another point we wish to make is that the analysis of variance is equivalent to regression on only categorical (or qualitative) variables, whereas "standard" regression is regression on only numerical (or quantitative) variables. Equation (5.271) represents regression on both categorical and numerical variables; such regression as defined above is called the analysis of covariance.

Returning to the linear model (5.271), we now present a computational scheme (Rao, 1965) which enables us to carry out statistical tests on various hypotheses of interest. The *normal equation* corresponding to the model (5.271) is now given by the following pair:

$$(\mathbf{XX'})\boldsymbol{\beta} + (\mathbf{XZ'})\boldsymbol{\gamma} = \mathbf{XY} \tag{5.273}$$

and

$$(\mathbf{ZX'})\boldsymbol{\beta} + (\mathbf{ZZ'})\boldsymbol{\gamma} = \mathbf{ZY}. \tag{5.274}$$

Let $\mathbf{b}_0$ be a solution vector that we obtain for the normal equation by ignoring the concomitant variables:

$$(\mathbf{XX'})\mathbf{b}_0 = \mathbf{XY}. \tag{5.275}$$

For the design matrix of (5.272), the last equation becomes

$$\begin{bmatrix} 35 & 18 & 8 \\ 18 & 18 & 0 \\ 8 & 0 & 8 \end{bmatrix} \begin{bmatrix} b_{00} \\ b_{01} \\ b_{02} \end{bmatrix} = \begin{bmatrix} \sum_{t=1}^{35} Y_t \\ \sum_{t=1}^{18} Y_t \\ \sum_{t=28}^{35} Y_t \end{bmatrix}. \tag{5.276}$$

Similarly, let vector $\mathbf{b}_j$ be a solution to the equation

$$(\mathbf{XX'})\mathbf{b}_j = \mathbf{XZ}_j, \qquad j = 1, 2, \ldots, k \tag{5.277}$$

which is the same as the normal equation (5.275) except that we now substitute $\mathbf{Z}_j$ for $\mathbf{Y}$.

Define the following residual sum of products:

$$\begin{aligned} Q_{ij} &= (\mathbf{Z}_i - \mathbf{X'b}_i)'(\mathbf{Z}_j - \mathbf{X'b}_j) \\ &= \mathbf{Z}_i'\mathbf{Z}_j - \mathbf{b}_i'\mathbf{XZ}_j, \quad \text{for} \quad i, j = 0, 1, \ldots, k \end{aligned} \tag{5.278}$$

where we interpret the subscript 0 for the response variable $\mathbf{Y}$, that is,

$$\mathbf{Z}_0 = \mathbf{Y}. \tag{5.279}$$

Therefore, Q_{00}, for example, is

$$\begin{aligned} Q_{00} &= (\mathbf{Y} - \mathbf{X'b}_0)'(\mathbf{Y} - \mathbf{X'b}_0) \\ &= \mathbf{Y'Y} - \mathbf{b}_0'\mathbf{XY}, \end{aligned} \tag{5.280}$$

which is the same as Q_w obtained earlier by the analysis of variance. Multiplying (5.273) by $\mathbf{b}_i$ and subtracting from the ith component of

(5.274), we obtain the following equation for the regression parameters:

$$\sum_{j=1}^{k} Q_{ij}\gamma_j = Q_{i0}, \qquad i = 1, 2, \ldots, k. \tag{5.281}$$

Then the solution $\hat{\boldsymbol{\beta}}$ satisfying the normal equations (5.273) and (5.274) is given by the following expression (Exercise 5.9.10):

$$\hat{\boldsymbol{\beta}} = \mathbf{b}_0 - \gamma_1\mathbf{b}_1 - \cdots - \gamma_k\mathbf{b}_k. \tag{5.282}$$

The form of this solution explicitly gives the adjustment to be made in $\mathbf{b}_0$ due to the concomitant variables: that is, the second through the last terms are adjustments to be made due to the work-load consideration. The sum of the squares of deviation about the regression plane is given by

$$Q_{aR} = Q_{00} - \sum_{j=1}^{k} Q_{0j}\gamma_j \tag{5.283}$$

with $n - (p + 1) - k$ degrees of freedom, where $p + 1$ represents the rank of the design matrix $\mathbf{X}$.

Now, most hypotheses of our interest are representable in the form

$$H^{(1)}: \mathbf{C}\boldsymbol{\beta} = \boldsymbol{\xi} \tag{5.284}$$

for some matrix $\mathbf{C}$ and vector $\boldsymbol{\xi}$. For example, the hypothesis H_3 of (5.247) earlier defined can be shown to be equivalent to (Exercise 5.9.10):

$$\beta_2 - \beta_3 = 0. \tag{5.285}$$

We have to find the minimum of the sum of deviations from the regression plane under the constraint (5.284):

$$Q_{aR}^{(1)} = \min_{\mathbf{C}\boldsymbol{\beta}=\boldsymbol{\xi}} (\mathbf{Y} - \mathbf{X}'\boldsymbol{\beta} - \mathbf{Z}'\boldsymbol{\gamma})'(\mathbf{Y} - \mathbf{X}'\boldsymbol{\beta} - \mathbf{Z}'\boldsymbol{\gamma}). \tag{5.286}$$

Let $Q_{ij}^{(1)}$ be the residual sums of squares and products as in (5.278) when $\boldsymbol{\beta}$ is subject to the restriction $H^{(1)}$. Let $\gamma_1^{(1)}, \gamma_2^{(1)}, \ldots, \gamma_k^{(1)}$ be the solutions using $Q_{ij}^{(1)}$ in the equation (5.281). Then the sum of the squares of deviation about the regression plane is now

$$Q_{aR}^{(1)} = Q_{00}^{(1)} - \sum_{j=1}^{k} Q_{0j}^{(1)}\gamma_j^{(1)}. \tag{5.287}$$

Thus, the statistic for testing the hypothesis (5.284) is given by the F-statistic:

$$F = \frac{(Q_{aR}^{(1)} - Q_{aR})/c}{Q_{aR}/(n - k - p - 1)}, \tag{5.288}$$

where c is the d.f. of the hypothesis (5.284).

Another hypothesis of practical interest is

$$H^{(0)}: \boldsymbol{\gamma} = \mathbf{0}. \tag{5.289}$$

The adjustment for concomitant variables is not profitable if $\boldsymbol{\gamma} = 0$; in order to test this hypothesis, we compute

$$\min_{\boldsymbol{\gamma}=0, \boldsymbol{\beta}} (\mathbf{Y} - \mathbf{X}'\boldsymbol{\beta} - \mathbf{Z}'\boldsymbol{\gamma})'(\mathbf{Y} - \mathbf{X}'\boldsymbol{\beta} - \mathbf{Z}'\boldsymbol{\gamma}) = Q_{00}, \tag{5.290}$$

which is the same as the quantity defined in (5.280). Therefore, the sum of the squares due to deviation from the hypothesis $H^{(0)}$ is

$$Q_{00} - Q_{aR} \tag{5.291}$$

on k degrees of freedom. The variance ratio for testing $H^{(0)}$ is given by

$$F = \frac{(Q_{00} - Q_{aR})/k}{Q_{aR}/(n - k - p - 1)}. \tag{5.292}$$

Exercises

5.9.10 Verify that $\boldsymbol{\beta}$ of (5.282) satisfies the normal equation.

5.9.11 Find the representations $H^{(1)}: \mathbf{C}\boldsymbol{\beta} = \boldsymbol{\xi}$ for hypotheses H_1, H_2, and H_3 of the previous section.

5.9.12 Carry out the analysis of covariance for the case study problem of the previous section. Compare the results with those obtained in that section.

5.9.13 Refer again to the case study problem. Can we conclude that the adjustment for the work-load variables was not profitable?

DISCUSSIONS FOR FURTHER READING

There are a number of subjects that are not covered in this chapter. Reduction of dimensionality is an important issue in the exploratory stages in data analysis. Histograms and other graphical presentations discussed in Sections 5.3 and 5.4 are extremely useful in the first stage of data analysis. However, there are other data analysis techniques that can be used in addition to the graphical plots in the *exploratory* stages in the construction of empirical models: They are techniques for reducing dimensionality of raw data. Such techniques as *principal component analysis, factor analysis* (a canonical representation), and *multidimensional classification and clustering* are among the best-known *multivariate statistical methods* for the reduction of dimensionality. Although similar in concept to the selection of regressors in multiple regression analysis, the principal component analysis and factor analysis usually transform the original multidimensional observables into a space of new coordinates (of reduced dimensionality). These derived coordinates do not necessarily correspond to directly interpretable measures; they are used in identifying statistical dependency or cluster patterns that may exist in the original set of observables. See Gnanadesikan (1977), Kendall and Stuart (1966), and references therein for the statistical methods of multivariate analysis. Anderson, Galati, and Reiser (1973) discuss an application of the principal component analysis to computer measurement data.

A number of papers discuss applications of regression models to evaluations of computer system changes. Bard (1971) and Bard and Suryanarayana (1972) report the regression method in modeling the overhead of CP-67, that is, the control program for IBM System/360 Model 67. Their work is also reviewed in an expository article on regression methods by Schatzoff and Bryant (1973). See Anderson and Sargent (1972) and Silverman and Yue (1973) also. One of the most critical steps in the construction of a multiple regression model is to select an appropriate response variable and a right set of predictor (or independent) variables for inclusion in the model. The stepwise regression method and other methods outlined in Section 5.9.4 are standard techniques to that end, and are well documented in advanced books on regression analysis (e.g., Draper and Smith, (1966)). Efroymson (1960) discusses a computation procedure useful in producing regression coefficients and additional quantities related to their significance tests and confidence intervals in multiple regression analysis. Regression methods should be used with extreme caution. In particular, one has to be cautious in interpreting regression coefficients when there is high correlation among the predictor variables. Mosteller and Tukey (1977) provide an excellent discussion of these problems. Seber (1977) provides a comprehensive theoretical discussion of recent advances in variable selection methods for multiple regression.

Statistical analysis of measurement data from real systems or simulators should be useful not only in the analysis of system changes or the comparison of configuration alternatives, but also in *system tuning*. Schatzoff and Bryant (1973) and Bard (1976) discuss the use of the *response surface method* to seek an optimal operating point of a running system. The basic idea behind this method is as follows. Conduct a series of experiments at different settings of controllable system parameters, and infer statistically the functional relationship between these parameters and the response variable. The measured data of the experiments are used to estimate a response surface by regression analysis: A quadratic regression model is often used to fit the response surface. As the number of parameters to be adjusted becomes large, however, the number of different combinations to be considered for experiments will become impractically large. An effective design of experiments, which can extract as much information per experiment as possible, becomes an important issue. The reader is referred to Box (1969). Mihram (1972) and Fishman (1973) discuss the subject as an experimental design for simulation experiments.

Time-series analysis (including spectral analysis) is a well-developed branch of the theory of statistics. So far, it has limited applications in computer system modeling. Fuchs and Jackson (1970) and Lewis and Yue (1972) discuss statistical characterizations of message traffic in a time-sharing system, and a teleprocessing information retrieval system, respectively. A characterization of computer system behavior from the time-series approach, in terms of the dynamic interaction between resource demands of programs and the resource allocation/managing policies of the operating system, is yet to be attempted. Lewis and Shedler (1977) review recent developments in statistical methods for the analysis of univariate and multivariate series of events (point processes), and discuss applications of point process methodology to computer system reliability and performance evaluation.

REFERENCES

Anderson, H. A. (1972). "An Empirical Investigation into Foreground-Background Scheduling for an Interactive Computing System." Ph.D. thesis, Syracuse University (June). Also IBM Research Report RC-3941, IBM T. J. Watson Research Center, Yorktown Heights, New York.

Anderson, H. A., G. L. Galati, and M. Reiser (1973). "The Classification of the Interactive Workload for a Virtual Memory Computer System." *Proceedings of Computer Science and Statistics: 7th Annual Symposium on the Interface*, Iowa State University (October).

Anderson, H. A., and R. Sargent (1972). "The Statistical Evaluation of the Performance of an Experimental APL/360 System." In W. Freiberger (ed.), *Statistical Computer Performance Evaluation*, pp. 73–98. New York:

Bard, Y. (1971). "Performance Criteria and Measurement for a Time-Sharing System." *IBM Systems Journal* **10** (3): 193–216.

Bard, Y. (1973). "Experimental Evaluation of System Performance." *IBM Systems Journal* **12** (3): 302–314.

Bard, Y. (1976). "An Experimental Approach to System Tuning." *Proceedings of the International Symposium on Computer Performance Modeling, Measurement and Evaluation*, P. S. Chen and M. Franklin (eds.), pp. 296–305. Harvard University, Cambridge, Massachusetts (March).

Bard, Y., and M. Schatzoff (1978). "Statistical Method in Computer Performance Analysis." In K. M. Chandy and R. T. Yeh (eds.), *Current Trends in Programming Methodology, Vol. III: Software Modeling*, pp. 1–51. Englewood Cliffs, N.J.: Prentice-Hall.

Bard, Y., and K. Suryanarayana (1972). "On the Structure of CP-67 Overhead." In W. Freiberger (ed.), *Statistical Computer Performance Evaluation*, pp. 329–346. New York: Academic Press.

Box, G. E. P. (1969). *Evolutionary Operation: A Statistical Method for Process Improvement.* New York: Wiley.

Chandy, K. M., and R. T. Yeh (eds.) (1977). *Current Trends in Programming Methodology, Vol. III: Software Modeling.* Englewood Cliffs, N.J.: Prentice-Hall.

Cox, D. R., and P. A. W. Lewis (1968). *The Statistical Analysis of Series of Events.* London: Methuen.

Daniel, C., and F. S. Wood (1971). *Fitting Equations to Data: Computer Analysis of Multifactor Data for Scientists and Engineers.* New York: Wiley.

Denning, P. J. (1968). "The Working Set Model for Program Behavior." *Communications of Association for Computing Machinery* **11** (5): 323–333.

Draper, N. R., and H. Smith (1966). *Applied Regression Analysis.* New York: Wiley.

Drummond, M. E., Jr. (1973). *Evaluation and Measurement Techniques for Digital Computer Systems.* Englewood Cliffs, N.J.: Prentice-Hall.

Efroymson, M. A. (1960). "Multiple Regression Analysis," In A. Ralston and H. S. Wilf (eds.), *Mathematical Methods for Digital Computers*, pp. 191–203. New York: Wiley.

Fisher, R. A. (1935). *Design of Experiments.* Edinburgh: Oliver and Boyd.

Fishman, G. S. (1973). *Concepts and Methods in Discrete Events Digital Simulation.* New York: Wiley.

Friedman, H. P., and G. Waldbaum (1975). "Evaluating System Changes Under Uncontrolled Workload: A Case Study." *IBM System Journal* **14** (4): 340–352.

Fuchs, E., and P. Jackson (1970). "Estimates of Distributions of Random Variables for Certain Computer Communication Traffic Models." *Communications of Association for Computing Machinery* **13** (12): 752–757.

Fuller, S. H. (1975). "Performance Evaluation." In H. S. Stone (ed.), *Introduction to Computer Architecture*, pp. 474–545. Chicago: Science Research Associates.

Gaver, D. P., S. S. Lavenberg, and T. G. Price, Jr. (1976). "Exploratory Analysis of Access Path Length Data for a Data Base Management System." *IBM Journal of Research and Development* **20** (5): 449–464.

Gnanadesikan, R. (1977). *Methods for Statistical Data Analysis of Multivariate Observations.* New York: Wiley.

Grenander, U., and R. F. Tsao (1972). "Quantitative Methods for Evaluating Computer System Performance: A Review and Proposals." In W. Freiberger (ed.), *Statistical Computer Performance Evaluation*, pp. 3–24. New York: Academic Press.

Guenther, W. G. (1964). *Analysis of Variance.* Englewood Cliffs, N.J.: Prentice-Hall.

Hald, A. (1952). *Statistical Theory with Engineering Applications.* New York: Wiley.

Hannan, E. J. (1960). *Time-Series Analysis.* London: Methuen.

Hooke, R. (1963). *Introduction to Scientific Inference.* San Francisco: Holden-Day.

Kendall, M. G., and A. Stuart (1958). *The Advanced Theory of Statistics, Vol. I: Distribution Theory.* London: Charles Griffin.

Kendall, M. G., and A. Stuart (1961). *The Advanced Theory of Statistics, Vol. II: Inference and Relationship.* London: Charles Griffin.

Kendall, M. G., and A. Stuart (1966). *The Advanced Theory of Statistics, Vol. III: Design and Analysis and Time-Series.* London: Charles Griffin.

Knuth, D. E. (1969). *The Art of Computer Programming: Vol. 2: Seminumerical Algorithms.* Reading, Mass.: Addison-Wesley.

Kobayashi, H. (1972). "Some Recent Progress in Analytic Studies of System Performance." *Proceedings of 1st USA-Japan Computer Conference,* Tokyo, Japan (October).

Lavenberg, S. S., and G. S. Shedler (1976). "Stochastic Modeling of Processor Scheduling with Application to Data Base Management Systems." *IBM Journal of Research and Development* **20** (5): 437–448.

Lewis, P. A. W., and G. S. Shedler (1973). "Empirically Derived Micromodels for Sequences of Page Exceptions." *IBM Journal of Research and Development* **17** (No. 3): 86–100.

Lewis, P. A. W., and G. S. Shedler (1976). "Statistical Analysis of Non-Stationary Series of Events in a Data Base System." *IBM Journal of Research and Development* **20** (5): 429–528.

Lewis, P. A. W., and G. S. Shedler (1977). "Analysis and Modeling of Point Processes in Computer Systems." IBM Research Report RJ 2011, San Jose, California. Presented at the 41st Session of the International Statistical Institute, New Delhi, India (December 1977).

Lewis, P. A. W., and P. C. Yue (1972). "Statistical Analysis of Series of Events in Computer Systems." In W. Freiberger (ed.), *Statistical Computer Performance Evaluation,* pp. 265–280. New York: Academic Press.

Lucas, H. (1971). "Performance Evaluation and Monitoring." *Computing Surveys* **3** (3): 79–91.

Mann, H. A. (1949). *Analysis and Design of Experiments.* New York: Dover.

Mihram, G. A. (1972). *Simulation: Statistical Foundations and Methodology.* New York: Academic Press.

Mosteller, F., and J. W. Tukey (1977). *Data Analysis and Regression.* Reading, Mass.: Addison-Wesley.

Owens, D. B. (1962). *Statistical Tables.* Reading, Mass.: Addison-Wesley.

Rao, C. R. (1965). *Linear Statistical Inference and Its Applications.* New York: Wiley.

Schatzoff, M., and P. Bryant (1973). "Regression Methods in Performance Evaluation: Some Comments on the State of the Art." *Proceedings of Computer Science and Statistics, 7th Annual Symposium on the Interface*, pp. 48–57. Iowa State University (October).

Schatzoff, M., and C. C. Tillman (1975). "Design of Experiments in Simulator Validation." *IBM Journal of Research and Development* **19** (3): 252–262.

Scheffe, H. (1959). *The Analysis of Variance.* New York: Wiley.

Seber, G. (1977). *Linear Regression.* New York: Wiley.

Silverman, H. F., and P. C. Yue (1973). "The Response Time Characteristics of an Information Retrieval System." *IBM Journal of Research and Development* **17** (5): 394–403.

Spirn, J. R. (1977). *Program Behavior: Models and Measurements.* New York: Elsevier.

Svobodova, L. (1976). "Computer System Measurability." *Computer* **9** (6): 9–17.

Tsao, R. F., L. W. Comeau, and B. H. Margolin (1972). "A Multi-Factor Paging Experiment: I. The Experiment and the Conclusions." In W. Freiberger (ed.), *Statistical Computer Performance Evaluation*, pp. 103–134. New York: Academic Press.

Tsao, R. F., and B. H. Margolin (1972). "A Multi-Factor Paging Experiment: II. Statistical Methodology." In W. Freiberger (ed.), *Statistical Computer Performance Evaluation*, pp. 135–158. New York: Academic Press.

Wood, F. S. (1972). *The Linear and Nonlinear Least-Square Curve Fitting Programs.* Program documentation numbers 360D-13.6.008 and 360D-13.6.007, SHARE Program Library Agency, Triangle University Computation Center, Research Triangle Park, North Carolina.

Yue, P. C. (1971). "Time-Series Techniques for Measurement Analysis." Unpublished note, IBM T. J. Watson Research Center, Yorktown Heights, New York.

Glossary
of
Principal
Symbols

The following is a list of the principal symbols that appear in this book. Pages or equation numbers indicating where the symbol is defined are included, along with a brief description. We do not list symbols that are special to one or two sections only.

The following conventions have been followed almost without exception:

1. Boldface roman is used for vectors and matrices.

2. A random variable is denoted by a capital letter. (But a capital letter is not always a random variable.)

3. The expectation (or the mean, the statistical average) of a random variable X is usually denoted by $E[X]$ or μ_X. This rule is violated in Chapter 3 [$\bar{T}$ (mean response time), $\bar{W}$ (mean waiting time), $\bar{N}$ (mean number of customers)], since in Chapter 3 the symbol μ is primarily used for the service completion rate.

4. The sample mean (or the empirical mean, the time average) of a random variable X is usually denoted by $\bar{X}$. (See above for exceptional usage.)

Symbol	Definition	Page or Equation Number
$A(t)$	Cumulative arrivals up to time t	(3.47)
$\{a_n\}$	Distribution of the number of customers seen by arrivals	152
$b(k; n, p)$	Binomial distribution	38
C	Service capacity or processing rate	98
C_X	Coefficient of variation of the random variable X	(2.108)
$C_i(n_i)$	Processing rate of service station i when $N_i(t) = n_i$	(3.200)
$\text{Cov}[X, Y]$	Covariance between X and Y	333
D	Deterministic distribution	115
$D(t)$	Total number of customers who have entered service by time t	(3.50)
$D^*(t)$	Total number of customers who have left the system by time t	(3.64)
$\det |\mathbf{A}|$	Determinant of matrix $\mathbf{A}$	85
$E[X]$	Expectation of the random variable X	(2.93)
$\mathbf{E}$	Square matrix with all entries 1's	(2.254)
E_k	k-stage Erlangian distribution	115
e_i	The ith element of $\mathbf{e}$; that is, the expected number of visits that a customer makes to station i	(3.222)
$\mathbf{e}$	Left eigenvector of $\mathbf{Q}$ associated with one	(3.239)
FCFS	First-come, first-served	99
F	F-value of the F-distribution	(5.106)
F_{n_1, n_2}	F-value with degrees of freedom of n_1 and n_2	(5.106)
$F_X(x)$	$P[X \le x]$	(2.42)
$F_X^c(x)$	$1 - F_X(x) = P[X > x]$	(2.97)
$F_W(x|n)$	Waiting-time distribution of a customer who finds n customers upon arrival	(3.115)
$f_N(A)$	Relative frequency of outcome A of an experiment of size N	(2.1)
$f_X(x)$	$\dfrac{dF_X(x)}{dx}$	(2.67)

Symbol	Definition	Page or Equation Number
$F_W(x \mid n)$	$\dfrac{dF_W(x \mid n)}{dx}$	(3.117)
G	General distribution	115
$G_X(z)$	$E[z^X]$: probability generating function of the random variable X	(2.135)
H	Hypothesis	361
$H(x)$	Cumulative histogram	325
H_k	k-stage (or k-phase) hyperexponential distribution	115
$h(x)$	Histogram	323
i	$\sqrt{-1}$	71
$\mathbf{I}$	Identity matrix	84
K	Number of customers in a closed queueing system	144
K	Size of storage capacity of a queueing system	142, 201
$\ln F^c(x)$	Log survivor function of the variable X	(5.27)
$\mathrm{mod}\ m$	Modulo m	(4.3)
M	Exponential distribution (M = Markovian)	115
$N(t)$	Number of customers in the system at time t	(3.65)
$\bar{N}$	$\lim\limits_{t \to \infty} E[N(t)]$	(3.108)
$N_i(t)$	The ith element of $\mathbf{N}(t)$; that is, the number of customers in station i at time t	(3.198)
$\mathbf{N}(t)$	Population size vector in a queueing network	(3.198)
N_k	Number of customers left behind in the system by the kth departing customer	(3.292)
N_k^*	N_k in a queueing system with a finite storage capacity	(3.351)
$N(\mu, \sigma^2)$	Normal (or Gaussian) distribution with mean μ and variance σ^2	77

Symbol	Definition	Page or Equation Number
n_i	The ith element of $\mathbf{n}$; that is, the value $N_i(t)$ takes on	162
$\mathbf{n}$	The value of the random process $\mathbf{N}(t)$	163
$n(\tau)$	The number of arrivals in $(0, \tau)$	101
$o(x)$	$\lim\limits_{x \to 0} \dfrac{o(x)}{x} = 0$	101
P	Percentile	327
$P[A]$	Probability of the event A	33
$P[B \mid A]$	Conditional probability of event B given A	(2.28)
$P[\mathbf{n}]$	$\lim\limits_{t \to \infty} P[\mathbf{N}(t) = \mathbf{n}]$	(3.202)
$P_n(t)$	$P[N(t) = n]$	(3.89)
$P(k; \lambda)$	$\dfrac{\lambda^k}{k!} e^{-\lambda}$: Poisson distribution	(3.170)
$\mathbf{P}(z)$	$\sum\limits_{t=0}^{\infty} \mathbf{p}(t) z^t$	(2.241)
$P(z)$	$\lim\limits_{k \to \infty} E[z^{N_k}]$	(3.295)
$P^*(z)$	$\lim\limits_{k \to \infty} E[z^{N_k^*}]$	(3.352)
$P(\lambda)$	Power spectrum	(5.56)
$\mathbf{p}(t)$	Probability distribution (vector) at time t	83
$p_i(n)$	Marginal distribution of $P[\mathbf{n}]$; that is, the distribution of the number of customers at station i	(3.254)
p_n	$\lim\limits_{t \to \infty} P_n(t)$	(3.92)
Q	Sum of the squares of errors	(5.128)
Q_T	Total sum of the squares of errors from the overall mean	(5.130)
Q_w	Sum of the squares of errors within treatment	(5.131)
Q_b	Sum of the squares of errors between treatments	(5.132)
Q_{bR}	Variation explained by regression	(5.232)
Q_{aR}	Variation not explained by regression	(5.228)

Symbol	Definition	Page or Equation Number
$Q(t)$	Number of customers in system at time t	120
$\bar{Q}$	Mean queue size in equilibrium	(3.60)
$Q(k;\lambda)$	$\displaystyle\sum_{i=0}^{k} P(i;\lambda)$	(3.171)
$\mathbf{Q}$	$[q_{ij}]$: (One-step) transition probability matrix of a homogeneous Markov chain	83
$Q(\mathbf{z})$	$E[z_1^{N_1}, z_2^{N_2} \cdots z_M^{z_M}]$: Probability generating function of $P[\mathbf{n}]$	(3.251)
$q_j \quad (0 \le j \le K)$	The distribution of the number of customers in $M/G/1$ with storage capacity K	(3.364)
q_{ij}	Probability that a customer leaving station i goes next to station j	163
$q_{ij}^{(n)}$	(i, j) element of $\mathbf{Q}^n$	84
$R_X(t_1, t_2)$	$E[X(t_1)X(t_2)]$	(2.226)
$R_X(\tau)$	Autocovariance function of the wide-sense stationary process $X(t)$	(2.228)
R_k	Autocovariance function of a wide-sense stationary sequence	(5.49)
$R_{Y\mathbf{X}}$	Multiple correlation coefficient between Y and $\mathbf{X}$	(5.236)
$R_{Y\mathbf{X}}^2$	Coefficient of determination (in multiple regression)	(5.237)
$\mathbf{R}$	Random vector (or random-number stream)	(4.75)
$\mathbf{R}^*$	$1-\mathbf{R}$: Antithetic partner of $\mathbf{R}$	(4.79)
r	$\dfrac{\mu}{\nu} = \dfrac{\text{Mean user response time}}{\text{Mean service time}}$	(3.152)
r_{YX}	Sample correlation coefficient between Y or X	(5.47), (5.190)
r_{YX}^2	Coefficient of determination or squared correlation coefficient	(5.193)
$r_{XY_j \cdot X \cdots X_p}$	Partial correlation coefficient	(5.240)
S	Service demand (or service time) variable	98
$\bar{S}$	$E[S]$: Mean service demand	98

Symbol	Definition	Page or Equation Number
$\bar{S}_i$	Mean service demand at station i	161
$\bar{S}_{\text{CPU}}$	Mean CPU service time	8
$\mathscr{S}$	Normalization coefficient of the queue distribution	(3.100)
$\mathscr{S}(N, M)$	Normalization constant in a closed queueing network	(3.236)
s^2	Sample variance	(5.9)
s_{XY}	Sample covariance between X and Y	(5.46)
s_b^2	Mean squared deviation between treatments	365
s_w^2	Mean squared deviation within treatments	365
$\bar{T}$	Mean response time	8
T_j	Response-time variable of customer j	117
t_j	Arrival time of customer j	118
t_j'	Time when customer j leaves the queue and enters service	118
t_j^*	Departure time of customer j	122
t	Student's t-statistic	(5.121)
t_n	Student's t-statistic with n degrees of freedom	346
$t_{\alpha/2;n}$	Upper $100 \times \alpha/2$ percentile of the t-distribution with n degrees of freedom	286
$\bar{U}$	Mean user response time	(3.147)
$\mathbf{U}$	Uncontrolled variables (vector)	353
$U(x)$	$\begin{cases} 1 & x > 0 \\ 0 & x \leq 0 \end{cases}$	(3.293)
u_p	Fractile (percentile) or the standard normal variable	(5.19)
$u(x)$	$\begin{cases} 1 & x \geq 0 \\ 0 & x < 0 \end{cases}$: unit step function	(3.323)
$V(t)$	Virtual waiting time or unfinished work	123
$\bar{V}_R$	$\dfrac{\lambda}{2} E[s^2]$: Mean remaining service time	(3.74)
$V(\hat{\boldsymbol{\beta}})$	Covariance matrix of $\hat{\boldsymbol{\beta}}$	(5.227)

Symbol	Definition	Page or Equation Number
$\bar{W}$	Mean waiting time	(3.59)
W_j	Waiting-time variable of customer j	117
$\bar{W}_{\mathrm{CPU}}$	Average CPU work per job	182
$\bar{W}_i$	$e_i \bar{S}_i$: Expected total work that a customer places on service station i	(3.223)
$\bar{W}_{\mathrm{FCFS}}$	Mean waiting time under FCFS	(3.81)
$W(f)$	Weight of function f	(3.276)
X_k	Number of customers who arrive while the kth customer is served in $M/G/1$	193
$\mathbf{X}$	Controlled variables (vector)	354
$\mathbf{X}$	Design matrix	(5.223)
$\mathbf{X}'$	Transpose of the design matrix $\mathbf{X}$	388
$\bar{X}$	$\dfrac{1}{n}\displaystyle\sum_{i=1}^{n} X_i$: Sample mean of $\{X_i\}$	(5.1)
x_k	$\displaystyle\sum_{i=1}^{M} \tau_i^k$	(3.281)
$Y(K)$	Normalized mean response time in the finite source model of size K	(3.175)
$\bar{Y}_{i\cdot}$	Sample mean of $\{Y_{it}\}$ over index t	(5.126)
$\bar{Y}_{i\cdot\cdot}$	Sample mean of $\{Y_{ijt}\}$ over indexes j,t	(5.161)
$\bar{Y}_{\cdot j\cdot}$	Sample mean of $\{Y_{ijt}\}$ over indexes i,t	(5.162)
$\bar{Y}_{\cdot t}$	Sample mean of $\{Y_{it}\}$ over index i	(5.142)
$\bar{Y}_{\cdot\cdot}$	Overall sample mean of $\{Y_{it}\}$	(5.129)
$\bar{Y}_{\cdots}$	Overall sample mean of $\{Y_{ijt}\}$	(5.158)
Z	Standard normal variable	(5.118)
$\mathbf{Z}$	Concomitant variables (vector)	405
$\mathbf{Z}'$	Transpose of $\mathbf{Z}$	(5.271)
$Z_{S_N}(x_1, x_2, \ldots, x_N)$	Cycle index polynomial of the symmetric group of degree N	(3.279)
$z_{\alpha/2}$	Upper $\alpha/2 \times 100$ percentile of the standard normal distribution	357
$z(x)$	Completion rate function or hazard function	340
α	Parameter of the gamma distribution	(3.25)
α	Linear regression coefficient	(5.116)
α	Confidence level	357
α_i	Main effect of factor X at level i	372

Symbol	Definition	Page or Equation Number
$\hat{\alpha}$	Least square estimate of α	(5.181)
β	Parameter of the gamma distribution	(3.25)
β	Regression coefficient	(5.116)
$\boldsymbol{\beta}$	Regression coefficients (vector)	(5.271)
$\hat{\beta}$	Least-square estimate of β	(5.180)
$\Gamma_i(n_i)$	$\displaystyle\prod_{i=1}^{n_i} C_i(n)$	(3.220)
$\Gamma(z)$	Gamma function	(3.26), (5.83)
γ_{ij}	Interaction effects between factor X at level i and factor Y at level j	(5.153)
$\boldsymbol{\gamma}$	Regression coefficients (vector) for concomitant variables $\mathbf{Z}$	(5.271)
Δ	$\det|\mathbf{I} - \mathbf{Q}z|$	85
$\delta(x)$	$\dfrac{du(x)}{dx}$; unit impulse function or Dirac delta function	(3.325) (3.326)
δ_{ij}	Kronecker's function	163
$\epsilon(\mathbf{U})$	Error due to the uncontrolled variables $\mathbf{U}$	(5.113)
$\Phi(x)$	Distribution function of the standard normal variable	(3.191)
$\Phi_X(s)$	$E[e^{sX}]$: The Laplace transform of the nonnegative random variable X	(2.170)
$\phi(x)$	$\dfrac{d\Phi(x)}{dx}$: Probability density function of the standard normal variable	357
$\phi_X(\theta)$	$E[e^{i\theta X}]$: The characteristic function of the random variable X	(2.109)
$\phi_{\mathbf{X}}(\boldsymbol{\theta})$	$E[e^{i<\boldsymbol{\theta},\mathbf{X}>}]$: The joint characteristic function of $\mathbf{X}$	(2.132)
χ_n^2	Chi-square variable with n degrees of freedom	(5.76)
$\psi_X(\theta)$	$\ln \phi_X(\theta)$: Cumulant generating function	(2.124)
κ_n	nth cumulants	(2.125)

Symbol	Definition	Page or Equation Number
$\Lambda(n)$	$\prod_{i=1}^{n} \lambda(i-1)$	(3.98)
λ	Arrival rate	101
$\lambda(n)$	Birth rate (or arrival rate) when $N(t) = n$	(3.85)
λ_i	Throughput (or arrival rate) at station i	(3.257)
$\lambda_t(K)$	Throughput in the finite source model of population size K	(3.174)
μ	$C/\bar{S}$: Completion rate	(3.1)
μ	Population mean of a random variable	(5.4)
μ_X	$E[X]$	(2.93), (2.94)
$\mu_X(t)$	$E[X(t)]$	(2.225)
$M(n)$	$\prod_{i=1}^{n} \mu(i)$	(3.99)
μ_{ij}	Mean first passage time from state i to state j	(2.245)
μ_{ii}	$1/\pi_i$: Mean recurrence time of state i	(2.251)
$\mu(n)$	Death rate (or completion rate) when $N(t) = n$	(3.86)
ν	$1/\bar{U}$: Request generation rate	(3.151)
π	$\lim_{t \to \infty} \mathbf{p}(t)$: The limit distribution (vector)	(2.247)
π_i	The ith element of π	(2.252)
$\{\pi_i; i = 1, 2, \ldots, k\}$	Probability that a customer is from the ith type in the k-stage hyperexponential distribution	(3.35)
ρ	$\lambda\bar{S}$: Utilization (factor)	(3.43)
ρ_{CPU}	CPU utilization	8
ρ_i	Utilization of station i	(3.255)
$\rho(K)$	Server utilization in a queueing system with source size K	(3.173)
ρ_k	R_k/R_0 = Autocorrelation function, or serial correlation coefficient of lag k	(5.50)

Symbol	Definition	Page or Equation Number
ρ_{XY}	Correlation coefficient between X and Y	(5.40)
σ_X^2	$E[(X - \mu_X)^2]$: Variance of the random variable X	(2.101)
σ_X	Standard deviation of the random variable X	(2.101)
σ_{XY}	Cov$[X, Y]$	(5.38)
τ_i	$\bar{W}_i/C_i = e_i/\mu_i$: Expected total time that a customer spends in station i	(3.250)
Ω	Sample space	29
ω	Sample point	29
$\{\omega\}$	Simple event	30
$\circledast$	Convolution	(2.116), (2.154)
$\cup$	Union	(2.10)
$\cap$	Intersection	(2.11)
1	A row vector of all 1's	90
1'	A column vector of all 1's	(2.253)

ABOUT THE AUTHOR

Hisashi Kobayashi is Senior Manager of Systems Analysis and Algorithms at the IBM T. J. Watson Research Center, Yorktown Heights, New York, and directs three research groups: "Performance Modeling Methodology," "Satellite Communications," and "Computer Network Measurement and Control." He has been with IBM since 1967 and has worked on data transmission theory and various signal processing projects, as well as on computer performance evaluation. He also taught at UCLA, the University of Hawaii, and Stanford University on sabbatical programs of IBM. He holds six U.S. patents and has published over 50 technical articles. He earned the B.S. and M.S. degrees in electrical engineering at the University of Tokyo, and the M.A. and Ph.D. degrees at Princeton University. He is an IEEE Fellow, a committee member of the IFIP Working Group on Computer System Modelling, a member of the U.S. National Committee of the International Union of Radio Science (URSI), and the Conference Chairman of the 1977 International Symposium on Computer Performance Modelling, Measurement, and Evaluation. He is an associate editor of the *IEEE Transactions on Computers* for the term of September 1977 through August 1979.

Author Index

427

Subject Index